The Compact Reader

SHORT ESSAYS BY METHOD AND THEME

Sixth Edition

THE COMPACT READER

SHORT ESSAYS BY METHOD AND THEME

Jane E. Aaron

BEDFORD/ST. MARTIN'S

Boston New York

For Bedford/St. Martin's
Developmental Editor: Aron Keesbury
Production Editor: Stasia Zomkowski
Production Supervisor: Joe Ford
Marketing Manager: Karen Melton
Editorial Assistant: Ellen Thibault
Production Assistants: Helaine Denenberg, Edward R. Tonderys
Copyeditor: Jane M. Zanichkowsky
Cover Design: Diana Coe
Cover Art: Henri Matisse, *The Snail.* © 1998 Succession H. Matisse, Paris/Artists Rights Society (ARS), New York. Courtesy of Tate Gallery, London/Art Resource, NY.
Composition: Pine Tree Composition, Inc.
Printing and Binding: Haddon Craftsmen, Inc.

President: Charles H. Christensen
Editorial Director: Joan E. Feinberg
Director of Editing, Design, and Production: Marcia Cohen
Managing Editor: Elizabeth M. Schaaf

Library of Congress Catalog Card Number: 98-87516

Manufactured in the United States of America.

3 2 1 0 9 8
f e d c b a

For information, write: Bedford/St. Martin's, 75 Arlington Street, Boston, MA 02116 (617-426-7440)

ISBN: 0-312-17165-X

Acknowledgments

Diane Ackerman, excerpt from *A Natural History of the Senses* by Diane Ackerman. Copyright © 1990 by Diane Ackerman. Reprinted by permission of Random House, Inc.

Acknowledgments and copyrights are continued at the back of the book on pages 359–61, which constitute an extension of the copyright page. It is a violation of the law to reproduce these selections by any means whatsoever without the written permission of the copyright holder.

Preface

Like its predecessor, the sixth edition of *The Compact Reader* offers three composition texts in one brief volume: a rhetorical reader, a thematic reader, and a short-essay reader. But this edition does more as well: in two new introductory chapters and in every rhetorical chapter, students receive detailed help with the elements of writing, from revising essays and paragraphs to editing sentences and words. This new material and other new features make *The Compact Reader* even more useful both for readers and writers in their first year of college and for their instructors.

Three Readers in One

The core of *The Compact Reader* remains its selections. The work of both established and emerging writers, thirty-four essays and twenty paragraphs provide interesting reading that will enliven class discussion and stimulate good writing. Three paragraphs and seventeen essays are new to this edition, and a student essay now illustrates every rhetorical method.

The Compact Reader's unique structure suits courses that take a rhetorical or a thematic approach and call for brief essays:

- In Chapters 4–13, three essays and two annotated paragraphs illustrate each rhetorical method, such as narration, comparison, and argument. Above all, the essays offer clear models, but they also show the methods at work in varied styles for varied purposes. Then Chapter 14 includes two annotated essays that demonstrate how writers combine methods to achieve their purposes.
- Each rhetorical chapter also has an overlapping thematic focus that shows the method developing the same general subject and provides diverse perspectives to spark students' discussion and writing. Four themes are new to this edition.

Description	Sensing the Natural World
Narration	Growing Up
Example	Using Language
Division or Analysis	Looking at Popular Culture
Classification	Sorting Thoughts and Behaviors
Process Analysis	Explaining Customs (new)
Comparison and Contrast	Challenging Misconceptions (new)
Definition	Clarifying Our Relationships
Cause-and-Effect Analysis	Exploring the Influence of Gender
Argument and Persuasion	Debating Cloning (new)
Combining Methods of Development	Articulating a Vision (new)

- The essays in *The Compact Reader* average just two to four pages apiece, so that students can read them quickly, analyze them thoroughly, and emulate them successfully. A few longer essays, such as Jessica Mitford's "Embalming Mr. Jones," help students make the transition to more challenging material.

An Introduction to Reading and Writing

The former introduction to critical reading and the writing process is now three full chapters:

- Chapter 1 demonstrates the reading process, showing a student's annotations on a sample passage and providing detailed analysis of a professional essay, Barbara Lazear Ascher's "The Box Man."
- Chapter 2 covers the initial stages of composing, from assessing the writing situation through drafting, following the work of the student as she responds to Ascher's essay and completes her first draft. The new material here includes sections on journal writing and brainstorming, using the methods of development to generate ideas for different purposes, and thinking in paragraphs.
- Chapter 3, almost entirely new, then discusses revising and editing, from rethinking the thesis through reshaping paragraphs to reworking sentences and changing words. The chapter includes new boxed checklists for each major stage as well as revised and final drafts by the student responding to Ascher's essay.

The Compact Reader's increased emphasis on writing carries through the entire book:

- Complementing the new Chapter 3, the introduction to each rhetorical method now features a new "Focus" box that covers an element of writing especially relevant to that method, such as verbs in narration, paragraph coherence in comparison and contrast, and tone in argument and persuasion. Each box falls within a revision and editing checklist that extends Chapter 3's more general checklists to the particular method.
- To help students find what they need in the book, a guide to the elements of writing appears inside the book's front cover. This index covers Chapters 2 and 3 as well as all the rhetorical introductions.

Unique Editorial Apparatus

In addition to the features already mentioned, *The Compact Reader* offers numerous aids for students and teachers:

- A detailed, practical introduction to each of the ten rhetorical methods discusses basic concepts, offers two sample paragraphs illustrating the method, and suggests strategies for starting, organizing, drafting, and revising and editing an essay using the method. The introductions now draw sharper connections among purpose, subject, and method, helping students analyze and respond to any writing situation. And a final "Note on Thematic Connections" explains how the chapter's paragraphs and essays relate to each other.
- Headnotes about the author and the essay place every selection in a context that helps focus students' reading.
- Detailed questions after each essay guide students' analysis of meaning, purpose and audience, method and structure, and language. A question labeled "Other Methods" highlights the author's use of combined methods.
- At least four writing topics after each selection give students specific direction for their own work. A new two-part topic, "Journal Response" and "Journal to Essay," prompts students' journal writing and helps them move from there to finished essays. A "Cultural Considerations" topic leads students to consider similarities and differences between cultures. And a "Connections" topic encourages students to make thematic or rhetorical links to other selections in the book.
- Additional writing topics appear at the ends of chapters. "Using

the Method" lists ideas for applying the chapter's method of development, and "Writing About the Theme" includes ideas for drawing on the chapter's resources to explore its topic.
- A glossary at the end of the book defines and illustrates more than a hundred terms, with specific cross-references to longer discussions in the text.

Helpful Instructor's Manual

Resources for Teaching THE COMPACT READER, bound into the instructor's edition of the book, aims to help teachers integrate the text into their courses and use it in class. It includes an overview of the book's organization and chapters, ideas for combining the reader with other course materials, and varied resources for each selection: teaching tips, a content quiz, a vocabulary quiz, and detailed answers to all questions. The manual also reprints one essay from each rhetorical chapter with annotations that highlight the author's thesis and methods.

Acknowledgments

A number of instructors helped to shape this edition of *The Compact Reader*, offering insights from their experience and suggestions for improvement. Special thanks to Brenda Brueggemann, Ohio State University; Tim Bywater, Dixie College; Elrod S. Ferreira, Delaware Technical and Community College; Joan Gagnon, Honolulu Community College; Margaret Jordan Gerard, Orange Coast College; Joseph Halabi, Saint John's University; Gwendolyn S. Jones, Tuskegee University; Anne M. Kincaid, John Jay College of Criminal Justice/City University of New York; Sarah Liggett, Louisiana State University; Japhet N. Makia, Southern Arkansas University; Inez Martinez, Kingsborough Community College, City University of New York; Jim Piper, Fresno City College; Ruth H. Reilly, Hocking College; Michael Schwartz, Bucks County Community College; Louise C. Silverman, Ocean County College; Ronni Soffian, Florida International University; Jacqueline Stark, Los Angeles Valley College; Robert Saltonstall Tapply, Fitchburg State College.

The people at and around Bedford/St. Martin's continue their tradition of supporting authors way beyond the call of mere duty. Chuck Christensen and Joan Feinberg provided the leadership and inspiration that their authors now rely on. Aron Keesbury earned his wings as a developmental editor, shaping the book's features and contents, managing myriad details, searching the Web for student work, and injecting intelligence, enthusiasm, and laughter into the entire project. Ellen Thibault assisted in development, proving a determined, creative, and cheerful researcher. David Gibbs contributed imaginatively to the questions and the instructor's manual. And Stasia Zomkowski pulled all the elements together, deftly overseeing production on a tight schedule. All deserve these happy thanks.

Contents

4 DESCRIPTION *Sensing the Natural World* 57

5 NARRATION *Growing Up* 84

Chapter 1

READING

This collection of essays has one purpose: to help you become a more proficient reader and writer. It combines examples of good writing with explanations of the writers' methods, questions to guide your reading, and ideas for your own writing. In doing so, it shows how you can adapt the processes and techniques of others as you learn to communicate clearly and effectively on paper.

Writing well is not an inborn skill but an acquired one: you will become proficient only by writing and rewriting, experimenting with different strategies, listening to the responses of readers. How, then, can it help to read the work of other writers?

- Reading others' ideas can introduce you to new information and give you new perspectives on your own experience. Many of the essays collected here demonstrate that personal experience is a rich and powerful source of material for writing. But the knowledge gained from reading can help pinpoint just what is remarkable in your experience. And by introducing varieties of behavior and ways of thinking that would otherwise remain unknown to you, reading can also help you understand where you fit in the scheme of things. Such insight not only reveals subjects for writing but also improves your ability to communicate with others whose experiences naturally differ from your own.

- Reading exposes you to a broad range of strategies and styles. Just seeing that these vary as much as the writers themselves should assure you that there is no fixed standard of writing, while it should also encourage you to find your own strategies and style. At the same time, you will see that writers do make choices to suit their subjects, their purposes, and especially their readers. Writing is rarely easy, even for the pros; but the more options you have to choose from, the more likely you are to succeed at it.
- Reading makes you sensitive to the role of audience in writing. As you become adept at reading the work of other writers critically, discovering intentions and analyzing choices, you will see how a writer's decisions affect you as audience. Training yourself to read consciously and critically is a first step to becoming a more objective reader of your own writing.

USING THIS BOOK FOR READING

The rest of this chapter offers strategies for making the most of your reading in this book and elsewhere. But first you should understand this book's overall organization. Most of the essays appear in Chapters 4–13, which introduce ten methods of developing a piece of writing:

description	process analysis
narration	comparison and contrast
example	definition
division or analysis	cause-and-effect analysis
classification	argument and persuasion

These methods correspond to basic and familiar patterns of thought and expression, common in our daily musings and conversations as well as in writing for all sorts of purposes and audiences: college term papers, lab reports, and examinations; business memos and reports; letters to the editors of newspapers; articles in popular magazines.

As writers we draw on the methods, sometimes unconsciously, to give order to our ideas and even to find ideas. For instance, a writer narrates, or tells, a story of her experiences to understand and convey the feeling of living her life. As readers, in turn, we have expectations for these familiar methods. When we read a narrative of someone's experiences, for instance, we expect enough details to understand what happened, we anticipate that events will be told primarily in the order they occurred, and we want the story to have a point—a reason for its being told and for our bothering to read it.

Making such expectations conscious can sharpen your skills as a critical reader and as a writer. The next chapter discusses all the methods in a bit more detail, and a full chapter on each one explains how it works, shows it at work in paragraphs, and gives advice for using it to develop your own essays. The three essays in each chapter provide clear examples that you can analyze and learn from (with the help of specific questions) and can refer to while writing (with the help of specific writing suggestions). In Chapter 14, two additional essays illustrate how writers combine the methods of development to suit their subjects and purposes.

To make your reading more interesting and also to stimulate your writing, the sample paragraphs and essays in Chapters 4–13 all focus on a common subject, such as growing up, popular culture, or cloning. You'll see how flexible the methods are when they help five writers produce five unique pieces on the same theme. You'll also have a springboard for producing your own unique pieces, whether you take up some of the book's writing suggestions or take off with your own topics.

READING CRITICALLY

When we look for something to watch on television or listen to on the radio, we often tune in one station after another, pausing just long enough each time to catch the program or music being broadcast before settling on one choice. Much of the reading we do is similar: we skim a newspaper, magazine, or online document, noting headings and scanning paragraphs to get the gist of the content. But such skimming is not really reading, for it neither involves us deeply in the subject nor engages us in interaction with the writer.

To get the most out of reading, we must invest something of ourselves in the process, applying our own ideas and emotions and attending not just to the substance but to the writer's interpretation of it. This kind of reading is **critical** because it looks beneath the surface of a piece of writing. (The common meaning of *critical* as "negative" doesn't apply here: critical reading may result in positive, negative, or even neutral reactions.)

Critical reading can be enormously rewarding, but of course it takes care and time. A good method for developing your own skill in critical reading is to prepare yourself beforehand and then read the work at least twice to uncover what it has to offer.

Preparing

Preparing to read need involve no more than a few minutes as you form some ideas about the author and the work:

- What is the author's background, what qualifications does he or she bring to the subject, and what approach is he or she likely to take? The biographical information provided before each essay in this book should help answer these questions; and many periodicals and books include similar information on their authors.
- What does the title convey about the subject and the author's attitude toward it? Note, for instance, the quite different attitudes conveyed by these three titles on the same subject: "Safe Hunting," "In Touch with Ancient Spirits," and "Killing Animals for Fun and Profit."
- For your reading in this book, what does the method of development suggest about how the author will handle the subject? Larry Woiwode's "Ode to an Orange," for instance, appears in the chapter on description, so you can assume that his essay describes an orange.

Reading Actively

After developing some expectations about the piece of writing, read it through carefully to acquaint yourself with the subject, the author's reason for writing about it, and the way the author presents it. (Each essay in this book is short enough to be read at one sitting.) Try not to read passively, letting the words wash over you, but instead interact directly with the work to discover its meaning, the author's intentions, and your own responses.

One of the best aids to active reading is to make notes on separate sheets of paper or, preferably (if you own the book), on the pages themselves. As you practice making notes, you will probably develop a personal code meaningful only to you. As a start, however, try this system:

- Underline or bracket passages that you find particularly effective or that seem especially important to the author's purpose.
- Circle words you don't understand so that you can look them up when you finish.
- Put question marks in the margins next to unclear passages.
- Jot down associations that occur to you, such as examples from your own experience, disagreements with the author's assumptions, or links to other works you've read.

When you have finished such an active reading, your annotations might look like those below. (The paragraph is from the end of the essay reprinted on pp. 6–10.)

The first half of our lives is spent stubbornly denying it. As children we acquire language to make ourselves understood and soon learn from the blank stares in response to our babblings that even these, our saviors, our parents, are strangers. In adolescence when we replay	true?
earlier dramas with peers in the place of parents, we begin the quest for the best friend, that person who will receive all thoughts as if they were (her) own. Later we assert that true love will find the way. True love finds many	What about <u>his</u> own? Audience = women?
ways, but no escape from exile. The shores are littered with us, <u>Annas</u> and Ophelias, <u>Emmas</u> and Juliets, all outcasts from the dream of perfect understanding. We might	*Ophelia + Juliet from Shakespeare. Others also?*
as well draw the night around us and find solace there and a friend in our own voice.	*In other words, just give up?*

Before leaving the essay after such an initial reading, try to answer your own questions by looking up unfamiliar words and figuring out the meaning of unclear passages. Then let the essay rest in your mind for at least an hour or two before approaching it again.

Rereading

When rereading the essay, write a one- or two-sentence summary of each paragraph—in your own words—to increase your mastery of the material. Aim to answer the following questions:

- Why did the author write about this subject?
- What impression did the author wish to make on readers?
- How do the many parts of the work—for instance, the sequencing of information, the tone, the evidence—contribute to the author's purpose?
- How effective is the essay, and why?

A procedure for such an analysis—and the insights to be gained from it—can best be illustrated by examining an actual essay.

READING A SAMPLE ESSAY

The paragraph on page 5 comes from "The Box Man" by the American writer Barbara Lazear Ascher. Born in 1946, Ascher attended Bennington College (B.A., 1968) and Cardozo School of Law (J.D., 1979) and practiced law for two years. Then she turned to writing full-time, publishing two books, *Playing After Dark* (1986) and *Landscape Without Gravity: A Memoir of Grief* (1993), along with essays in the *New York Times, Vogue, The Yale Review,* and other periodicals. "The Box Man" comes from *Playing After Dark.* The scene is New York City, where Ascher lives with her family.

Barbara Lazear Ascher

The Box Man

The Box Man was at it again. It was his lucky night. 1

The first stroke of good fortune occurred as darkness fell and the 2
night watchman at 220 East Forty-fifth Street neglected to close the door as he slipped out for a cup of coffee. I saw them before the Box Man did. Just inside the entrance, cardboard cartons, clean and with

their top flaps intact. With the silent fervor of a mute at a horse race, I willed him toward them.

It was slow going. His collar was pulled so high that he appeared headless as he shuffled across the street like a man who must feel Earth with his toes to know that he walks there. 3

Standing unselfconsciously in the white glare of an overhead light, he began to sort through the boxes, picking them up, one by one, inspecting tops, insides, flaps. Three were tossed aside. They looked perfectly good to me, but then, who knows what the Box Man knows? When he found the one that suited his purpose, he dragged it up the block and dropped it in a doorway. 4

Then, as if dogged by luck, he set out again and discovered, behind the sign at the parking garage, a plastic Dellwood box, strong and clean, once used to deliver milk. Back in the doorway the grand design was revealed as he pushed the Dellwood box against the door and set its cardboard cousin two feet in front—the usual distance between coffee table and couch. Six full shopping bags were distributed evenly on either side. 5

He eased himself with slow care onto the stronger box, reached into one of the bags, pulled out a *Daily News,* and snapped it open against his cardboard table. All done with the ease of IRT Express passengers whose white-tipped, fair-haired fingers reach into attaché cases as if radar-directed to the *Wall Street Journal.* They know how to fold it. They know how to stare at the print, not at the girl who stares at them. 6

That's just what the Box Man did, except that he touched his tongue to his fingers before turning each page, something grandmothers do. 7

One could live like this. Gathering boxes to organize a life. Wandering through the night collecting comforts to fill a doorway. 8

When I was a child, my favorite book was *The Boxcar Children.* If I remember correctly, the young protagonists were orphaned, and rather than live with cruel relatives, they ran away to the woods to live life on their own terms. An abandoned boxcar was turned into a home, a bubbling brook became an icebox. Wild berries provided abundant desserts and days were spent in the happy, adultless pursuit of joy. The children never worried where the next meal would come from or what February's chill might bring. They had unquestioning faith that berries would ripen and streams run cold and clear. And 9 unlike Thoreau,[1] whose deliberate living was self-conscious and purposeful, theirs had the ease of children at play.

10 Even now, when life seems complicated and reason slips, I long to live like a Boxcar Child, to have enough open space and freedom of movement to arrange my surroundings according to what I find. To turn streams into iceboxes. To be ingenious with simple things. To let the imagination hold sway.

11 Who is to say that the Box Man does not feel as Thoreau did in his doorway, not ". . . crowded or confined in the least," with "pasture enough for . . . imagination." Who is to say that his dawns don't bring back heroic ages? That he doesn't imagine a goddess trailing her garments across his blistered legs?

12 His is a life of the mind, such as it is, and voices only he can hear. Although it would appear to be a life of misery, judging from the bandages and chill of night, it is of his choosing. He will ignore you if you offer an alternative. Last winter, Mayor Koch[2] tried, coaxing him with promises and the persuasive tones reserved for rabid dogs. The Box Man backed away, keeping a car and paranoia between them.

13 He is not to be confused with the lonely ones. You'll find them everywhere. The lady who comes into our local coffee shop each evening at five-thirty, orders a bowl of soup and extra Saltines. She drags it out as long as possible, breaking the crackers into smaller and smaller pieces, first in halves and then halves of halves and so on until the last pieces burst into salty splinters and fall from dry fingers onto the soup's shimmering surface. By 6 P.M., it's all over. What will she do with the rest of the night?

14 You can tell by the vacancy of expression that no memories linger there. She does not wear a gold charm bracelet with silhouettes of boys and girls bearing grandchildren's birthdates and a chip of the appropriate birthstone. When she opens her black purse to pay, there is only a crumpled Kleenex and a wallet inside, no photographs spill onto her lap. Her children, if there are any, live far away and prefer not to visit. If she worked as a secretary for forty years in a downtown office, she was given a retirement party, a cake, a reproduction of an antique perfume atomizer and sent on her way. Old col-

[1] Henry David Thoreau (1817–62) was an American essayist and poet who for two years lived a solitary and simple life in the woods. He wrote of his experiences in *Walden* (1854). [Editor's note.]

[2] Edward Koch was the mayor of New York City from 1978 through 1989. [Editor's note.]

leagues—those who traded knitting patterns and brownie recipes over the water cooler, who discussed the weather, health, and office scandal while applying lipstick and blush before the ladies' room mirror—they are lost to time and the new young employees who take their places in the typing pool.

Each year she gets a Christmas card from her ex-boss. The envelope is canceled in the office mailroom and addressed by memory typewriter. Within is a family in black and white against a wooded Connecticut landscape. The boss, his wife, who wears her hair in a gray page boy, the three blond daughters, two with tall husbands and an occasional additional grandchild. All assembled before a worn stone wall. 15

Does she watch game shows? Talk to a parakeet, feed him cuttlebone, and call him Pete? When she rides the buses on her Senior Citizen pass, does she go anywhere or wait for something to happen? Does she have a niece like the one in Cynthia Ozick's story "Rosa," who sends enough money to keep her aunt at a distance? 16

There's a lady across the way whose lights and television stay on all night. A crystal chandelier in the dining room and matching Chinese lamps on Regency end tables in the living room. She has six cats, some Siamese, others Angora and Abyssinian. She pets them and waters her plethora of plants—African violets, a ficus tree, a palm, and geraniums in season. Not necessarily a lonely life except that 3 A.M. lights and television seem to proclaim it so. 17

The Box Man welcomes the night, opens to it like a lover. He moves in darkness and prefers it that way. He's not waiting for the phone to ring or an engraved invitation to arrive in the mail. Not for him a P.O. number. Not for him the overcrowded jollity of office parties, the hot anticipation of a singles' bar. Not even for him a holiday handout. People have tried and he shuffled away. 18

The Box Man knows that loneliness chosen loses its sting and claims no victims. He declares what we all know in the secret passages of our own nights, that although we long for perfect harmony, communion, and blending with another soul, this is a solo voyage. 19

The first half of our lives is spent stubbornly denying it. As children we acquire language to make ourselves understood and soon learn from the blank stares in response to our babblings that even these, our saviors, our parents, are strangers. In adolescence when we replay earlier dramas with peers in the place of parents, we begin the quest for the best friend, that person who will receive all thoughts as 20 if they were her own. Later we assert that true love will find the way. True love finds many ways, but no escape from exile. The shores are littered with us, Annas and Ophelias, Emmas and Juliets,[3] all outcasts from the dream of perfect understanding. We might as well draw the night around us and find solace there and a friend in our own voice.

One could do worse than be a collector of boxes. 21

Even read quickly, Ascher's essay would not be difficult to comprehend: the author draws on examples of three people to make a point at the end about solitude. In fact, a quick reading might give the impression that Ascher produced the essay effortlessly, artlessly. But close, critical reading reveals a carefully conceived work whose parts work independently and together to achieve the author's purpose.

One way to uncover underlying intentions and relations like those in Ascher's essay is to work through a series of questions about the work. The following questions proceed from the general to the specific—from overall meaning through purpose and method to word choices—and they parallel the more specific questions after the essays in this book. Here the questions come with possible answers for Ascher's essay. (The paragraph numbers can help you locate the appropriate passages in Ascher's essay as you follow the analysis.)

Meaning

What is the main idea of the essay—the chief point the writer makes about the subject, to which all other ideas and details relate? What are the subordinate ideas that contribute to the main idea?

Ascher states her main idea (or thesis) near the end of her essay: in choosing solitude, the Box Man confirms the essential aloneness of human beings (paragraph 19) but also demonstrates that we can "find solace" within ourselves (20). (Writers sometimes postpone stating their main idea, as Ascher does here. Perhaps more often, they

[3] These are all doomed heroines of literature. Anna is the title character of Leo Tolstoy's novel *Anna Karenina* (1876). Emma is the title character of Gustave Flaubert's novel *Madam Bovary* (1856). Ophelia and Juliet are in Shakespeare's plays—the lovers, respectively, of Hamlet and Romeo. [Editor's note.]

state it near the beginning of the essay. See pp. 17–18.) Ascher leads up to and supports her idea with three examples—the Box Man (paragraphs 1–7, 11–12) and, in contrast, two women whose loneliness seems unchosen (13–16, 17). These examples are developed with specific details from Ascher's observations (such as the nearly empty purse, 14) and from the imagined lives these observations suggest (such as the remote, perhaps nonexistent children, 14).

Occasionally, you may need to puzzle over some of the author's words before you can fully understand his or her meaning. Try to guess the word's meaning from its context first, and then check your guess in a dictionary. (To help master the word so that you know it next time and can draw on it yourself, use it in a sentence or more of your own.)

Purpose and Audience

Why did the author write the essay? What did the author hope readers would gain from it? What did the author assume about the knowledge and interests of readers, and how are these assumptions reflected in the essay?

Ascher seems to have written her essay for two interlocking reasons: to show and thus explain that solitude need not always be lonely and to argue gently for defeating loneliness by becoming one's own friend. In choosing the Box Man as her main example, she reveals perhaps a third purpose as well—to convince readers that a homeless person can have dignity and may achieve a measure of self-satisfaction lacking in some people who do have homes.

Ascher seems to assume that her readers, like her, are people with homes, people to whom the Box Man and his life might seem completely foreign: she comments on the Box Man's slow shuffle (paragraph 3), his mysterious discrimination among boxes (4), his "blistered legs" (11), how miserable his life looks (12), his bandages (12), the cold night he inhabits (12), the fearful or condescending approaches of strangers (12, 18). Building from this assumption that her readers will find the Box Man strange, Ascher takes pains to show the dignity of the Box Man—his "grand design" for furniture (5), his resemblance to commuters (6), his grandmotherly finger licking (7), his refusal of handouts (18).

Several other apparent assumptions about her audience also influence Ascher's selection of details, if less significantly. First, she assumes some familiarity with literature—at least with the writings of Thoreau (9, 11) and the characters named in paragraph 20. Second, Ascher seems to address women: in paragraph 20 she speaks of each person confiding in "her" friend, and she chooses only female figures from literature to illustrate "us, . . . all outcasts from the dream of perfect understanding." Finally, Ascher seems to address people who are familiar with, if not actually residents of, New York City: she refers to a New York street address (2); alludes to a New York newspaper, the *Daily News,* and a New York subway line, the IRT Express (6); and mentions the city's mayor (12). However, readers who do not know the literature Ascher cites, who are not women, and who do not know New York City are still likely to understand and appreciate Ascher's main point.

Method and Structure

What method or methods does the author use to develop the main idea, and how do the methods serve the author's subject and purpose? How does the organization serve the author's subject and purpose?

Ascher's primary support for her idea consists of three examples (Chapter 6)—specific instances of solitary people. The method of example especially suits Ascher's subject and purpose because it allows her to show contrasting responses to solitude: one person who seems to choose it and two people who don't.

As writers often do, Ascher relies on more than a single method, more than just example. She develops her examples with description (Chapter 4), vividly portraying the Box Man and the two women, as in paragraphs 6–7, so that we see them clearly. Paragraphs 1–7 in the portrayal of the Box Man involve retelling, or narrating (Chapter 5), his activities. Ascher uses division or analysis (Chapter 7) to tease apart the elements of her three characters' lives. And she relies on comparison and contrast (Chapter 10) to show the differences between the Box Man and the other two in paragraphs 13 and 17–18.

While using many methods to develop her idea, Ascher keeps her organization fairly simple. She does not begin with a formal introduction or a statement of her idea but instead starts right off with her main example, the inspiration for her idea. In the first seven paragraphs she narrates and describes the Box Man's activities. Then, in paragraphs 8–12, she explains what appeals to her about circumstances like the Box Man's and she applies those thoughts to what she imagines are his thoughts. Still delaying a statement of her main idea, Ascher contrasts the Box Man and two other solitary people, whose lives she sees as different from his (13–17). Finally, she returns to the Box Man (18–19) and zeroes in on her main idea (19–20). Though she has withheld this idea until the end, we see that everything in the essay has been controlled by it and directed toward it.

Language

How are the author's main idea and purpose revealed at the level of sentences and words? How does the author use language to convey his or her attitudes toward the subject and to make meaning clear and vivid?

One reason Ascher's essay works is that she uses specific language to portray her three examples—she *shows* them to us—and to let us know what she thinks about them. For instance, the language changes markedly from the depiction of the Box Man to the next-to-last paragraph on solitude. The Box Man comes to life in warm terms: Ascher watches him with "silent fervor" (paragraph 2); he seems "dogged by luck" (5); he sits with "slow care" and opens the newspaper with "ease" (6); his page turning reminds Ascher of "grandmothers" (7); it is conceivable that, in Thoreau's word, the Box Man's imagination has "pasture" to roam, that he dreams of "heroic ages" and a "goddess trailing her garments" (11). In contrast, isolation comes across as a desperate state in paragraph 20, where Ascher uses such words as "blank stares," "strangers," "exile," "littered," and "outcasts." The contrast in language helps to emphasize Ascher's point about the individual's ability to find comfort in solitude.

In describing the two other solitary people—those who evidently have not found comfort in aloneness—Ascher uses words that emphasize the heaviness of time and the sterility of existence. The first woman "drags" her meal out and crumbles crackers between "dry fingers" (13), a "vacancy of expression" on her face (14). She lacks even the trinkets of attachment—a "gold charm bracelet" with pictures of grandchildren (14). A vividly imagined photograph of her ex-boss and his family (15)—the wife with "her hair in a gray page boy," "the three blond daughters"—emphasizes the probable absence of such scenes in the woman's own life.

Ascher occasionally uses incomplete sentences (or sentence fragments) to stress the accumulation of details or the quickness of her impressions. For example, in paragraph 10 the incomplete sentences beginning "To . . ." sketch Ascher's dream. And in paragraph 18 the incomplete sentences beginning "Not . . ." emphasize the Box Man's withdrawal. Both of these sets of incomplete sentences gain emphasis from **parallelism,** the use of similar grammatical form for ideas of equal importance. (See p. 48) The parallelism begins in the complete sentences preceding each set of incomplete sentences—for example, ". . . I long to live like a Boxcar Child. . . . To turn streams into iceboxes. To be ingenious with simple things. To let the imagination hold sway." Although incomplete sentences can be unclear, these and the others in Ascher's essay are clear: she uses them deliberately and carefully, for a purpose. (Inexperienced writers often find it safer to avoid any incomplete sentences until they have mastered the complete sentence.)

These notes on Ascher's essay show how one can arrive at a deeper, more personal understanding of a piece of writing by attentive, thoughtful analysis. Guided by the questions at the end of each essay and by your own sense of what works and why, you'll find similar lessons and pleasures in all of this book's readings.

Chapter 2

WRITING

GETTING STARTED THROUGH DRAFTING

Analyzing a text in the way shown in the preceding chapter is valuable in itself: it can be fun, and the process helps you better understand and appreciate whatever you read. But it can make you a better writer, too, by showing you how to read your own work critically, increasing the strategies available to you, and suggesting topics for you to write about.

USING THIS BOOK FOR WRITING

Though it is mainly a collection of essays, *The Compact Reader* also contains a range of material designed to help you use your reading to write effectively.

The first element consists of this chapter and the next, on writing; you may want to refer to these chapters again and again as your writing skills develop. (See the inside front cover for a guide to the topics covered.) Offering specific ways to strengthen and clarify your work, the chapters also include a student's essay-in-progress from idea through final draft.

These two chapters follow the stages of the **writing process:** getting started, organizing, drafting, revising, and editing. Most writers experience such stages on their way to a finished piece of writing, and each stage tends to have a dominant activity, such as discovering ideas or shaping ideas or making corrections. But actually, the stages are quite arbitrary because writers rarely move in straight lines through fixed steps, like locomotives over tracks. Instead, just as they do when thinking, writers continually circle back over covered territory, each time picking up more information or seeing new relationships, until their meaning is clear to themselves and can be made clear to readers. No two writers proceed in exactly the same way, either, so that your writing process may differ considerably from your classmates'. Still, viewing the process in stages does help sort out its many activities so that you can develop the process or processes that work best for you.

Complementing this and the next chapter's overview of writing are the more specific introductions to the methods of development in Chapters 4–13—narration, comparison and contrast, definition, and so on. These method introductions follow the pattern set here by also proceeding from beginning to end of the writing process, but they take up particular concerns of the method, such as organizing a narrative or clarifying a definition.

Besides its advice on writing, *The Compact Reader* also contains scores of suggestions for what to write about. At least four writing topics follow each essay: some call for your analysis of the essay; others lead you to examine your own experiences or other sources in light of the essay's ideas. Two additional sets of topics fall at the end of each chapter: one group provides a range of subjects for using the chapter's method of development; the other encourages you to focus on thematic connections in the chapter.

GETTING STARTED

Every writing situation involves several elements: you communicate an *idea* about a subject to an *audience* of readers for a particular *purpose.* At first you may not be sure of your idea or your purpose. You may not know how you want to approach your readers, even when you know who they are. Your job in getting started, then, is to explore options and make choices.

Considering Your Subject and Purpose

A subject for writing may arise from any source, including your own experience or reading, a suggestion in this book, or an assignment specified by your instructor. In the previous chapter, Barbara Ascher's essay on a homeless man demonstrates how an excellent subject can be found from observing one's surroundings. Whatever its source, the subject should be something you care enough about to probe deeply and to stamp with your own perspective.

This personal stamp comprises both your main idea, the central point you want to make about the subject, and your **purpose,** your reason for writing. The purpose may be one of the following:

- To explain the subject so that readers understand it or see it in a new light.
- To persuade readers to accept or reject an opinion or to take a certain action.
- To entertain readers with a humorous or exciting story.
- To express the thoughts and emotions triggered by a revealing or instructive experience.

A single essay may sometimes have more than one purpose: for instance, a writer might both explain what it's like to be disabled and try to persuade readers to respect special parking zones for the disabled. Your purpose and your main idea may occur to you early on, arising out of the subject and its significance for you. But you may need to explore your subject for a while—even to the point of writing a draft—before it becomes clear to you.

Considering Your Thesis

How many times have you read a work of nonfiction and wondered, "What's the point?" Whether consciously or not, we expect a writer to *have* a point, a central idea that he or she wants readers to take away from the work. We expect that idea to determine the content of the work—so that everything relates to it—and we expect the content in turn to demonstrate or prove the idea.

Arriving at a main idea, or **thesis,** is thus an essential part of the writing process. Sometimes it will occur to you at the moment you hit on your subject—for instance, if you think of writing about the new grading policy because you want to make a point about its unfairness. At other times you may struggle through a draft or more to pin down just what you have to say. Even if your thesis will evolve, however, you'll probably benefit from focusing on it early so that it can help you generate ideas, seek information, organize your thoughts, and so on.

The best way to focus on your thesis is to write it out in a **thesis sentence** or sentences, an assertion about the subject. In these two sentences from the end of "The Box Man" (p. 10), Barbara Ascher asserts the point of her essay:

> [We are] all outcasts from the dream of perfect understanding. We might as well draw the night around us and find solace there and a friend in our own voice.

Because your thesis itself may change over the course of the writing process, your thesis sentence may also change, sometimes considerably. The following thesis sentences show how one writer shifted his opinion and moved from an explanatory to a persuasive purpose between the early stages of the writing process and the final draft.

> TENTATIVE With persistence, adopted children can often locate information about their birth parents.
>
> FINAL Adopted children are unfairly hampered in seeking information about their birth parents.

The final sentence makes a definite assertion ("Adopted children are unfairly hampered") and clearly conveys the persuasive purpose of the essay to come. Thus the sentence lets readers know what to expect: an argument that adopted children should be treated more fairly when they seek information about their birth parents. Readers will also expect some discussion of what hampers an adoptee's search, what is "unfair" and "fair" in this situation, and what changes the author proposes.

Most commonly, the thesis sentence comes near the beginning of an essay, sometimes in the first paragraph, where it serves as a promise to examine a particular subject from a particular perspective. But as Ascher demonstrates by stating her thesis at the end, the thesis sentence may come elsewhere as long as it controls the whole essay. The thesis may even go unstated, as other essays in this book illustrate, but it still must govern every element of the work as if it were announced.

Considering Your Audience

Either very early, when you first begin exploring your subject, or later, as a check on what you have generated, you may want to make a few notes on your anticipated audience. The notes are optional, but thinking about audience definitely is not. Your purpose and thesis as well as supporting ideas, details and examples, organization, style, tone, and language—all should reflect your answers to the following questions:

- What impression do you want to make on readers?
- What do readers already know about your subject? What do they need to know?
- What are readers' likely expectations and assumptions about your subject?
- How can you build on readers' previous knowledge, expectations, and assumptions to bring them around to your view?

These considerations are obviously crucial to achieve the fundamental purpose of all public writing: communication. Accordingly, they come up again and again in the chapter introductions and the questions after each essay.

Discovering Ideas

Ideas for your writing—whether your subject or your thesis or the many smaller ideas and details that build your thesis—may come to you in a rush, or you may need to search for them. Writers use a variety of searching techniques, from jotting down thoughts while they pursue other activities to writing concentratedly for a set period. Here are a few techniques you might try.

Journal Writing

Many writers keep a **journal**, a record of thoughts and observations. Whether in a notebook or in a computer file, journal entries give you an opportunity to explore ideas just for yourself, free of concerns about readers who will judge what you say or how you say it. Regular journal entries can also make you more comfortable with the act of writing and build your confidence. Indeed, writing teachers often require their students to keep journals for these reasons.

In a journal you can write about whatever interests, puzzles, or disturbs you. Here are just a few possible uses:

- Record your responses to your reading in this book and other sources.
- Prepare for a class by summarizing the week's reading or the previous class's discussion.
- Analyze a relationship that's causing you problems.
- Imitate a writer you admire, such as a poet or songwriter.
- Explore your reactions to a movie or a music album.
- Confide your dreams and fears.

Any of this material could provide a seed for a writing assignment, but you can also use a journal deliberately to develop ideas for assignments. One approach is built into this book: after every essay, a suggestion for "Journal Writing" prompts you to respond to the essay from your own experiences and observations. The following journal entry by a student, Grace Patterson, shows such a response to Barbara Ascher's "The Box Man" (pp. 6–10):

> Ascher gives an odd view of homelessness—hadn't really occurred to me that the homeless man on the street might want to be there. Always assumed that no one would want to live in filthy clothes, without a roof. What is a home anyway—shelter? decor? a clothes closet? Can your body and a few "possessions" = home?

Writing for herself, Patterson feels free to explore what's on her mind, without worrying about correctness and without trying to make it clear to external readers what she means or why they should accept her views. Indeed, she doesn't come to any conclusions herself, as the entry's final question makes clear. In journal writing, groping like Patterson's is not only appropriate but helpful. The aim is to *explore* ideas; presenting thought-out ideas for readers comes later.

Freewriting

To discover ideas for a particular assignment, you may find it useful to try **freewriting,** or writing without stopping for a set amount of time, usually ten to fifteen minutes. In freewriting you push yourself to keep writing, following ideas wherever they lead, paying no attention to completeness or correctness or even sense. When she began composing an essay response to Barbara Ascher's "The Box Man," Grace Patterson produced this freewriting:

> Something in Ascher's essay keeps nagging at me. Almost ticks me off. What she says about the Box Man is based on certain assumptions. Like she knows what he's been through, how he feels. Can he be as content as she says? What bothers me is, how much choice does the guy really have? Just cuz he manages to put a little dignity into his life on the street and refuses handouts—does that mean he chooses homelessness? Life in a shelter might be worse than life on the street.

Notice that this freewriting is rough: the tone is very informal, as if Patterson were speaking to herself; some thoughts are left dangling; some sentences are shapeless or incomplete; a word is misspelled (*cuz* for *because*). But none of this matters because the freewriting is just exploratory. Writing fluently, without halting to rethink or edit, actually pulled insights out of Patterson. She moved from being vaguely uneasy with Ascher's essay to conceiving an argument against it. Then, with a more definite focus, she could begin drafting in earnest.

If you have difficulty writing without correcting and you compose on a word processor, you might try **invisible writing:** turn the computer's monitor off while you freewrite, so that you can't see what you're producing. When your time is up, turn the monitor back on to work with the material.

Brainstorming

Another discovery technique that helps to pull ideas from you is **brainstorming,** listing ideas without stopping to censor or change them. As in freewriting, write without stopping for ten or fifteen minutes, jotting down everything that seems even remotely related to your subject. Don't stop to reread and rethink what you have written; just keep pulling and recording ideas, no matter how silly or dull or irrelevant they seem. When your time is up, look over the list to find the promising ideas and discard the rest. Depending on *how* promising the remaining ideas are, you can resume brainstorming, try freewriting about them, or begin a draft.

Considering Your Method of Development

The ten methods of development discussed in Chapters 4–13 can help you continue to expand your thinking or begin to focus and shape your ideas. You can use the methods singly, with one method dominating in an essay, or in combination, with different methods providing varied perspectives on your subject.

The sections below begin with questions suggested by each method. Asking these questions about your subject can open up approaches you may not have considered. Then the sections show how each method also provides a direction that may help you achieve your particular purpose for writing.

Description (Chapter 4)

How does the subject look, sound, smell, taste, and feel?

We use description to depict objects, places, people, and emotions through the evidence of our senses. It will come into play if you want to express your feelings about playing a sport, portray a friend, report on a laboratory procedure in biology or an observation session in psychology, file an insurance claim after a car accident, or show a denuded mountain as a way of arguing against clear-cutting forests.

Narration (Chapter 5)

What is the story in the subject? How did it happen?

Narration is storytelling, either fictional (as in novels) or nonfictional (as in recounting an experience you had). You can use narration to entertain readers by retelling an amusing or scary experience, to explain the sequence of events in a chemistry experiment, to summarize actions in a letter complaining about a product, to explain what went wrong in a ball game, or to persuade readers by means of several stories that the forestry industry is sincere about restoring clear-cut forests.

Example (Chapter 6)

How can the subject be illustrated? What are instances of it?

An example is evidence for a general statement, a particular instance of what the statement claims. We use examples constantly to clarify and support our general claims. You might use the method to entertain readers with the idea that you're accident prone, to demonstrate why your school should reduce maximum class size, to counter a prevailing view about your city, or to show by citing another company's policy how recycling could work in your company.

Division or Analysis (Chapter 7)

What are the subject's parts, and what is their relationship or significance?

Division or analysis (alternative names for the same process) is the method of taking apart and reassembling. With division or analysis, we peer into the insides of an object, institution, work of art, policy, or any other whole: we identify the parts, see how the parts relate, and draw on that vision to form conclusions about the whole. You can use division or analysis to write critically about a movie, poem, or journal article, to identify the flaws in a theory of schizophrenia, to explain a company's organization after a merger, to determine whether the company is now a good investment, or to argue that television talk shows do more good than harm.

Classification (Chapter 8)

What groups or categories can the subject be sorted into?

Classification takes many items that share at least one characteristic—writing students, tax laws, motorcycles—and arranges them into groups based on their similarities. You could draw on classification if you wanted to explain four styles of communicating by e-mail, argue that one type of campaign contribution is more corrupting than the others, propose new categories of nonsalaried employees, or explain the types of health-insurance policies.

Process Analysis (Chapter 9)

How does the subject work, or how does one do it?

Process analysis explains *how* a sequence of actions leads to an expected result: sending and receiving e-mail, manufacturing a car, training to be a registered nurse. Use process analysis when you want readers to understand how something works—for instance, in explaining how an electric car can save energy, how a congressional committee can shape legislation, or how a new kind of junction box can prevent household electrical fires. Also use process analysis when you want to tell readers how to do something, such as how to design a Web page, how to get the most from managed health care, or how to follow a new office procedure.

Comparison and Contrast (Chapter 10)

How is the subject similar to or different from something else?

A dual method, comparison and contrast allows us to explain or evaluate subjects by putting them side by side, showing how they are alike and different. You'll find the method useful if you want to explain that computer hackers are not like their popular image, to explain how nursing has changed in the past ten years, or to explain the likenesses between American football and rugby. Comparison and contrast is also useful for evaluating two or more subjects and perhaps arguing the superiority of one of them—for instance, two detective novels, three options for company health benefits, or two ways of routing traffic downtown.

Definition (Chapter 11)

What are the subject's characteristics and boundaries?

With definition we specify what something is and what it is not. We use definition often in sentences or paragraphs to explain our meaning—stopping to define *success,* for instance, in a paper on successful small businesses, or giving the sense of a technical term in an engineering study. But we may also define words at essay length, especially when they are abstract, complicated, or controversial. Drawing on other methods of development, such as example or comparison and contrast, you might devote an entire essay to the debated phrase *family values,* the current uses of the word *monopoly* in business, or the meanings of the term *personality* in a particular psychological theory.

Cause-and-Effect Analysis (Chapter 12)

Why did the subject happen? What were or may be its consequences?

By analyzing causes and effects, we determine the events that brought about an outcome (the causes) or the events that resulted or may result from an occurrence (the effects). Like everyone else, you probably consider causes and effects many times a day: Why is the traffic so heavy? What will happen if I major in communications rather than business? In writing you'll also draw often on cause-and-effect analysis, perhaps explaining why the school's basketball team has been so successful this year, what made a bridge collapse, or how a new stoplight has worsened rush-hour traffic. You'll use the method for persuasion, too, as in arguing that the family, not the mass media, bears responsibility for children's violence (focusing on causes) or that adult illiteracy threatens American democracy (focusing on possible effects).

Argument and Persuasion (Chapter 13)

Why do I believe as I do about the subject? Why do others have different opinions? How can I convince others to accept my opinion or believe as I do?

With argument and persuasion, purpose and method coincide: the aim is to find agreement with readers, change their minds, or move them to action. You'll construct arguments in your classes, as when you dispute someone else's interpretation of data, and also in work and in life, as when you identify and propose a solution for a problem or protest a tax bill. In writing argument and persuasion, you may draw on several or all of the other methods of development.

ORGANIZING

Writers vary in the extent to which they arrange their material before they begin drafting, but most do establish some plan. A good time to do so is after you've explored your subject and developed a good stock of ideas about it. Before you begin drafting, you can look over what you've got and consider the best ways to organize it.

Creating a Plan

A writing plan may consist of a list of key points, a fuller list including specifics as well, or even a detailed formal outline—whatever gives order to your ideas and provides some direction for your writing.

As you'll see in later chapters, many of the methods of development suggest specific structures, most notably description, narration, classification, process analysis, and comparison and contrast. But even when the organization is almost built into the method, you'll find that some subjects demand more thoughtful plans than others. You may be able to draft a straightforward narrative of a personal experience with very little advance planning. But a nonpersonal narrative, or even a personal one involving complex events and time shifts, may require more thought about arrangement.

Though some sort of plan is almost always useful when drafting, resist any temptation at this stage to pin down every detail in its proper place. A huge investment in planning can hamper you during drafting, making it difficult to respond to new ideas and even new directions that may prove fruitful.

Thinking in Paragraphs

Most essays consist of three parts, an introduction and a conclusion (discussed in the next section) and the **body,** the most substantial and longest part that develops the main idea or thesis.

As you explore your subject, you will discover both ideas that directly support your thesis and more specific examples, details, and other evidence that support these ideas. In the following outline of Grace Patterson's "A Rock and a Hard Place" (pp. 54–56), you can see how each supporting idea, or subpoint, helps to build the thesis sentence:

THESIS SENTENCE For the homeless people in America today, there are no good choices.

SUBPOINT A "good choice" is one made from a variety of options determined and narrowed down by the chooser.

SUBPOINT Homeless people do not necessarily choose to live on the streets.

SUBPOINT The streets are the only alternative to shelters, which are dangerous and dehumanizing.

Patterson uses specific evidence to develop each subpoint in a paragraph. In essence, the paragraphs are like mini-essays with their own main ideas and support. (See pp. 33–34 for more on paragraph structure.)

When you seek a plan in your ideas, look first for your subpoints, the main supports for your thesis. Use these as your starting points to work out your essay one chunk (or paragraph) at a time. You can fill in the supporting evidence, the details and examples, in your organizational plan, or you can wait until you begin drafting to get into the specifics.

Considering the Introduction and Conclusion

You'll probably have to be drafting or revising before you'll know for sure how you want to begin and end your essay. Still, it can be helpful to consider the introduction and conclusion earlier, so you have a sense of how you might approach readers and what you might leave them with.

The basic opening and closing serve readers by demonstrating your interest in their needs and expectations:

- The **introduction** draws readers into the essay and focuses their attention on the main idea and purpose—often stated in a thesis sentence.
- The **conclusion** ties together the elements of the essay and provides a final impression for readers to take away with them.

These basic forms allow considerable room for variation. Especially as you are developing your writing skills, you will find it helpful to state your thesis sentence near the beginning of the essay; but sometimes you can place it effectively at the end, or you can let it direct what you say in the essay but never state it at all. One essay may need two paragraphs of introduction but only a one-sentence conclusion, whereas another essay may require no formal introduction but a lengthy conclusion. How you begin and end depends on your subject and purpose, the kind of essay you are writing, and the likely responses of your readers. Specific ideas for opening and closing essays are included in each chapter introduction and in the Glossary under *introductions* and *conclusions*.

DRAFTING

Drafting is the chance for you to give expression to your ideas, filling them out, finding relationships, drawing conclusions. If you are like most writers, you will discover much of what you have to say while drafting. In fact, if your subject is complex or difficult for you to write about, you may need several drafts just to work out your ideas and their relationships.

Writing, Not Revising

Some writers draft rapidly, rarely looking up from the paper or keyboard. Others draft more in fits and starts, gazing out the window or doodling as much as writing. Any method that works is fine, but one method rarely works: collapsing drafting and revising into one stage, trying to do everything at once.

Write first; then revise. Concentrate on *what* you are saying, not on *how* you are saying it. You pressure yourself needlessly if you try to produce a well-developed, coherent, interesting, and grammatically correct paper all at once. You may have trouble getting words on paper because you're afraid to make mistakes, or you may be distracted by mistakes from exploring your ideas fully. Awkwardness, repetition, wrong words, grammatical errors, spelling mistakes—these and other more superficial concerns can be attended to in a later draft. The same goes for considering your readers' needs: like many writers, you may find that attention to readers during the first draft inhibits the flow of ideas.

If you experience writer's block or just don't know how to begin your draft, start writing the part you're most comfortable with. Writing in paragraph chunks, as described on pages 26–27, will also make drafting more manageable. You can start with your thesis sentence—or at least keep it in view while you draft—as a reminder of your purpose and main idea. But if you find yourself pulled away from the thesis by a new idea, you may want to let go and follow, at least for a while. If your purpose and main idea change as a result of such exploration, you can always revise your thesis accordingly.

Grace Patterson's First Draft

Some exploratory work by the student Grace Patterson appears on pages 20 and 21. What follows is the first draft she subsequently wrote on homelessness. The draft is very rough, with frequent repetitions, wandering paragraphs, and many other flaws. But such weaknesses are not important at this early stage. The draft gave Patterson the opportunity to discover what she had to say, explore her ideas, and link them in rough sequence.

Title?

In the essay, "The Box Man," Barbara Ascher says that a homeless man who has chosen solitude can show the rest of us how to "find . . . a friend in our own voice." Maybe. But her case depends on the Box Man's choice, her assumption that he <u>had</u> one.

Discussions of the homeless often use the word <u>choice</u>. Many people with enough money can accept the condition of the homeless in America when they tell themselves that many of the homeless chose their lives. That the streets are in fact what they want. But it's not fair to use the word <u>choice</u> here: the homeless don't get to choose their lives the way most of the rest of us do. For the homeless people in America today, there are no good choices.

What do I mean by a "good choice"? One made from a variety of options determined and narrowed down by the chooser. There is plenty of room for the chooser to make a decision that he will be satisfied with. When I choose a career, I expect to make a good choice. There is plenty of interesting fields worth investigating, and there is lots of rewarding work to be done. It's a choice that opens the world up and showcases its possibilities. If it came time for me to choose a career, and the mayor of my town came around and told me that I had to choose between a life of cleaning public toilets and operating a jackhammer on a busy street corner, I would object. That's a lousy choice, and I wouldn't let anyone force me to make it.

When the mayor of New York tried to take the homeless off the streets, some of them didn't want to go. People assumed that the homeless people who did not want to get in the mayor's car for a ride to a city shelter <u>chose</u> to live on the street. But just because some homeless people chose the street over the generosity of the mayor does not necessarily mean that life on the streets is their ideal. We allow ourselves as many options as we can imagine, but we allow the homeless only two: go to a shelter, or stay where you are. Who narrowed down the options for the homeless? Who benefits if they go to a shelter? Who suffers if they don't?

Homeless people are not always better off in shelters. I had a conversation with a man who had lived on the streets for a long time. The man said that he had spent some time in those shelters for the homeless, and he told me what they were like. The shelters are crowded and dirty and people have to wait in long lines for everything. People are constantly being herded around and bossed around. It's dangerous--drug dealers, beatings, theft. Dehumanizing. It matches my picture of hell. From the sound of it, I couldn't spend two hours in a shelter, never mind a whole night. I value my peace of mind and my sleep too much, not to mention my freedom and autonomy.

When homeless people sleep in the street, though, that makes the public uncomfortable. People with enough money wish the homeless would just disappear. They don't care where they go. Just out of sight. I've felt this way too but I'm as uneasy with that reaction as I am at the sight of a person sleeping on the sidewalk. And I tell myself that this is more than a question of my comfort. By and large I'm comfortable enough.

The homeless are in a difficult enough situation without having to take the blame for making the rest of us feel uncomfortable with our wealth. If we cannot offer the homeless a good set of choices, the opportunity to choose lives that they will be truly satisfied with then the least we can do is stop dumping on them (?). They're caught between a rock and a hard place: there are not many places for them to go, and the places where they can go afford nothing but suffering.

Chapter 3

WRITING

REVISING AND EDITING

The previous chapter took you through the first-draft stage of the writing process, when you have a chance to work out your meaning without regard for what others may think. This chapter describes the crucial next stages, when you actively consider your readers: revising to focus and shape the work and editing to clarify and polish.

REVISING

Revision means "re-seeing," looking at your draft as a reader sees it: mere words on a page that are only as clear, interesting, and significant as you have made them.

Looking at the Whole Draft

Revision involves seeing your draft as a whole, focusing mainly on your purpose and thesis, the support for your thesis, and the movement among ideas. You want to determine what will work and what won't for readers—where the draft strays from your purpose, leaves a hole in the development of your thesis, does not flow logically or smoothly, digresses, or needs more details. (See the revision checklist on p. 40.) Besides rewriting, you may need to cut whole paragraphs, condense paragraphs into sentences, add passages of explanation, or rearrange sections.

Revision is different from **editing.** In revising, you make fundamental changes in content and structure: you work below the surface of the draft. Then in editing, you make changes in the revised draft's sentences and words: you work on the surface, attending to style, grammar, punctuation, and the like. The separation of these two stages is important because attention to little changes distracts from a view of the whole. If you try to edit while you revise, you'll be more likely to miss the big picture. You may also waste effort perfecting sentences you'll later decide to cut.

Reading Your Own Work Critically

Perhaps the most difficult challenge in revising is reading your own work objectively, as a reader would. To gain something like a reader's critical distance from your draft, try one or more of the following techniques:

- Put your first draft aside for at least a few hours before attempting to revise it. You may have further thoughts in the interval, and you will be able to see your work more objectively when you return to it.
- Ask another person to read and comment on your draft. Your writing teacher may ask you and your classmates to exchange your drafts so that you can help each other revise. But even without such a procedure, you can benefit from others' responses. Keep an open mind to your readers' comments, and ask questions when you need more information.
- Make an outline of your draft by listing what you cover in each paragraph. Such an outline can show gaps, overlaps, and problems in organization. (See also pp. 26–27.)
- Read the draft aloud or into a tape recorder. Speaking the words and hearing them can help to create distance from them.
- Imagine you are someone else—a friend, perhaps, or a particular person in your intended audience—and read the draft through that person's eyes, as if for the first time.

- If you write on a word processor, print out a copy of your draft with double spacing. It's much easier to read text on paper than on a computer screen, and you can spread out the pages of a printout to see the whole paper at once. Once you've finished revising, making the changes on the computer requires little effort.

Revising for Purpose and Thesis

In the press of drafting, you may lose sight of why you are writing or what your main idea is. Both your purpose and your thesis may change as you work out your meaning, so that you start in one place and end somewhere else or even lose track of where you are.

Your first goal in revising, then, is to see that your essay is well focused. Readers should grasp a clear purpose right away, and they should find that you have achieved it at the end. They should see your main idea, your thesis, very early, usually by the end of the introduction, and they should think that you have proved or demonstrated the thesis when they reach the last paragraph.

Like many writers, you may sometimes start with one thesis and finish with another, in effect writing into your idea as you draft. To revise, you'll need to upend your essay, plucking your thesis out of the conclusion and starting over with it, providing the subpoints and details to develop it. You'll probably find the second draft much easier to write because you know better what you want to say, and the next round of revision will probably be much cleaner.

Revising for Unity

When a piece of writing has **unity,** all its parts are related: the sentences build the central idea of their paragraph, and the paragraphs build the central idea of the whole essay. Readers do not have to wonder what the essay is about or what a particular paragraph has to do with the rest of the piece.

Unity in Paragraphs

Earlier we saw how the body paragraphs of an essay are almost like mini-essays themselves, each developing an idea, or subpoint, that supports the thesis. (See pp. 26–27.) In fact, a body paragraph should have its own thesis, called its **topic,** usually expressed in a

topic sentence or sentences. The rest of the paragraph develops the topic with specifics.

In the following paragraph from the final draft of Grace Patterson's "A Rock and a Hard Place" (pp. 54–56), the topic sentence is italicized:

> *The fact is that homeless people are not always better off in shelters.* I recently had a conversation with a man named Alan who had lived on the streets for a long time. He said that he had spent some time in shelters for the homeless, and he told me what they are like. They're dangerous and dehumanizing. Drug dealing, beatings, and theft are common. The shelters are dirty and crowded, so that residents have to wait in long lines for everything and are constantly being bossed around. No wonder some homeless people, including Alan, prefer the street: it affords some space to breathe, some autonomy, some peace for sleeping.

Notice that every sentence of this paragraph relates to the topic sentence. Patterson achieved this unity in revision (see p. 43). In her draft her last sentences focused on herself rather than the conditions of homeless shelters:

> . . . It matches my picture of hell. From the sound of it, I couldn't spend two hours in a shelter, never mind a whole night. I value my peace of mind and my sleep too much, not to mention my freedom and autonomy.

If you look back at the full paragraph above, you'll see that Patterson deleted these sentences and substituted a final one that focused on the paragraph's topic, the conditions of the shelters for the homeless themselves.

Your topic sentences will not always fall at the very beginning of your paragraphs. Sometimes you'll need to create a transition from the preceding paragraph before stating the new paragraph's topic, or you'll build the paragraph to a topic sentence at the end, or you'll divide the statement between the beginning and the end. (Patterson's second paragraph, on p. 55, works this way, defining a good choice at the beginning and a bad choice at the end.) Sometimes, too, you'll write a paragraph with a topic but without a topic sentence. In all these cases, you'll need to have an idea for the paragraph and to unify the paragraph around that idea, so that all the specifics support and develop it.

Unity in Essays

Just as sentences must center on a paragraph's main idea, so paragraphs must center on the essay's main idea, or thesis. Readers who have to ask "What is the point?" or "Why am I reading this?" generally won't appreciate or accept the point.

Look back at the outline of Grace Patterson's essay on page 26. Her thesis sentences states, "For the homeless people in America today, there are no good choices," and each paragraph clearly develops this idea: what is a good choice, whether the homeless choose to live on the streets, and why shelters are not good alternatives to the streets.

This unity is true of Patterson's final draft but not of her first draft, where she drifted into considering how the homeless make other people uncomfortable. The topic could be interesting, but it blurred Patterson's focus on the homeless and their choices. Recognizing as much, Patterson deleted her entire second-to-last paragraph when she revised (see p. 43). Deleting this distracting passage also helped Patterson clarify her conclusion.

Like Patterson, you may be pulled in more than one direction by drafting, so that you digress from your thesis or pursue more than one thesis. Drafting and then revising are your chances to find and then sharpen your focus. Revising for unity strengthens your thesis.

Revising for Coherence

Writing is **coherent** when readers can follow it easily and can see how the parts relate to each other. The ideas develop in a clear sequence, the sentences and paragraphs connect logically, and the connections are clear and smooth. The writing flows.

Coherence in Paragraphs

Coherence starts as sentences build paragraphs. The example on the next page (also reprinted in Chapter 4 on description) shows several devices for achieving coherence in paragraphs:

- Repetition or restatement of key words (underlined twice in the example).
- Pronouns such as *it* or *they* that substitute for nouns such as *ice* or *birds* (circled in the example).
- Parallelism, the use of similar grammatical structures for related ideas of the same importance (underlined once in the example). See also page 48.

- Transitions that clearly link the parts of sentences and whole sentences (boxed in the example). See the Glossary, page 372, for a list of transitions.

> Pastel icebergs roamed around us, some tens of thousands of years old. Great pressure can push the air bubbles out of the ice and compact it. Free of air bubbles, it reflects light differently, as blue. The waters shivered with the gooseflesh of small ice shards. Some icebergs glowed like dull peppermint in the sun—impurities trapped in the ice (phytoplankton and algae) tinted them green. Ethereal snow petrels flew around the peaks of the icebergs, while the sun shone through their translucent wings. White, silent, the birds seemed to be pieces of ice flying with purpose and grace. As they passed in front of an ice floe, they became invisible. Glare transformed the landscape with such force that it seemed like a pure color. When we went out in the inflatable motorized rafts called Zodiacs to tour the iceberg orchards, I grabbed a piece of glacial ice and held it to my ear, listening to the bubbles cracking and popping as the air trapped inside escaped. And that night, though exhausted from the day's spectacles and doings, I lay in my narrow bunk, awake with my eyes closed, while sunstruck icebergs drifted across the insides of my lids, and the Antarctic peninsula revealed itself slowly, mile by mile, in the small theater of my closed eyes.
>
> —Diane Ackerman, from
> *A Natural History of the Senses*

Check all your paragraphs to be sure that each sentence connects with the one preceding and that readers will see the connection without having to stop and reread. You may not need all the coherence devices Ackerman uses, or as many as she uses, but every paragraph you write will require some devices to stitch the sentences into a seamless cloth.

Coherence in Essays

Reading a coherent essay, the audience does not have to ask "What does this have to do with the preceding paragraph?" or "Where is the writer going here?" The connections are apparent, and the organization is clear and logical.

Transitions work between paragraphs as well as within them to link ideas. When the ideas in two paragraphs are closely related, a simple word or phrase at the start of the second one may be all that's needed to show the relation. In each example below, the italicized transition opens the topic sentence of the paragraph:

> *Moreover,* the rising costs of health care have long outstripped inflation. . . .

> *However,* some kinds of health-care plans have proved much more expensive than others. . . .

When a paragraph is beginning a new part of the essay or otherwise changing direction, a sentence or more at the beginning will help explain the shift. In the next example, the first sentence summarizes the preceding paragraph, the second introduces the topic of the new paragraph, and the third gives the paragraph's topic sentence:

> Traditional health-care plans have *thus* become an unaffordable luxury for most individuals and businesses. The majority of those with health insurance *now* find themselves in so-called managed plans. Though they do vary, managed plans share at least two features: they pay full benefits only when the insured person consults an approved doctor, and they require prior approval for certain procedures. . . .

Notice that italicized transitions provide further cues about the relationship of ideas.

Though transitions can provide signposts to alert readers to movement from one idea to another, they can't achieve coherence by themselves. Just as important is an overall organization that directs readers in a familiar pattern:

- A **spatial organization** arranges information to parallel the way we scan people, objects, or places: top to bottom, left to right, front to back, near to far, or vice versa. This scheme is especially useful for description (Chapter 4).
- A **chronological organization** arranges events or steps as they occurred in time, first to last. Such an arrangement usually organizes a narrative (Chapter 5) or a process analysis (Chapter 9) and may also help with cause-and-effect analysis (Chapter 12).

- A **climactic organization** proceeds in order of climax, usually from least to most important, building to the most interesting example, the most telling point of comparison, the most significant argument. A climactic organization is most useful for example (Chapter 6), division or analysis (Chapter 7), classification (Chapter 8), comparison and contrast (Chapter 10), definition (Chapter 11), and argument and persuasion (Chapter 13), and it may also work for cause-and-effect analysis (Chapter 12).

The introduction to each method of development in Chapters 4–13 gives detailed advice on organizing with these arrangements and variations on them.

When revising your draft for coherence, try outlining it by jotting down the topic sentence of each paragraph and the key support for each topic. The exercise will give you some distance from your ideas and words, allowing you to see the structure like a skeleton. Will your readers grasp the logic of your arrangement? Will they see why you move from each idea to the next one? After checking the overall structure, be sure you've built in enough transitions between sentences and paragraphs to guide readers through your ideas.

Revising for Development

When you **develop** an idea, you provide concrete and specific details, examples, facts, opinions, and other evidence to make the idea vivid and true in readers' minds. Readers will know only as much as you tell them about your thesis and its support. Gaps, vague statements, and unsupported conclusions will undermine your efforts to win their interest and agreement.

Development begins in sentences, when you use the most concrete and specific words you can muster to explain your meaning. (See pp. 50–51.) At the level of the paragraph, these sentences develop the paragraph's topic. Then, at the level of the whole essay, these paragraphs develop the governing thesis.

The key to adequate development is a good sense of your readers' needs for information and reasons. The list of questions on page 19 can help you estimate these needs as you start to write; reconsidering the questions when you revise can help you see where your draft may fail to address, say, readers' unfamiliarity with your subject or possible resistance to your thesis.

The introduction to each method of development in Chapters 4–13 includes specific advice for meeting readers' needs when using the method to develop paragraphs and essays. When you sense that a paragraph or section of your essay is thin but you don't know how to improve it, you can also try the discovery techniques given on pages 19–21 or ask the questions for all the methods of development on pages 21–25.

Revising for Tone

The **tone** of writing is like the tone of voice in speech: it expresses the writer's attitude toward his or her subject and audience. In writing we express tone with word choice and sentence structure. Notice the marked differences in these two passages discussing the same information on the same subject:

> Voice mail can be convenient, sure, but for callers it's usually more trouble than it's worth. We waste time "listening to the following menu choices," when we just want the live person at the end. All too often, there isn't even such a person!

> For callers the occasional convenience of voice mail generally does not compensate for its inconveniences. Most callers would prefer to speak to a live operator but must wait through a series of choices to reach that person. Increasingly, companies with voice mail systems do not offer live operators at all.

The first passage is informal, expresses clear annoyance, and with *we* includes the reader in that attitude. The second passage is more formal and more objective, reporting the situation without involving readers directly.

Tone can range from casual to urgent, humorous to serious, sad to elated, pleased to angry, personal to distant. The particular tone you choose for a piece of writing depends on your purpose and your audience. For most academic and business writing, you will be trying to explain or argue a point to your equals or superiors. Your readers will be interested more in the substance of your writing than in a startling tone, and indeed an approach that is too familiar or unserious or hostile could put them off. In other kinds of writing, you have more latitude. A warm and lighthearted tone may be just right for a personal narrative, and a touch of anger may help to grab the reader's attention in a letter to a magazine editor.

Tone is something you want to evaluate in revision, along with whether you've achieved your purpose and whether you've developed your thesis adequately for your audience. But adjusting tone is largely a matter of replacing words and restructuring sentences, work that could distract you from an overall view of your essay. If you think your tone is off-base, you may want to devote a separate phase of revision to it, after addressing unity, coherence, and the other matters discussed in this section on revision.

For advice on sentence structures and word choices, see the section on editing, beginning on page 44.

Using a Revision Checklist

The checklist below summarizes the advice on revision given here. Use the checklist to remind yourself what to look for in your first draft. But don't try to answer all the questions in a single reading

CHECKLIST FOR REVISION

- What is your purpose in writing? Will it be clear to readers? Do you achieve it?
- What is your thesis? Where is it made clear to readers?
- How unified is your essay? How does each subpoint in your body paragraphs support your thesis? (Look especially at your topic sentences.) How does each sentence in the body paragraphs support the topic sentence of the paragraph?
- How coherent is your essay? Do repetition and restatement, pronouns, parallelism, and transitions link the sentences in paragraphs? Do transitions and overall organization smooth and clarify the flow of ideas?
- How well developed is your essay? Where might readers need more evidence to understand your ideas and find them convincing?
- What is the tone of your essay? How is it appropriate for your purpose and your audience?
- How does your introduction work to draw readers in and orient them to your purpose and thesis? How does your conclusion work to pull the essay together and give readers a sense of completion?

of the draft. Instead, take the questions one by one, rereading the whole draft for each. That way you'll be able to concentrate on each element with minimal distraction from the others.

Note that the introductions to the methods of development in Chapters 4–13 also have their own revision checklists. Combining this list with the one for the method you're using will produce a more targeted set of questions. (The guide inside the front cover will direct you to the discussion you want.)

Grace Patterson's Revised Draft

Considering questions like those in the revision checklist led the student Grace Patterson to revise the rough draft we saw on pages 28–30. Patterson's revision follows. Notice that she made substantial cuts, especially of digressions near the end of the draft. She also revamped the introduction, tightened many passages, improved the coherence of paragraphs, and wrote a wholly new conclusion to sharpen her point. She did not try to improve her style or fix errors at this stage, leaving these activities for later editing.

~~Title?~~ A Rock and a Hard Place

In the essay~~,~~ "The Box Man~~,~~" Barbara Ascher says that a homeless man who has chosen solitude can show the rest of us how to "find . . . a friend in our own voice." Maybe. But ~~her~~ Ascher's case depends on the Box Man's choice, her assumption that he *had* one.

Discussions of the homeless often use the word *choice*. Many ~~people with enough money can accept the condition of the homeless in America when they tell themselves~~ of us with homes would like to think that many of the homeless chose their lives. ~~That the streets are in fact what they want. But it's not fair to use the word *choice* here: the homeless don't get~~

~~to choose their lives the way most of the rest of us do.~~ *But* ~~F~~or the homeless people in America today, there are no good choices.

What do I mean by a "good choice"? *A good choice is* ~~One~~ made from a variety of options determined and narrowed down by the chooser. There is plenty of room for the chooser to make a decision that he will be satisfied with. When I choose a career, I expect to make a good choice. There is plenty of interesting fields worth investigating, and there is lots of rewarding work to be done. ~~It's a choice that opens the world up and showcases its possibilities.~~ *However,* ~~I~~f ~~it came time for me to choose a career, and~~ the mayor of my town came around and told me that I had to choose between a life of cleaning public toilets and operating a jackhammer on a busy street corner, I would object. That's a lousy choice, and I wouldn't let anyone force me to make it.

When the mayor of New York tried to take ~~the~~ homeless *people* off the streets, *he likewise offered them a bad choice.* ~~some of them didn't want to go. People assumed that the homeless people who did not want to~~ *They could* get in the mayor's car for a ride to a city shelter *or they could stay* ~~chose to live~~ on the street. ~~But just because some homeless people chose the street over the generosity of the mayor does not necessarily mean that life on the streets is their ideal.~~ *People assumed that the homeless people who refused a ride to the shelter wanted to live on the street. But that assumption is not necessarily true.*

We allow ourselves as many options as we can imagine, but

both unpleasant.

we allow the homeless only two/, ~~go to a shelter, or stay where you are. Who narrowed down the options for the homeless? Who benefits if they go to a shelter? Who suffers if they don't?~~

Homeless people are not always better off in

Last Sunday,

shelters.^I had a conversation with a man who had lived

He

on the streets for a long time. ~~The man~~ said that he had spent some time in those shelters for the homeless, and

They're dangerous and

he told me what they were like. ~~The shelters are crowded~~

dehumanizing. Drug dealing, beatings, and theft are common.

~~and dirty and people have to wait in long lines for~~

The shelters are dirty and crowded, so that residents have to wait in

~~everything. People are constantly being herded around and~~

long lines for everything and are constantly

^bossed around. ~~It's dangerous--drug dealers, beatings, theft. Dehumanizing. It matches my picture of hell. From~~

No wonder some homeless people prefer the street: some space to

~~the sound of it, I couldn't spend two hours in a shelter,~~

breathe, some autonomy, some peace for sleeping.

~~never mind a whole night. I value my peace of mind and my sleep too much, not to mention my freedom and autonomy.~~

~~When homeless people sleep in the street, though, that makes the public uncomfortable. People with enough money wish the homeless would just disappear. They don't care where they go. Just out of sight. I've felt this way too but I'm as uneasy with that reaction as I am at the sight of a person sleeping on the sidewalk. And I tell myself that this is more than a question of my comfort. By and large I'm comfortable enough.~~

The homeless are in a difficult enough situation without having to take the blame for making the rest of us feel uncomfortable with our wealth. If we cannot offer the homeless a good set of choices, the opportunity to choose lives that they will be truly satisfied with then the least we can do is stop dumping on them (?). They're caught between a rock and a hard place: there are not many places for them to go, and the places where they can go afford nothing but suffering.

Focusing on the supposed choices the homeless have may make us feel better, but it distracts attention from the kinds of choices that are really being denied the homeless. The options we take for granted—a job with decent pay, an affordable home—do not belong to the homeless. They're caught between no shelter at all and shelter that dehumanizes, between a rock and a hard place.

EDITING

In editing you turn from global issues of purpose, thesis, unity, coherence, development, and tone to more particular issues of sentences and words. In a sense revision occurs beneath the lines, in the deeper meaning and structure of the essay. Editing occurs more between the lines, on the surface of the essay.

Like revision, editing requires that you gain some distance from your work so that you can see it objectively. Try these techniques:

- Work on a clean copy of your revised draft. If you write on a computer, edit on a printout rather than on the computer: it's more difficult to read text and spot errors on a screen.
- Read your revised draft aloud or into a tape recorder so you can hear the words. But be sure to read what you have actually written, not what you may have intended to write but didn't.
- To catch errors, try reading your draft backward sentence by sentence. You'll be less likely to get caught up in the flow of your ideas.

- Profit from your past writing experiences by keeping a personal checklist of problems that others have pointed out to you. Add this personal checklist to the one on page 53.

Making Sentences Clear and Effective

Clear and effective sentences convey your meaning concisely and precisely. In editing you want to ensure that readers will understand you easily, follow your ideas without difficulty, and stay interested in what you have to say.

Conciseness

In drafting, we often circle around our ideas, making various attempts to express them. As a result, sentences may use more words than necessary to make their points. To edit for conciseness, focus on the following changes:

- *Put the main meaning of the sentence in its subject, verb, and any object of the verb.* Generally, the subject should name the agent of your idea, the verb should describe what the agent did or was, and an object of the verb may name the receiver of the action. Notice the difference in these two sentences (the subjects and verbs are italicized):

  WORDY According to some experts, the *use* of calculators by students *is* sometimes a reason why they fail to develop computational skills.

  CONCISE According to some experts, *students* who use calculators sometimes *fail* to develop computational skills.

  By focusing on the key elements of the idea, the students and their occasional failure, the edited sentence saves seven words and is easier to follow.

- *Delete repetition and padding.* Words that don't contribute to your meaning will interfere with readers' understanding and interest. Watch out for unneeded repetition or restatement, such as that italicized in the following sentence:

  WORDY Students *in the schools* should have ample practice in computational skills, *skills* such as long division and using fractions.

  CONCISE Students should have ample practice in computational skills, such as long division and using fractions.

Padding occurs most often often with empty phrases that add no meaning:

WORDY *In this particular regard, the nature of* calculators *is such that* they remove the drudgery from computation but can also *for all intents and purposes* interfere with the development of important cognitive skills.

CONCISE Calculators remove the drudgery from computation but can also interfere with the development of important cognitive skills.

- *Use the active voice.* In the active voice, a verb describes the action *by* the subject (*We grilled vegetables*), whereas in the passive voice a verb describes the action done *to* the subject (*Vegetables were grilled,* or, adding who did the action, *Vegetables were grilled by us*). The active voice usually conveys more information in fewer words than the passive. The active is also clearer, more direct, and more forceful because it always names the actor.

  WORDY PASSIVE Calculators *were withheld* from some classrooms by school administrators, and the math performance of students with and without the machines *was compared.*

  CONCISE ACTIVE School administrators *withheld* calculators from some classrooms and *compared* the math performance of students with and without the machines.

Emphasis

Once your sentences are as concise as you can make them, you'll want to see that they give the appropriate emphasis to your ideas. Readers will look for the idea of a sentence in its subject, verb, and any object of the verb (see also p. 45), and they will expect words and word groups to clarify or add texture to the idea by modifying it. You can emphasize the idea in various ways by altering the structure of the sentence:

- *Use subordination to stress the sentence's subject, verb, and object.* **Subordination** places less important information in words or word groups that modify the subject, verb, and object:

  UNEMPHATIC *Computers can manipulate film and photographs,* and *we can* no longer *trust these media* to represent reality. [The sentence has two subject-verb-object structures (both in italics), and they seem equally important.]

  EMPHATIC *Because* computers can manipulate film and photographs, we can no longer trust these media to represent reality.

[*Because* makes the first subject-verb-object group into a modifier, de-emphasizing the cause of the change and emphasizing the effect.]

The next example of subordination reduces word groups that are already subordinate to single words, thus emphasizing the main subject, verb, and object even more:

UNEMPHATIC In a computer-manipulated photograph, a person *who is living now* can shake hands with a person *who is already dead.*

EMPHATIC In a computer-manipulated photograph, a *living* person can shake hands with *a dead one.*

- *Use coordination to stress the equal importance of ideas.* **Coordination** uses *and, but, or,* or *nor* to join two or more ideas and emphasize their equality. It can link the ideas of separate sentences in one sentence:

  UNEMPHATIC Two people may be complete strangers. A photograph can show them embracing.

  EMPHATIC Two people may be complete strangers, *but* a photograph can show them embracing.

- *Place modifiers to give desired emphasis to ideas.* The end of a sentence is its most emphatic position, and the beginning is next most emphatic. Placing the sentence's subject, verb, and any object in one of these positions draws readers' attention to them. In these sentences the core idea is in italics:

  UNEMPHATIC With computerized images, *filmmakers can entertain us,* placing historical figures alongside today's actors.

  EMPHATIC With computerized images that place historical figures alongside today's actors, *filmmakers can entertain us.*

  EMPHATIC *Filmmakers can entertain us* with computerized images that place historical figures alongside today's actors.

- *Use short sentences to underscore points.* A very short sentence amid longer sentences will focus readers' attention on a key point:

  UNEMPHATIC Such images of historical figures and fictional characters have a disadvantage, however, in that they blur the boundaries of reality.

  EMPHATIC Such images of historical figures and fictional characters have a disadvantage, however. They blur the boundaries of reality.

Parallelism

Parallelism is the use of similar grammatical structures for elements of similar importance, either within or among sentences.

PARALLELISM WITHIN A SENTENCE Smoking can *worsen heart disease* and *cause lung cancer.*

PARALLELISM AMONG SENTENCES Smoking has less well-known effects, too. *It can cause* gum disease. *It can impair* circulation of blood and other fluids. And *it can reduce* the body's supply of vitamins and minerals.

Parallelism can help relate sequential sentences, improving paragraph coherence (see p. 35). It also clarifies when sentences or elements within them are equivalent, so that readers see the relationship automatically. Without the signal of parallelism in the first sentence below, the reader must stop to work out that both italicized elements are nonmedical consequences:

NONPARALLEL Smoking has nonmedical consequences as well, including *loss of productivity* for smokers at work and *insurance expenses are high* for smokers.

PARALLEL Smoking has nonmedical consequences as well, including smokers' *loss of productivity* at work and *high expenses for insurance.*

Variety

Variety in the structure and length of sentences helps keep readers alert and interested, but it also does more. By emphasizing important points and de-emphasizing less important points, varied sentences make your writing clearer and easier to follow. The first passage below is adapted from Jon Katz's "How Boys Become Men" (see p. 298). The second is the passage Katz actually wrote.

UNVARIED I was walking my dog last month past the playground near my house. I saw three boys encircling a fourth. They were laughing and pushing him. He was skinny and rumpled, and he looked frightened. One boy knelt behind him. Another pushed him from the front. The trick was familiar to any former boy. The victim fell backward.

VARIED Last month, walking my dog past the playground near my house, I saw three boys encircling a fourth, laughing and pushing him. He was skinny and rumpled, and he looked frightened. One boy knelt behind him while another pushed him from the front, a trick familiar to any former boy. He fell backward.

Katz's actual sentences work much better to hold and direct our attention because he uses several techniques to achieve variety:

- *Vary the lengths of sentences.* The eight sentences in the unvaried adaptation range from four to thirteen words. Katz's four sentences range from three to twenty-two words, with the long first sentence setting the scene and the short final sentence creating a climax.
- *Vary the beginnings of sentences.* Every sentence in the adaptation begins with its subject (*I, I, They, He, One boy, Another, The trick, The victim*). Katz, in contrast, begins one sentence with a transition and a modifier (*Last month, walking my dog past the playground near my house . . .*).
- *Vary the structure of sentences.* The sentences in the adaptation are all similar in structure, marching like soldiers down the page and making it difficult to pick out the important events of the story. Katz's version emphasizes the important events by making them the subjects and verbs of the sentences, turning the other information into modifiers that either precede or follow.

Choosing the Right Words

The words you use can have a dramatic effect on how readers understand your meaning, perceive your attitude, and respond to your thesis.

Denotation

The **denotation** of a word is its dictionary meaning, the literal sense without emotional overtones. Using a word with the wrong denotation muddies meaning. For instance, *reward* is different from *award,* and *sites* is different from *cites.* Substituting one for the other will confuse readers momentarily, and several such confusions can undermine readers' patience.

Consult a dictionary whenever you are unsure of a word's meaning. Be especially careful to distinguish between words with similar sounds but different meanings, such as *sites* and *cites* or *whether* and *weather,* and between words with related but distinct meanings, such as *reward* and *award* or *famous* and *infamous.* Keeping a list of the new words you acquire will help you build your vocabulary.

Connotation

A word's **connotations** are the emotional associations it produces in readers. *Bawling* denotes loud crying, but it connotes lack of control and dignity: we do not sympathize with bawlers. Writing that someone *bawled* will elicit a different reaction from readers than saying the person *wept* or *keened*—other kinds of crying with other connotations.

Using words with strong connotations can shape readers' responses to your ideas. For another example, consider the distinctions among *feeling, enthusiasm, passion,* and *mania.* Describing a group's *enthusiasm* for its cause is quite different from describing its *mania*: the latter connotes much more intensity, even irrationality. If your aim is to imply that the group's enthusiasm is excessive, and you think your readers will respond well to that characterization, then *mania* may be the appropriate word. But words can backfire if they set off inappropriate associations in readers.

A hardcover desk dictionary will usually distinguish among the connotations of words. You'll find a wider range of choices in a thesaurus, which lists words with similar meanings, but it won't provide definitions. Don't use a word from a thesaurus unless you are sure of its denotation and connotations, information you can find in a dictionary.

Choosing the Best Words

Attending to the established denotations and connotations of words will help you make correct and effective choices, but you can do more to convey your meaning clearly and interestingly if you opt for words that are specific, concrete, and fresh.

Concrete and Specific Words

Clear, exact writing balances abstract and general words, which provide outlines of ideas and things, with concrete and specific words, which limit and sharpen.

- **Abstract words** name ideas, qualities, attitudes, or states that we cannot perceive with our senses of sight, hearing, touch, smell, and taste: *liberty, hate, anxious, brave, idealistic.* **Concrete words**, in contrast, name objects, persons, places, or states that we can perceive with our senses: *newspaper, police officer, Mississippi River, red-faced, tangled, screeching.*

- **General words** name groups: *building, color, clothes.* **Specific words** name particular members of a group: *courthouse, red, trousers, black Levi's.*

You need abstract and general words for broad statements that set the course for your writing, conveying concepts or referring to entire groups. But you also need concrete and specific words to make meaning precise and vivid by appealing to readers' senses and experiences. The following examples show how much clearer and more interesting a sentence becomes when its abstractions and generalities are brought down to concrete and specific details:

VAGUE The pollution was apparent in the odor and color of the small stream.

EXACT The narrow stream, just four feet wide, smelled like rotten eggs and ran the greenish color of coffee with nonfat milk.

The first sentence leaves it to readers to imagine the size, odor, and color of the stream. A few readers may guess at details, but most won't bother: they'll just pass on without getting the picture. In contrast, the second sentence *shows* the stream just as the writer experienced it, in disturbing detail.

Concrete and specific language may seem essential only in description like that of the polluted stream, but it is equally crucial in any other kind of writing. Readers can't be expected to understand or agree with general statements unless they know what evidence the statements are based on. The evidence is in the details, and the details are in concrete and specific words.

Figures of Speech

You can make your writing concrete and specific, even lively and forceful, with **figures of speech,** expressions that imply meanings beyond or different from their literal meanings. Here are some of the most common figures:

- A **simile** compares two unlike things with the use of *like* or *as: The car spun around like a top. Coins as bright as sunshine lay glinting in the chest.*

- A **metaphor** also compares two unlike things, but more subtly, equating them without *like* or *as: The words shattered my fragile self-esteem. The laboratory was a prison, the beakers and test-tubes her guards.*
- **Personification** is a simile or metaphor that attributes human qualities or powers to things or abstractions: *The breeze sighed and whispered in the grasses. The city squeezed me tightly at first but then relaxed its grip.*
- **Hyperbole** is a deliberate overstatement or exaggeration: *The dentist filled the tooth with a bracelet's worth of silver. The children's noise shook the walls and rafters.*

By briefly translating experiences and qualities into vividly concrete images, figures of speech can be economical and powerful. But be careful not to combine figures and thus create confusing or absurd images in readers' minds. This mixed metaphor conjures up conflicting images of bees and dogs: *The troops swarmed the field like pit bulls ready for a fight.*

Fresh Language

In trying for concrete and specific words, we sometimes resort to **clichés,** worn phrases that have lost their descriptive power: *tried and true, ripe old age, hour of need.* Many clichés are exhausted figures of speech, such as *heavy as lead, thin as a rail,* or *goes on forever.*

If you have trouble recognizing clichés in your writing, be suspicious of any expression you have heard or read before. When you do find a cliché, cure it by substituting plain language (for instance, *reliable* for *tried and true*) or by substituting a fresh figure of speech (*thin as a sapling* for *thin as a rail*).

Using an Editing Checklist

The checklist on the facing page summarizes the editing advice given in this section and adds a few other technical concerns as well. Some of the items will be more relevant for your writing than others: you may have little difficulty with variety in sentences but may worry that your language is too general. Concentrate your editing efforts where they're needed most, and then survey your draft to check for other problems.

CHECKLIST FOR EDITING

- How clear and concise is each sentence? Have you put the main meaning in the subject, verb, and any object of the verb? Is there repetition and padding to delete? Have you relied on the active voice of verbs?
- How well do sentences emphasize their main ideas with subordination, coordination, modifier placement, or length?
- Where is parallelism needed within or between sentences to increase clarity and coherence?
- Where should groups of sentences be more varied in length and structure to improve clarity and readability?
- Which words should be changed either because they have the wrong denotations or because their connotations are inappropriate for your meaning or your audience?
- Where should you make your meaning less abstract and general with concrete and specific words or with figures of speech? Where do clichés need editing?
- Where do sentences need editing for grammar or punctuation—so that, for instance, pronouns such as *he* and *him* are used correctly, subjects and verbs agree, sentences are complete, and apostrophes fall in the right places? Concentrate on finding errors that readers have pointed out in your work before.
- Where might spelling be a problem? Look up any word you're not absolutely sure of, or use your computer's spelling checker. (You'll still have to proofread a spell-checked paper, though, because the programs can't catch everything.)

Grace Patterson's Editing and Final Draft

The paragraph on the next page comes from the edited draft of Grace Patterson's "A Rock and a Hard Place." Then Patterson's full final draft appears with notes in the margins highlighting its thesis, structure, and uses of the methods of development. If you compare the final version with the first draft on pages 28–30, you'll see clearly how Patterson's revising and editing transformed the essay from a rough exploration of ideas to a refined, and convincing, essay.

EDITED PARAGRAPH

~~What do I mean by~~ *A* ~~a~~ "good choice"~~?~~ ~~A good choice~~ is *one* made from a variety of options determined and narrowed down by the chooser. ~~There is plenty of room for the chooser to make a decision that he will be satisfied with.~~ When I choose a career, I expect to make a good choice. There *are many* ~~is plenty of~~ interesting fields *to* ~~worth~~ investigat*e,* ~~ing,~~ and there is *much* ~~lots of~~ rewarding work to *do.* ~~be done.~~ If the mayor of my town *suddenly* ~~around and~~ told me that I *would have* ~~had~~ to choose between a *career* ~~life~~ of cleaning public toilets and *one of* operating a jackhammer on a busy street corner, I would object. That's a *bad* ~~lousy~~ choice~~,~~. ~~and I wouldn't let anyone force me to make it.~~

FINAL DRAFT

A Rock and a Hard Place

In the essay "The Box Man" Barbara Ascher says that a homeless man who has chosen solitude can show the rest of us how to "find . . . a friend in our own voice." Maybe he can. But Ascher's case depends on the Box Man's choice, her assumption that he had one. Discussions of the homeless often involve the word choice. Many of us with homes would like to think that many of the homeless chose their lives. But for the homeless people in America today, there are no good choices.

Introduction: establishes point of contention with Ascher's essay

Thesis sentence (see pp. 17–18)

A "good choice" is one made from a variety of options determined and narrowed down by the chooser. When I choose a career, I expect to make a good choice. There are many interesting fields to investigate, and there is much rewarding work to do. If the mayor of my town suddenly told me that I would have to choose between a career of cleaning public toilets and one of operating a jackhammer on a busy street corner, I would object. That's a bad choice.

Definition and comparison of good choices *and* bad choices

Examples

When the mayor of New York tried to remove the homeless people from the streets, he offered them a similarly bad choice. They could get in the mayor's car for a ride to a city shelter, or they could stay on the street. People assumed that the homeless people who refused a ride to the shelter wanted to live on the street. But the assumption is not necessarily true. We allow ourselves as many options as we can imagine, but we allow the homeless only two, both unpleasant.

Application of definition to homeless; analysis of choice offered

The fact is that homeless people are not always better off in shelters. I recently had a conversation with a man named Alan who had lived on the streets for a long time. He said that he had spent some time in shelters for the homeless, and he told me what they are like. They're dangerous and dehumanizing. Drug dealing, beatings, and theft are common. The shelters are dirty and crowded, so that residents have to wait in long lines for

Cause-and-effect analysis: why homeless avoid shelters

Description of shelter

everything and are constantly being bossed around. No wonder some homeless people, including Alan, prefer the street: it affords some space to breathe, some autonomy, some peace for sleeping.

Comparison of shelter and street

Focusing on the supposed choices the homeless have may make us feel better. But it distracts our attention from something more important than our comfort: the options we take for granted--a job with decent pay, an affordable home--are denied the homeless. These people are caught between no shelter at all and shelter that dehumanizes, between a rock and a hard place.

Conclusion: returns to good vs. bad choices; sums up with a familiar image

Chapter 4

DESCRIPTION

Sensing the Natural World

USING THE METHOD

Whenever you use words to depict or re-create a scene, object, person, or feeling, you use **description.** You draw on the perceptions of your five senses—sight, hearing, smell, taste, and touch—to understand and communicate your experience of the world. Description is a mainstay of conversation between people, and it is likely to figure in almost any writing situation: a letter home may describe a new roommate's spiky yellow hair; a laboratory report may describe the colors and odors of chemicals; a business memo may distinguish between the tastes of two competitors' chicken potpies.

Your purpose in writing and your involvement with the subject will largely determine how objective or subjective your description is.

- In **objective description** you strive for precision and objectivity, trying to convey the subject impersonally, without emotion. This is the kind of description required in scientific writing—for instance, a medical diagnosis or a report on an experiment in psychology—where cold facts and absence of feeling are essential for readers to judge the accuracy of procedures and results. It is also the method of news reports and of reference works such as encyclopedias.

- In **subject description,** in contrast, you draw explicitly on your emotions, giving an impression of the subject filtered through your experience of it. Instead of withdrawing to the background, you invest feelings in the subject and let those feelings determine which details to describe and how to describe them. Your state of mind—perhaps loneliness, anger, joy—can be re-created by reference to sensory details such as numbness, heat, or sweetness.

In general, you should favor objective description when your purpose is explanation and subjective description when your purpose is self-expression or entertainment. But the categories are not exclusive, and most descriptive writing mixes the two. A news report on a tropical storm, for instance, might objectively describe bent and broken trees, fallen wires, and lashing rains, but your selection of details would give a subjective impression of the storm's fearsomeness.

Whether objective or subjective or a mixture of the two, effective description requires a **dominant impression**—a central theme or idea about the subject to which readers can relate all the details. The dominant impression may be something you see in the subject, such as the apparent purposefulness of city pedestrians or the expressiveness of an actor. Or it may derive from your emotional response to the subject, perhaps pleasure (or depression) at all the purposefulness, perhaps admiration (or disdain) for the actor's technique. Whatever its source, the dominant impression serves as a unifying principle that guides your selection of details and the reader's understanding of the subject.

One aid to creating a dominant impression is a consistent **point of view,** a position from which you approach the subject. Point of view in description has two main elements:

- You take a real or imagined *physical* relation to the subject: you could view a mountain, for instance, from the bottom looking up, from fifteen miles away across a valley, or from an airplane passing overhead. The first two points of view are fixed because you remain in one position and scan the scene from there; the third is moving because you change position.

- You take a *psychological* relation to the subject, a relation partly conveyed by pronouns. In subjective description, where your feelings are part of the message, you might use *I* and *you* freely to narrow the distance between yourself and the subject and between yourself and the reader. But in the most objective, impersonal description, you will use *one* ("One can see the summit . . .") or avoid self-reference altogether in order to appear distant from and unbiased toward the subject.

Once you establish a physical and psychological point of view, readers come to depend on it. Thus a sudden and inexplicable shift from one view to another—zooming in from fifteen miles away to the foot of a mountain, abandoning *I* for the more removed *one*—can disorient readers and distract them from the dominant impression you are trying to create.

ANALYZING DESCRIPTION IN PARAGRAPHS

David Mura (born 1952) is a poet, essayist, and critic. This paragraph comes from his book *Turning Japanese* (1991), a memoir of his time in Japan as a *sansei,* or a third-generation Japanese American. Mura describes Tokyo during the rainy season.

And then the rains of June came, the typhoon season. Every day endless streaks of gray drilled down from the sky. A note held, passing from monotone into a deeper, more permanent dirge. The air itself seemed to liquefy, like the insides of a giant invisible jellyfish. In the streets the patter grew into pools, then rushes and torrents. Umbrellas floated, black bobbing circles, close as the wings of bats in underground caves. In the empty lot across the street, the grass turned a deep, tropical green; then the earth itself seemed to bubble up in patches, foaming. In the country, square after square of rice field filled to the brim and overflowed. In the city, the city of labyrinths, the rain became another labyrinth, increased the density of inhabitants; everything seemed thicker, moving underwater.

Specific, concrete details (underlined once)

Figures of speech (underlined twice)

Point of view: moving; psychologically somewhat distant

Dominant impression: overwhelming, intense wetness

Diane Ackerman (born 1948) is a poet and essayist who writes extensively on the natural world. The following paragraph comes from *A Natural History of the Senses* (1991), a prose exploration of sight, hearing, touch, taste, and smell.

Pastel icebergs roamed around us, some tens of thousand of years old. Great pressure can push the air bubbles out of the ice and compact it. Free of air bubbles, it reflects light differently, as blue. The waters shivered with the gooseflesh of small ice shards. Some icebergs glowed like dull peppermint in the sun—impurities trapped in the ice (phytoplankton and algae) tinted them green. Ethereal snow petrels flew around the peaks of the icebergs, while the sun shone through their translucent wings. White, silent, the birds seemed to be pieces of ice flying with purpose and grace. As they passed in front of an ice floe, they became invisible. Glare transformed the landscape with such force that it seemed like a pure color. When we went out in the inflatable motorized rafts called Zodiacs to tour the iceberg orchards, I grabbed a piece of glacial ice and held it to my ear, listening to the bubbles cracking and popping as the air trapped inside escaped. And that night, though exhausted from the day's spectacles and doings, I lay in my narrow bunk, awake with my eyes closed, while sunstruck icebergs drifted across the insides of my lids, and the Antarctic peninsula revealed itself slowly, mile by mile, in the small theater of my closed eyes.

Specific, concrete details (underlined once)

Figures of speech (underlined twice)

Point of view: fixed, then moving; psychologically close

Dominant impression: awesome, chilly brightness

DEVELOPING A DESCRIPTIVE ESSAY

Getting Started

The subject for a descriptive essay may be any object, place, person, or state of mind that you have observed closely enough or experienced sharply enough to invest with special significance. A chair, a tree, a room, a shopping mall, a movie actor, a passerby on the street, a feeling of fear, a sense of achievement—anything you have a strong impression of can prompt effective description.

When you have your subject, specify in a sentence the impression that you want to create for readers. The sentence will help keep you on track while you search for details, and later it may serve as the thesis of your essay. It should evoke a quality or an atmosphere or an effect, as these examples do:

> His fierce anger at the world shows in every word and gesture.
>
> The mall is a thoroughly unnatural place, like a space station in a science-fiction movie.

A sentence like one of these should give you a good start in choosing the sensory details that will make your description concrete and vivid. Observe your subject directly, if possible, or recall it as completely as you can. Jot down the details that seem to contribute most to the impression you're trying to convey. You needn't write the description of them yet—that can wait for drafting—but you do want to capture the possibilities in your subject. While exploring, try to remain alert to any variations in your dominant impression so that it can continue to guide your search.

At this stage you should start to consider the needs and expectations of your readers. If the subject is something readers have never seen or felt before, you will need enough objective details to create a complete picture in their minds. A description of a friend, for example, might focus on his distinctive voice and laugh, but readers will also want to know something about his appearance. If the subject is essentially abstract, like an emotion, you will need details to make it concrete for readers. And if the subject is familiar to readers, as a shopping mall or an old spruce tree on campus probably would be, you will want to skip obvious objective information in favor of fresh observations that will make readers see the subject anew.

Organizing

Though the details of a subject may not occur to you in any particular order, you should arrange them so that readers are not confused by your shifts among features. You can give readers a sense of the whole subject in the introduction to the essay: objective details of location or size or shape, the incident leading to a state of mind, or the reasons for describing a familiar object. In the introduction, also, you may want to state your thesis—the dominant impression you will create. An explicit thesis is not essential in description; sometimes you may prefer to let the details build to a conclusion. But the thesis should hover over the essay nonetheless, governing the selection of every detail and making itself as clear to readers as if it were stated outright.

The organization of the body of the essay depends partly on point of view and partly on dominant impression. If you take a moving point of view—say, strolling down a city street—the details will probably arrange themselves naturally. But a fixed point of view, scanning a subject from one position, requires your intervention. When the subject is a landscape, a person, or an object, you'll probably want to use a spatial organization: near to far, top to bottom, left to right, or vice versa. (See also p. 37.) Other subjects, such as a shopping mall, might be better treated in groups of features: shoppers, main concourses, insides of stores. Or a description of an emotional state might follow the chronological sequence of the event that aroused it (thus overlapping description and narration, the subject of the next chapter). The order itself is not important, as long as there is an order that channels readers' attention.

Drafting

The challenge of drafting your description will be bringing the subject to life. Whether it is in front of you or in your mind, you may find it helpful to consider the subject one sense at a time—what you can see, hear, smell, touch, taste. Of course, not all senses will be applicable to all subjects; a chair, for instance, may not have a noticeable odor, and you're unlikely to know its taste. But proceeding sense by sense can help you uncover details, such as the smell of a tree or the sound of a person's voice, that you may have overlooked.

Examining one sense at a time is also one of the best ways to conceive of concrete words and figures of speech to represent sensations and feelings. For instance, does *acid* describe the taste of fear? Does an actor's appearance suggest the smell of soap? Does a shopping mall smell like new dollar bills? In creating distinct physical sensations for readers, such representations make meaning inescapably clear. (See pp. 50–51 and the box opposite for more on specific, concrete language and figures of speech.)

Revising and Editing

When you are ready to revise and edit, use the following questions and box as a guide.

- *Have you in fact created the dominant impression you intended to create?* Check that you have plenty of specific details and that each one helps to pin down one crucial feature of your subject. Cut irrelevant details that may have crept in. What counts is not the number of details but their quality and the strength of the impression they make.
- *Are your point of view and organization clear and consistent?* Watch for confusing shifts from one vantage point or organizational scheme to another. Watch also for confusing and unnecessary shifts in pronouns, such as from *I* to *one* or vice versa. Any shifts in point of view or organization should be clearly essential for your purpose and for the impression you want to create.

FOCUS ON CONCRETE AND SPECIFIC LANGUAGE

For readers to imagine your subject, you'll need to use concrete, specific language that appeals to their experiences and senses. (See pp. 50–51 for the meanings of *concrete* and *specific*.) The first sentence below shows a writer's first-draft attempt to describe something she saw. After editing, the second sentence is much more vivid.

VAGUE Beautiful, scented wildflowers were in the field.

CONCRETE AND SPECIFIC Backlighted by the sun and smelling faintly sweet, an acre of tiny lavender flowers spread away from me.

The writer might also have used figures of speech (see p. 51) to show what she saw: for instance, describing the field as "a giant's bed covered in a quilt of lavender dots" (a metaphor) or describing the backlighted flowers as "glowing like tiny lavender lamps" (a simile).

When editing your description, keep a sharp eye out for vague words such as *delicious, handsome, loud,* and *short* that force readers to create their own impressions or, worse, leave them with no impression at all. Using details that call on readers' sensory experiences, say why delicious or why handsome, how loud or how short. When stuck for a word, conjure up your subject and see it, hear it, touch it, smell it, taste it.

Note that *concrete* and *specific* do not mean "fancy": good description does not demand five-dollar words when nickel equivalents are just as informative. The writer who uses *rubiginous* instead of *rusty red* actually says less because fewer readers will understand the less common word and all readers will sense a writer showing off.

A NOTE ON THEMATIC CONNECTIONS

The writers represented in this chapter all set out to explore something in nature. They probably didn't decide consciously to write a description, but turned to the method intuitively as they chose to record the perceptions of their senses. In a paragraph, David Mura captures the dense unpleasantness of a seemingly endless downpour (p. 59). In another paragraph, Diane Ackerman describes the sharp, lasting images of a sea of icebergs (p. 60). Marta K. Taylor's essay on a nighttime car ride climaxes in a lightning storm (next page). Larry Woiwode's essay on oranges depicts his childhood anticipation and enjoyment of sweet, ripe fruit (p. 69). And Joan Didion's essay on a wind coming from the mountains above Los Angeles shows how an air current can transform a city (p. 75).

Marta K. Taylor

Marta K. Taylor was born in 1970 and raised in Los Angeles. She attended a "huge" public high school there before being accepted into Harvard University. She graduated from Harvard in 1992 with a bachelor's degree in chemistry and from Harvard Medical School in 1998. She is now a resident physician in Chapel Hill, North Carolina, where she specializes in head and neck surgery.

Desert Dance

Taylor wrote this description of a nighttime ride when she was a freshman in college taking the required writing course. The essay was published in the 1988–89 edition of Exposé, *a collection of student writing published by Harvard.*

We didn't know there was a rodeo in Flagstaff. All the hotels were filled, except the really expensive ones, so we decided to push on to Winslow that night. Dad must have thought we were all asleep, and so we should have been, too, as it was after one A.M. and we had been driving all day through the wicked California and Arizona desert on the first day of our August Family Trip. The back seat of our old station wagon was down, allowing two eleven-year-old kids to lie almost fully extended and still leaving room for the rusty green Coleman ice-chest which held the packages of pressed turkey breast, the white bread, and the pudding snack-pacs that Mom had cleverly packed to save on lunch expenses and quiet the inevitable "Are we there yet?" and "How much farther?" 1

Jon was sprawled out on his back, one arm up and one arm down, reminding me of Gumby or an outline chalked on the sidewalk in a murder mystery. His mouth was wide open and his regular breath rattled deeply in the back of his throat somewhere between his mouth and his nose. Beside the vibration of the wheels and the steady hum of the engine, no other sound disturbed the sacred silence of the desert night. 2

From where I lay, behind the driver's seat, next to my twin brother on the old green patchwork quilt that smelled like beaches 3 and picnics—salty and a little mildewed—I could see my mother's curly brown head slumped against the side window, her neck bent awkwardly against the seat belt, which seemed the only thing holding her in her seat. Dad, of course, drove—a motionless, soundless, protective paragon of security and strength, making me feel totally safe. The back of his head had never seemed more perfectly framed than by the reflection of the dashboard lights on the windshield; the short, raven-colored wiry hairs that I loved so much caught and played with, like tinsel would, the greenish glow with red and orange accents. The desert sky was starless, clouded.

Every couple of minutes, a big rig would pass us going west. The 4
lights would illuminate my mother's profile for a moment and then the roar of the truck would come and the sudden, the violent sucking rush of air and we would be plunged into darkness again. Time passed so slowly, unnoticeably, as if the whole concept of time were meaningless.

I was careful to make no sound, content to watch the rising and 5
falling of my twin's chest in the dim light and to feel on my cheek the gentle heat of the engine rising up through the floorboards. I lay motionless for a long time before the low rumbling, a larger sound than any eighteen-wheeler, rolled across the open plain. I lifted my head, excited to catch a glimpse of the rain that I, as a child from Los Angeles, seldom saw. A few seconds later, the lightning sliced the night sky all the way across the northern horizon. Like a rapidly growing twig, at least three or four branches, it illuminated the twisted forms of Joshua trees and low-growing cacti. All in silhouette—and only for a flash, though the image stayed many moments before my mind's eye in the following black.

The lightning came again, this time only a formless flash, as if 6
God were taking a photograph of the magnificent desert, and the long, straight road before us—empty and lonely—shone like a dagger. The trees looked like old men to me now, made motionless by the natural strobe, perhaps to resume their feeble hobble across the sands once the shield of night returned. The light show continued on the horizon though the expected rain never came. The fleeting, gnarled fingers grasped out and were gone; the fireworks flashed and frolicked and faded over and over—danced and jumped, acting out a drama in the quick, jerky movements of a marionette. Still in silence, still in darkness.

I watched the violent, gaudy display over the uninhabited, end- 7
less expanse, knowing I was in a state of grace and not knowing if I was dreaming but pretty sure I was awake because of the cramp in

my neck and the pain in my elbow from placing too much weight on it for too long.

Meaning

1. What does Taylor mean by "state of grace" in paragraph 7? What associations does this phrase have? To what extent does it capture the dominant impression of this essay?
2. If you do not know the meaning of any of the words below, try to guess it from its context in Taylor's essay. Test your guesses in a dictionary, and then try to use each word in a sentence or two of your own.

paragon (3)	gnarled (6)	marionette (6)
silhouette (5)	frolicked (6)	gaudy (7)
strobe (6)		

Purpose and Audience

1. Why does Taylor open with the sentence "We didn't know there was a rodeo in Flagstaff"? What purposes does the sentence serve?
2. Even readers familiar with the desert may not have had Taylor's experience of it in a nighttime lightning storm. Where does she seem especially careful about describing what she saw? What details surprised you?

Method and Structure

1. What impression or mood is Taylor trying to capture in this essay? How does the precise detail of the description help to convey that mood?
2. Taylor begins her description inside the car (paragraphs 1–5) and then moves out into the landscape (5–7), bringing us back into the car in her final thought. Why does she use such a sequence? Why do you think she devotes about equal space to each area?
3. Taylor's description is mainly subjective, invested with her emotions. Point to elements of the description that reveal emotion.
4. **Other Methods** Taylor's description relies in part on narration (Chapter 5). How does narrative strengthen the essay's dominant impression?

Language

1. How does Taylor's tone help convey the "state of grace" she feels inside the car? Point out three or four examples of language that establish that mood.

2. Why do you think Taylor titles her essay "Desert Dance"?
3. Notice the words Taylor uses to describe Joshua trees (paragraphs 5–6). If you're already familiar with the tree, how accurate do you find Taylor's description? If you've never seen a Joshua tree, what do you think it looks like, based on Taylor's description? (Next time you're in the library, look the tree up in an encyclopedia to test your impression.)
4. Taylor uses similes to make her description vivid and immediate. Find several examples, and comment on their effectiveness. (See p. 51 for more on similes.)
5. Taylor's last paragraph is one long sentence. Does this long sentence work with or against the content and mood of the paragraph? Why and how?

Writing Topics

1. **Journal Response** Taylor's description of the desert emerges from her memory of a childhood experience. Recall a vivid experience from your childhood—a visit to an unfamiliar place or an incident in your neighborhood, for instance. Jot down as many details from the experience as you can remember.

   Journal to Essay In an essay using subjective description, *show* readers what the experience was like for you. Be sure to convey a dominant impression.
2. Taylor's essay illustrates her feelings not only about the desert but also about her father, mother, and twin brother. Think of a situation when you were intensely aware of your feelings about another person (friend or relative). Describe the situation and the person in a way that conveys those feelings.
3. **Cultural Considerations** Though she had evidently seen the desert before, Taylor had not seen it the way she describes it in "Desert Dance." Write an essay in which you describe your first encounter with something new—for instance, a visit to the home of a friend from a different social or economic background, a visit to a big city or a farm, an unexpected view of your own backyard. Describe what you saw and your responses. How, if at all, did the experience change you?
4. **Connections** Both Taylor and Diane Ackerman (in the paragraph on p. 60) experience awe at a natural wonder. In a brief essay, analyze how these writers convey their sense of awe so that it is concrete, not vague. Focus on their words and especially on their figures of speech. (See pp. 51–52 for more on figures of speech.)

Larry Woiwode

A fiction writer, poet, and essayist, Larry Woiwode was born in 1941 in Carrington, North Dakota, and grew up in rural North Dakota and Illinois. His perceptions of the harsh climates and stark landscapes of the West and Midwest have influenced his work, in which natural detail often reflects and represents characters' feelings. Woiwode attended the University of Illinois in the early 1960s and has earned his living as a writer and teacher ever since. He has published two collections of stories, Neumiller Stories *(1989) and* Silent Passages *(1993); a book of poems,* Even Tide *(1975); five novels,* What I'm Going to Do, I Think *(1969),* Beyond the Bedroom Wall *(1975),* Poppa John *(1981),* Born Brothers *(1988), and* Indian Affairs *(1992); and a book of nonfiction,* Acts: A Writer's Reflections on the Church, Writing, and His Own Acts *(1993). In 1980 Woiwode received the fiction award from the American Academy and National Institute of Arts and Letters, and in 1995 he was made poet laureate of North Dakota, where he lives.*

Ode to an Orange

A critic has written that Woiwode's descriptions of nature can "hypnotize the senses" with their precision and vitality. In the following essay, first published in The Paris Review *in 1984, Woiwode turns his descriptive powers on a familiar fruit. While reading this description, recall your own experiences with oranges. When can you confirm Woiwode's impressions? When does he surprise you?*

---

1 Oh, those oranges arriving in the midst of the North Dakota winters of the forties—the mere color of them, carried through the door in a net bag or a crate from out of the white winter landscape. Their appearance was enough to set my brother and me to thinking that it might be about time to develop an illness, which was the surest way of receiving a steady supply of them.

2 "Mom, we think we're getting a cold."

3 "*We?* You mean, you two want an orange?"

4 This was difficult for us to answer or dispute; the matter seemed moved beyond our mere wanting.

5 "If you want an orange," she would say, "why don't you ask for one?"

6 "We want an orange."

7 "'We' again, '*We want an orange.*'"

8 "May we have an orange, please."

9 "That's the way you know I like you to ask for one. Now, why don't each of you ask for one in that same way, but separately?"

10 "Mom . . ." And so on. There was no depth of degradation that we wouldn't descend to in order to get one. If the oranges hadn't wended their way northward by Thanksgiving, they were sure to arrive before the Christmas season, stacked first in crates at the depot, filling that musty place, where pews sat back to back, with a springtime acidity, as if the building had been rinsed with a renewing elixir that set it right for yet another year. Then the crates would appear at the local grocery store, often with the top slats pried back on a few of them, so that we were aware of a resinous smell of fresh wood in addition to the already orangy atmosphere that foretold the season more explicitly than any calendar.

11 And in the broken-open crates (as if burst by the power of the oranges themselves), one or two of the lovely spheres would lie free of the tissue they came wrapped in—always purple tissue, as if that were the only color that could contain the populations of them in their nestled positions. The crates bore paper labels at one end—of an orange against a blue background, or of a blue goose against an orange background—signifying the colorful otherworld (unlike our wintry one) that these phenomena had arisen from. Each orange, stripped of its protective wrapping, as vivid in your vision as a pebbled sun, encouraged you to picture a whole pyramid of them in a bowl on your dining room table, glowing in the light, as if giving off the warmth that came through the windows from the real winter sun. And all of them came stamped with a blue-purple name as foreign as the otherworld that you might imagine as their place of origin, so that on Christmas day you would find yourself digging past everything else in your Christmas stocking, as if tunneling down to the country of China, in order to reach the rounded bulge at the tip of the toe which meant that you had received a personal reminder of another state of existence, wholly separate from your own.

12 The packed heft and texture, finally, of an orange in your hand—this is it!—and the eruption of smell and the watery fireworks as a knife, in the hand of someone skilled, like our mother, goes slicing through the skin so perfect for slicing. This gaseous spray can form a mist like smoke, which can then be lit with a match to

create actual fireworks if there is a chance to hide alone with a match (matches being forbidden) and the peel from one. Sputtery ignitions can also be produced by squeezing a peel near a candle (at least one candle is generally always going at Christmastime), and the leftover peels are set on the stove top to scent the house.

And the ingenious way in which oranges come packed into their 13
globes! The green nib at the top, like a detonator, can be bitten off, as if disarming the orange, in order to clear a place for you to sink a tooth under the peel. This is the best way to start. If you bite at the peel too much, your front teeth will feel scraped, like dry bone, and your lips will begin to burn from the bitter oil. Better to sink a tooth into this greenish or creamy depression, and then pick at that point with the nail of your thumb, removing a little piece of the peel at a time. Later, you might want to practice to see how large a piece you can remove intact. The peel can also be undone in one continuous ribbon, a feat which maybe your father is able to perform, so that after the orange is freed, looking yellowish, the peel, rewound, will stand in its original shape, although empty.

The yellowish whole of the orange can now be divided into sec- 14
tions, usually about a dozen, by beginning with a division down the middle; after this, each section, enclosed in its papery skin, will be able to be lifted and torn loose more easily. There is a stem up the center of the section like a mushroom stalk, but tougher; this can be eaten. A special variety of orange, without any pits, has an extra growth, or nubbin, like half of a tiny orange, tucked into its bottom. This nubbin is nearly as bitter as the peel, but it can be eaten, too; don't worry. Some of the sections will have miniature sections embedded in them and clinging as if for life, giving the impression that babies are being hatched, and should you happen to find some of these you've found the sweetest morsels of any.

If you prefer to have your orange sliced in half, as some people 15
do, the edges of the peel will abrade the corners of your mouth, making them feel raw, as you eat down into the white of the rind (which is the only way to do it) until you can see daylight through the orangy bubbles composing its outside. Your eyes might burn; there is no proper way to eat an orange. If there are pits, they can get in the way, and the slower you eat an orange, the more you'll find your fingers sticking together. And no matter how carefully you eat one, or bite into a quarter, juice can always fly or slip from a corner of your mouth; this happens to everyone. Close your eyes to be on the safe

side, and for the eruption in your mouth of the slivers of watery meat, which should be broken and rolled fine over your tongue for the essence of orange. And if indeed you have sensed yourself coming down with a cold, there is a chance that you will feel it driven from your head—your nose and sinuses suddenly opening—in the midst of the scent of a peel and eating an orange.

And oranges can also be eaten whole—rolled into a spongy mass and punctured with a pencil (if you don't find this offensive) or a knife, and then sucked upon. Then, once the juice is gone, you can disembowel the orange as you wish and eat away its pulpy remains, and eat once more into the whitish interior of the peel, which scours the coating from your teeth and makes your numbing lips and tip of your tongue start to tingle and swell up from behind, until, in the light from the windows (shining through an empty glass bowl), you see orange again from the inside. Oh, oranges, solid *o*'s, light from afar in the midst of the freeze, and not unlike that unspherical fruit which first went from Eve to Adam and from there (to abbreviate matters) to my brother and me. 16

"Mom, we think we're getting a cold." 17

"You mean, you want an orange?" 18

This is difficult to answer or dispute or even to acknowledge, finally, with the fullness that the subject deserves, and that each orange bears, within its own makeup, into this hard-edged yet insubstantial, incomplete, cold, wintry world. 19

Meaning

1. Woiwode opens and closes his essay with the same thought: his mother's question, "You mean, you want an orange?" was "difficult for us to answer or dispute" (paragraphs 4, 19). Why was it difficult? What did the orange signify to Woiwode that made "the matter" greater than "mere wanting"?
2. What dominant impression of the orange does Woiwode create?
3. If you're unsure of any of the following words, try to guess what they mean from the context of Woiwode's essay. Then look them up to see if you were right. Use each word in a sentence or two of your own.

ode (title)	resinous (10)	feat (13)
degradation (10)	heft (12)	abrade (15)
wended (10)	detonator (13)	disembowel (16)
elixir (10)		

Purpose and Audience

1. In repeating his reflection on his mother's question in paragraphs 4 and 19, Woiwode changes verb tense from past (for example, "This *was* difficult," 4) to present ("This *is* difficult," 19). What does this shift reveal about the grown Woiwode's reason for writing about his experiences and feelings as a child? To what extent are "North Dakota winters of the forties" (1) and "this . . . wintry world" (19) the same or different?
2. An ode usually praises some person or object. Is Woiwode's praise for the orange weakened by the unpleasant sensations he sometimes describes, such as bitterness (paragraph 14) or burning eyes (15)? Why, or why not?
3. Woiwode could expect his readers to be familiar with his subject: most of us have eaten an orange. To what extent does he succeed in making this familiar object and experience fresher and more significant? What details surprised you? What details evoked your own experiences?

Method and Structure

1. Woiwode mingles straightforward objective description and emotion-laden subjective description. Locate two or three examples of each kind in paragraphs 13–16. What does each kind contribute to the essay? How does combining the two types help Woiwode achieve his purpose?
2. In the body of the essay (paragraphs 10–16), Woiwode describes the orange from a number of perspectives. What topic does each of these paragraphs cover? Is the sequence of topics logical? Why, or why not?
3. **Other Methods** Woiwode uses several methods of development in addition to description—for instance, paragraphs 1–10 are narrative (Chapter 5), and paragraphs 13–14 divide the orange into its parts (Chapter 7). Most notably, paragraphs 13–16 analyze three processes (Chapter 9), three ways of eating an orange. Why does Woiwode explain these processes so painstakingly?

Language

1. An ode is usually a poem written in exalted language. Find language in Woiwode's essay that seems literary or poetic. What does Woiwode convey by such language? Is it excessive, do you think, or appropriate? Why?
2. In paragraph 11, Woiwode gradually shifts pronouns, from *we* and *our* to *you* and *your*. Do you find this shift disconcerting or effective? Why?

3. How many of the five senses does Woiwode appeal to in this extended description? Find words or phrases that seem especially precise in conveying sensory impressions.
4. To describe a bowl of oranges, Woiwode uses images of heat and light: it was "glowing in the light, as if giving off the warmth that came through the windows from the real winter sun" (paragraph 11). Locate other words or phrases in the essay that evoke heat and light. How does this imagery contribute to the essay?

Writing Topics

1. **Journal Response** Many people derive comfort from a childhood object throughout life: they may no longer sleep with a teddy bear, but the sight of it on the shelf provides security and a connection with the past. Think of such an object that exists for you—a Raggedy Ann doll, a model ship or car, a pillow, a ball, something in your parents' house. Describe the object as specifically as you can.
   Journal to Essay Describe the object of your attachment in an essay intended to reveal both its physical attributes and its significance to you.
2. Although Woiwode's essay is written with greater skill and range of vocabulary than a small boy would be capable of, the essay reveals the many facets of a small boy's emotional life. Write an essay in which you analyze the boyish concerns and observations evident in "Ode to an Orange," demonstrating how Woiwode captures the workings of a boy's mind. Consider, for example, the way he compares the orange to a hand grenade (paragraph 13).
3. **Cultural Considerations** Our attitudes toward foods are often influenced by the family, community, or larger culture in which we grew up. Think of feelings that you have about a particular food that seem due at least partly to others outside yourself. In an essay describe the food and your feelings about it and explain the origins of your feelings as best you can.
4. **Connections** Woiwode's tone when he describes oranges is almost reverential. Compare and contrast his attitude toward his subject with Joan Didion's attitude toward the Santa Ana wind (next page). Does Didion's tone indicate that she admires the destructive force she writes about? Be sure to include examples from both essays to support your comparison.

Joan Didion

One of America's leading nonfiction writers, Joan Didion consistently applies a journalist's eye for detail and a terse, understated style to the cultural dislocation pervading modern American society. She was born in 1934 in Sacramento, a fifth-generation Californian, and she has attended closely to the distinctive people and places of the American West. After graduating from the University of California at Berkeley in 1956, Didion lived for nearly a decade in New York City before returning permanently to California. She has contributed to many periodicals, and her essays have been published in Slouching Towards Bethlehem *(1968),* The White Album *(1979),* Salvador *(1983),* Essays and Conversations *(1984),* Miami *(1987), and* After Henry *(1992). Didion has also published five novels:* Run River *(1963),* Play It as It Lays *(1970),* A Book of Common Prayer *(1977),* Democracy *(1984), and* The Last Thing He Wanted *(1996). With her husband, the writer John Gregory Dunne, she has written screenplays for movies, among them* Panic in Needle Park *(1971),* A Star Is Born *(1976),* True Confessions *(1981), and* Up Close and Personal *(1996).*

The Santa Ana

In describing the violent effects of a hot, dry wind on Los Angeles, Didion ranges typically outward from herself to the people figuring in local news reports. "The Santa Ana" first appeared in The Saturday Evening Post *in 1967 and later appeared as part of "Los Angeles Notebook," an essay collected in* Slouching Towards Bethlehem.

There is something uneasy in the Los Angeles air this afternoon, some unnatural stillness, some tension. What it means is that tonight a Santa Ana will begin to blow, a hot wind from the northeast whining down through the Cajon and San Gorgonio Passes, blowing up sandstorms out along Route 66, drying the hills and the nerves to the flash point. For a few days now we will see smoke back in the canyons, and hear sirens in the night. I have neither heard nor read that a Santa Ana is due, but I know it, and almost everyone I have seen today knows it too. We know it because we feel it. The baby frets. The maid sulks. I rekindle a waning argument with the 1 telephone company, then cut my losses and lie down, given over to whatever it is in the air. To live with the Santa Ana is to accept, consciously or unconsciously, a deeply mechanistic view of human behavior.

I recall being told, when I first moved to Los Angeles and was liv- 2
ing on an isolated beach, that the Indians would throw themselves into the sea when the bad wind blew. I could see why. The Pacific turned ominously glossy during a Santa Ana period, and one woke in the night troubled not only by the peacocks screaming in the olive trees but by the eerie absence of surf. The heat was surreal. The sky had a yellow cast, the kind of light sometimes called "earthquake weather." My only neighbor would not come out of her house for days, and there were no lights at night, and her husband roamed the place with a machete. One day he would tell me that he had heard a trespasser, the next a rattlesnake.

"On nights like that," Raymond Chandler[1] once wrote about the 3
Santa Ana, "every booze party ends in a fight. Meek little wives feel the edge of the carving knife and study their husbands' necks. Anything can happen." That was the kind of wind it was. I did not know then that there was any basis for the effect it had on all of us, but it turns out to be another of those cases in which science bears out folk wisdom. The Santa Ana, which is named for one of the canyons it rushes through, is a *foehn* wind, like the *foehn* of Austria and Switzerland and the *hamsin* of Israel. There are a number of persistent malevolent winds, perhaps the best known of which are the mistral of France and the Mediterranean sirocco, but a *foehn* wind has distinct characteristics: it occurs on the leeward slope of a mountain range and, although the air begins as a cold mass, it is warmed as it comes down the mountain and appears finally as a hot dry wind. Whenever and wherever a *foehn* blows, doctors hear about headaches and nausea and allergies, about "nervousness," about "depression." In Los Angeles some teachers do not attempt to conduct formal classes during a Santa Ana, because the children become unmanageable. In Switzerland the suicide rate goes up during the *foehn,* and in the courts of some Swiss cantons the wind is considered a mitigating circumstance for crime. Surgeons are said to watch the wind, because blood does not clot normally during a *foehn.* A few years ago an Israeli physicist discovered that not only during such winds, but

[1] Chandler (1888–1959) is best known for his detective novels featuring Philip Marlowe. [Editor's note.]

for the ten or twelve hours which precede them, the air carries an unusually high ratio of positive to negative ions. No one seems to know exactly why that should be; some talk about friction and others suggest solar disturbances. In any case the positive ions are there, and what an excess of positive ions does, in the simplest terms, is make people unhappy. One cannot get much more mechanistic than that.

Easterners commonly complain that there is no "weather" at all in 4
Southern California, that the days and the seasons slip by relentlessly, numbingly bland. That is quite misleading. In fact the climate is characterized by infrequent but violent extremes: two periods of torrential subtropical rains which continue for weeks and wash out the hills and send subdivisions sliding toward the sea; about twenty scattered days a year of the Santa Ana, which, with its incendiary dryness, invariably means fire. At the first prediction of a Santa Ana, the Forest Service flies men and equipment from northern California into the southern forests, and the Los Angeles Fire Department cancels its ordinary nonfirefighting routines. The Santa Ana caused Malibu to burn the way it did in 1956, and Bel Air in 1961, and Santa Barbara in 1964. In the winter of 1966–67 eleven men were killed fighting a Santa Ana fire that spread through the San Gabriel Mountains.

Just to watch the front-page news out of Los Angeles during a 5
Santa Ana is to get very close to what it is about the place. The longest single Santa Ana period in recent years was in 1957, and it lasted not the usual three or four days but fourteen days, from November 21 until December 4. On the first day 25,000 acres of the San Gabriel Mountains were burning, with gusts reaching 100 miles an hour. In town, the wind reached Force 12, or hurricane force, on the Beaufort Scale; oil derricks were toppled and people ordered off the downtown streets to avoid injury from flying objects. On November 22 the fire in the San Gabriels was out of control. On November 24 six people were killed in automobile accidents, and by the end of the week the Los Angeles *Times* was keeping a box score of traffic deaths. On November 26 a prominent Pasadena attorney, depressed about money, shot and killed his wife, their two sons, and himself. On November 27 a South Gate divorcée, twenty-two, was murdered and thrown from a moving car. On November 30 the San Gabriel fire was still out of control, and the wind in town was blowing eighty miles an hour. On the first day of December four people died violently, and on the third the wind began to break.

It is hard for people who have not lived in Los Angeles to realize 6
how radically the Santa Ana figures in the local imagination. The city

burning is Los Angeles's deepest image of itself: Nathanael West perceived that, in *The Day of the Locust;* and at the time of the 1965 Watts riots what struck the imagination most indelibly were the fires.[2] For days one could drive the Harbor Freeway and see the city on fire, just as we had always known it would be in the end. Los Angeles weather is the weather of catastrophe, of apocalypse, and, just as the reliably long and bitter winters of New England determine the way life is lived there, so the violence and the unpredictability of the Santa Ana affect the entire quality of life in Los Angeles, accentuate its impermanence, its unreliability. The wind shows us how close to the edge we are.

Meaning

1. Does Didion describe purely for the sake of describing, or does she have a thesis she wants to convey? If so, where does she most explicitly state this thesis?
2. What is the dominant impression Didion creates of the Santa Ana wind? What effect does it have on residents of Los Angeles?
3. Explain what Didion means by a "mechanistic view of human behavior" (paragraph 1). What would the opposite of such a view of human behavior be?
4. How might Didion's last sentence have two meanings?
5. Based on their context in the essay, try to guess the meanings of any of the following words that you don't know. Test your guesses in a dictionary, and then try out your knowledge of each word by using it in sentences of your own.

flash point (1)	malevolent (3)	derricks (5)
mechanistic (1)	leeward (3)	indelibly (6)
ominously (2)	cantons (3)	apocalypse (6)
surreal (2)	mitigating (3)	accentuate (6)
machete (2)	incendiary (4)	

Purpose and Audience

1. Why do you think Didion felt compelled to write about the Santa Ana? Consider whether she might have had a dual purpose.

[2] *The Day of the Locust* (1939), a novel about Hollywood, ends in riot and fire. The August 1965 disturbances in the Watts neighborhood of Los Angeles resulted in millions of dollars in damage from fires. [Editor's note.]

2. What kind of audience is Didion writing for? Primarily people from Los Angeles? How do you know? Does Didion identify herself as an Angelina?

Method and Structure

1. Didion doesn't describe the Santa Ana wind itself as much as its effects. Why does she approach her subject this way? What effects does she focus on?
2. Didion alternates between passages of mostly objective and mostly subjective description. Trace this movement throughout the essay.
3. What is the function of the quotation from Raymond Chandler at the beginning of paragraph 3? How does it serve as a transition?
4. **Other Methods** The essay is full of examples (Chapter 6) of the wind's effects on human beings. How do these examples help Didion achieve her purpose?

Language

1. Note Didion's frequent use of the first person (*I* and *we*) and of the present tense. What does she achieve with this point of view?
2. What is the effect of the vivid imagery in paragraph 2? In what way is this imagery "surreal" (fantastic or dreamlike)?

Writing Topics

1. **Journal Response** Think of something that drives people crazy where you live, such as bumper-to-bumper traffic at a certain time of day, long lines at the bank on Fridays, or a new flu everyone catches. Write down as many details as you can about the ways this phenomenon affects people. How, specifically, do they react? What strategies do they develop to cope with it?

   Journal to Essay Using Didion's essay as a model, write a descriptive essay about the phenomenon you have chosen. You may use examples from your own experiences and observations, from experiences you have read or heard about, or, like Didion, from both sources.
2. Didion tries to explain the Santa Ana phenomenon scientifically in paragraph 3 as having something to do with an excess of positive ions in the air. But she admits that nobody knows why there are more positive than negative ions or why that fact should translate into human unhappiness. To what extent do you think our moods can be explained by science? Are our emotions simply the by-products of brain chemistry, as some

scientists would suggest? Write an essay, using description and narration (Chapter 5), about someone you know (or know of) whose moods are affected by forces beyond his or her control. Be sure to include enough detail to create a vivid portrait for your readers.

3. **Cultural Considerations** Didion perceives the Santa Ana as a cultural phenomenon in Los Angeles that affects the attitudes, relationships, and activities of residents "just as the reliably long and bitter winters of New England determine the way life is lived there" (paragraph 6). Consider a place you know well and describe how some aspect of the climate or weather affects the culture, "the way life is lived," not only during a particular event or season but throughout the year.
4. **Connections** Both Didion and Marta K. Taylor, in "Desert Dance" (p. 65), describe dramatic natural phenomena that occur in the American West. Compare the way Taylor describes a desert lightning storm in paragraphs 5 and 6 of her essay to Didion's description, in paragraph 2, of the surreal landscape of the Santa Ana. How does each writer combine striking images and original figures of speech to convey a strong sense of mood and a feeling in the reader that he or she is there? Do you think one author's description is more successful than the other's? Why?

Writing with the Method

Description

Choose one of the following topics, or any topic they suggest, for an essay developed by description. The topic you decide on should be something you care about so that description is a means of communicating an idea, not an end in itself.

PEOPLE

1. An exceptionally neat or messy person
2. A person whose appearance and mannerisms are at odds with his or her real self
3. A person you admire or respect
4. An irritating child
5. A person who intimidates you (teacher, salesperson, doctor, police officer, fellow student)

PLACES

6. A shopping mall
7. A frightening place
8. A place near water (ocean, lake, pond, river, swimming pool)
9. A place you daydream about
10. A prison cell, police station, or courtroom
11. A cellar, attic, or garage
12. Your room

ANIMALS AND THINGS

13. Birds at a bird feeder
14. A work of art
15. A pet or an animal in a zoo
16. A favorite childhood toy
17. A prized possession
18. The look and taste of a favorite or detested food

SCENES

19. The devastation caused by a natural disaster
20. A scene of environmental destruction
21. A yard sale or flea market
22. Late night or early morning
23. The scene at a concert (rock, country, folk, classical, jazz)

SENSATIONS

24. Waiting for important news
25. Being freed of some restraint
26. Sunday afternoon
27. Writing
28. Skating, running, body surfing, skydiving, or some other activity
29. Extreme hunger, thirst, cold, heat, or fatigue

Writing About the Theme

Sensing the Natural World

1. Some of the writers in this chapter recognize that nature can be difficult to cope with. Joan Didion's description of the Santa Ana wind (p. 75) and David Mura's description of rain (p. 59) are most notable in this respect, but even Larry Woiwode's celebration of the orange (p. 69) mentions that parts of it are bitter and that the peel can abrade the corners of one's mouth. Write a descriptive essay about a place or thing that is special to you, paying close attention to its blemishes as well as its beauty.
2. All of the writers in this chapter demonstrate strong feelings for the place, thing, or phenomenon they describe, but the writers vary considerably in the way they express their feelings. For example, Joan Didion's own discomfort in the Santa Ana wind colors all of her perceptions, whereas Larry Woiwode's description of oranges is celebratory. Write an essay analyzing the tone of these and the three other selections in this chapter: David Mura's paragraph on typhoons, Diane Ackerman's paragraph on icebergs (p. 60), and Marta K. Taylor's "Desert Dance" (p. 65). Discuss which pieces you find most effective and why.
3. Each writer in this chapter vividly describes a specific place or thing that represents some larger, abstract concept: for example, Larry Woiwode's oranges represent childhood, and Marta Taylor's desert lightning represents the awesomeness of nature. Think of a specific, tangible place or thing in your life that represents some larger, abstract idea and write a descriptive essay exploring this relationship.

Chapter 5

NARRATION

Growing Up

USING THE METHOD

To **narrate** is to tell a story, to relate a sequence of events that are linked in time. We narrate when we tell of a funny experience, report a baseball game, or trace a historical event. By arranging events in an orderly progression, we illuminate the stages leading to a result.

Sometimes the emphasis in narration is on the story itself, as in fiction, biography, autobiography, some history, and much journalism. But often a narrative serves some larger point, as when a paragraph or a brief story about an innocent person's death helps to strengthen an argument for stricter handling of drunk drivers. When used as a primary means of developing an essay, such pointed narration usually relates a sequence of events that led to new knowledge or had a notable outcome. The point of the narrative—the idea the reader is to take away—then determines the selection of events, the amount of detail devoted to them, and their arrangement.

Though narration arranges events in time, narrative time is not real time. An important event may fill whole pages, even though it took only minutes to unfold; and a less important event may be dispensed with in a sentence, even though it lasted hours. Suppose, for instance, that a writer wants to narrate the experience of being mugged in order to show how courage came unexpectedly to his aid. He might provide a slow-motion account of the few minutes' encounter with the muggers, including vivid details of the setting and of the attackers' appearance, a moment-by-moment replay of his emotions, and exact dialogue. At the same time, he will compress events that merely fill in background or link main events, such as how he got to the scene of the mugging or the follow-up questioning by a police detective. And he will entirely omit many events, such as a conversation overheard at the police station, that have no significance for his point.

The point of a narrative influences not only which events are covered and how fully but also how the events are arranged. There are several possibilities:

- A straight chronological sequence is usually the easiest to manage because it relates events in the order of their actual occurrence. It is particularly useful for short narratives, for those in which the last event is the most dramatic, or for those in which the events preceding and following the climax contribute to the point being made.
- The final event, such as a self-revelation, may come first, followed by an explanation of the events leading up to it.
- The entire story may be summarized first and then examined in detail.
- **Flashbacks**—shifts backward rather than forward in time—may recall events whose significance would not have been apparent earlier. Flashbacks are common in movies and fiction: a character in the midst of one scene mentally replays another.

In addition to providing a clear organization, you can also help readers by adopting a consistent **point of view**, a position relative to the events, conveyed in two main ways:

- Pronouns indicate your place in the story: the first-person *I* if you are a direct participant; the third-person *he, she, it,* and *they* if you are an observer or reporter.

- Verb tense indicates your relation in time to the sequence of events: present (*is, run*) or past (*was, ran*).

Combining the first-person pronoun with the present tense can create great immediacy ("I feel the point of the knife in my back"). At the other extreme, combining third-person pronouns with the past tense creates more distance and objectivity ("He felt the point of the knife in his back"). In between extremes, you can combine first person with past tense ("I felt . . .") or third person with present tense ("He feels . . ."). The choice depends on your actual involvement in the narrative and on your purpose.

ANALYZING NARRATION IN PARAGRAPHS

Michael Ondaatje (born 1943) is a poet, fiction writer, essayist, and filmmaker. The following paragraph is from *Running in the Family* (1982), Ondaatje's memoir of his childhood in Ceylon, now called Sri Lanka, off the southern tip of India.

After my father died, a grey cobra came into the house. My stepmother loaded the gun and fired at point blank range. The gun jammed. She stepped back and reloaded but by then the snake had slid out into the garden. For the next month this snake would often come into the house and each time the gun would misfire or jam, or my stepmother would miss at absurdly short range. The snake attacked no one and had a tendency to follow my younger sister Susan around. Other snakes entering the house were killed by the shotgun, lifted with a long stick and flicked into the bushes, but the old grey cobra led a charmed life. Finally one of the old workers at Rock Hill told my stepmother what had become obvious, that it was my father who had come to protect his family. And in fact, whether it was because the chicken farm closed down or because of my father's presence in the form of a snake, very few other snakes came into the house again.

Chronological order

Past tense

Transitions (underlined)

Point of view: participant

Purpose: to relate a colorful, mysterious story

Andre Dubus (born 1936) writes essays and fiction. This paragraph comes from his essay "Under the Lights," which was published first in *The Village Voice* and then in Dubus's collection *Broken Vessels* (1991).

In the spring of 1948, in the first softball game during the afternoon hour of physical education in the dusty schoolyard, the two captains chose teams and, as always, they chose other boys until only two of us remained. I batted last, and first came to the plate with two or three runners on base, and while my teammates urged me to try for a walk, and the players on the field called Easy out, Easy out, I watched the softball coming in waist-high, and stepped and swung, and hit it over the right fielder's head for a double. My next time at bat I tripled to center. From then on I brought my glove to school, hanging from a handlebar.

Chronological order

Past tense

Transitions (underlined)

Point of view: direct participant

Purpose: to relate the author's transformation into a baseball player

DEVELOPING A NARRATIVE ESSAY

Getting Started

You'll find narration useful whenever relating a sequence of events can help you make a point, sometimes to support the thesis of a larger paper, sometimes *as* the thesis of a paper. If you're assigned a narrative essay, probe your own experiences for a situation such as an argument involving strong emotion, a humorous or embarrassing incident, a dramatic scene you witnessed, or a learning experience like a job. If you have the opportunity to do research, you might choose a topic dealing with the natural world (such as the Big Bang scenario for the origin of the universe) or an event in history or politics (such as how a local activist worked to close down an animal-research lab).

Whatever your subject, you should have some point to make about it: Why was the incident or experience significant? What does it teach or illustrate? Phrase this point in a sentence if you can at this stage (later it can serve as your thesis sentence). For instance:

> I used to think small-town life was boring, but one taste of the city made me appreciate the leisurely pace of home.
>
> A recent small earthquake demonstrated the hazards of inadequate civil-defense measures.

Sometimes you may need to draft your story before the point of it becomes clear to you, especially if the experience was personal and too recent to have sunk in.

Explore your subject by listing all the events in sequence as they happened. At this stage you may find the traditional journalist's questions helpful:

- Who was involved?
- What happened?
- When did it happen?
- Where did it happen?
- Why did it happen?
- How did it happen?

These questions will lead you to examine your subject from all angles. Then you need to decide which events should be developed in great detail because they are central to your point; which merit compression because they merely contribute background or tie the main events together; and which should be omitted altogether because they add nothing to your point and might clutter your narrative.

While you are weighing the relative importance of events, consider also what your readers need to know in order to understand and appreciate your narrative.

- What information will help locate readers in the narrative's time and place?
- How will you expand and compress events to keep readers' attention?
- What details about people, places, and feelings will make the events vivid for readers?
- What is your attitude toward the subject—lighthearted, sarcastic, bitter, serious?—and how will you convey it to readers in your choice of events and details?
- What should your point of view be? Do you want to involve readers intimately by using the first person and the present tense? Or does that seem overdramatic, less appropriate than the more detached, objective view that would be conveyed by the past tense or the third person or both?

Organizing

Narrative essays often begin without formal introductions, instead drawing the reader in with one of the more dramatic events in the sequence. But you may find an introduction useful to set the scene for your narrative, summarize the events leading up to it, or otherwise establish the context for it. Such an opening may lead to a statement of your thesis so that readers know why you are bothering to tell them your story. Then again, to intensify the drama of your story you may decide to withhold your thesis sentence for the conclusion or omit it altogether. (Remember, though, that the thesis must be evident to readers even if it isn't stated: the narrative needs a point.)

The arrangement of events in the body of your essay depends on the actual order in which they occurred and the point you want to make. To narrate a trip during which one thing after another went wrong, you might find a strict chronological order most effective. To narrate an earthquake that began and ended in an instant, you might sort simultaneous events into groups—say, what happened to buildings and what happened to people—or you might arrange a few people's experiences in order of increasing drama. To narrate your experience of city life, you might interweave events in the city with contrasting flashbacks to your life in a small town, or you might start by relating one especially bad experience in the city, drop back to explain how you ended up in that situation, and then go on to tell what happened afterward. Narrative time can be manipulated in any number of ways, but your scheme should have a purpose that your readers can see, and you should stick to it.

Let the ending of your essay be determined by the effect you want to leave with readers. You can end with the last event in your sequence, or the one you have saved for last, if it conveys your point and provides a strong finish. Or you can summarize the aftermath of the story if it contributes to the point. You can also end with a formal conclusion that states your point—your thesis—explicitly. Such a conclusion is especially useful if your point unfolds gradually throughout the narrative and you want to emphasize it at the finish.

Drafting

Drafting a narrative can be less of a struggle than drafting other kinds of papers, especially if you're close to the events and you use a straight chronological order. But the relative ease of storytelling can be misleading if it causes you to describe events too quickly or write without making a point. While drafting, be as specific as possible. Tell what the people in your narrative were wearing, what expressions their faces held, how they gestured, what they said. Specify the time of day, and describe the weather and the surroundings (buildings, vegetation, and the like). All these details may be familiar to you, but they won't be to your readers.

At the same time, try to remain open to what the story means to you, so that you can convey that meaning in your selection and description of events. If you know before you begin what your thesis is, let it guide you. But the first draft may turn out to be a search for your thesis, so that you'll need another draft to make it evident in the way you relate events.

In your draft you may want to experiment with dialogue—quotations of what participants said, in their words. Dialogue can add immediacy and realism as long as it advances the narrative and doesn't ramble beyond its usefulness. In reconstructing dialogue from memory, try to recall not only the actual words but also the sounds of speakers' voices and the expressions on their faces—information that will help you represent each speaker distinctly. And keep the dialogue natural sounding by using constructions typical of speech. For instance, most speakers prefer contractions like *don't* and *shouldn't* to the longer forms *do not* and *should not;* and few speakers begin sentences with *although,* as in the formal-sounding "Although we could hear our mother's voice, we refused to answer her."

Whether you are relating events in strict chronological order or manipulating them for some effect, try to make their sequence in real time and the distance between them clear to readers. Instead of signaling sequence with the monotonous *and then . . . and then . . . and then . . .* or *next . . . next . . . next,* use informative transitions that signal the order of events (*afterward, earlier*), the duration of events (*for an hour, in that time*), or the amount of time between events (*the next morning, a week later*). (See the Glossary under *transitions* for a list of such expressions.)

Revising and Editing

When your draft is complete, revise and edit it by answering the following questions and considering the information in the box.

- *Is the point of your narrative clear, and does every event you relate contribute to it?* Whether or not you state your thesis, it should be obvious to readers. They should be able to see why you have lingered over some events and compressed others, and they should not be distracted by insignificant events and details.

- *Is your organization clear?* Be sure that your readers will understand any shifts backward or forward in time.
- *Have you used transitions to help readers follow the sequence of events?* Transitions such as *meanwhile* or *soon afterward* serve a dual purpose: they keep the reader on track, and they link sentences and paragraphs so that they flow smoothly. (For more information, see pp. 36 and 37 and the Glossary under *transitions.*)
- *If you have used dialogue, is it purposeful and natural?* Be sure all quoted speeches move the action ahead. And read all dialogue aloud to check that it sounds like something someone would actually say.

FOCUS ON VERBS

Narration depends heavily on verbs to clarify and enliven events. Strong verbs sharpen meaning and encourage you to add other informative details:

WEAK The wind *made* an awful noise.

STRONG The wind *roared* around the house and *rattled* the trees.

Forms of *make* (as in the example above) and forms of *be* (as in the next example) can sap the life from narration:

WEAK The noises *were* alarming to us.

STRONG The noises *alarmed* us.

Verbs in the active voice (the subject does the action) usually pack more power into fewer words than verbs in the passive voice (the subject is acted upon):

WEAK PASSIVE We *were besieged* in the basement by the wind, as the water at our feet *was swelled* by the rain.

STRONG ACTIVE The wind *besieged* us in the basement, as the rain *swelled* the water at our feet.

(See also p. 46 on active versus passive voice.)

While strengthening verbs, also ensure that they're consistent in tense. The tense you choose for relating events, present or past, should not shift unnecessarily.

INCONSISTENT TENSES We *held* a frantic conference to consider our options. It *takes* only a minute to decide to stay put.

CONSISTENT TENSE We *held* a frantic conference to consider our options. It *took* only a minute to decide to stay put.

A NOTE ON THEMATIC CONNECTIONS

All the authors in this chapter saw reasons to articulate key events in their childhoods, and for that purpose narration is the obvious choice. Michael Ondaatje, in a paragraph, recalls his stepmother's inability to kill a cobra, perhaps because it embodied his dead father (p. 86). Andre Dubus, in another paragraph, records his transformation from a bench warmer to a baseball player (p. 87). Langston Hughes's essay pinpoints the moment during a church revival when he lost his faith (next page). Lionel Prokop's essay recounts the writer's boyhood experience of his father's funeral (p. 98). And Annie Dillard's essay recounts the ecstasy of being chased by an adult for pelting his car with a snowball (p. 102).

Langston Hughes

A poet, fiction writer, playwright, critic, and humorist, Langston Hughes described his writing as "largely concerned with depicting Negro life in America." He was born in 1902 in Joplin, Missouri, and grew up in Illinois, Kansas, and Ohio. After dropping out of Columbia University in the early 1920s, Hughes worked at odd jobs while struggling to gain recognition as a writer. His first book of poems, The Weary Blues *(1925), helped seed the Harlem Renaissance, a flowering of African American music and literature centered in the Harlem district of New York City during the 1920s. The book also generated a scholarship that enabled Hughes to finish college at Lincoln University. In all of his work—including* The Negro Mother *(1931),* The Ways of White Folks *(1934),* Shakespeare in Harlem *(1942),* Montage of a Dream Deferred *(1951),* Ask Your Mama *(1961), and* The Best of Simple *(1961)—Hughes captured and projected the rhythms of jazz and the distinctive speech, subtle humor, and deep traditions of African American people. He died in New York City in 1967.*

Salvation

A chapter in Hughes's autobiography, The Big Sea *(1940), "Salvation" is a simple yet compelling narrative about a moment of deceit and disillusionment for a boy of twelve. As you read Hughes's account, notice how the opening two sentences set up every twist of the story.*

I was saved from sin when I was going on thirteen. But not really saved. It happened like this. There was a big revival at my Auntie Reed's church. Every night for weeks there had been much preaching, singing, praying, and shouting, and some very hardened sinners had been brought to Christ, and the membership of the church had grown by leaps and bounds. Then just before the revival ended, they held a special meeting for children, "to bring the young lambs to the fold." My aunt spoke of it for days ahead. That night, I was escorted to the front row and placed on the mourner's bench with all the other young sinners, who had not yet been brought to Jesus. 1

My aunt told me that when you were saved you saw a light, and something happened to you inside! And Jesus came into your life! 2

And God was with you from then on! She said you could see and hear and feel Jesus in your soul. I believed her. I have heard a great many old people say the same thing and it seemed to me they ought to know. So I sat there calmly in the hot, crowded church, waiting for Jesus to come to me.

The preacher preached a wonderful rhythmical sermon, all moans and shouts and lonely cries and dire pictures of hell, and then he sang a song about the ninety and nine safe in the fold, but one little lamb was left out in the cold. Then he said: "Won't you come? Won't you come to Jesus? Young lambs, won't you come?" And he held out his arms to all us young sinners there on the mourner's bench. And the little girls cried. And some of them jumped up and went to Jesus right away. But most of us just sat there. *3*

A great many old people came and knelt around us and prayed, old women with jet-black faces and braided hair, old men with work-gnarled hands. And the church sang a song about the lower lights are burning, some poor sinners to be saved. And the whole building rocked with prayer and song. *4*

Still I kept waiting to *see* Jesus. *5*

Finally all the young people had gone to the altar and were saved, but one boy and me. He was a rounder's son named Westley. Westley and I were surrounded by sisters and deacons praying. It was very hot in the church, and getting late now. Finally Westley said to me in a whisper: "God damn! I'm tired o' sitting here. Let's get up and be saved." So he got up and was saved. *6*

Then I was left all alone on the mourner's bench. My aunt came and knelt at my knees and cried, while prayers and songs swirled all around me in the little church. The whole congregation prayed for me alone, in a mighty wail of moans and voices. And I kept waiting serenely for Jesus, waiting, waiting—but he didn't come. I wanted to see him, but nothing happened to me. Nothing! I wanted something to happen to me, but nothing happened. *7*

I heard the songs and the minister saying: "Why don't you come? My dear child, why don't you come to Jesus? Jesus is waiting for you. He wants you. Why don't you come? Sister Reed, what is this child's name?" *8*

"Langston," my aunt sobbed. *9*

"Langston, why don't you come? Why don't you come and be saved? Oh, Lamb of God! Why don't you come?" *10*

Now it was really getting late. I began to be ashamed of myself, holding everything up so long. I began to wonder what God thought *11* about Westley, who certainly hadn't seen Jesus either, but who was now sitting proudly on the platform, swinging his knickerbockered legs and grinning down at me, surrounded by deacons and old women on their knees praying. God had not struck Westley dead for taking his name in vain or for lying in the temple. So I decided that maybe to save further trouble, I'd better lie, too, and say that Jesus had come, and get up and be saved.

So I got up. 12

Suddenly the whole room broke into a sea of shouting, as they 13
saw me rise. Waves of rejoicing swept the place. Women leaped in the air. My aunt threw her arms around me. The minister took me by the hand and led me to the platform.

When things quieted down, in a hushed silence, punctuated by a 14
few ecstatic "Amens," all the new young lambs were blessed in the name of God. Then joyous singing filled the room.

That night, for the last time in my life but one—for I was a big 15
boy twelve years old—I cried. I cried, in bed alone, and couldn't stop. I buried my head under the quilts, but my aunt heard me. She woke up and told my uncle I was crying because the Holy Ghost had come into my life, and because I had seen Jesus. But I was really crying because I couldn't bear to tell her that I had lied, that I had deceived everybody in the church, that I hadn't seen Jesus, and that now I didn't believe there was a Jesus anymore, since he didn't come to help me.

Meaning

1. What is the main point of Hughes's narrative? What change occurs in him as a result of his experience?
2. What finally makes Hughes decide to get up and be saved? How does this decision affect him afterward?
3. What do you make of the title and the first two sentences? What is Hughes saying here about "salvation"?
4. If you are unfamiliar with any of the following words, try to guess what they mean from the context of Hughes's essay. Test your guesses in a dictionary, and then try to use each word in a sentence or two of your own.

dire (3)
rounder (6)
deacons (6)

Purpose and Audience

1. Why do you think Hughes wrote "Salvation" as part of his autobiography more than two decades after the experience? Was his purpose simply to express feelings prompted by a significant event in his life? Did he want to criticize his aunt and the other adults in the congregation? Did he want to explain something about childhood or about the distance between generations? What passages support your answer?
2. What does Hughes seem to assume about his readers' familiarity with the kind of service he describes? What details help make the procedure clear?
3. How do dialogue, lines from hymns, and details of other sounds (paragraphs 3–10) help re-create the increasing pressure Hughes feels? What other details contribute to this sense of pressure?

Method and Structure

1. Why do you think Hughes chose narration to explore the themes of this essay? Can you imagine an argumentative essay (Chapter 13) that would deal with the same themes? What might its title be?
2. Where in his narrative does Hughes insert explanations, compress time by summarizing events, or jump ahead in time by omitting events? Where does he expand time by drawing moments out? How does each of these insertions and manipulations of time relate to Hughes's main point?
3. In paragraph 1 Hughes uses several transitions to signal the sequence of events and the passage of time: "for weeks," "Then just before," "for days ahead," "That night." Where does he use similar signals in the rest of the essay?
4. **Other Methods** Hughes's narrative also explains a process (Chapter 9): we learn how a revival meeting works. Why is this process analysis essential to the essay?

Language

1. What does Hughes's language reveal about his adult attitudes toward his experience? Does he feel anger? bitterness? sorrow? guilt? shame? amusement? What words and passages support your answer?
2. Hughes relates his experience in an almost childlike style, using many short sentences and beginning many sentences with *And*. What effect do you think he is trying to achieve with this style?
3. Hughes expects to "see" Jesus when he is saved (paragraphs 2, 5, 7), and afterward his aunt thinks that he has "seen" Jesus (15). What does each

of them mean by *see?* What is the significance of the difference in Hughes's story?

Writing Topics

1. **Journal Response** Do you have childhood memories of one or more experiences with religion that comforted, thrilled, distressed, bored, or challenged you? If not, try to think of another experience that was memorable for either good or bad reasons: for instance, watching or performing in a play or concert, participating in a spelling bee, attending a family reunion, playing a sport. Write down as much as you can remember of the experience.

   Journal to Essay Write a narrative essay about your experience that uses details to explain to your readers exactly how and why the experience affected you.
2. Hughes says, "I have heard a great many old people say the same thing and it seemed to me they ought to know" (paragraph 2). Think of a piece of information or advice that you heard over and over again from adults when you were a child. Write a narrative essay about an experience in which you were helped or misled by that information or advice.
3. **Cultural Considerations** It seems that Hughes wants to be saved largely because of the influence of his family and his community. Westley (paragraphs 6 and 11) represents another kind of influence, peer pressure, that often works against family and community. Think of an incident in your own life when you felt pressured by peers to go against your parents, religion, school, or another authority. Write a narrative essay telling what happened and making it clear why the situation was important to you. What were the results?
4. **Connections** When Hughes doesn't see Jesus and then lies to satisfy everyone around him, he feels betrayed and pained. How does Hughes's experience differ from the one cheerfully reported by Michael Ondaatje (paragraph, p. 86), in which a potentially deadly snake is said to be Ondaatje's dead father, "come to protect his family"? Write an essay analyzing what elements these narratives have in common and any significant differences between them.

Lionel L. Prokop

Lionel L. Prokop was born in 1949 in Stratton, Nebraska, and raised in Colby, Kansas. He attended the Colby public schools, graduating in 1968, and after working for some years graduated from Colby Community College in 1995 with training in restaurant management. He now lives in North Platte, Nebraska, and operates a barbecue restaurant. The barbecue sauce, he says, is his "secret recipe."

In the Eyes of a Little Boy

Relating his father's funeral through his then-baffled senses, Prokop conveys both the innocence and the awareness of childhood. He wrote this essay for a freshman composition class, and it was then published in the 1994 volume of The Colby College Collection, *an anthology of students' writing.*

There are lots of people. Actually, there are more than the church can even hold. The lady in a blue dress hugs me as tears run down her cheeks. As I turn around, a bald man in a black suit takes my hand and leads me to the front of the church. Sitting down on the red cushion in the pew, I wonder why all the people look sad and many are wiping at their eyes. I see flowers all around. There are red roses, pink carnations, yellow mums, and white lilies. I can smell the sweet aroma as it fills the air. Music begins coming from the organ. 1

Some men are walking down the aisle; there is a large metal box between them and the priest is following with a cross. Carrying a bucket of water, a young boy is following the priest. There is another young boy swinging a smoking lantern. I smell a funny odor and my eyes begin to burn. Looking around, I see the sunlight coming through the stained-glass windows as the red, blue, and yellow colors dance on the metal box. There is a large man in the box. I know the man—it's my dad. Why is he sleeping in the box? 2

The priest stops talking as the sad music begins again. Coming to the front of the church, the people are walking past my dad and crying. He isn't waking up; they are going out the door. Everyone is gone now except for my family. My brother is holding my mom and 3 they are both crying. My sisters are hugging each other. I feel a tear run down my own cheek; it tastes salty. Why are we all crying?

Some man is closing the top on the box now. He pushes the box out of the door where six men put it into a big black car. We all get into another car to follow the black one. 4

After a long ride, we are on top of a hill and there is a large hole in the ground. I see big stones standing like statues by piles of dirt. There are flowers on some of the dirt piles and some are just grass. The six men take the box out of the black car and set it over the hole. People are standing close together all around the box. The priest starts talking again. When he finishes, the men put their flowers on top of the closed box. 5

Before they leave, the women are hugging my mom. The men are talking about my dad. I hear them say that he was their friend, that he helped them build their barns, that he could pick the most corn, that he played funny pranks, that he made the best home brew, that he loved his family and was the only father with his own softball team. As a man carrying his hat walks by, he pats me on the head. A bearded man picks me up and gives me a tight squeeze. Most of the people are gone now. Walking to the car with my family, I look back and see some men putting the box in the ground. Where is my dad? 6

Meaning

1. What is the implied main idea of this essay? In other words, what notion is the reader expected to come away with after reading the narrative?
2. What is never explicitly said in this essay? What word is never spoken, and what effect does this omission achieve?
3. The "smoking lantern" whose "funny odor" makes the narrator's eyes burn (paragraph 2) is a censer that burns incense. Why doesn't Prokop use its real name?
4. What kind of community does the narrator live in? How can you infer this?

Purpose and Audience

1. What do you think Prokop's purpose was in narrating this event? Is there a clear point to the narrative?
2. Is there anything in the essay to indicate that Prokop had a particular audience in mind? Is this an essay best appreciated by readers with cer-

tain backgrounds or attitudes? Do *you* appreciate the essay? Why, or why not?

Method and Structure

1. Why do you think Prokop chose narration to convey his experience of his father's death?
2. What is the effect of the use of the present tense throughout the essay?
3. Analyze the narrative time in paragraphs 3–5. Which events does Prokop linger on? Which ones does he gloss over or compress? Why, do you think?
4. Prokop holds back certain information at the beginning of the essay, so that the reader doesn't immediately understand what's going on. When did you realize what ceremony was being performed? When did you realize who had died? What effect is created by the delay?
5. **Other Methods** This essay is almost as descriptive (Chapter 4) as it is narrative. How many senses does Prokop appeal to? Point out some especially effective examples.

Language

1. What is the effect of the narrator's questions, "Why is he sleeping in the box?" (paragraph 2), "Why are we all crying?" (3), and "Where is my dad?" (6)? To whom are they addressed? How does their placement contribute to their effect?
2. How would you characterize the tone of the essay? Is the narrator very emotionally involved in the events he is recounting? How does this tone affect you as reader?

Writing Topics

1. **Journal Response** Think of a momentous event from your childhood, an event that marked you, even though you may not have understood its importance at the time. Write down as many details as you can: what happened, what you saw, what was said, what you felt.

   Journal to Essay Write a narrative essay using your notes. You may decide, like Prokop, to take the limited point of view of your young self. Or you may prefer to write with the hindsight of age.
2. Experiment with verb tenses by writing a paragraph or two of personal narrative, first using the present tense throughout and then rewriting to use the past tense throughout. How do the two narratives differ in effect? Which verb tense seems more appropriate for your story? Why?

3. **Cultural Considerations** Think of how Prokop's confusion as a child at a funeral might resemble the confusion of a young child who has just moved to the United States from another country. Imagine a specific situation in which a lack of context would be especially disorienting—for instance, a basketball game or, for a child who doesn't speak English, the first day of school. Write a narrative essay in which you recount the event or situation from the child's point of view. (If you have actually *been* the child immigrating to the United States, then you may want to write from your experience.)
4. **Connections** Jessica Mitford, in "Embalming Mr. Jones" (p. 209), criticizes the American practice of beautifying a corpse for public display before the funeral. What do you think Mitford would have said about Prokop's experience? Is it possible for a child to understand death when it is made to resemble sleep? Does the grieving process require that we be able to see the loved one a last time, or is this a morbid tradition? Write an essay in which you examine Prokop's narrative through Mitford's eyes.

Annie Dillard

A poet and essayist, Annie Dillard is part naturalist, part mystic. She was born in 1945 in Pittsburgh. Growing up in that city, she was an independent child given to exploration and reading. (As an adult, she reads nearly a hundred books a year.) After graduating from Hollins College in the Blue Ridge Mountains of Virginia, Dillard settled in the area to investigate her natural surroundings and to write. Her early books were Tickets for a Prayer Wheel *(1974), a collection of poems, and* Pilgrim at Tinker Creek *(1974), a series of related essays that demonstrate Dillard's intense, passionate involvement with the world of nature and the world of the mind.* Pilgrim *earned her national recognition and a Pulitzer Prize. It was followed by* Holy the Firm *(1977), a prose poem;* Teaching a Stone to Talk *(1982), a collection of essays;* Living by Fiction *(1982), a collection of critical essays;* Encounters with Chinese Writers *(1984); the autobiography* An American Childhood *(1987);* The Writing Life *(1989); and* The Living *(1992), a novel that takes place in Washington Territory in the nineteenth century. Currently living in Connecticut, Dillard teaches at Wesleyan University.*

The Chase

In her autobiography, An American Childhood, *Dillard's enthusiasm for life in its many forms colors her recollections of her own youth. "The Chase" (editor's title) is a self-contained chapter from the book that narrates a few minutes of glorious excitement.*

Some boys taught me to play football. This was fine sport. You thought up a new strategy for every play and whispered it to the others. You went out for a pass, fooling everyone. Best, you got to throw yourself mightily at someone's running legs. Either you brought him down or you hit the ground flat out on your chin, with your arms empty before you. It was all or nothing. If you hesitated in fear, you would miss and get hurt: you would take a hard fall while the kid got away, or you would get kicked in the face while the kid got away. But if you flung yourself wholeheartedly at the back of his knees—if you gathered and joined body and soul and pointed them diving fearlessly—then you likely wouldn't get hurt, and you'd stop the ball. 1

Your fate, and your team's score, depended on your concentration and courage. Nothing girls did could compare with it.

Boys welcomed me at baseball, too, for I had, through enthusias- 2
tic practice, what was weirdly known as a boy's arm. In winter, in the snow, there was neither baseball nor football, so the boys and I threw snowballs at passing cars. I got in trouble throwing snowballs, and have seldom been happier since.

On one weekday morning after Christmas, six inches of new 3
snow had just fallen. We were standing up to our boot tops in snow on a front yard on trafficked Reynolds Street, waiting for cars. The cars traveled Reynolds Street slowly and evenly; they were targets all but wrapped in red ribbons, cream puffs. We couldn't miss.

I was seven; the boys were eight, nine, and ten. The oldest two 4
Fahey boys were there—Mikey and Peter—polite blond boys who lived near me on Lloyd Street, and who already had four brothers and sisters. My parents approved of Mikey and Peter Fahey. Chickie McBride was there, a tough kid, and Billy Paul and Mackie Kean too, from across Reynolds, where the boys grew up dark and furious, grew up skinny, knowing, and skilled. We had all drifted from our houses that morning looking for action, and had found it here on Reynolds Street.

It was cloudy but cold. The cars' tires laid behind them on the 5
snowy street a complex trail of beige chunks like crenellated castle walls. I had stepped on some earlier; they squeaked. We could have wished for more traffic. When a car came, we all popped it one. In the intervals between cars we reverted to the natural solitude of children.

I started making an iceball—a perfect iceball, from perfectly 6
white snow, perfectly spherical, and squeezed perfectly translucent so no snow remained all the way through. (The Fahey boys and I considered it unfair actually to throw an iceball at somebody, but it had been known to happen.)

I had just embarked on the iceball project when we heard tire 7
chains come clanking from afar. A black Buick was moving toward us down the street. We all spread out, banged together some regular snowballs, took aim, and, when the Buick drew nigh, fired.

A soft snowball hit the driver's windshield right before the dri- 8
ver's face. It made a smashed star with a hump in the middle.

Often, of course, we hit our target, but this time, the only time 9
in all of life, the car pulled over and stopped. Its wide black door

opened; a man got out of it, running. He didn't even close the car door.

He ran after us, and we ran away from him, up the snowy Reynolds sidewalk. At the corner, I looked back; incredibly, he was still after us. He was in city clothes: a suit and tie, street shoes. Any normal adult would have quit, having sprung us into flight and made his point. This man was gaining on us. He was a thin man, all action. All of a sudden, we were running for our lives. *10*

Wordless, we split up. We were on our turf; we could lose ourselves in the neighborhood backyards, everyone for himself. I paused and considered. Everyone had vanished except Mike Fahey, who was just rounding the corner of a yellow brick house. Poor Mikey, I trailed him. The driver of the Buick sensibly picked the two of us to follow. The man apparently had all day. *11*

He chased Mikey and me around the yellow house and up a backyard path we knew by heart: under a low tree, up a bank, through a hedge, down some snowy steps, and across the grocery store's delivery driveway. We smashed through a gap in another hedge, entered a scruffy backyard and ran around its back porch and tight between houses to Edgerton Avenue; we ran across Edgerton to an alley and up our own sliding woodpile to the Halls' front yard; he kept coming. We ran up Lloyd Street and wound through mazy backyards toward the steep hilltop at Willard and Lang. *12*

He chased us silently, block after block. He chased us silently over picket fences, through thorny hedges, between houses, around garbage cans, and across streets. Every time I glanced back, choking for breath, I expected he would have quit. He must have been as breathless as we were. His jacket strained over his body. It was an immense discovery, pounding into my hot head with every sliding, joyous step, that this ordinary adult evidently knew what I thought only children who trained at football knew: that you have to fling yourself at what you're doing, you have to point yourself, forget yourself, aim, dive. *13*

Mikey and I had nowhere to go, in our own neighborhood or out of it, but away from this man who was chasing us. He impelled us forward; we compelled him to follow our route. The air was cold; every breath tore my throat. We kept running, block after block; we kept improvising, backyard after backyard, running a frantic course and choosing it simultaneously, failing always to find small places or hard places to slow him down, and discovering always, exhilarated, *14* dismayed, that only bare speed could save us—for he would never give up, this man—and we were losing speed.

He chased us through the backyard labyrinths of ten blocks be- 15
fore he caught us by our jackets. He caught us and we all stopped.

We three stood staggering, half blinded, coughing, in an obscure 16
hilltop backyard: a man in his twenties, a boy, a girl. He had released our jackets, our pursuer, our captor, our hero: he knew we weren't going anywhere. We all played by the rules. Mikey and I unzipped our jackets. I pulled off my sopping mittens. Our tracks multiplied in the backyard's new snow. We had been breaking new snow all morning. We didn't look at each other. I was cherishing my excitement. The man's lower pants legs were wet; his cuffs were full of snow, and there was a prow of snow beneath them on his shoes and socks. Some trees bordered the little flat backyard, some messy winter trees. There was no one around: a clearing in a grove, and we the only players.

It was a long time before he could speak. I had some difficulty at 17
first recalling why we were there. My lips felt swollen; I couldn't see out of the sides of my eyes; I kept coughing.

"You stupid kids," he began perfunctorily. 18

We listened perfunctorily indeed, if we listened at all, for the 19
chewing out was redundant, a mere formality, and beside the point. The point was that he had chased us passionately without giving up, and so he had caught us. Now he came down to earth. I wanted the glory to last forever.

But how could the glory have lasted forever? We could have run 20
through every backyard in North America until we got to Panama. But when he trapped us at the lip of the Panama Canal, what precisely could he have done to prolong the drama of the chase and cap its glory? I brooded about this for the next few years. He could only have fried Mikey Fahey and me in boiling oil, say, or dismembered us piecemeal, or staked us to anthills. None of which I really wanted, and none of which any adult was likely to do, even in the spirit of fun. He could only chew us out there in the Panamanian jungle, after months or years of exalting pursuit. He could only begin, "You stupid kids," and continue in his ordinary Pittsburgh accent with his normal righteous anger and the usual common sense.

If in that snowy backyard the driver of the black Buick had cut 21
off our heads, Mikey's and mine, I would have died happy, for nothing has required so much of me since as being chased all over Pittsburgh in the middle of winter—running terrified, exhausted—by this

sainted, skinny, furious red-headed man who wished to have a word with us. I don't know how he found his way back to his car.

Meaning

1. What lesson did Dillard learn from the experience of the chase? Where is her point explicitly revealed?
2. In paragraph 2 Dillard writes, "I got in trouble throwing snowballs, and have seldom been happier since." What exactly is Dillard saying about the relationship between trouble and happiness? Do you think she is recommending "getting in trouble" as a means to happiness? Why, or why not?
3. If you do not know the meanings of the following words, try to guess them from the context of Dillard's essay. Test your guesses in a dictionary, and then try to use each word in a sentence or two of your own.

crenellated (5)	compelled (14)	perfunctorily (18, 19)
translucent (6)	improvising (14)	redundant (19)
embarked (7)	labyrinths (15)	exalting (20)
impelled (14)	obscure (16)	

Purpose and Audience

1. What seems to be Dillard's purpose in "The Chase": to encourage children to get into trouble? to encourage adults to be more tolerant of children who get into trouble? something else?
2. In her first paragraph, Dillard deliberately shifts from the first-person point of view (using *me*) to the second (using *you*). What is the effect of this shift, and how does it contribute to Dillard's purpose?

Method and Structure

1. Why do you think Dillard chose narration to illustrate her point about the difference between children and adults? What does she gain from this method? What other methods might she have used?
2. In this straightforward narrative, Dillard expands some events and summarizes others: for instance, she provides much more detail about the chase in paragraph 12 than in paragraphs 13 and 14. Why might she first provide and then pull back from the detail in paragraph 12?
3. How does the last sentence of paragraph 2—"I got in trouble throwing snowballs, and have seldom been happier since"—serve to set up the story Dillard is about to tell?

4. **Other Methods** Dillard makes extensive use of description (Chapter 4). Locate examples of this method and analyze what they contribute to the essay as a whole.

Language

1. How would you characterize Dillard's style? How does the style reflect the fact that the adult Dillard is writing from a child's point of view?
2. What does Dillard mean by calling the man who chases her "sainted" (paragraph 21)? What is her attitude toward this man? What words and passages support your answer?
3. Consider Dillard's description of cars: traveling down the street, they looked like "targets all but wrapped in red ribbons, cream puffs" (paragraph 3), and their tires in the snow left "a complex trail of beige chunks like crenellated castle walls" (5). What is the dominant impression created here?

Writing Topics

1. **Journal Response** What incidents in your childhood seem to you momentous even now? List three or four of these significant incidents, along with some notes about their importance to you then and now.

   Journal to Essay Choose one significant incident from your journal list and narrate it as vividly as you can, using the first-person *I*. Use strong, suggestive verbs (as Dillard uses "popped" in paragraph 5 and "smashed" in paragraph 12) and plenty of other descriptive details to render the event vividly.
2. Write a narrative essay about a time you discovered that "an ordinary adult" knew some truth you thought only children knew. What was that truth, and why did you believe until that moment that only children knew it? What did this adult do to change your mind?
3. Though Dillard focuses on a time when no harm was done, the consequences of throwing snowballs at moving cars could be quite serious. Rewrite the essay from the point of view of someone who would *not* glorify the children's behavior—the man driving the Buick, for instance, or one of the children's parents. How might one of these people narrate these events? On what might he or she focus?
4. **Cultural Considerations** Childhood pranks like throwing snowballs at cars are tolerated more in some cultural groups than in others. In a narrative essay, retell an event in your childhood when you felt you were testing the rules of behavior in your culture. Make your motivations as clear as possible, and reflect on the results of your action.

Connections Annie Dillard and Larry Woiwode ("Ode to an Orange," p. 69) share an exuberant attitude toward their childhoods, at least toward the small portions they describe in their essays. But Woiwode focuses on a concrete, specific object, while Dillard focuses on an event. Write an essay examining the effects each essay has on you, and why. What techniques does each writer use to create these effects?

Writing with the Method

Narration

Choose one of the following topics, or any other topic they suggest, for an essay developed by narration. The topic you decide on should be something you care about so that narration is a means of communicating an idea, not an end in itself.

FRIENDS AND RELATIONS

1. Gaining independence
2. A friend's generosity or sacrifice
3. A significant trip with your family
4. A wedding or funeral
5. An incident from family legend

THE WORLD AROUND YOU

6. An interaction you witnessed while taking public transportation
7. A storm, flood, earthquake, or other natural event
8. The history of your neighborhood
9. The most important minutes of a particular game in baseball, football, basketball, or some other sport
10. A school event, such as a meeting, demonstration, or celebration
11. A time when a poem, story, film, song, or other work left you feeling changed

LESSONS OF DAILY LIFE

12. Acquiring and repaying a debt, either psychological or financial
13. An especially satisfying run, tennis match, bicycle tour, one-on-one basketball game, or other sports experience
14. A time when you confronted authority
15. A time when you had to deliver bad news
16. A time when a new, eagerly anticipated possession proved disappointing
17. Your biggest social blunder

FIRSTS

18. Your first day of school, as a child or more recently
19. The first time you met someone who became important to you
20. The first performance you gave
21. A first date

ADVENTURES

22. An episode of extrasensory perception
23. An intellectual journey: discovering a new field, pursuing a subject, solving a mystery
24. A trip to an unfamiliar place

Writing About the Theme

Growing Up

1. While growing up inevitably involves fear, disappointment, and pain, there is usually security and joy as well. Michael Ondaatje clearly finds comfort in his dead father's reappearance as a cobra (p. 86), Andre Dubus finally earns the respect of his classmates on the softball field (p. 87), and Annie Dillard relishes the thrill of being chased (p. 102). Write a narrative essay about a similarly mixed experience from your childhood, making sure to describe your feelings vividly so that your readers share them with you.
2. The vulnerability of children is a recurring theme in the essays and paragraphs in this chapter. Andre Dubus, Langston Hughes (p. 93), and Lionel Prokop (p. 98) all write in some way about psychological pain. After considering each writer's situation individually, write an essay analyzing the differences among these situations. Based on these narratives, which writers seem to have the most in common? Which of their responses seem unique to children? Which are most likely to be outgrown?
3. Childhood is full of epiphanies, or sudden moments of realization, insight, or understanding. Langston Hughes and Annie Dillard both report such moments at the ends of their essays: Hughes loses faith in a Jesus who would not help him in church, and Dillard recognizes that any experience of glorious happiness must end. Write a narrative essay in which you tell of events leading to an epiphany when you were growing up. Make sure both the events themselves and the nature of the epiphany are vividly clear.

Chapter 6

EXAMPLE

Using Language

USING THE METHOD

An **example** represents a general group or an abstract concept or quality. Steven Spielberg is an example of the group of movie directors. A friend's calling at 2:00 A.M. is an example of her inconsiderateness—or desperation. We habitually use examples to bring general and abstract statements down to earth so that listeners or readers will take an interest in them and understand them.

As this definition indicates, the chief purpose of examples is to make the general specific and the abstract concrete. Since these operations are among the most basic in writing, it is easy to see why illustration or exemplification (the use of example) is among the most common methods of writing. Examples appear frequently in essays developed by other methods. In fact, as diverse as they are, all the essays in this book employ examples for clarity, support, and liveliness. If the writers had not used examples, we might have only a vague sense of their meaning or, worse, might supply mistaken meanings from our own experiences.

While nearly indispensable in any kind of writing, examples may also serve as the dominant method of developing a thesis. For instance:

- Generalizations about trends: "The cable box could become the most useful machine in the house."
- Generalizations about events: "Some members of the audience at *The Rocky Horror Picture Show* were stranger than anything in the movie."
- Generalizations about institutions: "A mental hospital is no place for the mentally ill."
- Generalizations about behaviors: "The personalities of parents are sometimes visited on their children."
- Generalizations about rituals: "A funeral benefits the dead person's family and friends."

Each of the quoted ideas could form the central assertion (the thesis) of an essay, and as many examples as necessary would then support it.

How many examples are necessary? That depends on your subject, your purpose, and your intended audience. Two basic patterns are possible:

- A single **extended example** of several paragraphs or several pages fills in needed background and gives the reader a complete view of the subject from one angle. For instance, the purpose of a funeral might be made clear with a narrative and descriptive account of a particular funeral, the family and friends who attended it, and the benefits they derived from it.
- **Multiple examples,** from a few to dozens, illustrate the range covered by the generalization. The strangeness of a movie's viewers might be captured with three or four very strange examples. But supporting the generalization about mental hospitals might demand many examples of patients whose illnesses worsened in the hospital or (from a different angle) many examples of hospital practices that actually harm patients.

Sometimes a generalization merits support from both an extended example and several briefer examples, a combination that provides depth along with range. For instance, half the essay on mental hospitals might be devoted to one patient's experiences and the other half to brief summaries of others' experiences.

ANALYZING EXAMPLES IN PARAGRAPHS

Lewis Thomas (1913–93) was a medical doctor, researcher, and administrator widely known for his engaging, perceptive essays on science, health, and society. The following paragraph is from "Communication," an essay in Thomas's last collection, *The Fragile Species* (1992).

No amount of probing with electrodes inserted into the substance of the brain, no array of electroencephalographic tracings, can come close to telling you what the brain is up to, while a simple declarative sentence can sometimes tell you everything. Sometimes a phrase will do to describe what human beings in general are like, and even how they look at themselves. There is an ancient Chinese phrase, dating back millennia, which is still used to say that someone is in a great hurry, in too much of a hurry. It is *zou-ma guan-hua; zou* means "traveling," *ma* means "horse," *guan* is "looking at," *hua* is "flowers." The whole phrase means riding on horseback while looking, or trying to look, at the flowers. Precipitously, as we might say, meaning to look about while going over a cliff.

Generalization and topic sentence (underlined)

Single detailed example

William Lutz (born 1940) is an expert on doublespeak, which he defines as "language that conceals or manipulates thought. It makes the bad seem good, the negative appear positive, the unpleasant appear attractive or at least tolerable." In this paragraph from his book *Doublespeak* (1989), Lutz illustrates one use of this deceptive language.

Because it avoids or shifts responsibility, doublespeak is particularly effective in explaining or at least glossing over accidents. An Air Force colonel in charge of safety wrote in a letter that rocket boosters weighing more than 300,000 pounds "have an explosive force upon surface impact that is sufficient to exceed the accepted overpressure threshold of physiological damage for exposed

Generalization and topic sentence (underlined)

Two examples

personnel." In English: if a 300,000-pound booster rocket falls on you, you probably won't survive. In 1985 three American soldiers were killed and sixteen were injured when the first stage of a Pershing II missile they were unloading suddenly ignited. There was no explosion, said Maj. Michael Griffen, but rather "an unplanned rapid ignition of solid fuel."

DEVELOPING AN ESSAY BY EXAMPLE

Getting Started

You will need examples whenever your experiences, observations, or reading lead you to make a general statement: the examples give readers evidence for the statement, so that they see its truth. An appropriate subject for an example paper is likely to be a general idea you have formed about people, things, the media, or any other feature of your life. Say, for instance, that over the past several years you have seen many made-for-television movies dealing effectively with a sensitive issue such as incest, domestic violence, or AIDS. There is your subject: some TV movies do a good job of dramatizing and explaining difficult social issues. It is a generalization about TV movies based on what you know of individual movies. This statement could serve as the thesis of an essay, the point you want readers to take away. A clear thesis is crucial for an example paper because without it readers can only guess what your illustrations are intended to show.

After arriving at your thesis, you should make a list of all the pertinent examples. This stage may take some thought and even some further reading or observation. While making the list, keep your intended readers at the front of your mind: what do they already know about your subject, and what do they need to know in order to accept your thesis? In illustrating the social value of TV movies for readers who believe television is worthless or even harmful, you might concentrate on the movies that are most relevant to readers' lives, providing enough detail about each to make readers see the relevance.

Organizing

Most example essays open with an introduction that engages readers' attention and gives them some context to relate to. You might begin the paper on TV movies, for instance, by briefly narrating the plot of one movie. The opening should lead into your thesis sentence so that readers know what to expect from the rest of the essay.

Organizing the body of the essay may not be difficult if you use a single example, for the example itself may suggest a distinct method of development (such as narration) and thus an arrangement. But an essay using multiple examples usually requires close attention to arrangement so that readers experience not a list but a pattern. Some guidelines:

- With a limited number of examples—say, four or five—use a climactic organization (p. 38), arranging examples in order of increasing importance, interest, or complexity. Then the strongest and most detailed example provides a dramatic finish.
- With very many examples—ten or more—find some likenesses among examples that will allow you to treat them in groups. For instance, instead of covering fourteen TV movies in a shapeless list, you might group them by subject into movies dealing with family relations, those dealing with illness, and the like. (This is the method of classification discussed in Chapter 8.) Covering each group in a separate paragraph or two would avoid the awkward string of choppy paragraphs that might result from covering each example independently. And arranging the groups themselves in order of increasing interest or importance would further structure your presentation.

To conclude your essay, you may want to summarize by elaborating on the generalization of your thesis now that you have supported it. But the essay may not require a conclusion at all if you believe your final example emphasizes your point and provides a strong finish.

Drafting

While you draft your essay, remember that your examples must be plentiful and specific enough to support your generalization. If you use fifteen different examples, their range should allow you to treat each one briefly, in one or two sentences. But if you use only three examples, say, you will have to describe each one in sufficient detail to make up for their small number. And, obviously, if you use only a single example, you must be as specific as possible so that readers see clearly how it illustrates your generalization.

Revising and Editing

To be sure you've met the expectations that most readers hold for examples, revise and edit your draft by considering the following questions and the information in the box.

- *Are all examples, or parts of a single example, obviously relevant to your generalization?* Be careful not to get sidetracked by interesting but unrelated information.
- *Are the examples specific?* Examples bring a generalization down to earth only if they are well detailed. Simply naming representative TV movies and their subjects would not demonstrate their social value. Each movie would need a plot summary that shows how the movie fits and illustrates the generalization.
- *Do the examples, or the parts of a single example, cover all the*

FOCUS ON SENTENCE VARIETY

While accumulating and detailing examples during drafting, you may find yourself writing strings of similar sentences:

> UNVARIED One example of a movie about a disease is *In the Forest*. Another example is *The Beating Heart*. Another is *Tree of Life*. These three movies treat misunderstood or little-known diseases in a way that increases the viewer's sympathy and understanding. *In the Forest* deals with a little boy who suffers from cystic fibrosis. *The Beating Heart* deals with a middle-aged woman who is weakening from multiple sclerosis. *Tree of Life* deals with a father of four who is dying from AIDS. All three movies show complex, struggling human beings caught blamelessly in desperate circumstances.

The writer of this paragraph was clearly pushing to add examples and to expand them—both essential for a successful essay—but the resulting passage needs editing so that the writer's labor isn't so obvious and the sentences are more varied and interesting:

> VARIED Three movies dealing with disease are *In the Forest, The Beating Heart,* and *Tree of Life*. In these movies little-known or misunderstood diseases become subjects for the viewer's sympathy and understanding. A little boy suffering from cystic fibrosis, a middle-aged woman weakening from multiple sclerosis, a father of four dying from AIDS—these complex, struggling human beings are caught blamelessly in desperate circumstances.

For more on sentence variety, see page 48.

territory mapped out by your generalization? To support your generalization, you need to present a range of instances that fairly represents the whole. An essay on the social value of TV movies would be misleading if it failed to acknowledge that not *all* TV movies have social value. It would also be misleading if it presented several TV movies as representative examples of socially valuable TV when in fact they were the *only* instances of such TV.

- *Do your examples support your generalization?* You should not start with a broad statement and then try to drum up a few examples to prove it. A thesis such as "Children do poorly in school because they watch too much television" would require factual support gained from research, not the lone example of your little brother. If your little brother performs poorly in school and you attribute his performance to his television habits, then narrow your thesis so that it accurately reflects your evidence—perhaps "In the case of my little brother, at least, the more time spent watching television the poorer the grades."

A NOTE ON THEMATIC CONNECTIONS

The authors represented in this chapter all had something to say about language—how we use it, abuse it, or change from it. Their ideas probably came to them through examples as they read, talked, and listened, so naturally they use examples to demonstrate those ideas. In one paragraph, Lewis Thomas draws on a single example to show how much meaning a phrase can pack (p. 114). In another, William Lutz uses two examples to illustrate how evasive doublespeak can be (p. 114). Kim Kessler's essay explores the emergence of the expression "blah blah blah" to end sentences (next page). Michael W. Miller's essay probes the uses of so-called smileys, or emoticons, to express emotions in electronic mail (p. 124). And Perri Klass's essay grapples with why doctors use peculiar and often cruel jargon and how it affects them (p. 130).

Kim Kessler

Kim Kessler was born in 1975 in New York City and grew up mostly in Greenwich, Connecticut, graduating from high school there. In 1997 she graduated from Brown University and took a job at Vanity Fair *magazine. She lives in New York City.*

Blah Blah Blah

Kessler published this essay in the Brown Daily Herald *in 1996, after noticing, she says, that she and her friends "had basically stopped talking to each other in complete sentences." With ample examples and analysis, Kessler questions the uses of the title expression in place of words that the speaker, for some reason, doesn't want to utter.*

"So he says to me, 'Well it just happened. I was this and that and blah blah blah.'" 1

That's an actual quote. That was the statement one of my oh-so-articulate friends made as an explanation of a certain situation. The thing about it is that I figured I knew exactly what he meant. The more important thing about it, the thing that makes this quote notable, is that I feel as though I've been hearing it all over the place these days. It has come to my attention in the last few weeks, maybe even in the last couple of months, that it is common for peers of mine to finish their sentences with "blah blah blah." Some people have their own less common versions of the phrase—e.g., "yadda yadda" or "etc., etc."—but it all amounts to the same thing. Rather than completing a thought or detailing an explanation, sentences simply fade away into a symbol of generic rhetoric. 2

I'm not quite sure what I think about this recently noticed phenomenon quite yet. What does it mean that I can say "blah blah blah" to you and you consider it to be an acceptable statement? 3

I guess that there are a couple of good reasons for why this is going on. First, it's a commentary on just how trite so many of those conversations we spend our time having really are. Using the phrase is a simple acknowledgment of the fact that what is about to be said 4 has been said so many times before that it is pretty much an exercise in redundancy to say it again. Some folks "blah blah blah" me (yeah, it's a verb) when they're using the phrase as a shortcut; they are eager to get to the part of their story that *does* distinguish it from all the other stories out there. Other times people "blah blah blah" me when they think that it is not worth their time or their energy to actually recount a story for my sake. In this case I feel dismissed, rejected. You can get "blah blahed" (past tense) in an inclusive way, too. In this scenario the "blah blah" construction is used to refer to something that both you and the speaker understand. This reflects a certain intimacy between the speaker and the listener, an intimacy that transcends the need for the English language that strangers would need in order to communicate.

I have discovered quite a different use for the phrase. I have found that because "blah blah" is an accepted part of our everyday discourse, and because people assume that with this phrase what you are referring to is indeed the same thing that they are thinking of, it is very easy to use this construction to lie. Well, maybe "lie" isn't the best word. It's usually more of a coverup than a lie. I'll give an example to demonstrate my meaning here. 5

I'm walking across campus at some time on some Monday. I get accosted by some acquaintance and have the gratuitous "How was your weekend?" conversation. He's asking me about my Saturday night. I reply: "It was good, you know . . . went out to dinner then to a party, blah blah blah." The acquaintance smiles and nods and then goes merrily on his way, his head filled with thoughts of me and my normal Saturday night. What he will never know (as long as he's not reading this) is that I ended that night walking many, many blocks home alone in the rain without a coat, carrying on my back, of all things, a trombone. He also does not know about the mini-breakdown and moment of personal evaluation that my lonely, wet, trombone-carrying state caused me to have under a streetlight in the middle of one of those many blocks. He does not know these things because he has constructed his own end to my night to fill in for my "blah blah blah." (I hope you can all handle that open display of vulnerability. It's not very often that I share like that.) 6

"Blah blah blah" implies the typical. I tend to use it in place of the atypical, usually the atypical of the most embarrassing sort. For me, it's a cop-out. The accepted use of the phrase has allowed me a refuge, a wall of meaningless words with which to protect myself. I'm definitely abusing the term. 7

Maybe there are a couple of you readers who would want to interject here and remind me that not everybody tells the *whole* truth *all* of the time. (I'd guess that there would even be a hint of sarcasm in your voice as you said this to me.) Well, I realize that. I just feel the slightest twinge of guilt because my withholding of the truth has a deceptive element to it. 8

But, hey, maybe I'm not the only one. Maybe everyone is manipulating the phrase "blah blah blah." What if none of us really knows what anyone else is talking about anymore? What are the repercussions of this fill-in-the-blank type of conversation? I feel myself slipping into that very annoying and much too often frequented realm of the overly analytical, so I'm going to stop myself. To those of you who are concerned about this "blah blah" thing I am going to offer the most reasonable solution that I know of—put on your Walkman and avoid it all. The logic here is that the more time you spend with your Walkman on, the less time you spend having those aforementioned gratuitous conversations, and therefore the fewer "blah blahs" you'll have to deal with. 9

Meaning

1. How does Kessler's use of the phrase "blah blah blah" differ from the normal use, and why does her use bother her?
2. What is the "symbol of generic rhetoric" referred to in paragraph 2? What does Kessler mean by these words? (Consult a dictionary if you're not sure.) Does this sentence state Kessler's main idea? Why, or why not?
3. Try to guess the meanings of any of the following words you are unsure of, based on their context in Kessler's essay. Look the words up in a dictionary to test your guesses, and then use each word in a sentence of your own.

articulate (2)	transcends (4)	atypical (7)
phenomenon (3)	discourse (5)	interject (8)
trite (4)	accosted (6)	repercussions (9)
redundancy (4)	gratuitous (6)	

Purpose and Audience

1. What seems to be Kessler's purpose in this essay: to explain the various ways the phrase "blah blah blah" can be used? to argue against the overuse of the phrase? something else?

2. Whom did Kessler assume as her audience? (Look back at the note on the essay, p. 119, if you're not sure.) How do her subject, evidence, and tone reflect such an assumption?

Method and Structure

1. Why do you think Kessler chose to examine this linguistic phenomenon through examples? How do examples help her achieve her purpose in a way that another method might not? (Hint: What is lost when you skip from paragraph 5 to 7?)
2. What generalizations do the examples in paragraphs 4 and 6 support?
3. Which paragraphs fall into the introduction, body, and conclusion of Kessler's essay? What function does each part serve?
4. **Other Methods** Kessler's essay attempts to define the indefinable, an expression that would seem to have no meaning. What meanings does she find for "blah blah blah"? How does this use of definition (Chapter 11) help Kessler achieve her purpose?

Language

1. How would you characterize Kessler's tone: serious? light? a mix of both? How does this tone reflect her intended audience and her attitude toward her subject?
2. Point out instances of irony in the essay. (See *irony* in the Glossary.)
3. What does Kessler achieve by addressing the reader directly throughout the essay?

Writing Topics

1. **Journal Response** Think of other conversational fillers that might be compared to "blah blah blah," such as "like" or "you know." Pick one such phrase and make as complete a list of its uses as you can. Listen carefully to your friends' speech, dialogue in television shows and movies, and overheard conversations for possible source material.
   Journal to Essay Form a generalization about the phrase you have chosen that explains how it functions, the purpose or purposes it serves. Write an essay modeled on Kessler's in which you use examples to support your generalization.
2. Write an essay expressing your opinion of Kessler's essay. For instance, how did you react to her complaint that most of her conversations with

her peers were "trite"or "gratuitous"? Do you think she is too critical of her peers? Agree or disagree with Kessler, supporting your opinion with your own examples.

3. **Cultural Considerations** Although Kessler never explicitly says so, the phenomenon she writes about seems to apply mainly to people of her own generation. Think of an expression that you use when among a group to which you belong (family, ethnic group, others of your own gender, and so on) but feel constrained from using outside the group. Write an essay explaining and illustrating the uses of the expression in the group and the problems you experience using it elsewhere.
4. **Connections** To what extent, if at all, does "blah blah blah" resemble the jargon of the medical profession as discussed by Perri Klass in "She's Your Basic L.O.L. in N.A.D." (p. 130)? After reading Klass's essay, list the purposes she believes medical jargon serves. Does "blah blah blah" serve similar or different purposes for Kessler and her peers? Spell your answer out in an essay, drawing on Klass's and Kessler's essays as well as your own experience for evidence.

Michael W. Miller

Born in 1962 in New York City, Michael W. Miller is a journalist specializing in business. He graduated from Harvard University, where he majored in English and was the managing editor of the Harvard Crimson. *In 1983 Miller joined the* Wall Street Journal *as an intern, and from 1984 to 1993 he covered the technology industry from the paper's San Francisco and New York bureaus. Since 1993 he has worked as the* Journal's *senior special writer on health care, as the news editor for media and marketing, and currently as the "Marketplace" editor. Miller has also published a book,* Beyond Crossword Puzzles. *He lives with his family in Manhattan.*

The Type That Turns Heads in Computer Circles

Smileys, or emoticons—little sideways faces made up of punctuation—pervade electronic mail. In this essay from the Wall Street Journal *in 1992, Miller explores the origins and uses of the symbols as expressions of emotion and individuality. Fans say the symbols enrich e-mail communication; critics say they make poor substitutes for words. What do you think?*

The subject is uncontrollable scalp flaking. On a computer bulletin board called the Well, "Casey," as she calls herself online, is proposing a novel remedy. "I found that rinsing my scalp with vinegar will cut down on it for a while," her electronic message advises. "If you don't mind smelling like a salad :-)" 1

Elsewhere on the Well, a debate rages over the rules of etiquette for newlyweds. Scott Marley of Albany, Calif., joins in: "I believe Miss Manners insists that the thank-you notes must be sent before the divorce :-)" 2

All over the country these days, electronic-mail messages are concluding with this odd little punctuation sequence :-) or one of its many variants, like :-(3

These are "smileys," so-called because when you tilt your head to the left, they look like little faces with a colon for eyes and a hyphen for a nose. Thus, when a message ends :-) it means "just kidding." If 4 it ends :-(it means "I'm depressed." If it ends 7:^] it means "I resemble Ronald Reagan."

You may have thought that the only people who use smiley faces 5
in written communication are motivational consultants and teenagers in love. But the electronic smiley is spreading like a virus in the new medium of e-mail, used by thousands as a form of emotional punctuation.

One smiley dictionary circulating on computer bulletin boards 6
lists 664 distinct variations, including:

:-D I'm laughing.
B-) I'm cool.
:*) I'm drunk.
:-'| I have a cold.
{(:-) I have a toupee.
}(:-(I have a toupee and it's windy.

Smileys started popping up on computer screens more than a decade ago. The MIT Press's *New Hacker's Dictionary* attributes the very first smiley to a 1980 message by a Carnegie-Mellon computer scientist named Scott Fahlman. "I wish I had saved the original post or at least recorded the date for posterity," he later wrote, "but I had no idea that I was starting something that would soon pollute all the world's communication channels."

Today it's hard to log on to a bulletin board without tripping 7
over someone's electronic face. On some boards, it's de rigueur to use a noseless version known as "midget smiley," which looks like the original, ubiquitous 1970s happy face :) The CompuServe network, where 1.1 million computer buffs swap messages, has its own smiley alternative, representing the word "grin." A recent usage: "Women irrational? Nahhhhhhh! Can't be <g>"

Dvorak's Guide to PC Telecommunications, a popular technical 8
tome, devotes four pages to the symbols. It soberly explains: "These are called emoticons and are used to express online the emotions of normal voice communication." The guide lists 105 essential examples, including :-8 (I'm talking out of both sides of my mouth) and =|:-)= (I'm Uncle Sam).

Why is this happening now, when for thousands of years writers 9
have found it possible to express emotions without using little sideways smiley faces? The smiley's roots may well go back to the science fiction "fanzines" of the '40s and '50s, homemade cult publications

such as *Spaceship* and *Rhodomagnetic Digest.* The writer Harlan Ellison, a pioneering fanzine publisher, recalls that contributors commonly punctuated their inside jokes with a simple sideways smile in quotation marks, like so: ")"

Today smiley scholars (there are already a handful) attribute the 10
trend to the hybrid quality of e-mail, which at times is less like an exchange of letters than like a telephone conversation. Without some device to suggest a tone of voice, they say, e-mail is uniquely ripe for misunderstanding.

In a computer conversation, "It is difficult for a sender to convey 11
nuance, communicate a sense of individuality, or exercise dominance or charisma," write social scientists Lee Sproull of Boston University and Sara Kiesler of Carnegie-Mellon in a study of "electronic communities" that examines the rise of smileys.

David Gans, an Oakland radio producer and bulletin-board 12
devotee, began using smileys when he found his "deeply sarcastic" tone was getting lost in transmission. "I found that if you're going to say something really rude, you damn well better defuse it," he says. Today, he sprinkles his messages generously with his favorite smiley ("sort of a three-quarters-view") :^)

Sometimes the smiley also helps in the difficult business of flirting 13
via computer. Consider this exchange on the Well:

> She: "In general I hate the smell of perfumes and deodorants, while the smell of certain people's fresh sweat turns me into a gooey gibbering mass of slithery lust."
>
> He: "hmmmmm . . . i work out tuesday and thursday . . . :-)"

In the same context, a popular alternative is the "winky" ;-)

The world's most elaborate electronic flirting signal was invented 14
in 1987 by a Silicon Valley engineer named Alan Chamberlain. It drew heavily on the appearance of its creator's own face. "In those days I had my hair real short, I wore shades, I had a brash in-your-face personality," Mr. Chamberlain recalls. He called his creation the "kissy" and typed it like this #!^~

There are computer users whose faces wrinkle with distaste at the 15
whole smiley phenomenon.

"I cringe when I see them," says the movie critic Roger Ebert, a 16
habitué of CompuServe, interviewed via e-mail. On the other hand, he adds, "smileys might be a real help for today's students, raised on TV and unskilled at spotting irony without a laugh track."

An even fiercer anti-smiley is the comedian/magician Penn Jil- 17
lette, who runs a computer bulletin board with his partner Teller and

writes the "Micro Mephisto" column in *PC Computing* magazine. His scornful verdict: "As soon as you put one in you've killed the joke." In a recent column, he described the smiley as "the hateful :) which means 'just kidding' and is used by people who would dot their *i*'s with little circles and should have their eyes dotted with Drano."

Ms. Sproull and Ms. Kiesler, the e-mail scholars, discuss a limita- 18
tion of smileys in their book *Connections: New Ways of Working in the Networked Organization.* "Although such cues weakly signal mood, they are flat and stereotyped. . . . Mild amusement looks no different from hilarity," the scholars write.

Flat and stereotyped? Hey, Sproull and Kiesler, do some real re- 19
search! :-) Joe Flower, a Sausalito, Calif., writer, recently sent an electronic message about his brutal book schedule—"a chapter every ten days, counting weekends and holidays, for five months." Then he signed off by hanging his tongue out with exhaustion :-+

Meaning

1. What generalization do most of Miller's examples of smileys support? What is Miller's thesis? Where does he state it?
2. Miller's title contains a pun, or a play on the different senses of the same words. What is it?
3. Explain the concept of "emotional punctuation" (paragraph 5). What does punctuation like commas and question marks do? How are smileys similar?
4. If any of the following words are unfamiliar to you, try to determine their meanings from their context in Miller's essay. Test your guesses using a dictionary, and then make up sentences of your own using the words.

etiquette (2)	ubiquitous (7)	charisma (11)
attributes (6)	tome (8)	gibbering (13)
posterity (6)	hybrid (10)	slithery (13)
de rigueur (7)	nuance (11)	habitué (16)

Purpose and Audience

1. Why do you think Miller wrote this essay: to criticize the excessive use of smiley faces and their variants in e-mail? to teach readers how to interpret these symbols? Or do you think he had some other purpose in mind?

2. What assumptions are made about the readers of the essay? What knowledge on their part is taken for granted? Is Miller writing exclusively for computer users?

Method and Structure

1. Why do you think Miller chose the method of example to examine the rise of symbols in e-mail correspondence? How does the method lend itself to his subject and his purpose?
2. Miller supports the generalization of his thesis with a series of subpoints, also generalizations, that are in turn supported by an example or examples. Try to identify each subpoint and the examples used to demonstrate it. (For example, the generalization in paragraph 3 is supported by the examples in paragraphs 1 and 2.) Don't worry if you can't make everything fit neatly into the category of generalization and example: some passages offer background.
3. Miller does not make the subject of the essay clear until the third paragraph and indeed misleads us about the subject in his opening sentence ("The subject is uncontrollable scalp flaking"). Why do you think he waits so long to clarify his subject? Is this a flaw in the essay?
4. **Other Methods** Where in the essay can you find an instance of definition (Chapter 11)? How is this definition central to Miller's purpose?

Language

1. What is the tone of the essay? Is it appropriate, given Miller's purpose?
2. Does Miller let his own opinion of the smiley phenomenon show through? What do you think his opinion is?
3. The word *emoticon* (paragraph 8) is a hybrid, like *guesstimate.* What two words does *emoticon* contain, and what meaning do they produce when put together?

Writing Topics

1. **Journal Response** Do you use smileys or emoticons in your e-mail or other Internet postings? Do the people you correspond with? Copy as many examples of the symbols as you can find, and define each one in words as well as possible.

   Journal to Essay Separate the symbols you have found into different categories, based on what they are used for. For example, some symbols may express surprise, others may indicate irony, and still others may flirt. Write an essay in which you discuss the different possible uses of the symbols, giving representative examples of each use.

2. Does Miller satisfactorily answer the question he poses at the beginning of paragraph 9? Why can't writers of e-mail use the same rhetorical strategies for expressing emotion and irony in language that have been used for centuries? Write an essay that either defends the usefulness of smileys and their cousins in electronic communication or criticizes e-mailers for relying on them as crutches.
3. How did you react to Roger Ebert's comment in paragraph 16 about today's students being "raised on TV and unskilled at spotting irony without a laugh track"? Respond to Ebert's accusation in an essay, citing examples to confirm or disprove his view.
4. **Cultural Considerations** Do you think of cyberspace as a place of limitless freedom, where differences in the "real" world become irrelevant and people can assume identities contrary to the ones the world assigns them? Or are our cultural identities too ingrained in us to check at the door when we turn on the computer? Write an essay in which you examine the possibilities of playing with identity online (in terms of gender, race, age, sexual orientation, and so on), using examples you know of from real life that were either successful or unsuccessful.
5. **Connections** In "Gender Gap in Cyberspace" (p. 292), Deborah Tannen points out several differences in the way men and women use e-mail. Have you noticed these differences, or others? Do you find that women, whom Tannen says are more likely to seek connection and harmony in spoken conversation, tend to qualify or temper their online speech more than men, either with smileys or with other interpretive cues? Or is the opposite true? Write an essay using examples from real computer communication in which you examine the real or perceived gender gap in cyberspace.

Perri Klass

Perri Klass is a pediatrician and a writer of both fiction and nonfiction. She was born in 1958 in Trinidad and grew up in New York City and New Jersey. After obtaining a B.A. from Harvard University in 1979, she began graduate work in biology but then switched to medicine. Klass finished Harvard Medical School in 1986 and practices pediatrics in Boston. Her publications are extensive: short stories in Mademoiselle, Antioch Review, *and other magazines; a collection of stories,* I Am Having an Adventure *(1986); two novels,* Recombinations *(1985) and* Other Women's Children *(1990); essays for the* New York Times, Discover, *and other periodicals; and two collections of essays,* A Not Entirely Benign Procedure *(1987) and* Baby Doctor: A Pediatrician's Training *(1992). She is the mother of two sons and one daughter.*

She's Your Basic L.O.L. in N.A.D.

Most of us have felt excluded, confused, or even frightened by the jargon of the medical profession—that is, by the special terminology and abbreviations for diseases and procedures. In this essay Klass uses examples of such language, some of it heartless, to illustrate the pluses and minuses of becoming a doctor. The essay first appeared in 1984 as a "Hers" column in the New York Times.

"Mrs. Tolstoy is your basic L.O.L. in N.A.D., admitted for a soft 1
rule-out M.I.," the intern announces. I scribble that on my patient list. In other words Mrs. Tolstoy is a Little Old Lady in No Apparent Distress who is in the hospital to make sure she hasn't had a heart attack (rule out a myocardial infarction). And we think it's unlikely that she has had a heart attack (a *soft* rule-out).

If I learned nothing else during my first three months of working 2
in the hospital as a medical student, I learned endless jargon and abbreviations. I started out in a state of primeval innocence, in which I didn't even know that "s̄ C.P., S.O.B., N/V" meant "without chest pain, shortness of breath, or nausea and vomiting." By the end I took the abbreviations so for granted that I would complain to my mother

the English Professor, "And can you believe I had to put down *three* NG tubes last night?"

"You'll have to tell me what an NG tube is if you want me to sympathize properly," my mother said. NG, nasogastric—isn't it obvious? 3

I picked up not only the specific expressions but also the patterns of speech and the grammatical conventions; for example, you never say that a patient's blood pressure fell or that his cardiac enzymes rose. Instead, the patient is always the subject of the verb: "He dropped his pressure." "He bumped his enzymes." This sort of construction probably reflects that profound irritation of the intern when the nurses come in the middle of the night to say that Mr. Dickinson has disturbingly low blood pressure. "Oh, he's gonna hurt me bad tonight," the intern may say, inevitably angry at Mr. Dickinson for dropping his pressure and creating a problem. 4

When chemotherapy fails to cure Mrs. Bacon's cancer, what we say is, "Mrs. Bacon failed chemotherapy." 5

"Well, we've already had one hit today, and we're up next, but at least we've got mostly stable players on our team." This means that our team (group of doctors and medical students) has already gotten one new admission today, and it is our turn again, so we'll get whoever is next admitted in emergency, but at least most of the patients we already have are fairly stable, that is, unlikely to drop their pressures or in any other way get suddenly sicker and hurt us bad. Baseball metaphor is pervasive: a no-hitter is a night without any new admissions. A player is always a patient—a nitrate player is a patient on nitrates, a unit player is a patient in the intensive-care unit and so on, until you reach the terminal player. 6

It is interesting to consider what it means to be winning, or doing well, in this perennial baseball game. When the intern hangs up the phone and announces, "I got a hit," that is not cause for congratulations. The team is not scoring points; rather, it is getting hit, being bombarded with new patients. The object of the game from the point of view of the doctors, considering the players for whom they are already responsible, is to get as few new hits as possible. 7

These special languages contribute to a sense of closeness and professional spirit among people who are under a great deal of stress. As a medical student, it was exciting for me to discover that I'd finally cracked the code, that I could understand what doctors said and wrote and could use the same formulations myself. Some people seem to become enamored of the jargon for its own sake, perhaps because 8 they are so deeply thrilled with the idea of medicine, with the idea of themselves as doctors.

I knew a medical student who was referred to by the interns on the team as Mr. Eponym because he was so infatuated with eponymous terminology,[1] the more obscure the better. He never said "capillary pulsation" if he could say "Quincke's pulses." He would lovingly tell over the multinamed syndromes—Wolff-Parkinson-White, Lown-Ganong-Levine, Henoch-Schonlein—until the temptation to suggest Schleswig-Holstein or Stevenson-Kefauver or Baskin-Robbins became irresistible to his less reverent colleagues. 9

And there is the jargon that you don't ever want to hear yourself using. You know that your training is changing you, but there are certain changes you think would be going a little too far. 10

The resident was describing a man with devastating terminal pancreatic cancer. "Basically he's C.T.D.," the resident concluded. I reminded myself that I had resolved not to be shy about asking when I didn't understand things. "C.T.D.?" I asked timidly. 11

The resident smirked at me. "Circling The Drain." 12

The images are vivid and terrible. "What happened to Mrs. Melville?" 13

"Oh, she boxed last night." To box is to die, of course. 14

Then there are the more pompous locutions that can make the beginning medical student nervous about the effects of medical training. A friend of mine was told by his resident, "A pregnant woman with sickle-cell represents a failure of genetic counseling." 15

Mr. Eponym, who tried hard to talk like the doctors, once explained to me, "An infant is basically a brainstem preparation." A brainstem preparation, as used in neurological research, is an animal whose higher brain functions have been destroyed so that only the most primitive reflexes remain, like the sucking reflex, the startle reflex, and the rooting reflex. 16

The more extreme forms aside, one most important function of medical jargon is to help doctors maintain some distance from their patients. By reformulating a patient's pain and problems into a language that the patient doesn't even speak, I suppose we are in some sense taking those pains and problems under our jurisdiction and also reducing their emotional impact. This linguistic separation between 17

[1] *Eponymous* means "named after"—in this case, medical terminology is named after researchers. [Editor's note.]

doctors and patients allows conversations to go on at the bedside that are unintelligible to the patient. "Naturally, we're worried about adreno-C.A.," the intern can say to the medical student, and lung cancer need never be mentioned.

I learned a new language this past summer. At times it thrills me 18
to hear myself using it. It enables me to understand my colleagues, to communicate effectively in the hospital. Yet I am uncomfortably aware that I will never again notice the peculiarities and even atrocities of medical language as keenly as I did this summer. There may be specific expressions I manage to avoid, but even as I remark them, promising myself I will never use them, I find that this language is becoming my professional speech. It no longer sounds strange in my ears—or coming from my mouth. And I am afraid that as with any new language, to use it properly you must absorb not only the vocabulary but also the structure, the logic, the attitudes. At first you may notice these new alien assumptions every time you put together a sentence, but with time and increased fluency you stop being aware of them at all. And as you lose that awareness, for better or for worse, you move closer and closer to being a doctor instead of just talking like one.

Meaning

1. What point does Klass make about medical jargon in this essay? Where does she reveal her main point explicitly?
2. What useful purposes does medical jargon serve, according to Klass? Do the examples in paragraphs 9–16 serve these purposes? Why, or why not?
3. Try to guess the meanings of any of the following words that are unfamiliar. Check your guesses in a dictionary, and then use each word in a sentence or two of your own.

primeval (2)	syndromes (9)	locutions (15)
terminal (6)	reverent (9)	jurisdiction (17)
perennial (7)	pompous (15)	

Purpose and Audience

1. What does Klass imply when she states that she began her work in the hospital "in a state of primeval innocence" (paragraph 2)? What does this phrase suggest about her purpose in writing the essay?

2. From what perspective does Klass write this essay: that of a medical professional? someone outside the profession? a patient? someone else? To what extent does she expect her readers to share her perspective? What evidence in the essay supports your answer?
3. Given that she is writing for a general audience, does Klass take adequate care to define medical terms? Support your answer with examples from the essay.

Method and Structure

1. Why does Klass begin the essay with an example rather than a statement of her main idea? What effect does this example produce? How does this effect support her purpose in writing the essay?
2. Although Klass uses many examples of medical jargon, she avoids the dull effect of a list by periodically stepping back to make a general statement about her experience or the jargon—for instance, "I picked up not only the specific expressions but also the patterns of speech and the grammatical conventions" (paragraph 4). Locate other places—not necessarily at the beginnings of paragraphs—where Klass breaks up her examples with more general statements.
3. **Other Methods** Klass uses several other methods besides example, among them classification (Chapter 8), definition (Chapter 11), and cause-and-effect analysis (Chapter 12). What effects—positive and negative—does medical jargon have on Klass, other students, and doctors who use it?

Language

1. What is the tone of this essay? Is Klass trying to be humorous or tongue-in-cheek about the jargon of the profession, or is she serious? Where in the essay is the author's attitude toward her subject the most obvious?
2. Klass refers to the users of medical jargon as both *we/us* (paragraphs 1, 5, 6, 17) and *they/them* (7), and sometimes she shifts from *I* to *you* within a paragraph (4, 18). Do you think these shifts are effective or distracting? Why? Do the shifts serve any function?
3. Klass obviously experienced both positive and negative feelings about mastering medical jargon. Which words and phrases in the last paragraph (18) reflect positive feelings, and which negative?

Writing Topics

1. **Journal Response** Perri Klass discovered a new language and new attitudes when she went to medical school. Many students have a similar experience when they go to college. Think about the ways college has changed you. Have you been confronted by different kinds of people

(professors, other students) from the ones you knew before? Have you found yourself embracing ideas you never thought you would, or speaking differently? Have others noticed a change in you that you may not have been aware of? Have you noticed changes in your precollege friends? Write down some reflections on the effects college has had on you.

Journal to Essay Using Klass's essay as a model, write an essay about the effects of a college education based on your personal experiences. Does college change people for the better, for the worse, or both? Give plenty of detailed examples.

2. Klass likens her experience learning medical jargon to that of learning a new language (paragraph 18). If you are studying or have learned a second language, write an essay in which you explain the "new alien assumptions" you must make "every time you put together a sentence." Draw your examples not just from the new language's grammar and vocabulary but from its underlying logic and attitudes. For instance, does one speak to older people differently in the new language? make requests differently? describe love or art differently?
3. Klass's essay explores the "separation between doctors and patients" (paragraph 17). Has this separation affected you as a patient or as the relative or friend of a patient? If so, write an essay about your experiences. Did the medical professionals rely heavily on jargon? Was their language comforting, frightening, irritating? Based on your experience and on Klass's essay, do you believe that the separation between doctors and patients is desirable? Why, or why not?
4. **Cultural Considerations** Most groups focused on a common interest have their own jargon. If you belong to such a group—for example, runners, football fans, food servers, engineering students—spend a few days listening to yourself and others use this language and thinking about the purposes it serves. Which aspects of this language seem intended to make users feel like insiders? Which seem to serve some other purpose, and what is it? In an essay, explain what this jargon reveals about the group and its common interest, using as many specific examples as you can.
5. **Connections** Klass says that one reason doctors use jargon is to hide potentially painful truths from patients and their families. The narrator in Lionel L. Prokop's "In the Eyes of a Little Boy" (p. 98) seems to have been spared the painful truth that his father died. Write an essay in which you give examples of when it is or is not appropriate to hold back the truth. Your examples may be from the two essays or from your own experience, but be sure to flesh them out with narration and description.

Writing with the Method

Example

Choose one of the following statements, or any other statement they suggest, and agree *or* disagree with it in an essay developed by one or more examples. The statement you decide on should concern a topic you care about so that the example or examples are a means of communicating an idea, not an end in themselves.

FAMILY

1. In happy families, talk is the main activity.
2. Grandparents relate more closely to their grandchildren than to their children.
3. Sooner or later, children take on the personalities of their parents.

BEHAVIOR AND PERSONALITY

4. Rudeness is on the rise.
5. Gestures and facial expressions often communicate what words cannot say.
6. Our natural surroundings when we are growing up contribute to our happiness or unhappiness as adults.

EDUCATION

7. The best courses are the difficult ones.
8. Education is an easy way to get ahead in life.
9. Students at schools with enforced dress codes behave better than students at schools without such codes.

POLITICS AND SOCIAL ISSUES

10. Talk radio can influence public policy.
11. Drug or alcohol addiction does not happen just to "bad" people.
12. True-life crime mimics TV and movies.
13. Unemployment is hardest on those over 50 years old.

MEDIA AND CULTURE

14. Bumper stickers are a form of conversation among Americans.
15. The Internet divides people instead of connecting them.
16. Good art can be ugly.

17. A craze or fad reveals something about the culture it arises in.
18. The best rock musicians treat social and political issues in their songs.
19. Television news programs are beauty pageants for untalented journalists.
20. The most rewarding books are always easy to read.

RULES FOR LIVING

21. Murphy's Law: If anything can go wrong, it will go wrong, and at the worst possible moment.
22. With enough motivation, a person can accomplish anything.
23. Lying may be justified by the circumstances.
24. Friends are people you can't always trust.

Writing About the Theme

Using Language

1. Lewis Thomas (p. 114), William Lutz (p. 114), and Perri Klass (p. 130) discuss the power of language with a good deal of respect. Thomas refers to its descriptive powers, Lutz to its effectiveness "in explaining . . . accidents," and Klass to its support as she became a doctor. Think of a time when you were in some way profoundly affected by language, and write an essay about this experience. Provide as many examples as necessary to illustrate both the language that affected you and how it made you feel.
2. Kim Kessler (p. 119) and Michael Miller (p. 124) both write about language that *isn't* language as we conventionally think of it—that is, words in sentences. As you see it, what are the advantages and disadvantages of communicating without words? How effective (or not) are Kessler's "blah blah blah" and Miller's smileys as communicators? Write an essay offering your definition of *communication* and answering these questions. Use examples from the essays and your own experience. (If you need help with definition, see Chapter 11.)
3. Perri Klass writes that medical jargon "contribute[s] to a sense of closeness and professional spirit among people who are under a great deal of stress" (paragraph 8) and that it helps "doctors maintain some distance from their patients" (17). Write an essay in which you analyze the function of "doublespeak," as presented by William Lutz. Who, if anyone, is such language designed to help? The accident victims? Survivors of these victims? Someone else? Can a positive case be made for this language?

Chapter 7

DIVISION OR ANALYSIS

Looking at Popular Culture

USING THE METHOD

Division and **analysis** are interchangeable terms for the same method. *Division* comes from a Latin word meaning "to force asunder or separate." *Analysis* comes from a Greek word meaning "to undo." Using this method, we separate a whole into its elements, examine the relations of the elements to one another and to the whole, and reassemble the elements into a new whole informed by the examination. The method is essential to understanding and evaluating objects, works, and ideas.

Analysis (as we will call it) is a daily occurrence in our lives, whether we ponder our relationships with others, decide whether a certain movie was worthwhile, or try to understand a politician's campaign promises. We also use analysis throughout this book, when looking at paragraphs and essays. And it is the basic operation in at least four other methods discussed in this book: classification

(Chapter 8), process analysis (Chapter 9), comparison and contrast (Chapter 10), and cause-and-effect analysis (Chapter 12).

At its most helpful, analysis builds on the separation into elements, leading to a conclusion about the meaning, significance, or value of the whole. This approach is essential to college learning, whether in discussing literature, reviewing a psychology experiment, or interpreting a business case. It is fundamental to work, from choosing a career to making sense of market research. And it informs and enriches life outside school or work, in buying a car, looking at art, or deciding whom to vote for. The method is the foundation of **critical thinking,** the ability to see beneath the surface of things, images, events, and ideas; to uncover and test assumptions; to see the importance of context; and to draw and support independent conclusions.

The subject of any analysis is usually singular—a freestanding, coherent unit, such as a bicycle or a poem, with its own unique constitution of elements. (In contrast, classification, the subject of the next chapter, usually starts with a plural subject, such as bicycles or the poems of the Civil War, and groups them according to their shared features.) You choose the subject and with it a **principle of analysis,** a framework that determines how you divide the subject and thus what elements you identify.

Sometimes the principle of analysis will be self-evident, especially when the subject is an object, such as a bicycle or a camera, that can be "undone" in only a limited number of ways. Most of the time, however, the principle you choose will depend on your view of the whole. In academic disciplines, businesses, and the professions, distinctive principles are part of what the field is about and are often the subject of debate within the field. In art, for instance, some critics see a painting primarily as a visual object and concentrate on its composition, color, line, and other formal qualities; other critics see a painting primarily as a social object and concentrate on its content and context (cultural, economic, political, and so on). Both groups use a principle of analysis that is a well-established way of looking at painting; yet each group finds different elements and thus meaning in a work.

There is, then, a great deal of flexibility in choosing a principle of analysis. But it should be appropriate for the subject and the field or discipline; it should be significant; and it should be applied thoroughly and consistently. Analysis is not done for its own sake but for a larger goal of illuminating the subject, perhaps concluding something about it, perhaps evaluating it. But even when the method culminates in evaluation—in the writer's judgment of the subject's value—the analysis should represent the subject as it actually is, in all its fullness and complexity. In analyzing a movie, for instance, a writer may emphasize one element, such as setting, and even omit some elements, such as costumes; but the characterization of the whole must still apply to *all* the elements. If it does not, readers can be counted on to notice; so the writer must single out any wayward element(s) and explain why they do not substantially undermine the framework and thus weaken the opinion.

ANALYZING DIVISION OR ANALYSIS IN PARAGRAPHS

Jon Pareles (born 1953) is the chief critic of popular music for the *New York Times.* The following paragraph comes from "Gather No Moss, Take No Prisoners, but Be Cool," a review of a concert by the rock guitarist Keith Richards.

Principle of analysis (topic sentence underlined): elements of Richards's "not showing off"

Mr. Richards shows off by not showing off. He uses rhythm chords as a goad, not a metronome, slipping them in just ahead of a beat or skipping them entirely. The distilled twang of his tone has been imitated all over rock, but far fewer guitarists have learned his guerrilla timing, his coiled silences. When he switches to lead guitar, Mr. Richards goes not for long lines, but for serrated riffing, zinging out three or four notes again and again in various permutations, wringing from them the essence of the blues. The phrasing is poised and suspenseful, but it also carries a salutary rock attitude: that less is more, especially when delivered with utter confidence.

1. Rhythm chords as goad (or prod)

2. Timing

3. Silences

4. Riffing (or choppy playing)

5. Confident, less-is-more attitude

Luci Tapahonso (born 1953) is a poet and teacher. This paragraph is from her essay "The Way It Is," which appears in *Sign Language,* a book of photographs (by Skeet McAuley) of life on the reservation for some Navajo and Apache Indians.

Principle of analysis (topic sentence underlined at end): elements of the commercial that appealed to Indians

It is rare and, indeed, very exciting to see an Indian person in a commercial advertisement. Word travels fast when that happens. Nunzio's Pizza in Albuquerque,

New Mexico, ran commercials featuring Jose Rey Toledo of Jemez Pueblo talking about his "native land—Italy" while wearing typical Pueblo attire—jewelry, moccasins, and hair tied in a chongo. Because of the ironic humor, because Indian grandfathers specialize in playing tricks and jokes on their grandchildren, and because Jose Rey Toledo is a respected and well-known elder in the Indian communities, word of this commercial spread fast among Indians in New Mexico. It was the cause of recognition and celebration of sorts on the reservations and in the pueblos. His portrayal was not in the categories which the media usually associate with Indians but as a typical sight in the Southwest. It showed Indians as we live today—enjoying pizza as one of our favorite foods, including humor and fun as part of our daily lives, and recognizing the importance of preserving traditional knowledge.

1. Rarity of an Indian in a commercial
2. Indian dress
3. Indian humor
4. Indian tradition
5. Respected Indian spokesperson
6. Realism

DEVELOPING AN ESSAY BY DIVISION OR ANALYSIS

Getting Started

Analysis is one of the readiest methods of development: almost anything whole can be separated into its elements, from a lemon to a play by Shakespeare to an economic theory. In college and work, many writing assignments will demand analysis with a verb such as *analyze, criticize, discuss, evaluate, interpret,* or *review.* If you need to develop your own subject for analysis, think of something whose meaning or significance puzzles or intrigues you and whose parts you can distinguish and relate to the whole—an object such as a machine, an artwork such as poem, a media product such as a news broadcast, an institution such as a hospital, a relationship such as stepparenting, a social issue such as sheltering the homeless.

If you begin by seeking meaning or significance, you will be more likely to find a workable principle of analysis and less likely to waste time on a hollow exercise. Each question on the facing page suggests a distinct approach to the subject's elements—a distinct principle—that makes it easier to isolate the elements and show their connection to one another. Each question could lead to a thesis sentence that states an opinion and reveals the principle of analysis.

QUESTION To what extent is an enormously complex hospital a community in itself?

THESIS SENTENCE The hospital encompasses such a wide range of personnel and services that it resembles a good-sized town.

QUESTION What is the appeal of the front-page headlines in the local tabloid newspaper?

THESIS SENTENCE The newspaper's front page routinely appeals to readers' fear of crime, anger at criminals, and sympathy for victims.

QUESTION Why did a certain movie have such a powerful effect on you and your friends?

THESIS SENTENCE The film is a unique and important statement of the private terrors of adolescence.

Note that all three thesis sentences imply an explanatory purpose—an effort to understand something and share that understanding with the reader. The third thesis sentence, however, conveys a persuasive purpose as well: the writer hopes that readers will accept her evaluation of the film. (See p. 146 for more on thesis sentences in division or analysis.)

Of course, the thesis must develop from and be supported by the evidence of the analysis—the elements of the subject, their interconnections, and their relation to the whole. Dissect your subject, looking at the actual, physical thing if possible, imagining it in your mind if necessary. Make detailed notes of all the elements you see, their distinguishing features, and how they help answer your starting question about meaning or significance. In analyzing someone's creation, tease out the creator's influences, assumptions, intentions, conclusions, and evidence. You may have to go outside the work for some of this information—researching an author's background, for instance, to uncover the political biases that may underlie his or her opinions. Even if you do not use all this information in your final draft, it will help you see the elements and help keep your analysis true to the subject.

At this point you should consider your readers' needs as well as the needs of your subject and your own framework:

- If the subject is familiar to readers (as, say, the newspaper's headlines might be), then your principle of analysis may not require much justification (as long as it's clear), but your details and examples must be vivid and convincing.
- If the subject is unfamiliar, then you should carefully explain your principle of analysis, define all specialized terms, distinguish parts from one another, and provide ample illustrations.
- If readers know your subject but may dispute your way of looking at it, then you should justify as well as explain your principle of analysis. You should also account for any evidence that may seem not to support your opinion by showing either why, in fact, the evidence is supportive or why it is unimportant. (If contrary evidence refuses to be dispensed with, you may have to rethink your approach.)

Organizing

In the introduction to your essay, let readers know why you are bothering to analyze your subject: Why is the subject significant? How might the essay relate to the experiences of readers or be useful to them? A subject unfamiliar to readers might be summarized or described, or part of it (an anecdote or quotation, say) might be used to tantalize readers. A familiar subject might be introduced with a surprising fact or unusual perspective. An evaluative analysis might open with an opposing viewpoint.

In the body of the essay you'll need to explain your principle of analysis according to the guidelines above. The arrangement of elements and analysis should suit your subject and purpose: you can describe the elements and then offer your analysis, or you can introduce and analyze elements one by one. You can arrange the elements themselves from least to most important, least to most complex, most to least familiar, spatially, or chronologically. Devote as much space to each element as it demands: there is no requirement that all elements be given equal space and emphasis if their complexity or your framework dictates otherwise.

Most analysis essays need a conclusion that assembles the elements, returning readers to a sense of the whole subject. The conclusion can restate the thesis, summarize what the essay has contributed, consider the influence of the subject or its place in a larger picture, or (especially in an evaluation) assess the effectiveness or worth of the subject.

Drafting

If your subject or your view of it is complex, you may need at least two rough drafts of an analysis essay—one to discover what you think and one to clarify your principle, cover each element, and support your points with concrete details and vivid examples (including quotations if the subject is a written work). Plan on two drafts if you're uncertain of your thesis when you begin: you'll probably save time in the long run by attending to one goal at a time. Especially because the analysis essay says something about the subject by explaining its structure, you need to have a clear picture of the whole and relate each part to it.

Revising and Editing

When you revise and edit your essay, use the following questions and the box on the next page to uncover any weaknesses remaining in your analysis.

- *Is your principle of analysis clear?* The significance of your analysis and your view of the subject should be apparent throughout your essay.
- *Is your analysis complete?* Have you identified all elements according to your principle of analysis and determined their relations to one another and to the whole? If you have omitted some elements from your discussion, will the reason for their omission be clear to readers?
- *Is your analysis consistent?* Is your principle of analysis applied consistently to the entire subject (including any elements you have omitted)? Do all elements reflect the same principle, and are they clearly separate rather than overlapping? You may find it helpful to check your draft against your list of elements or your outline or to outline the draft itself.
- *Is your analysis well supported?* Is the thesis supported by clear assertions about parts of the subject, and are the assertions supported by concrete, specific evidence (sensory details, facts, quotations, and so on)? Do not rely on your readers to prove your thesis.
- *Is your analysis true to the subject?* Is your thesis unforced, your analysis fair? Is your new whole (your reassembly of the

FOCUS ON THE THESIS SENTENCE

A clear, informative thesis sentence (or sentences) is crucial in division or analysis because readers need to know your purpose in analyzing the subject and your principle of analysis. The sample sentences on page 143 convey both kinds of information. The following sentence, however, does not—with "do anything," it overstates and yet fails to specify a framework for analysis:

VAGUE Advertisers will do anything to sell their products.

Compare this thesis sentence with the one from Shafeeq Sadiq's essay later in this chapter (p. 152). Here it is apparent that the writer will focus on the racist and sexist elements in advertising:

CLEAR In general, these gimmicks [in advertisements] seem to enforce racial stereotypes and to view women in a negative way.

A well-focused thesis sentence benefits not only your readers but also you as writer, because it gives you a yardstick to judge the completeness, consistency, and supportiveness of your analysis. Don't be discouraged, though, if your thesis sentence doesn't come to you until *after* you've written a first draft and had a chance to discover your interest. Writing about your subject may be the best way for you to find its meaning and significance.

For more on thesis sentences, see pages 17–18.

elements) faithful to the original? Be wary of leaping to a conclusion that distorts the subject.

A NOTE ON THEMATIC CONNECTIONS

Because it is everywhere, and everywhere taken for granted, popular culture is a tempting and challenging target for writers. Having chosen to write critically about a disturbing, cheering, or intriguing aspect of popular culture, all the authors represented in this chapter naturally pursued the method of division or analysis. A paragraph by Jon Pareles dissects the unique playing style of the rock guitarist Keith Richards (p. 141). Another paragraph, by Luci Tapahonso, analyzes a pizza commercial that especially appealed to Native Americans (p. 141). Emily Prager's essay looks at just who or what the dolls Barbie and Ken represent (next page). Shafeeq Sadiq's essay finds plenty of political incorrectness in advertising (p. 152). And Margaret Visser's essay considers what besides food we buy when we visit McDonald's (p. 157).

Emily Prager

An essayist and fiction writer, Emily Prager was born in 1952 and grew up in Texas, Asia, and New York City. She graduated from Barnard College. Prager has written humor, satire, and criticism for periodicals as diverse as The National Lampoon, Viva, *the* Village Voice, *and* Penthouse. *Her fiction combines a satirical wit and a lively prose style to analyze gender relations, ethnic friction, and other anxieties of contemporary life. Among other books, Prager has published* A Visit from the Footbinder and Other Stories *(1982),* Clea and Zeus Divorce *(1987), and* Eve's Tattoo *(1991). She has also acted in several films and in the TV soap opera* The Edge of Night.

Our Barbies, Ourselves

The Barbie doll debuted in 1959, when Prager was seven years old, and ever since has dominated the "fashion doll" market. In this essay from Interview *magazine in 1991, Prager explains how a chance bit of information changed her framework for analyzing Barbie.*

I read an astounding obituary in the *New York Times* not too long ago. It concerned the death of one Jack Ryan. A former husband of Zsa Zsa Gabor, it said, Mr. Ryan had been an inventor and designer during his lifetime. A man of eclectic creativity, he designed Sparrow and Hawk missiles when he worked for the Raytheon Company, and the notice said, when he consulted for Mattel he designed Barbie.[1] 1

If Barbie was designed by a man, suddenly a lot of things made sense to me, things I'd wondered about for years. I used to look at Barbie and wonder, What's wrong with this picture? What kind of woman designed this doll? Let's be honest: Barbie looks like someone who got her start at the Playboy Mansion. She could be a regular 2

[1] Since Prager wrote this essay, a "biography" of Barbie and statements by a founder of Mattel have clarified Ryan's role in Barbie's creation. Barbie's prototype was a hard-edged adult doll made in Germany after World War II. At the direction of Mattel's founders, Ryan oversaw the transformation of this version into a toy for American girls. [Editor's note.]

guest on *The Howard Stern Show*. It is a fact of Barbie's design that her breasts are so out of proportion to the rest of her body that if she were a human, she'd fall flat on her face.

If it's true that a woman didn't design Barbie, you don't know how much saner that makes me feel. Of course, that doesn't ameliorate the damage. There are millions of women who are subliminally sure that a thirty-nine-inch bust and a twenty-three-inch waist are the epitome of lovability. Could this account for the popularity of breast implant surgery? 3

I don't mean to step on anyone's toes here. I loved my Barbie. Secretly, I still believe that neon pink and turquoise are the only colors in which to decorate a duplex condo. And like many others of my generation, I've never married, simply because I cannot find a man who looks as good in clam diggers as Ken. 4

The question that comes to mind is, of course, Did Mr. Ryan design Barbie as a weapon? Because it *is* odd that Barbie appeared about the same time in my consciousness as the feminist movement—a time when women sought equality and small breasts were king. Or is Barbie the dream date of weapons designers? Or perhaps it's simpler than that: perhaps Barbie is Zsa Zsa if she were eleven inches tall. No matter what, my discovery of Jack Ryan confirms what I have always felt: there is something indescribably masculine about Barbie—dare I say it, phallic. For all her giant breasts and high-heeled feet, she lacks a certain softness. If you asked a little girl what kind of doll she wanted for Christmas, I just don't think she'd reply, "Please, Santa, I want a hard-body." 5

On the other hand, you could say that Barbie, in feminist terms, is definitely her own person. With her condos and fashion plazas and pools and beauty salons, she is definitely a liberated woman, a gal on the move. And she has always been sexual, even totemic. Before Barbie, American dolls were flat-footed and breastless, and ineffably dignified. They were created in the image of little girls or babies. Madame Alexander was the queen of doll makers in the '50s, and her dollies looked like Elizabeth Taylor in *National Velvet*. They represented the kind of girls who looked perfect in jodhpurs, whose hair was never out of place, who grew up to be Jackie Kennedy—before she married Onassis. Her dolls' boyfriends were figments of the imagination, figments with large portfolios and three-piece suits and presidential aspirations, figments who could keep dolly in the style to which little girls of the '50s were programmed to become accus- 6 tomed, a style that spasmed with the '60s, and the appearance of Barbie. And perhaps what accounts for Barbie's vast popularity is that she was also a '60s woman: into free love and fun colors, anti-class, and possessed of a real, molded boyfriend, Ken, with whom she could chant a mantra.

But there were problems with Ken. I always felt weird about him. He had no genitals, and, even at age ten, I found that ominous. I mean, here was Barbie with these humongous breasts, and that was O.K. with the toy company. And then, there was Ken with that truncated, unidentifiable lump at his groin. I sensed injustice at work. Why, I wondered, was Barbie designed with such obvious sexual equipment and Ken not? Why was his treated as if it were more mysterious than hers? Did the fact that it was treated as such indicate that somehow his equipment, his essential maleness, was considered more powerful than hers, more worthy of the dignity of concealment? And if the issue in the mind of the toy company was obscenity and its possible damage to children, I still object. How do they think I felt, knowing that no matter how many water beds they slept in, or hot tubs they romped in, or swimming pools they lounged by under the stars, Barbie and Ken could never make love? No matter how much sexuality Barbie possessed, she would never turn Ken on. He would be forever withholding, forever detached. There was a loneliness about Barbie's situation that was always disturbing. And twenty-five years later, movies and videos are still filled with topless women and covered men. As if we're all trapped in Barbie's world and can never escape. 7

Meaning

1. "If Barbie was designed by a man," Prager writes in her second paragraph, "suddenly a lot of things make sense to me." What are these "things," and how do they relate to Prager's main idea? What is that idea?
2. In paragraph 5 Prager asks, "Did Mr. Ryan design Barbie as a weapon?" What do you think she means here? A weapon against what?
3. Try to guess the meanings of any of the following words with which you may be unfamiliar. Check a dictionary to see if your guesses were right, and then practice using each word in a sentence or two of your own.

obituary (1)	ameliorate (3)	epitome (3)
eclectic (1)	subliminally (3)	phallic (5)

totemic (6)
ineffably (6)
jodhpurs (6)
figments (6)
portfolios (6)
aspirations (6)
mantra (6)
ominous (7)
humongous (7)
truncated (7)

Purpose and Audience

1. Why do you think Prager wrote this essay? What did she hope her readers would gain?
2. In her next-to-last sentence, Prager states that "twenty-five years later, movies and videos are still filled with topless women and covered men." What does this statement reveal about Prager's biases and the assumptions she makes about her audience?

Method and Structure

1. What elements of Barbie does Prager analyze, and how does she reassemble these elements into a new whole? Support your answer with evidence from the essay.
2. Why is division or analysis essential for Prager to make her claims about Barbie? Is an analysis of Barbie's features important even to readers already familiar with the doll?
3. Prager waits until the end of her essay to make the connection between Barbie and today's movies featuring "topless women and covered men." What is the effect of this decision? How might the essay be different if she had opened with a straightforward thesis statement such as "The Barbie doll is partly responsible for the double standards regarding male and female nudity in the movies today"?
4. **Other Methods** In addition to analysis, Prager uses description (Chapter 4) in her essay to create a clear, concrete image of Barbie. In paragraph 6 she also uses comparison and contrast (Chapter 10), comparing Barbie to the American dolls who came before her. How did these dolls differ from Barbie, and what does this comparison contribute to Prager's overall purpose?

Language

1. Prager's diction includes some words and phrases that are colloquial ("condo," "dream date," "gal," "humongous," "turn . . . on") and others that are more formal ("ameliorate," "subliminally," "epitome," "totemic," "ineffably"). What purpose do these different levels of language serve? (If necessary, see *colloquial language* in the Glossary.)
2. In paragraph 6 Prager says of Barbie, "With her condos and fashion plazas and pools and beauty salons, she is definitely a liberated woman,

a gal on the move." How would you characterize the tone of this statement? Where else in the essay can you locate this tone?

Writing Topics

1. **Journal Response** Think of a toy or game that you played with as a child (G.I. Joe, *Star Wars* action figures, Risk, Monopoly, Life) that may have had other meanings besides pure entertainment. Make a list of messages that the makers of the toy or game might intentionally or unintentionally have been sending to children—for example, Monopoly could be seen as teaching children the values of capitalism.
   Journal to Essay Using Prager's essay as a model, write an analysis of the toy or game you explored in your journal, making sure to examine each element for its contribution to the intentional or unintentional meanings you identified. Your essay may be serious or humorous, but it should include plenty of description to make the elements clear and support your analysis.
2. Defend Barbie or Ken: write an essay analyzing the positive lessons about women and men that children might learn from either or both of these dolls. Your essay may, but need not, directly challenge Prager's essay.
3. In paragraph 4 Prager writes that "like many others of my generation, I've never married, simply because I cannot find a man who looks as good in clam diggers as Ken." Her tone here is ironic; clearly Prager does not really expect her readers to believe this explanation for her choice to remain single. What might it mean to a girl to come of age during the 1960s as opposed to the 1950s? How might the feminist movement have influenced a girl's expectations, goals, and desires? Write an essay in which you suggest a serious explanation for why Prager and women of her generation might choose not to marry.
4. **Cultural Considerations** As explained in the footnote on page 147, Barbie was adapted from a German adult doll into a doll specifically for American girls. What characteristics of Barbie and Ken strike you as especially American? How might the dolls be different in other cultures? Write an essay analyzing Barbie and Ken in which you answer these questions. The characteristics you identify may come from Prager's analysis, but be sure to explain why you think they are distinctly American.
5. **Connections** Prager writes of a double standard for men and women regarding nudity in the movies. How does this concept relate to the double standard that Judy Brady focuses on in her essay "I Want a Wife" (p. 261)? Write an essay analyzing these writers' attitudes toward relationships between men and women. How much do Prager and Brady seem to have in common? Use evidence from both essays to support your response.

Shafeeq Sadiq

Shafeeq Sadiq was born in 1977 in Stockton, California, the son of Pakistani immigrants. He grew up in Stockton, graduated from high school in nearby Manteca, and obtained an A.A. degree from San Joaquin Delta College in Stockton. Sadiq now majors in economics at the University of California at Davis and enjoys body building in his free time.

Racism and Sexism in Advertising

In this strong critique of advertising tactics, Sadiq offers detailed examples to support his assertions. The essay was published in the 1997 Delta Winds, *a collection of student writing from San Joaquin Delta College.*

It seems as if everywhere you turn, someone is trying to be politically correct. Whether it involves minorities or women, racist and sexist comments are no longer tolerated in places such as the school yard and the workplace. Why is it, then, that minorities and women are constantly being exploited in everyday advertisements? Television, magazines, and billboards no longer show products, but rather show gimmicks in order to sell their product. In general, these gimmicks seem to enforce racial stereotypes and to view women in a negative way. 1

It appears that on every channel, there is another television commercial trying to sell its product with beautiful women. These commercials can range from selling beer to selling cars. Who can forget the gorgeous blonde standing next to the green Geo Storm, proudly exclaiming, "A man likes a woman who knows how to drive a stick!"? Advertisements like these, though seemingly aimed towards women, are exploiting them en route to the actual target: men. This commercial would routinely air during sporting events, when the majority of the viewers are male. It fits in well with the other commercials which, more often than not, have to do with beer. 2

Beer companies have been notorious for exploiting women in their everyday promotions. Watching a football game, you can usu- 3 ally find an attractive young lady being swept off her feet by a less than attractive man after he opens the beer of his choice. Or, if you are lucky, you can witness several young women materializing on a desert island with the male drinker after, of course, he opens his can of beer. These advertisements present women as a goal, a trophy if you will, that can only be attained with the proper beverage. These women seldom have anything to say besides "Yes," making them seem like unintelligent sex objects.

Unfortunately, the exploitation does not stop with women. Beer commercials exploit minorities as well. Black Entertainment Television frequently airs malt liquor commercials directed at African-American buyers. These ads usually involve a hip-hop rap artist who visits an unusually quiet ghetto community. When he brings the malt liquor, the entire neighborhood breaks into song and dance, with the very attractive African-American woman saying, "Things are back to the way they used to be." How did things used to be? Were there no peaceful afternoons in the 'hood? African-Americans can't be happy in a calm, serene environment? Though there are no racial slurs uttered, the entire commercial perpetuates stereotypes of the African-American community. They must sing and dance in the streets, trying to live life the way it used to be, before they were confined to the monotony of a good job and a quiet neighborhood. Perhaps the commercial maker is trying to say that African-Americans, as a whole, have been subdued by society. 4

African-Americans are not the only minority group exploited in advertising; Arab Americans are victims as well. On September 16, 1996, *Newsweek* magazine printed a two-page advertisement for a well-known computer company. This ad depicted an Arab man from an unknown Arab country, wearing his native garb and standing next to a camel. There are boxes of computer parts in the corner of the page. The ad reads, "Some computer companies don't make their own parts. Makes you wonder where they get them." This advertisement insinuates that if these parts were made in an Arab country, they would somehow be inferior. Though the country is not mentioned by name, the message is still very clear. 5

Perhaps the most stereotyped people, when it comes to advertising, are Indian-Americans, those whose family originated in India. To my recollection, there has never been a major commercial involving an Indian-American who didn't speak with a ridiculously exaggerated accent. The most recent perpetrator, MCI, promotes a dime-a-minute service featuring an Indian-American with a very thick and pro- 6 nounced accent stereotypically driving a New York City taxicab. The actor will never be an American who happens to be of Indian descent. For the company, using Indian-Americans in this manner might add to the comic value of the commercial. But it is safe to say that to most Indian-Americans, it is no laughing matter.

Racism and sexism are problems that go unnoticed in advertising 7
today. Nevertheless, they must be dealt with. The only winners in these types of ads are the advertisers themselves, who make money when you buy the product. There needs to be a public awakening, for racism and sexism should not be used in any situation, especially not to sell products. Advertisers need to take responsibility for their own actions and to end this type of exploitation. If they do not, we the consumer can always force them. After all, we have the dollars and the sense.

Meaning

1. What is Sadiq's thesis? Where does he state it explicitly?
2. In your own words, explain the process, described in paragraphs 2 and 3, by which advertisers use women to sell products to men. What, besides the product, are they selling?
3. What is wrong, in Sadiq's opinion, with a beer company's depicting African Americans having a good time?
4. What does Sadiq mean in paragraph 6 when he says, "The actor will never be an American who happens to be of Indian descent"? As opposed to what?
5. If you are unfamiliar with any of the following words, try to guess their meanings from the context in which Sadiq uses them. Look the words up in the dictionary to check your guesses, and then use each one in a sentence or two of your own.

gimmicks (1)	materialize (3)	monotony (4)
notorious (3)	perpetuates (4)	perpetrator (6)

Purpose and Audience

1. What do you think Sadiq's purpose was in writing this essay: to ask readers who think that racism and sexism have disappeared from advertising to reconsider? to convince advertisers to change their ways? something else?

2. What assumptions does Sadiq seem to make about his readers—their gender or age, their attitudes toward stereotypes of gender or race, their attitudes toward advertising, and so on?

Method and Structure

1. Why do you think Sadiq chose the method of analysis to talk about sexism and racism in advertising? How does the method help Sadiq achieve his purpose?
2. Each example Sadiq cites is a mini-analysis of a television commercial or magazine ad. By breaking down the commercial into its elements, he creates a new whole, a new way of looking at the commercial, that might not have been apparent before. Show how this analysis works in paragraph 5 of the essay, using the annotated paragraphs on pages 141–42 as a guide.
3. What does Sadiq accomplish in his first and last paragraphs? How do they function differently from the equivalent paragraphs in the previous essay, by Emily Prager?
4. Why do you think Sadiq cites more examples of racism than of sexism in advertising? Does he seem to think racism is more important or more widespread?
5. **Other Methods** The advertisements Sadiq analyzes are all examples (Chapter 6) used to illustrate racism or sexism in advertising, and each of these examples includes description (Chapter 4). What does this description contribute to Sadiq's thesis?

Language

1. How would you describe Sadiq's tone? How seriously does he take his subject? Is the tone appropriate, given his purpose?
2. Sadiq occasionally uses irony in analyzing advertisements, as in "Or, if you are lucky, you can witness several young women materializing on a desert island with the male drinker after, of course, he opens his can of beer" (paragraph 3) or "Were there no peaceful afternoons in the 'hood? African-Americans can't be happy in a calm, serene environment?" (4). Is the irony effective? Why, or why not? (See *irony* in the Glossary.)

Writing Topics

1. **Journal Response** Think of a commercial that you object to. It doesn't necessarily have to be sexist or racist, just offensive or annoying in some way. Write down as many reasons for why it bothers you as you can

think of. Alternately, choose a commercial you think is unusually entertaining, amusing, or moving, and write down the reasons why it works.
Journal to Essay Write a brief essay (a page or two) analyzing the commercial, choosing the strongest points from your journal entry. Make sure your essay has some controlling thesis that draws together all the points of your analysis, explaining why the commercial has the effect it does.

2. How did you react to Sadiq's essay? Do you agree with him that too many commercials remain sexist or racist in an age of supposed tolerance? Or do you find his complaints to be exaggerated, the offenses he points out rare or minor? Write an essay of your own responding to Sadiq's essay. Be sure to include examples to support your view.
3. **Cultural Considerations** Sadiq is critical of an advertisement on Black Entertainment Television that he sees as depicting African Americans in a negative light. However, what if the ad was created by African Americans for African Americans? Would it still seem to stereotype? And if so, do the members of a minority group have a license to employ stereotypes about themselves, either in jest or as a way of deflating the stereotypes? Write an essay in which you state your position on this issue and support it using examples.
4. **Connections** Write a two-paragraph comparison of paragraph 4 of Sadiq's essay and the paragraph by Luci Tapahonso on page 141. Each paragraph analyzes a single advertisement, but their tones are quite different. How do the words used by each author convey his or her attitude toward the advertisement?

Margaret Visser

Born in 1940 in South Africa, Margaret Visser was raised in Zambia and lived in England, France, Iraq, and the United States before settling in Toronto, Canada. (She is a naturalized citizen of Canada.) Visser was educated at the University of Toronto, where she earned a B.A. (1970), an M.A. (1973), and a Ph.D. in classics (1980). She taught classics at York University in Toronto and has published articles in scholarly and popular periodicals. Visser also appears on television and radio, discussing her discoveries about the history and social mythology of everyday life. "The extent to which we take everyday objects for granted," she says, "is the precise extent to which they govern and inform our lives." Three books illuminate this important territory: Much Depends on Dinner *(1986),* The Rituals of Dinner *(1991), and* The Way We Are *(1994).*

The Ritual of Fast Food

In this excerpt from The Rituals of Dinner, *an investigation of table manners, Visser analyzes the fast-food restaurant. What do we seek when we visit such a place? How does the management oblige us? Success hinges on predictability.*

An early precursor of the restaurant meal was dinner served to the public at fixed times and prices at an eating house or tavern. Such a meal was called, because of its predetermined aspects, an "ordinary," and the place where it was eaten came to be called an "ordinary," too. When a huge modern business conglomerate offers fast food to travellers on the highway, it knows that its customers are likely to desire No Surprises. They are hungry, tired, and not in a celebratory mood; they are happy to pay—provided that the price looks easily manageable—for the safely predictable, the convenient, the fast and ordinary. 1

Ornamental formalities are pruned away (tables and chairs are bolted to the floor, for instance, and "cutlery" is either nonexistent or not worth stealing); but rituals, in the sense of behaviour and expectations that conform to preordained rules, still inform the proceedings. People who stop for a hamburger—at a Wendy's, a Harvey's, a 2

McDonald's, or a Burger King—know exactly what the building that houses the establishment should look like; architectural variations merely ring changes on rigidly imposed themes. People want, perhaps even need, to *recognize* their chain store, to feel that they know it and its food in advance. Such an outlet is designed to be a "home away from home," on the highway, or anywhere in the city, or for Americans abroad.

Words and actions are officially laid down, learned by the staff from handbooks and teaching sessions, and then picked up by customers in the course of regular visits. Things have to be called by their correct names ("Big Mac," "large fries"); the McDonald's rubric in 1978 required servers to ask "Will that be with cheese, sir?" "Will there be any fries today, sir?" and to close the transaction with "Have a nice day." The staff wear distinctive garments; menus are always the same, and even placed in the same spot in every outlet in the chain; prices are low and predictable; and the theme of cleanliness is proclaimed and tirelessly reiterated. The company attempts also to play the role of a lovable host, kind and concerned, even parental: it knows that blunt and direct confrontation with a huge faceless corporation makes us suspicious, and even badly behaved. So it stresses its love of children, its nostalgia for cozy warmth and for the past (cottagy roofs, warm earth tones), or its clean, brisk modernity (glass walls, smooth surfaces, red trim). It responds to social concerns—when they are insistent enough, sufficiently widely held, and therefore "correct." McDonald's for example, is at present busy showing how much it cares about the environment. 3

Fast-food chains know that they are ordinary. They *want* to be ordinary, and for people to think of them as almost inseparable from the idea of everyday food consumed outside the home. They are happy to allow their customers time off for feasts—on Thanksgiving, Christmas, and so on—to which they do not cater. Even those comparatively rare holiday times, however, are turned to a profit, because the companies know that their favourite customers—law-abiding families—are at home together then, watching television, where carefully placed commercials will spread the word concerning new fast-food products, and re-imprint the image of the various chain stores for later, when the long stretches of ordinary times return. 4

Families are the customers the fast-food chains want: solid citizens in groups of several at a time, the adults hovering over their children, teaching them the goodness of hamburgers, anxious to bring 5 them up to behave typically and correctly. Customers usually maintain a clean, restrained, considerate, and competent demeanour as they swiftly, gratefully, and informally eat. Fast-food operators have recently faced the alarming realization that crack addicts, craving salt and fat, have spread the word among their number that French fries deliver these substances easily, ubiquitously, cheaply, and at all hours. Dope addicts at family "ordinaries"! The unacceptability of such a thought was neatly captured by a news story in *The Economist* (1990) that spelled out the words a fast-foods proprietor can least afford to hear from his faithful customers, the participants in his polite and practiced rituals: the title of the story was "Come on Mabel, let's leave." The plan to counter this threat included increasing the intensity of the lighting in fast-food establishments—drug addicts, apparently, prefer to eat in the dark.

The formality of eating at a restaurant belonging to a fast-food 6
chain depends upon the fierce regularity of its product, its simple but carefully observed rituals, and its environment. Supplying a hamburger that adheres to perfect standards of shape, weight, temperature, and consistency, together with selections from a pre-set list of trimmings, to a customer with fiendishly precise expectations is an enormously complex feat. The technology involved in performing it has been learned through the expenditure of huge sums on research, and after decades of experience—not to mention the vast political and economic ramifications involved in maintaining the supplies of cheap beef and cheap buns. But these costs and complexities are, with tremendous care, hidden from view. We know of course that, say, a Big Mac is a cultural construct: the careful control expended upon it is one of the things we are buying. But McDonald's manages—it must do so if it is to succeed in being ordinary—to provide a "casual" eating experience. Convenient, innocent simplicity is what the technology, the ruthless politics, and the elaborate organization serve to the customer.

Meaning

1. In paragraph 6 Visser writes, "Supplying a hamburger that adheres to perfect standards of shape, weight, temperature, and consistency . . . to a customer with fiendishly precise expectations is an enormously complex feat." How does this statement illustrate Visser's main idea?

2. What do you think Visser means by the statement that "a Big Mac is a cultural construct" (paragraph 6)?
3. If any of the following words are new to you, try to guess their meanings from the context of Visser's essay. Test your guesses in a dictionary, and then use each new word in a sentence or two.

precursor (1)	cater (4)	ubiquitously (5)
conglomerate (1)	hovering (5)	proprietor (5)
pruned (2)	demeanour (5)	expenditure (6)
preordained (2)	(American spelling:	ramifications (6)
rubric (3)	demeanor)	
reiterated (3)		

Purpose and Audience

1. What is Visser's purpose in writing this essay: to propose more interesting surroundings and menus at fast-food restaurants? to argue that the patrons of these establishments are too demanding? to explain how these chains manage to satisfy so many customers? something else?
2. Whom does Visser seem to imagine as her audience? Is she writing for sociologists? for managers at corporations such as McDonald's and Burger King? for diners who patronize fast-food restaurants? What evidence in the essay supports your answer?

Method and Structure

1. How does Visser's analysis, breaking the fast-food experience down into its elements, help her achieve her purpose?
2. Into what elements does Visser divide the fast-food restaurant? Be specific, supporting your answer with examples from the text.
3. **Other Methods** In addition to analysis, Visser employs example (Chapter 6) and description (Chapter 4) to illustrate the predictable nature of fast-food restaurants, most extensively in paragraph 3. In paragraph 5 she also uses cause-and-effect analysis (Chapter 12) to explain both why crack addicts began to frequent chain restaurants and why these restaurants couldn't risk including addicts among their clientele. What does this cause-and-effect analysis add to the analysis of fast-food restaurants? How would addicts, whose money is presumably as good as anyone else's, interfere with the operation of these restaurants?

Language

1. What is Visser's tone? How seriously does she take her subject?
2. Visser writes that McDonald's used to require its servers to ask patrons, depending on their order, "Will that be with cheese, sir?" or "Will there be any fries today, sir?" (paragraph 3). What would be the purpose of such questions? How would you characterize this use of language?
3. According to Visser, people who patronize fast-food restaurants "want, perhaps even need, to *recognize* their chain store" (paragraph 2); they are looking for "the safely predictable, the convenient, the fast and ordinary" (1). Find other instances in the essay where Visser describes the people who eat in these restaurants. What portrait emerges of these customers? How does this portrait contribute to Visser's overall message?

Writing Topics

1. **Journal Response** Think of an activity you do often, such as shopping for groceries, doing your laundry at a laundromat, getting gas at a self-service pump, or shopping for and trying on clothes in a department store. Make a list of all the elements that constitute this activity and the setting in which it takes place.
   Journal to Essay Using "The Ritual of Fast Food" as a model, write an essay in which you analyze your chosen activity, examining each element to see what it contributes to the whole. Be sure your principle of analysis is clear to readers.
2. In her last paragraph, Visser writes that the "costs and complexities" of providing "a 'casual' eating experience" in a fast-food restaurant are "hidden from view." Does this seem appropriate to you, or would you rather know what the corporation feeding you puts into its operation, such as the "economic ramifications involved in maintaining the supplies of cheap beef and cheap buns"? Write an essay exploring the issues this question raises for you.
3. **Cultural Considerations** All of us have probably experienced a particular moment (or perhaps many moments) when we were willing to dine out on anything *but* fast food. What, at these moments, do you think we are seeking? Following Visser's example, write an essay analyzing the "culture" of a particular *non*chain restaurant. How does the management deliver what the customer wants?
4. **Connections** Like Visser, Emily Prager, in "Our Barbies, Ourselves" (p. 147), writes seriously about a subject that some people would consider trivial and unworthy of serious attention. How informative and useful do you find such analyses of elements of popular culture?

Where does each essay tell us something significant about ourselves, or, in contrast, where does it fail in trying to make the trivial seem important? Is popular culture—magazines, television, Hollywood movies, self-help books, toys, fast-food restaurants—best looked at critically, best ignored, or best simply enjoyed, do you think? Explain your answers in an essay, using plenty of examples to support your thesis.

Writing with the Method

Division or Analysis

Choose one of the following topics, or any other topic they suggest, for an essay developed by analysis. The topic you decide on should be something you care about so that analysis is a means of communicating an idea, not an end in itself.

PEOPLE, ANIMALS, OBJECTS

1. The personality of a friend or relative
2. The personality of a typical politician, teacher, or other professional
3. An animal such as a cat, dog, horse, cow, spider, or bat
4. A machine or appliance such as a car engine, harvesting combine, laptop computer, hair dryer, toaster, or sewing machine
5. A nonmotorized vehicle such as a skateboard, in-line skate, bicycle, or snowboard
6. A building such as a hospital, theater, or sports arena

IDEAS

7. The perfect city
8. The perfect crime
9. A theory or concept in a field such as psychology, sociology, economics, biology, physics, engineering, or astronomy
10. The evidence in a political argument (written, spoken, or reported in the news)
11. A liberal arts education

ASPECTS OF CULTURE

12. A style of dress or "look" such as that associated with the typical businessperson, jock, rap musician, or outdoors enthusiast
13. A typical hero or villain in science fiction, romance novels, war movies, or movies or novels about adolescents
14. A television or film comedy
15. A literary work: short story, novel, poem, essay
16. A visual work: painting, sculpture, building
17. A musical work: song, concerto, symphony, opera
18. A performance: sports, acting, dance, music, speech
19. The slang of a particular group or occupation

Writing About the Theme

Looking at Popular Culture

1. The essays by Emily Prager (p. 147), Shafeeq Sadiq (p. 152), and Margaret Visser (p. 157) all include the theme that what you see—whether in dolls, advertising, or fast-food restaurants—is not all you get. Think of something you have used, seen, or otherwise experienced that made you suspect a hidden message or agenda. Consider, for example, a childhood toy, a popular breakfast cereal, a political speech, a magazine, a textbook, a video game, a movie, or a visit to a theme park such as Disney World. Using the essays in this chapter as models, write an analysis of your subject, making sure to divide it into distinct elements, and conclude by reassembling these elements into a new whole.
2. Margaret Visser writes that "a Big Mac is a cultural construct: the careful control expended upon it is one of the things we are buying." Emily Prager illustrates that Barbie is also a cultural construct, involving the expectations that girls should play with dolls and that a woman should have large breasts, a tiny waist, and minimal power in the world, except in regard to choosing her wardrobe. In what way is Keith Richards's guitar playing, as described by Jon Pareles (p. 141), also part of a cultural construct? Consider the myths surrounding guitars and famous rock-and-roll guitar players, such as Elvis Presley, Chuck Berry, Jimi Hendrix, and Eric Clapton. Write an essay explaining the attitudes and expectations invested in rock guitar playing in our society. Examine the language, setting, and atmosphere surrounding guitars and guitarists, whether in clubs, at rock concerts, or on music videos.
3. Luci Tapahonso (p. 141) and Shafeeq Sadiq both analyze television advertising. Sadiq calls for a "public awakening" to racist and sexist advertising. Tapahonso, in contrast, thinks that Native Americans found cause for celebration in a positive commercial that showed "Indians as we live today." What do you think of television advertising? Is Sadiq's concern justified, or are the ads he singles out unusual? How common are ads like the one Tapahonso analyzes? Consider ads you've seen, or pay close attention to the ads as you're watching television over a week or so. Then write an essay addressing whether advertisers seem to treat the differences among people fairly or to exploit those differences. Are there notable exceptions in either case?

Chapter 8

CLASSIFICATION

Sorting Thoughts and Behaviors

USING THE METHOD

We **classify** when we sort things into groups: kinds of cars, styles of writing, types of psychotherapy. Because it creates order, classification helps us make sense of our physical and mental experience. With it, we see the correspondences among like things and distinguish them from unlike things. We can name things, remember them, discuss them.

Writers classify primarily to explain a pattern in a subject that might not have been noticed before: for instance, a sportswriter might observe that basketball players tend to fall into one of three groups based on the aggressiveness of their play. Sometimes, writers also classify to persuade readers that one group is superior: the sportswriter might argue that one style of basketball play is more effective than the other two.

Classification is a three-step process:

- Separate things into their elements, using the method of division or analysis (previous chapter).
- Isolate the similarities among the elements.
- Group or classify the things based on those similarities, matching like with like.

The diagram below illustrates a classification essay that appears later in this chapter, "The People Next Door" by Jonathan R. Gould, Jr. (p. 178). Gould's subject is neighbors, and he sees four distinct kinds:

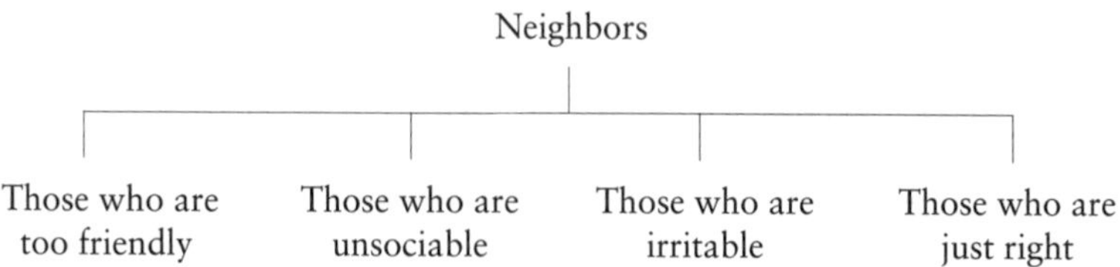

All the members of Gould's overall group share at least one characteristic: they have been Gould's neighbors. The members of each subgroup also share at least one characteristic: they are too friendly, for instance, or unsociable. The people in each subgroup are independent of each other, and none of them is essential to the existence of the subgroup: the kind of neighbor would continue to exist even if at the moment Gould didn't live next door to such a person.

The number of groups in a classification scheme depends entirely on the basis for establishing the classes in the first place. There are two systems:

- In a complex classification like that used for neighbors, each individual fits firmly into one class because of at least one distinguishing feature shared with all members of that class but not with any members of any other classes. All the too-friendly neighbors are overly friendly, but none of the unsociable, irritable, or just-right neighbors is.
- In a binary or two-part classification, two classes are in opposition to each other, such as constructive and destructive neighbors. Often, one group has a certain characteristic that the other group lacks. For instance, neighbors could be classified into those who respect your privacy and those who don't. A binary scheme

is useful to emphasize the possession of a particular characteristic, but it is limited if it specifies nothing about the members of the "other" class except that they lack the trait. (An old joke claims that there are two kinds of people in the world—those who classify, and all others.)

Sorting items demands a **principle of classification** that determines the groups by distinguishing them. For instance, Gould's principle in identifying four groups of neighbors is their behavior toward him and his family. Principles for sorting a year's movies might be genre (action-adventures, comedies, dramas); place of origin (domestic, foreign); or cost of production (low-budget, medium-priced, high-budget). Your choice of a principle depends on your interest.

Although you may emphasize one class over the others, the classification itself must be complete and consistent. A classification of movies by genre would be incomplete if it omitted comedies. It would be inconsistent if it included action-adventures, comedies, dramas, low-budget films, and foreign films: such a system mixes *three* principles (genre, cost, origin); it omits whole classes (what of high-budget domestic dramas?); and it overlaps other classes (a low-budget foreign action-adventure would fit in three different groups).

ANALYZING CLASSIFICATION IN PARAGRAPHS

Max Eastman (1883–1969) was a political organizer and tract writer and also a poet and scholar of Russian. This paragraph comes from his book *Enjoyment of Poetry* (1913).

A simple experiment will distinguish two types of
human nature. Gather a throng of people and pour
them into a ferry-boat. By the time the boat has
swung into the river you will find that a certain proportion have taken the trouble to climb upstairs in 1
order to be out on deck and see what is to be seen
as they cross over. The rest have settled indoors to
think what they will do upon reaching the other 2
side, or perhaps lose themselves in apathy or tobacco smoke. But leaving out those apathetic, or
addicted to a single enjoyment, we may divide all
the alert passengers on the boat into two classes:

Principle of classification (topic sentences underlined toward end): attitude toward experience and goals

1. Poetic people: focused on experience

2. Practical people: focused on goals

those who are interested in crossing the river, and 1
those who are merely interested in getting across. 2
And we may divide all the people on the earth, or
all the moods of people, in the same way. Some of
them are chiefly occupied with attaining ends, and 2
some with receiving experiences. The distinction of 1
the two will be more marked when we name the
first kind practical, and the second poetic, for common knowledge recognizes that a person poetic or 1
in a poetic mood is impractical, and a practical per- 2
son is intolerant of poetry.

Daniel Goleman (born 1940) is a psychologist who consults and writes on "emotional intelligence." He previously wrote for the *New York Times*, and the following paragraph comes from a 1992 *Times* column headlined "As Addiction Medicine Gains, Experts Debate What It Should Cover."

Dr. [Harvey] Milkman, in a theory often cited by those who are stretching the boundaries of addiction, proposed in the mid-1980s that there are three kinds of addiction, each marked by the change they produce in emotional states. The first involves substances or activities that are calming, including alcohol, tranquilizers, overeating, and even watching television. The second involves becoming energized, whether by cocaine and amphetamines, gambling, sexual activity, or high-risk sports like parachute-jumping. The third kind of addiction is to fantasy, whether induced by psychedelic drugs or, for example, by sexual thoughts.

Principle of classification (topic sentence underlined): change produced in emotional states

1. Calming addiction

2. Energizing addiction

3. Fantasy-producing addiction

DEVELOPING AN ESSAY BY CLASSIFICATION

Getting Started

Classification essays are often assigned in college courses. When you need to develop your own subject for a classification essay, think of one large class of things whose members you've noticed fall into subclasses, such as study habits, midnight grocery shoppers, or political fund-raising appeals. Be sure that your general subject forms a class in its own right—that all its members share at least one important quality. Then look for your principle of classification, the quality or qualities that distinguish some members from others, providing poles for the members to group themselves around. One such principle for political fund-raising appeals might be the different methods of delivery, including letters, telephone calls, advertisements, telethons, social gatherings, and rallies.

Your principle of classification may suggest a thesis sentence, but be sure the sentence also conveys a *reason* for the classification so that the essay does not become a dull list of categories. The following tentative thesis sentence is mechanical; the revision is more interesting.

> TENTATIVE THESIS SENTENCE Political fund-raising appeals are delivered in any of six ways.
>
> REVISED THESIS SENTENCE Of the six ways to deliver political fund-raising appeals, the three that rely on personal contact are generally the most effective.

(Note that the revised thesis sentence implies a further classification based on whether the appeals involve personal contact or not.)

While generating ideas for your classification, keep track of them in a list, diagram, or outline to ensure that your principle is applied thoroughly (all classes) and consistently (each class relating to the principle). Fill in the list, diagram, or outline with the distinguishing features of each class and with examples that will clarify your scheme. Be sure to consider your readers' needs. The principle for classifying a familiar subject such as study habits might need little justification, although the classes themselves would need to be enlivened with vivid examples. An unfamiliar subject, in contrast, might require considerable care in explaining the principle of classification as well as attention to the details.

Organizing

The introduction to a classification essay should make clear why the classification is worthwhile: What situation prompted the essay? What do readers already know about the subject? What use might they make of the information you will provide? Unless your principle of classification is self-evident, you may want to explain it briefly—though save extensive explanation for the body of the essay. Do state your principle in a thesis sentence, so that readers know where you're taking them.

In the body of the essay the classes may be arranged in order of decreasing familiarity or increasing importance or size—whatever pattern provides the emphasis you want and clarifies your scheme for readers. You should at least mention each class, but some classes may demand considerable space and detail.

A classification essay often ends with a conclusion that restores the wholeness of the subject. Among other uses, the conclusion might summarize the classes, comment on the significance of one particular class in relation to the whole, or point out a new understanding of the whole subject gained from the classification.

Drafting

For the first draft of your classification, your main goal will be to establish your scheme: spelling out the purpose and principle of classification and defining the groups so that they are complete and consistent, covering the subject without mixing principles or overlapping. The more you've been able to plan your scheme, the less difficult the draft will be. If you can also fill in the examples and other details needed to develop the groups, do so. But you may want to save this important work for revision, as discussed in the box opposite.

Revising and Editing

The following questions and the information in the box opposite can help you revise and edit your classification.

- *Will readers see the purpose of your classification?* Let readers know early why you are troubling to classify your subject, and keep this purpose evident throughout the essay.
- *Is your classification complete?* Your principle of classification should create categories that encompass every representative of the general subject. If some representatives will not fit the scheme, you may have to create a new category or revise the existing categories to include them.
- *Is your classification consistent?* Consistency is essential to save readers from confusion or irritation. Make sure all the classes reflect the same principle and that they do not overlap. Remedy flaws by adjusting the classes or creating new ones.

FOCUS ON PARAGRAPH DEVELOPMENT

A crucial aim of revising a classification is to make sure each group is clear: what's counted in, what's counted out, and why. You'll provide the examples and other details that make the groups clear as you develop the paragraph(s) devoted to each group.

The following paragraph gives just the outline of one group in a four-part classification of ex-smokers into zealots, evangelists, the elect, and the serene:

> The second group, evangelists, does not condemn smokers but encourages them to quit. Evangelists think quitting is easy, and they preach this message, often earning the resentment of potential converts.

Contrast this bare-bones adaptation with the actual paragraphs written by Franklin E. Zimring in his essay "Confessions of a Former Smoker" (p. 183):

> By contrast, the antismoking evangelist does not condemn smokers. Unlike the zealot, he regards smoking as an easily curable condition, as a social disease, and not a sin. The evangelist spends an enormous amount of time seeking and preaching to the unconverted. He argues that kicking the habit is not *that* difficult. After all, *he* did it; moreover, as he describes it, the benefits of quitting are beyond measure and the disadvantages are nil.
>
> The hallmark of the evangelist is his insistence that he never misses tobacco. Though he is less hostile to smokers than the zealot, he is resented more. Friends and loved ones who have been the targets of his preachments frequently greet the resumption of smoking by the evangelist as an occasion for unmitigated glee.

In the second sentence of both paragraphs, Zimring explicitly contrasts evangelists with zealots, the group he previously defined. And he does more as well: he provides specific examples of the evangelist's message (first paragraph) and of others' reactions to him (second paragraph). These details pin down the group, making it distinct from other groups and clear in itself.

For more on paragraph development through specifics, see pages 38–39.

A NOTE ON THEMATIC CONNECTIONS

Writers classify the thoughts and behaviors of human beings more than any other subject, perhaps because the method gives order and even humor to our many psychological quirks and curious actions. The authors in this chapter mine thoughts and behaviors for information and for humor. In a paragraph Max Eastman identifies two classes of people, the practical and the poets (p. 167). Also in a paragraph Daniel Goleman sorts addictions by the emotional changes they produce (p. 168). Russell Baker's essay takes a wry view of the ways in which objects foil their human users (next page). Jonathan Gould's essay finds four kinds of next-door neighbors (p. 178). And Franklin Zimring's essay explores the four varieties of ex-smokers (p. 182).

Russell Baker

A distinguished journalist, prize-winning memoirist, and treasured humorist, Russell Baker has informed and amused readers for more than fifty years. He was born in 1925 in Baltimore, served as a flyer during World War II, and graduated from Johns Hopkins University in 1947. That same year he began his journalism career at the Baltimore Sun *and in 1954 he moved to the* New York Times, *covering the president, the State Department, and Congress. In 1962 he launched a regular column for the* Times *titled "Observer," now appearing twice weekly on the op-ed page. Baker has received two Pulitzer Prizes, one for distinguished commentary in 1979 and one for his memoir,* Growing Up *(1982). He has also published many collections of his columns and edited two books of humor. These days he is a television star as well, hosting PBS's* Masterpiece Theatre.

The Plot Against People

Classifying inanimate objects, Baker here provides a funny take on how we relate to our cars, keys, flashlights, and other things. The essay was first published in 1968 in the New York Times.

Inanimate objects are classified scientifically into three major categories—those that don't work, those that break down and those that get lost. 1

The goal of all inanimate objects is to resist man and ultimately to defeat him, and the three major classifications are based on the method each object uses to achieve its purpose. As a general rule, any object capable of breaking down at the moment when it is most needed will do so. The automobile is typical of the category. 2

With the cunning typical of its breed, the automobile never breaks down while entering a filling station with a large staff of idle mechanics. It waits until it reaches a downtown intersection in the middle of the rush hour, or until it is fully loaded with family and luggage on the Ohio turnpike. 3

Thus it creates maximum misery, inconvenience, frustration and irritability among its human cargo, thereby reducing its owner's life span. 4

Washing machines, garbage disposals, lawn mowers, light bulbs, 5
automatic laundry dryers, water pipes, furnaces, electrical fuses, television tubes, hose nozzles, tape recorders, slide projectors all are in league with the automobile to take their turn at breaking down whenever life threatens to flow smoothly for their human enemies.

Many inanimate objects, of course, find it extremely difficult to 6
break down. Pliers, for example, and gloves and keys are almost totally incapable of breaking down. Therefore, they have had to evolve a different technique for resisting man.

They get lost. Science has still not solved the mystery of how they 7
do it, and no man has ever caught one of them in the act of getting lost. The most plausible theory is that they have developed a secret method of locomotion which they are able to conceal the instant a human eye falls upon them.

It is not uncommon for a pair of pliers to climb all the way from 8
the cellar to the attic in its single-minded determination to raise its owner's blood pressure. Keys have been known to burrow three feet under mattresses. Women's purses, despite their great weight, frequently travel through six or seven rooms to find hiding space under a couch.

Scientists have been struck by the fact that things that break 9
down virtually never get lost, while things that get lost hardly ever break down.

A furnace, for example, will invariably break down at the depth 10
of the first winter cold wave, but it will never get lost. A woman's purse, which after all does have some inherent capacity for breaking down, hardly ever does; it almost invariably chooses to get lost.

Some persons believe this constitutes evidence that inanimate ob- 11
jects are not entirely hostile to man, and that a negotiated peace is possible. After all, they point out, a furnace could infuriate a man even more thoroughly by getting lost than by breaking down, just as a glove could upset him far more by breaking down than by getting lost.

Not everyone agrees, however, that this indicates a conciliatory 12
attitude among inanimate objects. Many say it merely proves that furnaces, gloves and pliers are incredibly stupid.

The third class of objects—those that don't work—is the most 13
curious of all. These include such objects as barometers, car clocks, cigarette lighters, flashlights and toy-train locomotives. It is inaccu-

rate, of course, to say that they never work. They work once, usually for the first few hours after being brought home, and then quit. Thereafter, they never work again.

In fact, it is widely assumed that they are built for the purpose of not working. Some people have reached advanced ages without ever seeing some of these objects—barometers, for example—in working order. 14

Science is utterly baffled by the entire category. There are many theories about it. The most interesting holds that the things that don't work have attained the highest state possible for an inanimate object, the state to which things that break down and things that get lost can still only aspire. 15

They have truly defeated man by conditioning him never to expect anything of them, and in return they have given man the only peace he receives from inanimate society. He does not expect his barometer to work, his electric locomotive to run, his cigarette lighter to light or his flashlight to illuminate, and when they don't it does not raise his blood pressure. 16

He cannot attain that peace with furnaces and keys, and cars and women's purses as long as he demands that they work for their keep. 17

Meaning

1. What is Baker's thesis? How is it ironic? (See *irony* in the Glossary.)
2. How have things that don't work "defeated man" (paragraph 16)?
3. If you are unsure of any of the following words, try to guess their meanings from the context in Baker's essay. Look up the words in a dictionary to test your guesses. Then use each word in a sentence or two of your own.

cargo (4) locomotion (7) inherent (10)
plausible (7) invariably (10) conciliatory (12)

Purpose and Audience

1. How can we tell that Baker intends to entertain us with his essay? What are some of the elements of his humor?
2. What assumptions does Baker make about the readers of his essay? Are the assumptions correct in your case?

Method and Structure

1. How does Baker use the method of classification for comic effect? In what ways does classification lend itself particularly well to a humorous subject such as this one?
2. What is Baker's principle of classification?
3. Where in the essay does Baker take pains to distinguish his classes of objects?
4. How does Baker make the transition between his discussion of objects that break down and his discussion of objects that get lost?
5. **Other Methods** For each of his classes, Baker offers specific examples (Chapter 6). What functions do these examples serve? Can you think of other objects that would fit in each class?

Language

1. Baker's tone is often quite serious, from the abrupt opening assertion to the concluding statement about spiritual "peace." How do you account for such seriousness in a humorous essay?
2. Find three places where Baker uses hyperbole (see p. 52 for a definition). What is the effect of this figure of speech?
3. What does the word "cunning" mean (paragraph 3)? What are its connotations? In what way does the word set a pattern for Baker's use of words to describe objects?

Writing Topics

1. **Journal Response** Can you think of other ways to classify inanimate objects? For instance, a scheme centering on student life might include objects no student can live without, objects no student would be caught dead with, objects that cause students problems, and perhaps other categories as well. Play with some classification schemes in your journal, making lists or drawing charts to find one that works well.

   Journal to Essay Write a brief, humorous essay based on a classification scheme from your journal entry. To achieve humor, you might want to draw on some of Baker's techniques, such as a mock-serious tone, exaggeration, attributing human qualities to things, and appeals to science. But make your scheme thorough and consistent at the same time.
2. Are we the helpless victims of our things, as Baker holds, or can we get the upper hand? What advice would you give Baker for taming his things? Write him a letter in which you offer this advice, either seriously or mock-seriously.

3. **Cultural Considerations** What can you infer from the examples used in this essay about Baker's age and economic status? Does he seem to assume his audience is similar? (Remember, this essay first appeared in the *New York Times.*) Are readers who don't match those assumptions (perhaps you yourself) likely to enjoy Baker's essay as much as those who do match? Write an essay in which you analyze Baker's apparent assumptions, explaining whether and how they strengthen the essay, weaken it, or don't affect it.
4. **Connections** Baker and Franklin E. Zimring, in "Confessions of a Former Smoker" (p. 182), use similar means to achieve humorous effects. Write an essay in which you compare and contrast the tone, style, and use of language in each essay. How does each writer make his readers laugh? Is one more successful than the other, and why?

Jonathan R. Gould, Jr.

Jonathan R. Gould, Jr., was born in 1968 in Little Falls, New York, and grew up on a dairy farm in nearby Ft. Plain. Graduating from Little Falls Baptist Academy, he was valedictorian of his class. He served three years in the U.S. Army, specializing in administration and computer programming. At the State University of New York at Oneonta, he was an honors student, received the Provost Award for academic distinction, and obtained a B.S. in mathematics education. Gould currently works for an Internet service provider in Oneonta, where he lives with his wife and three children.

The People Next Door

From his experiences in many different settings, Gould identifies four types of neighbors, only one of which could be considered truly neighborly. Gould wrote this essay in 1994 for a writing course at SUNY.

I have moved more often than I care to remember. However, one thing always stays the same no matter where I have been. There is always a house next door, and that house contains neighbors. Over time, I have begun putting my neighbors into one of four categories: too friendly, unsociable, irritable, and just right. 1

Neighbors who are too friendly can be seen just about anywhere. I mean that both ways. They exist in every neighborhood I have ever lived in and seem to appear everywhere I go. For some strange reason these people become extremely attached to my family and stop in as many as eight to ten times a day. No matter how tired I appear to be, nothing short of opening the door and suggesting they leave will make them go home at night. (I once told an unusually friendly neighbor that his house was on fire, in an attempt to make him leave, and he still took ten minutes to say goodbye.) What is truly interesting about these people is their strong desire to cook for us even though they have developed no culinary skill whatsoever. (This has always proved particularly disconcerting since they stay to watch us eat every bite as they continually ask if the food "tastes good.") 2

The unsociable neighbor is a different story altogether. For reasons of his own, he has decided to pretend that we do not exist. I 3 have always found that one or two neighbors of this type are in my neighborhood. It is not easy to identify these people, because they seldom leave the shelter of their own house. To be honest, the only way I know that someone lives in their building is the presence of a name on the mailbox and the lights shining through the windows at night. My wife often tries to befriend these unique people, and I have to admire her courage. However, even her serenity is shaken when she offers our neighbors a fresh-baked apple pie only to have them look at her as if she intended to poison them.

Probably the most difficult neighbor to deal with is the irritable 4
neighbor. This individual probably has several problems, but he has reduced all those problems down to one cause—the proximity of my family to his residence. Fortunately, I have only encountered this type of neighbor in a handful of settings. (He is usually too busy with one group of "troublemakers" to pick up a new set.) The times that I have encountered this rascal, however, have proved more than enough for my tastes. He is more than willing to talk to me. Unfortunately, all he wants to tell me is how miserable my family is making him. Ignoring this individual has not worked for me yet. (He just adds my "snobbishness" to his list of faults that my family displays.) Interestingly, this fellow will eat anything my wife (bless her soul) might make in an attempt to be sociable. Even though he never has anything good to say about the food, not a crumb will be left on the plate when he is finished (which leads me to wonder just how starved and impoverished he must be).

At the risk of sounding like Goldilocks, there is also a neighbor 5
who is "just right." One of the most wonderful things about this neighbor is that there has always been at least one everywhere I have gone. We meet often (though not too often), and our greetings are always sincere. Occasionally, our families will go out to eat or to shop, or just sit and talk. We tend to spend as much time at their house as they do at ours (two to three times a month), and everyone knows just when it is time to say goodnight. For some reason, this neighbor knows how to cook, and we frequently exchange baked goods as well as pleasantries. For obvious reasons, this type of neighbor is my favorite.

As I mentioned before, each type of neighbor I have encountered is 6
a common sight in any neighborhood. I have always felt it was important to identify the type of neighbors that were around me. Then I am better able to maintain a clear perspective on our relationship and understand their needs. After all, people do not really change; we just learn how to live with both the good and the bad aspects of their behavior.

Meaning

1. Where does Gould state his thesis?
2. What is the difference between unsociable and irritable neighbors in Gould's classification?
3. From their context in Gould's essay, try to guess the meanings of any of the following words that are unfamiliar to you. Check your definitions against a dictionary's, and then write a sentence or two using each new word.

culinary (2)
disconcerting (2)
proximity (4)
impoverished (4)
pleasantries (5)

Purpose and Audience

1. Why do you suppose Gould wrote this essay? Where does he give the clearest indication?
2. Does Gould make any assumptions about his audience? Does he seem to be writing for a certain type of reader?

Method and Structure

1. Why do you think Gould chose the method of classification to write about the subject of neighbors? How does the method help him achieve his purpose?
2. What is Gould's principle of classification? Do you think his classification is complete and consistent? How else might he have sorted neighbors?
3. Why do you think Gould stresses the fact that he has encountered most of these types of neighbors everywhere he has lived?
4. What does Gould accomplish in his conclusion?
5. **Other Methods** Gould's categories lend themselves to comparison and contrast (Chapter 10). Based on his descriptions, what are the differences between the too-friendly neighbor and the just-right neighbor?

Language

1. What is Gould's tone? How seriously does he take the problem of difficult neighbors?
2. Point out several instances of hyperbole or overstatement in the essay. What effect do these have?

Writing Topics

1. **Journal Response** Think of a group to which you belong—perhaps a religious organization, your family, a club or committee, even a writing class. Write down all the ways you can think of to classify the members of this group. Consider both two-part classifications (for example, students who study throughout the semester versus students who procrastinate) and complex classifications, like Gould's.

   Journal to Essay Write a classification essay in which you sort the group's members into categories according to a clear principle of classification. Be sure to label and define each type for your readers, to provide examples, and to position yourself in one of the categories. What does your classification reveal about the group as a whole?
2. Most of us have had at least one colorful or bothersome neighbor at some time or another—a busybody, a recluse, a peeping Tom. Write a descriptive essay (with some narration) about an interesting neighbor you have known or a narrative essay (with some description) about a memorable run-in with a neighbor.
3. Television has provided us with a large array of eccentric neighbors—from the Nortons in *The Honeymooners* to Rhoda Morgenstern in *The Mary Tyler Moore Show* to Cosmo Kramer in *Seinfeld*. Write an essay in which you classify the kinds of neighbors depicted on TV. You may borrow Gould's principle of classification if it fits, or come up with an alternative one of your own.
4. **Cultural Considerations** "Good fences make good neighbors," says a character in Robert Frost's poem "Mending Wall," and many people in our live-and-let-live society would seem to agree. Is the best neighbor an invisible one? Or do we lose something when we ignore those who are literally closest to us? Write an essay giving a definition of what it means to be a good neighbor. Or, if you prefer, write an essay in which you compare and contrast neighboring habits in different types of communities you have lived in or know of.
5. **Connections** Russell Baker's "The Plot Against People" (p. 173), like Gould's essay, takes a dauntingly large group (inanimate objects) and sorts its members into a small number of classes. Both essays are written at least partly to amuse. And yet the two essays are very different in tone, style, and organization. Write an essay comparing and contrasting the two essays. What are the strengths and weaknesses of each approach?

Franklin E. Zimring

A teacher and scholar of the law, Franklin E. Zimring writes soberly about pornography, capital punishment, drug control, and other fiery subjects. He was born in 1942 in Los Angeles, received a B.A. in 1963 from Wayne State University, and earned a doctorate in law in 1967 from the University of Chicago. He taught law at Chicago until 1985 and also directed the Center for Studies in Criminal Justice. Then he moved to the University of California at Berkeley, where he now teaches and also directs the Earl Warren Legal Institute. In addition to numerous articles for scholarly and popular periodicals, Zimring has written a number of distinguished books, among them Confronting Youth Crime *(1978),* Capital Punishment and the American Agenda *(with Gordon Hawkins, 1986), and* American Youth Violence *(1998). Calling himself "an involuntary writer," Zimring believes that "to undertake research is to commit oneself to report it."*

Confessions of a Former Smoker

In this essay Zimring reports research somewhat off his usual legal path: an ex-smoker himself, he carefully classifies four kinds of quitters. The essay appeared first in Newsweek *on April 20, 1987.*

Americans can be divided into three groups—smokers, nonsmokers, and that expanding pack of us who have quit. Those who have never smoked don't know what they're missing, but former smokers, ex-smokers, reformed smokers can never forget. We are veterans of a personal war, linked by that watershed experience of ceasing to smoke and by the temptation to have just one more cigarette. For almost all of us ex-smokers, smoking continues to play an important part in our lives. And now that it is being restricted in restaurants around the country and will be banned in almost all indoor public places in New York state starting next month, it is vital that everyone understand the different emotional states cessation of smoking can cause. I have observed four of them; and in the interest of sci- 1 ence I have classified them as those of the zealot, the evangelist, the elect, and the serene. Each day, each category gains new recruits.

Not all antitobacco zealots are former smokers, but a substantial number of fire-and-brimstone opponents do come from the ranks of the reformed. Zealots believe that those who continue to smoke are degenerates who deserve scorn, not pity, and the penalties that will deter offensive behavior in public as well. Relations between these people and those who continue to smoke are strained. 2

One explanation for the zealot's fervor in seeking to outlaw tobacco consumption is his own tenuous hold on abstaining from smoking. But I think part of the emotional force arises from sheer envy as he watches and identifies with each lung-filling puff. By making smoking in public a crime, the zealot seeks reassurance that he will not revert to bad habits; give him strong social penalties and he won't become a recidivist. 3

No systematic survey has been done yet, but anecdotal evidence suggests that a disproportionate number of doctors who have quit smoking can be found among the fanatics. Just as the most enthusiastic revolutionary tends to make the most enthusiastic counterrevolutionary, many of today's vitriolic zealots include those who had been deeply committed to tobacco habits. 4

By contrast, the antismoking evangelist does not condemn smokers. Unlike the zealot, he regards smoking as an easily curable condition, as a social disease, and not a sin. The evangelist spends an enormous amount of time seeking and preaching to the unconverted. He argues that kicking the habit is not *that* difficult. After all, *he* did it; moreover, as he describes it, the benefits of quitting are beyond measure and the disadvantages are nil. 5

The hallmark of the evangelist is his insistence that he never misses tobacco. Though he is less hostile to smokers than the zealot, he is resented more. Friends and loved ones who have been the targets of his preachments frequently greet the resumption of smoking by the evangelist as an occasion for unmitigated glee. 6

Among former smokers, the distinctions between the evangelist and the elect are much the same as the differences between proselytizing and nonproselytizing religious sects. While the evangelists preach the ease and desirability of abstinence, the elect do not attempt to convert their friends. They think that virtue is its own reward and subscribe to the Puritan theory of predestination. Since they have proved themselves capable of abstaining from tobacco, they are 7 therefore different from friends and relatives who continue to smoke. They feel superior, secure that their salvation was foreordained. These ex-smokers rarely give personal testimony on their conversion. They rarely speak about their tobacco habits, while evangelists talk about little else. Of course, active smokers find such bluenosed[1] behavior far less offensive than that of the evangelist or the zealot, yet they resent the elect simply because they are smug. Their air of self-satisfaction rarely escapes the notice of those lighting up. For active smokers, life with a member of the ex-smoking elect is less stormy than with a zealot or evangelist, but it is subtly oppressive nonetheless.

I have labeled my final category of former smokers the serene. 8
This classification is meant to encourage those who find the other psychic styles of ex-smokers disagreeable. Serenity is quieter than zealotry and evangelism, and those who qualify are not as self-righteous as the elect. The serene ex-smoker accepts himself and also accepts those around him who continue to smoke. This kind of serenity does not come easily, nor does it seem to be an immediate option for those who have stopped. Rather it is a goal, an end stage in a process of development during which some former smokers progress through one or more of the less-than-positive psychological points en route. For former smokers, serenity is thus a positive possibility that exists at the end of the rainbow. But all former smokers cannot reach that promised land.

What is it that permits some former smokers to become serene? I 9
think the key is self-acceptance and gratitude. The fully mature former smoker knows he has the soul of an addict and is grateful for the knowledge. He may sit up front in an airplane, but he knows he belongs in the smoking section in back. He doesn't regret that he quit smoking, nor any of his previous adventures with tobacco. As a former smoker, he is grateful for the experience and memory of craving a cigarette.

Serenity comes from accepting the lessons of one's life. And ex- 10
smokers who have reached this point in their worldview have much to be grateful for. They have learned about the potential and limits of change. In becoming the right kind of former smoker, they developed a healthy sense of self. This former smoker, for one, believes that it is better to crave (one hopes only occasionally) and not to smoke than

[1] *Bluenosed* means straitlaced and moralistic, deriving perhaps from the perceived character of people from cold northern climates. [Editor's note.]

never to have craved at all. And by accepting that fact, the reformed smoker does not need to excoriate, envy, or disassociate himself from those who continue to smoke.

Meaning

1. What is the author's thesis? What reasons does he give for classifying?
2. In which category does Zimring place himself, and what does he say about this group in relation to the others?
3. Try to guess the meanings of any of the following words that are unfamiliar. Test your guesses in a dictionary, and then come up with a sentence or two using each new word.

watershed (1)	deter (2)	nil (5)
cessation (1)	tenuous (3)	unmitigated (6)
zealot (1)	abstaining (3)	proselytizing (7)
evangelist (1)	recidivist (3)	predestination (7)
elect (1)	anecdotal (4)	foreordained (7)
serene (1)	vitriolic (4)	excoriate (10)
degenerates (2)		

Purpose and Audience

1. What do you suppose Zimring's purpose is? Do you think his classification is really motivated by "the interest of science" (paragraph 1)?
2. Who is Zimring's intended audience? What in the text supports your answer?
3. What do you think of Zimring's categories? Are they complete? convincing? If you know people in these categories, do they match Zimring's description?

Method and Structure

1. How does or doesn't the method of classification lend itself to Zimring's purpose?
2. Summarize each of the groups Zimring identifies (even those he does not discuss in detail). What is their relation to one another?
3. What do you notice about Zimring's organization and the space he devotes to each category? Why would he present his categories at different lengths? Do some of the categories get shortchanged?
4. **Other Methods** In addition to classification, Zimring uses a number of other methods to convey his ideas effectively: description (Chapter 4),

example (Chapter 6), division or analysis (Chapter 7), comparison and contrast (Chapter 10), definition (Chapter 11), and cause-and-effect analysis (Chapter 12). Locate at least one instance of each, and consider how these methods contribute to the discussion as a whole.

Language

1. Consider the labels Zimring devises for each category. What connotations do these words have? How do these words and their connotations contribute to Zimring's overall tone? (If necessary, see p. 50 on connotation and pp. 39–40 on tone.)
2. Zimring uses a lot of "five-dollar words," many of which appear in the vocabulary list. He also avoids use of the first-person *I*. How do his diction and point of view relate to his purpose and to his audience?

Writing Topics

1. **Journal Response** Write a reaction to Zimring's essay. Does it amuse you? irritate you? something else? Do you find the categories and the descriptions of people fair, given that Zimring is not entirely serious? Does Zimring's essay lead you to sympathize with ex-smokers? What general category do you fall into: nonsmoker, smoker, or ex-smoker? How does your position influence your reaction to the essay?
   Journal to Essay From your journal response, extract an idea that you can develop into a brief essay. For instance, you could defend one or more of the groups of ex-smokers that Zimring apparently considers inferior to the serene. You could narrate the experiences of someone you know (or you yourself) who fits into one of Zimring's ex-smoker categories. You could object to Zimring's view that smoking (or quitting smoking) is something to be written about lightly.
2. Using Zimring's essay as a model, write an essay classifying some group of people with whom you are quite familiar (teachers, bosses, or sales clerks, for example). Sort your subject into classes according to a consistent principle, and make sure to provide plenty of details to clarify the classes you decide on. Write an essay in which you explain your classification.
3. **Cultural Considerations** Smoking is a battlefield in our culture, with feelings running high on all sides. In a thoughtful, well-reasoned essay, establish your position on smoking in outdoor places, such as outdoor restaurants, sports stadiums, or the street. In expressing your opinion, consider and acknowledge opposing views—for instance, the smoker's right to enjoy smoke or the nonsmoker's right to enjoy smoke-free air.

4. **Connections** In his paragraph on page 168, Daniel Goleman writes about addictions as calming, energizing, or fantasy-producing. Based on what you know about smoking, either from experience or from reading about or observing smokers, does it fall into one or more of these categories? Write a brief essay in which you explain what you understand smokers gain from their addiction. In other words, why do people smoke?

Writing with the Method

Classification

Choose one of the following topics, or any other topic they suggest, for an essay developed by classification. The topic you decide on should be something you care about so that classification is a means of communicating an idea, not an end in itself.

PEOPLE

1. People you like (or dislike)
2. Boring people
3. Laundromat users
4. Teachers or students
5. Friends or co-workers
6. Computer users
7. Mothers or fathers

PSYCHOLOGY AND BEHAVIOR

8. Friendships
9. Ways of disciplining children
10. Ways of practicing religion
11. Obsessions
12. Diets
13. Dreams

THINGS

14. Buildings on campus
15. Junk foods
16. Computer games
17. Trucks

SPORTS AND PERFORMANCE

18. Styles of baseball pitching, tennis serving, football tackling, or another sports skill
19. Runners
20. Styles of dance, guitar playing, acting, or another performance art

COMMUNICATIONS MEDIA

21. Young male or female movie stars
22. Talk-show hosts
23. Electronic discussion groups
24. Sports announcers
25. Television programs
26. Radio stations
27. Magazines or newspapers

Writing About the Theme

Sorting Thoughts and Behaviors

1. Max Eastman (p. 167) claims that there are two types of human beings: those who are poetic and those who are practical. Write an essay in which you apply Eastman's classification to Franklin Zimring's categories of reformed smokers (p. 182). Be sure to define each type for your readers and explain why you assign Zimring's groups the way you do. Remember to use evidence from Zimring's essay to support your idea.
2. Jonathan Gould (p. 178) and Franklin Zimring classify and label people with some intention to amuse readers. However, not all labels used to classify people are harmless. Consider, for example, labels based on gender or race or sexual orientation. Write an essay in which you discuss both the benefits and the costs of assigning labels to people—for those using the labels, for those being labeled, and for society as a whole. Give plenty of specific examples.
3. Taking off from Russell Baker's "The Plot Against People" (p. 173), create your own classification of people's relationships with objects. Try adapting the categories of one of the other writers to this subject. For instance, are some object owners poetic and some practical, using Max Eastman's scheme? Or do people seek calm, energy, or fantasy from objects, using Daniel Goleman's scheme (p. 168)? Or are people zealots, evangelists, the elect, and the serene, using Franklin Zimring's scheme?

Chapter 9

PROCESS ANALYSIS

Explaining Customs

USING THE METHOD

Game rules, car-repair manuals, cookbooks, science textbooks—these and many other familiar works are essentially process analyses. They explain how to do something (play Monopoly, tune a car), how to make something (a carrot cake), or how something happens (how our hormones affect our behavior, how a computer stores and retrieves data). That is, they explain a sequence of actions with a specified result (the **process**) by dividing it into its component steps (the **analysis**). Almost always, the purpose of process analysis is to explain, but sometimes a parallel purpose is to prove something about the process or to evaluate it: to show how easy it is to change a tire, for instance, or to urge dieters to follow a weight-loss plan on the grounds of its safety and effectiveness.

Process analysis overlaps several other methods discussed in this book. The analysis is actually the method examined in Chapter 7—dividing a thing or concept into its elements. And we analyze a process much as we analyze causes and effects (Chapter 12), except that cause-and-effect analysis asks mainly *why* something happens or *why* it has certain results, whereas process analysis asks mainly *how* something happens. Process analysis also overlaps narration (Chapter 5), for the steps of the process are almost always presented in chronological sequence. But narration recounts a unique sequence of events with a unique result, whereas process analysis explains a series of steps with the same predictable result. You might narrate a particularly exciting baseball game, but you would analyze the process—the rules—of any baseball game.

Processes occur in several varieties, including mechanical (a car engine), natural (cell division), psychological (acquisition of sex roles), and political (the electoral process). Process analyses generally fall into one of two types:

- In a **directive** process analysis, you tell how to do or make something: bake a cake, repair a bicycle, negotiate a deal, write a process analysis. You outline the steps in the process completely so that the reader who follows them can achieve the specified result. Generally, you address the reader directly, using the second-person *you* ("You should concentrate on the words that tell you what to do") or the imperative (commanding) mood of verbs ("Add one egg yolk and stir vigorously"). (See also p. 197.)
- In an **explanatory** process analysis, you provide the information necessary for readers to understand the process, but more to satisfy their curiosity than to teach them how to perform it. You may address the reader directly, but the third-person *he, she, it,* and *they* are more common.

Whether directive or explanatory, process analyses usually follow a chronological sequence. Most processes can be divided into phases or stages, and these in turn can be divided into steps. The stages of changing a tire, for instance, may be jacking up the car, removing the flat, putting on the spare, and lowering the car. The steps within, say, jacking up the car may be setting the emergency brake, blocking the other wheels, loosening the bolts, positioning the jack, and raising the car. Following a chronological order, you cover the stages in sequence and, within each stage, cover the steps in sequence.

To ensure that the reader can duplicate the process or understand how it unfolds, you must fully detail each step and specify the reasons for it. In addition, you must be sure that the reader grasps the sequence of steps, their duration, and where they occur. To this end, transitional expressions that signal time and place—such as *after five minutes, meanwhile, to the left,* and *below*—can be invaluable in process analysis.

Though a chronological sequence is usual for process analysis, you may have to interrupt or modify it to suit your material. You may need to pause in the sequence to provide definitions of specialized terms or to explain why a step is necessary or how it relates to the preceding and following steps. In an essay on how to change a tire, for instance, you might stop briefly to explain that the bolts should be slightly loosened *before* the car is jacked up in order to prevent the wheel from spinning afterward.

ANALYZING PROCESSES IN PARAGRAPHS

Monica Haena (born 1973) was a student at San Joaquin Delta College in Stockton, California, when she wrote the essay "Scented," which includes the following paragraph. The essay was published in the spring 1993 issue of *Delta Winds,* a collection of student writing.

Once we were home I'd watch my Pops comb his hair. I would sit on the counter and hold his Pomade jar in one hand and his little black pocket comb in the other. He would drape a towel around his shoulder, then partially wet his hair with his hands. Next, he would comb it straight back. After that, he would stick his three middle fingers in the Pomade jar and scoop the goop. He would slap his hands together and run it through his hair. Finally, he would comb the grease into his hair, spreading it evenly. The Pomade worked perfectly to hold each and every strand of hair down. The outcome would be a shiny, slicked back, neat hair style. Afterwards, he would wipe his comb and place it in his Ben Davis shirt pocket, right next to his eyeglass pouch.

Explanatory process analysis: tells how author's grandfather combed his hair

Transitions signaling sequence (underlined)

Process divided into five steps

Result of the process

L. Rust Hills (born 1924) has been a magazine editor, writing teacher, and full-time writer. This paragraph comes from "How to Eat an Ice-Cream Cone," which appears in his book *How to Do Things Right* (1972).

In trying to make wise and correct decisions about the ice-cream cone in your hand, you should always keep the objectives in mind. The main objective, of course, is to get the cone under control. Secondarily, one will want to eat the cone calmly and with pleasure. Real pleasure lies not simply in eating the cone but in eating it *right*. Let us assume that you have darted to your open space and made your necessary emergency repairs. The cone is still dangerous—still, so to speak, "live." But you can now proceed with it in an orderly fashion. First, revolve the cone through the full three hundred and sixty degrees, snapping at the loose gobs of ice cream; turn the cone by moving the thumb away from you and the forefinger toward you, so the cone moves counterclockwise. Then with the cone still "wound," which will require the wrist to be bent at the full right angle toward you, apply pressure with the mouth and tongue to accomplish overall realignment, straightening and settling the whole mess. Then, unwinding the cone back through the full three hundred and sixty degrees, remove any trickles of ice cream. From here on, some supplementary repairs may be necessary, but the cone is now defused.

Directive process analysis: tells how to eat an ice-cream cone

Goals of the process

Transitions signaling sequence, time, and place (underlined)

Process divided into three distinct steps

Test for correct performance of step

Reason for step

Result of the process

DEVELOPING AN ESSAY BY PROCESS ANALYSIS

Getting Started

You'll find yourself writing process analyses for your courses in school (for instance, explaining how a drug affects brain chemistry), in memos at work (recommending a new procedure for approving cost estimates), or in life outside work (giving written directions to your home). To find a subject when an assignment doesn't make one obvious, examine your interests or hobbies or think of something whose workings you'd like to research in order to understand them better. Explore the subject by listing chronologically all the necessary stages and steps.

While you are exploring your subject, decide on the point of your analysis and express it in a thesis sentence that will guide your writing and tell your readers what to expect. The simplest thesis states what the process is and its basic stages. For instance:

> Building a table is a three-stage process of cutting, assembling, and finishing.

But you can increase your readers' interest in the process by also conveying your reason for writing about it. You might assert that a seemingly difficult process is actually quite simple, or vice versa:

> Changing a tire does not require a mechanic's skill or strength; on the contrary, a ten-year-old child can do it.

> Windsurfing may look easy, but it demands the knowledge of an experienced sailor and the balance of an acrobat.

You might show how the process demonstrates a more general principle:

> The process of getting a bill through Congress illustrates majority rule at work.

Or you might assert that a process is inefficient or unfair:

> The overly complicated registration procedure forces students to waste two days each semester standing in line.

Remember your readers while you are generating ideas and formulating your thesis. Consider how much background information they need, where specialized terms must be defined, and where examples must be given. Especially if you are providing directions, consider what special equipment readers will need, what hitches they may encounter, and what the interim results should be. To build a table, for instance, what tools would readers need? What should they do if the table wobbles even after the corners are braced? What should the table feel like after the first sanding or the first varnishing?

Organizing

Many successful process analyses begin with an overview of the process to which readers can relate each step. In such an introduction you can lead up to your thesis sentence by specifying when or where the process occurs, why it is useful or interesting or controversial, what its result is, and the like. Especially if you are providing directions, you can also use the introduction (perhaps a separate paragraph) to provide essential background information, such as the materials readers will need.

After the introduction, you should present the stages distinctly, perhaps one or two paragraphs for each, and usually in chronological order. Within each stage, also chronologically, you then cover the necessary steps. This chronological sequence helps readers see how a process unfolds or how to perform it themselves. Try not to deviate from it unless you have good reason to—perhaps because your process requires you to group simultaneous steps or your readers need definitions of terms, reasons for steps, connection between separated steps, and other explanations.

A process essay may end simply with the result. But you might conclude with a summary of the major stages, with a comment on the significance or usefulness of the process, or with a recommendation for changing a process you have criticized. For an essay providing directions, you might state the standards by which readers can measure their success or give an idea of how much practice may be necessary to master the process.

Drafting

While drafting your process analysis, concentrate on getting in as many details as you can: every step, how each relates to the one before and after, how each contributes to the result. In revising you can always delete unnecessary details and connective tissue if they seem cumbersome, but in the first draft it's better to overexplain than underexplain.

Drafting a process analysis is a good occasion to practice a straightforward, concise writing style, for clarity is more important than originality of expression. Stick to plain language and uncomplicated sentences. If you want to dress up your style a bit, you can always do so after you have made yourself clear.

Revising and Editing

When you've finished your draft, ask a friend to read it. If you have explained a process, he or she should be able to understand it. If you have given directions, he or she should be able to follow them, or imagine following them. Then examine the draft yourself against the following questions and the information in the box.

- *Have you adhered to a chronological sequence?* Unless there is a compelling and clear reason to use some other arrangement, the stages and steps of your analysis should proceed in chronological order. If you had to depart from that order—to define or explain or to sort out simultaneous steps—the reasons should be clear to your readers.

- *Have you included all necessary steps and omitted any unnecessary digressions?* The explanation should be as complete as pos-

FOCUS ON CONSISTENCY

While drafting a directive process analysis, telling readers how to do something, you may start off with subjects or verbs in one form and then shift to another form because the original choice felt awkward. These shifts occur most often with the subjects *a person* or *one:*

> INCONSISTENT To keep the car from rolling while changing the tire, *one* should first set the car's emergency brake. Then *one* should block the three other tires with objects like rocks or chunks of wood. Before raising the car, *you* should loosen the bolts of the wheel. . . .

To repair the inconsistency here, you could stick with *one* for the subject (*one should loosen*), but that usually sounds stiff. It's better to revise the earlier subjects to be *you*:

> CONSISTENT To keep the car from rolling while changing the tire, *you* should set the car's emergency brake. Then *you* should block the three other tires with objects like rocks or chunks of wood. Before raising the car, *you* should loosen the bolts of the wheel. . . .

Sometimes, writers try to avoid *one* or *a person* or even *you* with passive verbs that don't require actors:

> INCONSISTENT To keep the car from rolling while changing the tire, you should first set the car's emergency brake. . . . Before raising the car, the bolts of the wheel *should be loosened*. . . .

But the passive is wordy and potentially confusing, especially when directions should be making it clear who does what. (See p. 46 for more on passive verbs.)

One solution to the problem of inconsistent subjects and passive verbs is to use the imperative, or commanding, form of verbs, in which *you* is understood as the subject:

> CONSISTENT To keep the car from rolling while changing the tire, first *set* the car's emergency brake. Then *block* the three other tires. . . . Before raising the car, *loosen* the bolts of the wheel. . . .

But the imperative verbs should be consistent, too: don't shift back and forth between *set* or *block* and *you should set* or *you should block*.

sible but not cluttered with information, however interesting, that contributes nothing to the readers' understanding of the process.

- *Have you accurately gauged your readers' need for information?* You don't want to bore readers with explanations and details they don't need. But erring in the other direction is even worse, for your essay will achieve little if readers cannot understand it.
- *Have you shown readers how each step fits into the whole process and relates to the other steps?* If your analysis seems to break down into a multitude of isolated steps, you may need to organize them more clearly into stages.
- *Have you used plenty of informative transitions?* Transitions such as *at the same time* and *on the other side of the machine* indicate when steps start and stop, how long they last, and where they occur. (A list of such expressions appears in the Glossary under *transitions.*) The expressions should be as informative as possible; signals such as *first . . . second . . . third . . . fourteenth* and *next . . . next* do not help indicate movement in space or lapses in time, and they quickly grow tiresome.

A NOTE ON THEMATIC CONNECTIONS

The authors represented in this chapter set out to explain the workings of a personal or family or societal custom, and for that purpose process analysis is the natural choice of method. Monica Haena, in a paragraph, outlines her grandfather's painstaking process of combing his hair (p. 193). L. Rust Hills, in another paragraph, provides meticulous instructions for eating an ice-cream cone without making a mess (p. 193). Cortney Keim's essay directs readers in the art of making a bed, a daily chore with larger implications (next page). Leo Buscaglia's essay describes his family's ritual celebration of wine making (p. 204). And Jessica Mitford's essay analyzes the technique of embalming a corpse, which turns out to be gruesomely funny (p. 209).

Cortney Keim

Born in 1978 in New York City, Cortney Keim grew up mostly in Connecticut, graduating from high school in Westport. She is a theater major at Boston University's School for the Arts, class of 2001. Keim volunteers at a teen hotline and at Planned Parenthood, which named her volunteer of the year in 1995. She also writes monologues and one-act plays and intends to pursue a career as an actor and singer.

Making the Bed

In this essay Keim adds an interesting twist to a tedious daily chore. Her instructions offer a model of process analysis, but they might seem absurdly precise if they didn't serve a larger purpose. Keim wrote this piece especially for The Compact Reader.

"Cooort, are you ready?" 1

It is 7:25 on a Tuesday morning. I have showered, brushed my teeth, dressed, plucked, powdered, and curled my eyelashes. I grab my bag, shut my door, and head for the stairs, only to be stopped by my father, waiting always in dismay. 2

"Have you made your bed?" 3

"Well, I shut the door so when I . . ." 4

"Cortney, just a few minutes, I'll . . ." 5

He'll wait, I know. 6

I turn around like a good girl and walk back to my room. I open the door and see my twisted sheets and depressed comforter, confronting me once again with a dreary routine. 7

I never really understood why I had to make my bed, but I did it because I am, after all, a good girl. But gradually, after I'd made the bed hundreds of times, I began to see that the routine offers a chance to pull myself together in the morning, to smooth my jumble of imperfections and unfinished business into defined layers. With just a little attention to detail, you too can turn this mundane task into a beneficial ritual. 8

At all times during the following procedure, be careful to bend from the hips and knees, not the waist, to prevent back and joint strain. Remember, making the bed is an activity for easing the burdens of life, not creating new ones. 9

Begin making the bed by tearing it apart. Depending on how much time you have, place or throw the bedding on the floor—in the opposite order in which it will be placed on the bed. Then put the bottom sheet (usually a fitted sheet) on the bed so that it is centered in the middle of the mattress. The fitted sheet may or may not have elastic at the edges, but elastic is preferable because it is easier and allows you, later, to have more control. At this point it does not matter if you are on the left or right side of the bed—whichever makes you more comfortable. Tuck the hem of the fitted sheet well under the designated mattress corner (options: top, left or right; bottom, left or right). The fitted sheet will unwrinkle on its own as the corners that are tucked under the mattress take up the slack in the middle. 10

A warning about the fitted sheet: expect a corner you've already finished to pop out as you attend to the opposite diagonal corner. You may need several tries to master the difficult art of balanced distribution. Make sure that the fitted sheet is even under each corner and that your tug to fit a corner under the mattress is not too rough. I advise much patience here because sheets tend to pick up on frustration, and that only complicates matters. When the sheet is secure, smooth out any remaining bumps with the palm of the hand. 11

When the bottom sheet is in place, pick up the top sheet and center this material also in the middle of the bed. The not-pretty side of the sheet should face up, to be covered later by the blanket. "The pretty side is for God," my mom says—and for you when you lie in bed. 12

When spreading the top sheet across the mattress, leave extra sheet at the foot of the bed. Lift the mattress at the bottom, and tuck the sheet in there. This, ideally, keeps you in bed, helping to hold you still and secure. Pull the remaining sheet tight to the top of the bed, without untucking, and smooth out wrinkles with your palms from the bottom up and the center out. You'll be a kind of human iron pressing out problems, regrouping each time for more steam. 13

Pick up the quilt or the comforter with the pattern facing God, because no one wants to look at the mess of stitching and seams underneath. Then spread the blanket smoothly and evenly so that its surface covers the bed. (I have seen the sides and bottom of comforters tucked under, creating a sort of cocoon, but I like mine out for show and for more air under the accumulated covers while sleeping.) 14

Move then to the head of the bed, and take the loose sheet and comforter in hand. Fold both sides of this upper bedding toward the center of the bed, revealing the vulnerable fitted sheet underneath and allowing a bit of top sheet to show off once the pillows are in place. This is one of the most important tasks, the finishing touch that makes the event special, the mandatory pumpkin pie after Thanksgiving dinner, no matter how full you are. Continue smoothing the cover if necessary.

For the final and most technical stage, push each pillow into the open side of its case tag first, so the tag doesn't scratch your face in the middle of the night. Then, holding the open corners of the pillowcase in both hands, bang the pillow against your knee for fluff. (Repeat if more than one pillow.) Place the pillow in the empty space between the headboard and your turned-down blanket. If you choose to add stuffed animals or decorative pillows (both of which I am personally against because of all the unnecessary clutter), place them on the surface for style. The ritual is complete. 15

When I've finished making my bed, with one foot out the door and into Tuesday, I glance back at my creation and decide to leave the door open. I actually feel good about starting this day. My math homework, not yet completed, seems doable, and the book I have yet to read, well, I think I may start tonight. In just seven days God created the entire world. In a seven-minute ceremony I've managed to re-create order in my little part of that world. 16

Meaning

1. What is Keim's thesis? Does she have a point to make beyond the process analysis itself?
2. The following words may be new to you. If so, try to guess their meanings from the context of Keim's essay. Then test your guesses in a dictionary, and use each new word in a sentence or two.

   regrouping (13)
   mandatory (14)

Purpose and Audience

1. Why do you think Keim wrote this essay? To teach readers how to make a bed? Or is she trying to help readers in some other way?

2. Who is the ideal reader for this essay? Are Keim's instructions thorough enough for someone who has never made a bed? What does her process analysis have to offer for the reader already familiar with the art of bed making?

Method and Structure

1. Assuming Keim has a larger purpose in mind than merely teaching readers how to make a bed, how does her process analysis help accomplish this purpose?
2. Where does the process analysis begin? What shift in the language of the essay indicates a transition into the process analysis itself?
3. Point out transitional words and phrases that Keim uses as guideposts in her process analysis.
4. **Other Methods** What is the function of the mini-narrative that starts off the essay? What would be lost if Keim had started with paragraph 8?

Language

1. How seriously does Keim take her subject? How can you tell?
2. Point out examples of metaphor and personification in the essay. (See p. 52 if you need help with these figures of speech.)

Writing Topics

1. **Journal Response** Think of a daily routine that helps to create a sense of order in your life and that you feel guilty about skipping. Some examples might be an early morning jog, putting on or taking off your makeup, or a daily phone call to an important person in your life. Write down all the steps involved in your routine and the ritual that surrounds it.

   Journal to Essay Write a process analysis, modeled on Keim's (although it need not be directive), in which you break down your routine into its component parts and explain how it helps to compose your day.
2. Even though she is a "good girl," Keim would probably resist her father's insistence that she make her bed every day if she were not a naturally neat person herself. Write an essay in which you contrast the habits of neat people with those of messy people. Be sure to use concrete examples, and consider not only the obvious, surface differences, but also the differences in character and behavior of the two groups.
3. **Cultural Considerations** Why do we bother making the bed? Is there a point to all those little chores—dusting, washing the car, raking the

leaves—that seem to be undone almost as soon as we do them? Write an essay in which you either defend the need for such tasks or explain why they are a waste of time.

4. **Connections** Both this essay and Margaret Visser's (p. 157) deal with the notion of "ritual"—Keim's from a personal perspective and Visser's from a sociological perspective. What importance does each writer ascribe to ritual in our daily lives? What do they see as the benefits and the disadvantages of ritual?

Leo Buscaglia

When he died in 1998, his New York Times *obituary described Leo Buscaglia as "the cuddly television guru who preached love with single-minded fervor." He had become a familiar figure in the media, lecturing and writing about human relationships. Buscaglia was born in 1924 in East Los Angeles and obtained a B.A. from Wayne State University and an M.A. and Ph.D. from the University of Southern California. At USC from 1968 to 1984 he was an assistant professor and then a professor of psychology. He wrote scores of articles and books, including* Love *(1972) and* Loving Each Other *(1984). The* New York Times *bestseller list once included five of his books in a single week. In 1984 Buscaglia founded the Felice Foundation, and in 1991 he established the Leo F. Buscaglia Scholarship for Inner City Teacher Education. He died in Lake Tahoe, Nevada.*

Alla Salute!

Buscaglia often spoke warmly of the large and close-knit Italian American family in which he grew up. In an appreciation of his father, Papa, My Father *(1989), he included this description of the family's custom of making wine.* Alla salute *(Buscaglia's last line) means "to your health" in Italian.*

Like all good Italians, Papa loved his wine, although I never knew him to drink to excess. A glass or two of wine to accompany his dinner was his limit. He never touched hard liquor. 1

Papa's love of wine went far beyond the simple enjoyment of drinking it. He was truly an oenophile, a connoisseur. He always made his own wine, from ripened grapes to dated label. His cool, dark cellar was full of dusty bottles and cylindrical, wooden barrels of varying sizes, all carefully marked to indicate the type of grape and the year of the harvest. 2

When I was growing up, we had many festivities in our home. None, except Christmas and Easter, topped the one night each year that we made the new wine. The anticipation and preparation began in July and August, long before the eventful September evening when the truckload of grapes was delivered. By then Papa had made several visits to his friends—grape growers in Cucamonga, about forty miles 3 from our home—to observe the progress of his grapes. He had spent hours scouring the barrels in which the wine would be made and stored and applying antirust varnish on every visible metal part of the wine-making equipment. The fermenting vat had been filled with water to swell the wood.

On the appointed evening, the truck would arrive after night- 4
fall, brimming with small, tough-skinned, sweet-smelling Cabernet grapes. The boxes of grapes were hand-carried about two hundred feet to the garage, where a giant empty vat awaited. A hand-powered crusher was positioned precariously on top of the vat, ready to grind noisily into the night, as thousands of grapes were poured into it. It was an all-male operation that included Papa, his relatives, and friends. Dressed in their undershirts, bodies glistening with perspiration, they took turns cranking the crusher handle. My job was to stack the empty crates neatly out of the way as a prelude to what for me was the most exciting part of the evening.

After all the grapes had been mashed and the empty boxes 5
stacked, it was time for us to remove our shoes, socks, and pants and slip into the cool, dark moisture for the traditional grape stomping. This was done, of course, to break up the skins, but I couldn't have cared less why it was necessary. For me it was a sensual experience unlike any other, feeling the grape residue gushing between my toes and watching as the new wine turned my legs the rich, deep color of Cabernet Sauvignon.

While this "man's work" was being accomplished, the "woman's 6
work" was progressing in the kitchen. The heady fragrance of the crushed grapes, mingled with the savory aromas of dinner wafting from the house, caused our feet to move in step with our growing appetites. The traditional main course for our wine-making dinner was gnocchi, a small, dumplinglike pasta that would be cooked to perfection and topped with a wonderful sauce that had been simmering for hours.

Like Christmas Eve, this particular night was unique in many 7
ways. Throughout the rest of the year, we routinely sat down to dinner by 5:30 each evening. But for this occasion dinner was never served until the wine making was finished, sometimes as late as 10 P.M. By then, we were all purple from grape juice, exhausted, and famished.

No matter how tired and hungry we were, however, Papa always 8
prefaced the dinner with a dissertation on "the wine experience." This ceremony called for his finest wines, which had been aging in his

modest but efficient wine cellar. Drinking wine, he would remind us, was a highly respected activity, not to be taken lightly. The nectar of the grape had brought joy to human beings long before recorded history.

"Wine is a delight and a challenge and is never meant to be drunk quickly. It's to be savored and sipped slowly," he'd tell us. "All the senses are awakened when you drink wine. You drink with your eyes, your tongue, your throat, your nose. Notice the colors the wine makes in the glass—all the way from dark purple, like a bishop's robe, to the golden amber of an aspen leaf." 9

He would hold up the glass to the light as if we were about to share a sacrament, then swirl the wine around in his glass, guiding us through the whole ritual, from the first sip to the final, all-important swallow. 10

"Alla salute!" 11

Meaning

1. What is Buscaglia's statement of thesis? How does it attract readers' interest to the process he will describe?
2. How does "from ripened grapes to dated label" (paragraph 2) serve as a shorthand? What does it refer to?
3. Does Buscaglia indicate whether his father was still alive when this selection was written? How might this knowledge affect your reading of the essay?
4. If you are uncertain of the meanings of any words below, try to guess them from the context of Buscaglia's essay. Then look up the words to see how close your definitions were to the dictionary's. Test out the new words by using each of them in a sentence or two.

oenophile (2)	prelude (4)	dissertation (8)
connoisseur (2)	residue (5)	nectar (8)
cylindrical (2)	savory (6)	sacrament (10)
precariously (4)	wafting (6)	

Purpose and Audience

1. Is this a directive process analysis or an explanatory one? Is Buscaglia's purpose to show readers how to make and enjoy wine, or does he have other purposes in mind? If so, what might they be?
2. Instead of just assuming his readers' interest in his family's tradition, how does Buscaglia try to *earn* that interest?

Method and Structure

1. Why do you think Buscaglia chose to write a process analysis instead of simply narrating one of his experiences of the day in question? In other words, what does he gain by emphasizing the yearly repetition and the steps of the process?
2. Where does Buscaglia's process analysis begin? Where does it end? Does it include more than just the winemaking itself?
3. What is the function of the first two paragraphs?
4. **Other Methods** Buscaglia's essay is full of rich, telling description (Chapter 4). How many senses does he appeal to? (Give examples.) How do these sensory details play an important part in the essay, given the subject matter?

Language

1. What is Buscaglia's tone? How does he feel about his subject?
2. What is the effect of "like all good Italians" (paragraph 1)?
3. What effect does Buscaglia achieve by using *would* in his verbs, as in "the truck would arrive" (paragraph 4) or "pasta that would be cooked to perfection" (6)?

Writing Topics

1. **Journal Response** Think of a celebration or ritual that holds a special importance for a group you belong to, such as your family, your church, or your ethnic or national group. What are the elements that constitute the event? Write them down in order, in as much detail as you can.
   Journal to Essay Write a process analysis based on your journal notes, clarifying and enlivening the process with description, as Buscaglia does. Try to draw some kind of conclusion about the process, such as why it is important or what it symbolizes for its participants.
2. Write an essay about something you love doing that might be hard to appreciate without some background or training—for instance, listening to jazz or opera, figure skating or playing ice hockey, making a special dish or working on cars. Your essay may or may not incorporate a process analysis, but it should communicate to an outsider what makes your activity special.
3. **Cultural Considerations** Buscaglia's family seems to have had definite ideas about what was "man's work" and what was "woman's work" (paragraphs 4–6). Write an essay about the division of domestic labor in your family when you were growing up. Were certain chores always done by the males and others by the females? Did this division seem to

occur naturally, or was it a source of conflict? Are certain household tasks more suited to one sex than to the other?

4. **Connections** Like this essay, Larry Woiwode's "Ode to an Orange" (p. 69) is a song of praise to a treasured experience of childhood. Compare and contrast the two writers' techniques for recapturing that experience. You might consider their tones, their uses of images, or their uses of both description and process analysis.

Jessica Mitford

Tough-minded, commonsensical, and witty, Jessica Mitford was described by Time *as the "Queen of Muckrakers." She was born in England in 1917, the sixth of Lord and Lady Redesdale's seven children, and was educated entirely at home. Her highly eccentric family is the subject of novels by her sister Nancy Mitford and of her own autobiographical* Daughters and Rebels *(1960). In 1939, a few years after she left home, Mitford took up permanent residence in the United States, becoming a naturalized American citizen in 1944. Shortly afterward, moved by her long-standing antifascism and the promise of equality in a socialist society, she joined the American Communist party; her years as a "Red Menace" are recounted in* A Fine Old Conflict *(1977). In the late 1950s she turned to investigative journalism, researching and exposing numerous instances of deception, greed, and foolishness in American society. Her articles appeared in* The Nation, Esquire, The Atlantic, *and other magazines, and many of them are collected in* Poison Penmanship: The Gentle Art of Muckraking *(1979). Her book-length exposés include* The Trial of Dr. Spock *(1969),* Kind and Usual Punishment: The Prison Business *(1973), and* The American Way of Birth *(1992). Mitford died in 1996.*

Embalming Mr. Jones

In 1963 Mitford published The American Way of Death, *a daring and influential look at the standard practices of the American funeral industry. (*The American Way of Death Revisited, *nearly complete at Mitford's death, was published in 1998.) Mitford pegs the modern American funeral as "the most irrational and weirdest" custom of our affluent society, in which "the trappings of Gracious Living are transformed, as in a nightmare, into the trappings of Gracious Dying." This excerpt from the book, an analysis of the process of embalming a corpse and restoring it for viewing, demonstrates Mitford's sharp eye for detail, commanding style, and caustic wit.*

The drama begins to unfold with the arrival of the corpse at the mortuary. 1

Alas, poor Yorick![1] How surprised he would be to see how his counterpart of today is whisked off to a funeral parlor and is in short order, sprayed, sliced, pierced, pickled, trussed, trimmed, creamed, 2

[1] A line from Shakespeare's *Hamlet,* spoken by Hamlet in a graveyard as he contemplates the skull of the former jester in his father's court. [Editor's note.]

waxed, painted, rouged, and neatly dressed—transformed from a common corpse into a Beautiful Memory Picture. This process is known in the trade as embalming and restorative art, and is so universally employed in the United States and Canada that the funeral director does it routinely, without consulting corpse or kin. He regards as eccentric those few who are hardy enough to suggest that it might be dispensed with. Yet no law requires embalming, no religious doctrine commends it, nor is it dictated by considerations of health, sanitation, or even of personal daintiness. In no part of the world but in Northern America is it widely used. The purpose of embalming is to make the corpse presentable for viewing in a suitably costly container; and here too the funeral director routinely, without first consulting the family, prepares the body for public display.

Is all this legal? The processes to which a dead body may be sub- 3
jected are after all to some extent circumscribed by law. In most states, for instance, the signature of next of kin must be obtained before an autopsy may be performed, before the deceased may be cremated, before the body may be turned over to a medical school for research purposes; or such provision must be made in the decedent's will. In the case of embalming, no such permission is required nor is it ever sought.[2] A textbook, *The Principles and Practices of Embalming,* comments on this: "There is some question regarding the legality of much that is done within the preparation room." The author points out that it would be most unusual for a responsible member of a bereaved family to instruct the mortician, in so many words, to *"embalm"* the body of a deceased relative. The very term *embalming* is so seldom used that the mortician must rely upon custom in the matter. The author concludes that unless the family specifies otherwise, the act of entrusting the body to the care of a funeral establishment carries with it an implied permission to go ahead and embalm.

Embalming is indeed a most extraordinary procedure, and one 4
must wonder at the docility of Americans who each year pay hun-

[2]In 1982, nineteen years after this was written, the Federal Trade Commission issued comprehensive regulations on the funeral industry, including the requirement that funeral providers prepare an itemized price list for their goods and services. The list must include a notice that embalming is not required by law, along with an indication of the charge for embalming and an explanation of the alternatives. Consumers must give permission for embalming before they may be charged for it. Shortly before her death, however, Mitford wrote that thirteen years after the ruling the FTC had "watered down" the regulations and "routinely ignored" consumer complaints against the funeral industry, enforcing the regulations only forty-two times. [Editor's note.]

dreds of millions of dollars for its perpetuation, blissfully ignorant of what it is all about, what is done, how it is done. Not one in ten thousand has any idea of what actually takes place. Books on the subject are extremely hard to come by. They are not to be found in most libraries or bookshops.

In an era when huge television audiences watch surgical opera- 5
tions in the comfort of their living rooms, when, thanks to the animated cartoon, the geography of the digestive system has become familiar territory even to the nursery school set, in a land where the satisfaction of curiosity about all matters is a national pastime, the secrecy surrounding embalming can, surely, hardly be attributed to the inherent gruesomeness of the subject. Custom in this regard has within this century suffered a complete reversal. In the early days of American embalming, when it was performed in the home of the deceased, it was almost mandatory for some relative to stay by the embalmer's side and witness the procedure. Today, family members who might wish to be in attendance would certainly be dissuaded by the funeral director. All others, except apprentices, are excluded by law from the preparation room.

A close look at what does actually take place may explain in 6
large measure the undertaker's intractable reticence concerning a procedure that has become his major *raison d'être.*[3] Is it possible he fears that public information about embalming might lead patrons to wonder if they really want this service? If the funeral men are loath to discuss the subject outside the trade, the reader may, understandably, be equally loath to go on reading at this point. For those who have the stomach for it, let us part the formaldehyde curtain. . . .

The body is first laid out in the undertaker's morgue—or rather, 7
Mr. Jones is reposing in the preparation room—to be readied to bid the world farewell.

The preparation room in any of the better funeral establishments 8
has the tiled and sterile look of a surgery, and indeed the embalmer–restorative artist who does his chores there is beginning to adopt the term "dermasurgeon" (appropriately corrupted by some mortician-writers as "demisurgeon") to describe his calling. His equipment, consisting of scalpels, scissors, augers, forceps, clamps, needles, pumps, tubes, bowls and basins, is crudely imitative of the surgeon's, as is his technique, acquired in a nine- or twelve-month post–high-school course in an embalming school. He is supplied by an advanced

[3] French, meaning "reason for being." [Editor's note.]

chemical industry with a bewildering array of fluids, sprays, pastes, oils, powders, creams, to fix or soften tissue, shrink or distend it as needed, dry it here, restore the moisture there. There are cosmetics, waxes, and paints to fill and cover features, even plaster of Paris to replace entire limbs. There are ingenious aids to prop and stabilize the cadaver: a Vari-Pose Head Rest, the Edwards Arm and Hand Positioner, the Repose Block (to support the shoulders during the embalming), and the Throop Foot Positioner, which resembles an old-fashioned stocks.

Mr. John H. Eckels, president of the Eckels College of Mortuary Science, thus describes the first part of the embalming procedure: "In the hands of a skilled practitioner, this work may be done in a comparatively short time and without mutilating the body other than by slight incision—so slight that it scarcely would cause serious inconvenience if made upon a living person. It is necessary to remove the blood, and doing this not only helps in the disinfecting, but removes the principal cause of disfigurements due to discoloration." 9

Another textbook discusses the all-important time element: "The earlier this is done, the better, for every hour that elapses between death and embalming will add to the problems and complications encountered. . . ." Just how soon should one get going on the embalming? The author tells us, "On the basis of such scanty information made available to this profession through its rudimentary and haphazard system of technical research, we must conclude that the best results are to be obtained if the subject is embalmed before life is completely extinct—that is, before cellular death has occurred. In the average case, this would mean within an hour after somatic death." For those who feel that there is something a little rudimentary, not to say haphazard, about this advice, a comforting thought is offered by another writer. Speaking of fears entertained in early days of premature burial, he points out, "One of the effects of embalming by chemical injection, however, has been to dispel fears of live burial." How true; once the blood is removed, chances of live burial are indeed remote. 10

To return to Mr. Jones, the blood is drained out through the veins and replaced by embalming fluid pumped in through the arteries. As noted in *The Principles and Practices of Embalming,* "every operator has a favorite injection and drainage point—a fact which becomes a handicap only if he fails or refuses to forsake his favorites when conditions demand it." Typical favorites are the carotid artery, femoral artery, jugular vein, subclavian vein. There are various 11 choices of embalming fluid. If Flextone is used, it will produce a "mild, flexible rigidity. The skin retains a velvety softness, the tissues are rubbery and pliable. Ideal for women and children." It may be blended with B. and G. Products Company's Lyf-Lyk tint, which is guaranteed to reproduce "nature's own skin texture . . . the velvety appearance of living tissue." Suntone comes in three separate tints: Suntan; Special Cosmetic Tint, a pink shade "especially indicated for young female subjects"; and Regular Cosmetic Tint, moderately pink.

About three to six gallons of a dyed and perfumed solution of 12
formaldehyde, glycerin, borax, phenol, alcohol, and water is soon circulating through Mr. Jones, whose mouth has been sewn together with a "needle directed upward between the upper lip and gum and brought out through the left nostril," with the corners raised slightly "for a more pleasant expression." If he should be bucktoothed, his teeth are cleaned with Bon Ami and coated with colorless nail polish. His eyes, meanwhile, are closed with flesh-tinted eye caps and eye cement.

The next step is to have at Mr. Jones with a thing called a trocar. 13
This is a long, hollow needle attached to a tube. It is jabbed into the abdomen, poked around the entrails and chest cavity, the contents of which are pumped out and replaced with "cavity fluid." This done, and the hole in the abdomen sewn up, Mr. Jones's face is heavily creamed (to protect the skin from burns which may be caused by leakage of the chemicals), and he is covered with a sheet and left unmolested for a while. But not for long—there is more, much more, in store for him. He has been embalmed, but not yet restored, and the best time to start the restorative work is eight to ten hours after embalming, when the tissues have become firm and dry.

The object of all this attention to the corpse, it must be remem- 14
bered, is to make it presentable for viewing in an attitude of healthy repose. "Our customs require the presentation of our dead in the semblance of normality . . . unmarred by the ravages of illness, disease or mutilation," says Mr. J. Sheridan Mayer in his *Restorative Art.* This is a rather large order since few people die in the full bloom of health, unravaged by illness and unmarked by some disfigurement. The funeral industry is equal to the challenge: "In some cases the gruesome appearance of a mutilated or disease-ridden subject may be quite discouraging. The task of restoration may seem impossible and shake the confidence of the embalmer. This is the time for intestinal fortitude and determination. Once the formative work is begun and affected tissues are cleaned or removed, all doubts of success vanish.

It is surprising and gratifying to discover the results which may be obtained."

The embalmer, having allowed an appropriate interval to elapse, returns to the attack, but now he brings into play the skill and equipment of sculptor and cosmetician. Is a hand missing? Casting one in plaster of Paris is a simple matter. "For replacement purposes, only a cast of the back of the hand is necessary; this is within the ability of the average operator and is quite adequate." If a lip or two, a nose or an ear should be missing, the embalmer has at hand a variety of restorative waxes with which to model replacements. Pores and skin texture are simulated by stippling with a little brush, and over this cosmetics are laid on. Head off? Decapitation cases are rather routinely handled. Ragged edges are trimmed, and head joined to torso with a series of splints, wires and sutures. It is a good idea to have a little something at the neck—a scarf or high collar—when time for viewing comes. Swollen mouth? Cut out tissue as needed from inside the lips. If too much is removed, the surface contour can easily be restored by padding with cotton. Swollen necks and cheeks are reduced by removing tissue through vertical incisions made down each side of the neck. "When the deceased is casketed, the pillow will hide the suture incisions . . . as an extra precaution against leakage, the suture may be painted with liquid sealer." *15*

The opposite condition is more likely to present itself—that of emaciation. His hypodermic syringe now loaded with massage cream, the embalmer seeks out and fills the hollowed and sunken areas by injection. In this procedure the backs of the hands and fingers and the under-chin area should not be neglected. *16*

Positioning the lips is a problem that recurrently challenges the ingenuity of the embalmer. Closed too tightly they tend to give a stern, even disapproving expression. Ideally, embalmers feel, the lips should give the impression of being ever so slightly parted, the upper lip protruding slightly for a more youthful appearance. This takes some engineering, however, as the lips tend to drift apart. Lip drift can sometimes be remedied by pushing one or two straight pins through the inner margin of the lower lip and then inserting them between the two upper front teeth. If Mr. Jones happens to have no teeth, the pins can just as easily be anchored in his Armstrong Face Former and Denture Replacer. Another method to maintain lip closure is to dislocate the lower jaw, which is then held in its new position by a wire run through holes which have been drilled through the *17* upper and lower jaws at the midline. As the French are fond of saying, *il faut souffrir pour être belle.*[4]

If Mr. Jones has died of jaundice, the embalming fluid will very likely turn him green. Does this deter the embalmer? Not if he has intestinal fortitude. Masking pastes and cosmetics are heavily laid on, burial garments and casket interiors are color-correlated with particular care, and Jones is displayed beneath rose-colored lights. Friends will say, "How *well* he looks." Death by carbon monoxide, on the other hand, can be rather a good thing from the embalmer's viewpoint: "One advantage is the fact that this type of discoloration is an exaggerated form of a natural pink coloration." This is nice because the healthy glow is already present and needs but little attention. 18

The patching and filling completed, Mr. Jones is now shaved, washed, and dressed. Cream-based cosmetic, available in pink, flesh, suntan, brunette, and blond, is applied to his hands and face, his hair is shampooed and combed (and, in the case of Mrs. Jones, set), his hands manicured. For the horny-handed son of toil special care must be taken; cream should be applied to remove ingrained grime, and the nails cleaned. "If he were not in the habit of having them manicured in life, trimming and shaping is advised for better appearance —never questioned by kin." 19

Jones is now ready for casketing (this is the present participle of the verb "to casket"). In this operation his right shoulder should be depressed slightly "to turn the body a bit to the right and soften the appearance of lying flat on the back." Positioning the hands is a matter of importance, and special rubber positioning blocks may be used. The hands should be cupped slightly for a more lifelike, relaxed appearance. Proper placement of the body requires a delicate sense of balance. It should lie as high as possible in the casket, yet not so high that the lid, when lowered, will hit the nose. On the other hand, we are cautioned, placing the body too low "creates the impression that the body is in a box." 20

Jones is next wheeled into the appointed slumber room where a few last touches may be added—his favorite pipe placed in his hand or, if he was a great reader, a book propped into position. (In the case of little Master Jones a Teddy bear may be clutched.) Here he will hold open house for a few days, visiting hours 10 A.M. to 9 P.M. 21

[4] French, meaning "It is necessary to suffer in order to be beautiful." [Editor's note.]

Meaning

1. According to Mitford, what is the purpose of embalming and restoration (see paragraphs 2 and 14)? If they are not required by law or religion or "considerations of health, sanitation, or even of personal daintiness," why are they routinely performed?
2. Why do Americans know so little about embalming (paragraphs 3–6)? Does Mitford blame Americans themselves, the funeral industry, or both?
3. Some of the following words may be new to you. Before looking them up in a dictionary, try to guess their meanings from their context in Mitford's essay. Then use each new word in a sentence or more.

mortuary (1)	mandatory (5)	cadaver (8)
counterpart (2)	apprentices (5)	somatic (10)
circumscribed (3)	intractable (6)	rudimentary (10)
decedent (3)	reticence (6)	haphazard (10)
bereaved (3)	loath (6)	pliable (11)
docility (4)	formaldehyde (6)	semblance (14)
perpetuation (4)	augers (8)	jaundice (18)
inherent (5)	distend (8)	

Purpose and Audience

1. What does Mitford reveal about her purpose when she questions whether the undertaker "fears that public information about embalming might lead patrons to wonder if they really want this service" (paragraph 6)? To discover how different the essay would be if Mitford had wanted only to explain the process, reread the essay from the point of view of an undertaker. What comments and details would the undertaker object to or find embarrassing?
2. Mitford's chief assumption about her readers is evident in paragraph 4. What is it?
3. Most readers find Mitford's essay humorous. Assuming you did, too, which details or comments struck you as especially amusing? How does Mitford use humor to achieve her purpose?

Method and Structure

1. Why do you think Mitford chose the method of process analysis to explore this particular social custom? What does the method allow her to convey about the custom? How does this information help her achieve her purpose?

2. Despite the fact that her purpose goes beyond mere explanation, does Mitford explain the process of embalming and restoration clearly enough for you to understand how it's done and what the reasons for each step are? Starting at paragraph 7, what are the main steps in the process?
3. Mitford interrupts the sequence of steps in the process several times. What information does she provide in paragraphs 8, 10, and 14 to make the interruptions worthwhile?
4. **Other Methods** Mitford occasionally uses other methods to develop her process analysis—for instance, in paragraph 8 she combines description (Chapter 4) and classification (Chapter 8) to present the embalmer's preparation room and tools; and in paragraph 5 she uses contrast (Chapter 10) to note changes in the family's knowledge of embalming. What does this contrast suggest about our current attitudes toward death and the dead?

Language

1. How would you characterize Mitford's tone? Support your answer with specific details, sentence structures, and words in the essay. (See pp. 39–40 for a discussion of *tone.*)
2. Mitford is more than a little ironic—that is, she often says one thing when she means another or deliberately understates her meaning. Here are two examples from paragraph 10: "the all-important time element" in the embalming of a corpse; "How true; once the blood is removed, chances of live burial are indeed remote." What additional examples do you find? What does this persistent irony contribute to Mitford's tone? (For a fuller explanation of *irony,* consult the Glossary.)
3. Mitford's style in this essay is often informal, even conversational, as in "The next step is to have at Mr. Jones with a thing called a trocar" (paragraph 13). But equally often she seems to imitate the technical, impersonal style of the embalming textbooks she quotes so extensively, as in "Another method to maintain lip closure is to dislocate the lower jaw" (17). What other examples of each style do you find? What does each style contribute to Mitford's purpose? Is the contrast effective, or would a consistent style, one way or the other, be more effective? Why?

Writing Topics

1. **Journal Response** Think of a modern custom or practice that you find ridiculous, barbaric, tedious, or otherwise objectionable. Write down all of the steps of that process in a detailed list.

   Journal to Essay Write an essay that analyzes the process by which your chosen custom or practice unfolds. Following Mitford's model, explain the process clearly while also conveying your attitude toward it.

2. Elsewhere in her book *The American Way of Death,* Mitford notes that the open casket at funerals, which creates the need for embalming and restoration, is "a custom unknown in other parts of the world. Foreigners are astonished by it." Write an essay in which you explore the possible reasons for the custom in the United States. Or, if you have strong feelings about closed or open caskets at funerals—derived from religious beliefs, family tradition, or some other source—write an essay agreeing or disagreeing with Mitford's treatment of embalming and restoration.
3. **Cultural Considerations** Read about funeral customs in another country. (The library's catalog or a periodical guide such as the *Social Sciences Index* can direct you to appropriate books or articles.) Write an essay in which you analyze the process covered in your sources and use it as the basis for agreeing or disagreeing with Mitford's opinion of embalming and restoration.
4. **Connections** In "The Ritual of Fast Food" (p. 157), Margaret Visser claims that "a Big Mac is a cultural construct: the careful control extended upon it is one of the things we are buying." Write an essay analyzing embalming and restoration—which Mitford notes are widely practiced only in North America—as a cultural construct. What expectations and assumptions lie behind these practices? What is the customer really buying?

Writing with the Method

Process Analysis

Choose one of the following topics, or any other topic they suggest, for an essay developed by process analysis. The topic you decide on should be something you care about so that process analysis is a means of communicating an idea, not an end in itself.

TECHNOLOGY AND THE ENVIRONMENT

1. How an engine or other machine works
2. How the Internet works
3. Winterizing a car
4. Setting up a recycling program in a home or office
5. How solar energy can be converted to electricity

EDUCATION AND CAREER

6. How children learn to dress themselves, play with others, read, or write
7. Reading a newspaper
8. Interviewing for a job
9. Succeeding in biology, history, computer science, or another course
10. Learning a foreign language
11. Coping with a bad boss

ENTERTAINMENT AND HOBBIES

12. Keeping a car in good shape
13. Making a model car, airplane, or ship
14. Performing a magic trick
15. Playing a board or card game, or performing one maneuver in that game
16. Throwing a really *bad* party
17. Playing a sport or a musical instrument
18. Making great chili or some other dish

HEALTH AND APPEARANCE

19. Getting physically fit
20. Climbing a mountain
21. Dieting
22. Cutting or dyeing one's own hair

FAMILY AND FRIENDS

23. Offering constructive criticism to a friend
24. Driving your parents, brother, sister, friend, or roommate crazy
25. Minimizing sibling rivalry
26. Making new friends in a new place

Writing About the Theme

Explaining Customs

1. What do the selections by Cortney Keim (p. 199), Leo Buscaglia (p. 204), and Jessica Mitford (p. 209) tell you about the purpose or purposes of customs? In other words, what is gained by participating in a practice that is habitual or traditional? Write an essay exploring the answer to this question for Keim, for Buscaglia and his family, and for those who decide to have their deceased relatives embalmed. You may find a dictionary's or encyclopedia's definitions of *custom* and *ritual* helpful as background for your ideas.
2. Several of the authors in this chapter discuss processes that can have negative sides: L. Rust Hills equates an ice-cream cone with a live bomb (p. 193); Cortney Keim's view of bed making as a soothing ritual compensates for its being a dreary routine; and the embalmers Jessica Mitford describes sometimes require "intestinal fortitude." Using these works as models, write a process analysis about an activity you find simultaneously boring or difficult *and* rewarding, making sure to convey both feelings to your readers.
3. Monica Haena (p. 193), L. Rust Hills, and Cortney Keim all explain personal customs: habits practiced by individuals. What do you think of these personal customs? Does each seem worthwhile to you, needlessly fussy, a waste of effort, or what? Write an essay defining a worthwhile personal custom: what would it consist of and accomplish? If you like, write your definition in the form of a process analysis of a particular custom, taking care to show *why* it is worthwhile.

Chapter 10

COMPARISON AND CONTRAST

Challenging Misconceptions

USING THE METHOD

An insomniac watching late-night television faces a choice between two World War II movies broadcasting at the same time. To make up his mind, he uses the dual method of comparison and contrast.

- **Comparison** shows the similarities between two or more subjects: the similar broadcast times and topics of the two movies force the insomniac to choose between them.
- **Contrast** shows the differences between subjects: the different actors, locations, and reputations of the two movies make it possible for the insomniac to choose one.

As in the example, comparison and contrast usually work together because any subjects that warrant side-by-side examination usually resemble each other in some respects and differ in others. (Since comparison and contrast are so closely related, the terms *comparison* and *compare* will be used from now on to designate both.)

You'll generally write a comparison for one of two purposes:

- To explain the similarities and differences between subjects so as to make either or both of them clear.
- To evaluate subjects so as to establish their advantages and disadvantages, strengths and weaknesses.

The explanatory comparison does not take a position on the relative merits of the subjects; the evaluative comparison does, and it usually concludes with a preference or a suggested course of action. In an explanatory comparison you might show how new income-tax laws differ from old laws. In an evaluative comparison on the same subject, you might argue that the old laws were more equitable than the new ones are.

Whether explanatory or evaluative, comparisons treat two or more subjects in the same general class or group: tax laws, religions, attitudes toward marriage, diseases, advertising strategies, diets, contact sports, friends. You may define the class to suit your interest—for instance, you might focus on Tuesday night's television shows, on network news programs, or on old situation comedies. The class likeness ensures that the subjects share enough features to make comparison worthwhile. With subjects from different classes, such as an insect and a tree, the similarities are so few and differences so numerous—and both are so obvious—that explaining them would be pointless.

In writing a comparison, you not only select subjects from the same class but also, using division or analysis, identify the features shared by the subjects. These **points of comparison** are the attributes of the class and thus of the subjects within the class. For instance, the points of comparison for diets may be forbidden foods, allowed foods, speed of weight loss, and nutritional quality; for air pollutants they may be sources and dangers to plants, animals, and humans. These points help you arrange similarities and differences between subjects, and, more important, they ensure direct comparison rather than a random listing of unrelated characteristics.

In an effective comparison a thesis or controlling idea governs the choice of class, points of comparison, and specific similarities and differences, while also making the comparison worthwhile for the reader. The thesis of an evaluative comparison generally emerges naturally because it coincides with the writer's purpose of supporting a preference for one subject over another:

> THESIS SENTENCE (EVALUATION) The two diets result in similarly rapid weight loss, but Harris's requires much more self-discipline and is nutritionally much riskier than Marconi's.

In an explanatory comparison, however, the thesis does more than merely reflect the general purpose of explaining. It should go beyond the obvious and begin to identify the points of comparison. For example:

> TENTATIVE THESIS SENTENCE (EXPLANATION) Rugby and American football are the same in some respects and different in others.
>
> REVISED THESIS SENTENCE (EXPLANATION) Though rugby requires less strength and more stamina than American football, the two games are very much alike in their rules and strategies.

The examples above suggest other decisions you must make when writing a comparison:

- Should the subjects be treated in equal detail, or should one be emphasized over the others? Generally, give the subjects equal emphasis when they are equally familiar or are being evaluated (as the diets are in the example above). Stress one subject over the others when it is less familiar (as rugby is in this country).
- Should the essay focus on similarities or differences, or both? Generally, stress them equally when all the points of comparison are equally familiar or important. Stress the differences between subjects usually considered similar (such as diets) or the similarities between subjects usually considered different (such as rugby and American football).

With two or more subjects, several points of comparison, many similarities and differences, and a particular emphasis, comparison clearly requires a firm organizational hand. You have two options for arranging a comparison:

- **Subject-by-subject,** in which you group the points of comparison under each subject so that the *subjects* are covered one at a time.
- **Point-by-point,** in which you group the subjects under each point of comparison so that the *points* are covered one at a time.

The following brief outlines illustrate the different arrangements as they might be applied to diets:

Subject-by-subject	*Point-by-point*
Harris's diet	Speed of weight loss
Speed of weight loss	Harris's diet
Required self-discipline	Marconi's diet
Nutritional risk	Required self-discipline
Marconi's diet	Harris's diet
Speed of weight loss	Marconi's diet
Required self-discipline	Nutritional risk
Nutritional risk	Harris's diet
	Marconi's diet

Since the subject-by-subject arrangement presents each subject as a coherent unit, it is particularly useful for comparing impressions of subjects: the dissimilar characters of two friends, for instance. However, covering the subjects one at a time can break an essay into discrete pieces and strain readers' memories, so this arrangement is usually confined to essays that are short or that compare several subjects briefly. For longer papers requiring precise treatment of the individual points of comparison—say, an evaluation of two proposals for a new student-aid policy—the point-by-point arrangement is more useful. Its chief disadvantage is that the reader can get lost in details and fail to see any subject as a whole. Because each arrangement has its strengths and weaknesses, you may sometimes combine the two in a single work, using the divided arrangement to introduce or summarize overall impressions of the subjects and using the alternating arrangement to deal specifically with the points of comparison.

ANALYZING COMPARISON AND CONTRAST IN PARAGRAPHS

Michael Dorris (1945–97) was a fiction and nonfiction writer who, as a member of the Modoc tribe, explored Native American issues and experiences. The following paragraph comes from "Noble Savages? We'll Drink to That," first published in the *New York Times* in April 1992.

For centuries, flesh and blood Indians have been assigned the role of a popular-culture metaphor. Today, their evocation instantly connotes fuzzy images of Nature, the Past, Plight, or Summer Camp. War-bonneted

Subject-by-subject organization

apparitions pasted to football helmets or baseball caps act as opaque, impermeable curtains, solid walls of white noise that for many citizens block or distort all vision of the nearly two million native Americans today. And why not? Such honoring relegates Indians to the long-ago and thus makes them magically disappear from public consciousness and conscience. What do the 300 federally recognized tribes, and their various complicated treaties governing land rights and protections, their crippling teenage suicide rates, their manifold health problems have in common with jolly (or menacing) cartoon caricatures, wistful braves, or raven-tressed Mazola girls?

1. The image in popular culture

Comparison clarified by transitions (underlined once) and repetition and restatement (underlined twice) (see p. 231)

2. The reality of Native American life

Gretel Ehrlich (born 1946) is an essayist who often writes about the high country of Wyoming, where she has lived for more than two decades. This paragraph comes from the essay "About Men," which appeared in Ehrlich's collection *The Solace of Open Spaces* (1985).

When I'm in New York but feeling lonely for Wyoming I look for the Marlboro ads in the subway. What I'm aching to see is horseflesh, the glint of a spur, a line of distant mountains, brimming creeks, and a reminder of the ranchers and cowboys I've ridden with for the last eight years. But the men I see in those posters with their stern, humorless looks remind me of no one I know here. In our hellbent earnestness to romanticize the cowboy we've ironically disesteemed his true character. If he's "strong and silent" it's because there's probably no one to talk to. If he "rides away into the sunset" it's because he's been on horseback since four in the morning moving cattle and he's trying, fifteen hours later, to get home to his family. If he's "a rugged individualist" he's also part of a team: ranch work is teamwork and even the glorified open-range cowboys of the 1880s rode up and down the Chisholm Trail in the company of twenty or thirty other riders. Instead of the

Point-by-point organization

Comparison clarified by transitions (underlined once) and repetition and restatement (underlined twice) (see p. 231)

1. Strength and silence

2. Riding into sunset

3. Individualism

macho, trigger-happy man our culture has perversely wanted him to be, the cowboy is more apt to be convivial, quirky, and softhearted. To be "tough" on a ranch has nothing to do with conquests and displays of power. More often than not, circumstances—like the colt he's riding or an unexpected blizzard—are overpowering him. It's not toughness but "toughing it out" that counts. In other words, this macho, cultural artifact the cowboy has become is simply a man who possesses resilience, patience, and an instinct for survival. "Cowboys are just like a pile of rocks—everything happens to them. They get climbed on, kicked, rained and snowed on, scuffed up by wind. Their job is 'just to take it,'" one old-timer told me.

4. Machismo

5. Toughness

DEVELOPING AN ESSAY BY COMPARISON AND CONTRAST

Getting Started

Whenever you observe similarities or differences between two or more members of the same general class—activities, people, ideas, things, places—you have a possible subject for comparison and contrast. Just be sure that the subjects are worth comparing and that you can do the job in the space and time allowed. For instance, if you have a week to complete a three-page paper, don't try to show all the similarities and differences between country-and-western music and rhythm-and-blues. The effort can only frustrate you and irritate your readers. Instead, limit the subjects to a manageable size—for instance, the lyrics of a representative song in each type of music—so that you can develop the comparisons completely and specifically.

To generate ideas for a comparison, explore each subject separately to pick out its characteristics, and then explore the subjects together to see what characteristics one suggests for the other. Look for points of comparison. Early on, you can use division or analysis (Chapter 7) to identify points of comparison by breaking the subjects' general class into its elements. A song lyric, for instance, could be divided into story line or plot, basic emotion, and special language such as dialect or slang. After you have explored your subjects fully, you can use classification (Chapter 8) to group your characteristics under the points of comparison. For instance, you might classify characteristics of two proposals for a new student-aid policy into qualifications for aid, minimum and maximum amounts to be made available, and repayment terms.

While you are shaping your ideas, you should begin formulating your controlling idea, your thesis. As discussed on pages 223–24, the thesis should reflect your answers to these questions:

- Do the ideas suggest an explanatory or evaluative comparison?
- If explanatory, what point will the comparison make so that it does not merely recite the obvious?
- If evaluative, what preference or recommendation will you express?
- Will you emphasize both subjects equally or stress one over the other?
- Will you emphasize differences or similarities, or both?

As you gain increasing control over your material, consider also the needs of your readers:

- Do they know your subjects well, or should you take special care to explain one or both of them?
- Will your readers be equally interested in similarities and differences, or will they find one more enlightening than the other?
- If your essay is evaluative, are your readers likely to be biased against your preference? If so, you will need to support your case with plenty of specific reasons.

Most readers know intuitively how a comparison works, so they will expect you to balance your comparison feature for feature. In other words, all the features you mention for the first subject should be mentioned as well for the second, and any features not mentioned for the first subject should not suddenly materialize for the second.

Organizing

Your readers' needs and expectations can also help you plan your essay's organization. An effective introduction to a comparison essay often provides some context for readers—the situation that prompts the comparison, for instance, or the need for the comparison. Placing your thesis sentence in the introduction also informs readers of your purpose and point, and it may help keep you focused while you write.

For the body of the essay, choose the arrangement that will present your material most clearly and effectively. Remember that the subject-by-subject arrangement suits brief essays comparing dominant impressions of the subjects, whereas the point-by-point arrangement suits longer essays requiring emphasis on the individual points of comparison. If you are torn between the two—wanting both to sum up each subject and to show the two side by side—then a combined arrangement may be your wisest choice.

A rough outline like the models on page 225 can help you plan the basic arrangement of your essay and also the order of the subjects and points of comparison. If your subjects are equally familiar to your readers and equally important to you, then it may not matter which subject you treat first, even in a subject-by-subject arrangement. But if one subject is less familiar or if you favor one, then that one should probably come second. You can also arrange the points themselves to reflect their importance and your readers' knowledge: from least to most significant or complex, from most to least familiar. Be sure to use the same order for both subjects.

The conclusion to a comparison essay can help readers see the whole picture: the chief similarities and differences between two subjects compared in a divided arrangement, or the chief characteristics of subjects compared in an alternating arrangement. In addition, you may want to comment on the significance of your comparison, advise readers on how they can use the information you have provided, or recommend a specific course of action for them to follow. As with all other methods of development, the choice of conclusion should reflect the impression you want to leave with readers.

Drafting

Drafting your essay gives you the chance to spell out your comparison so that it supports your thesis or, if your thesis is still tentative, to find your idea by writing into it. You can use paragraphs to help manage the comparison as it unfolds:

- In a subject-by-subject arrangement, if you devote two paragraphs to the first subject, try to do the same for the second subject. For both subjects, try to cover the points of comparison in the same order and group the same ones in paragraphs.
- In a point-by-point arrangement, balance the paragraphs as you move back and forth between subjects. If you treat several points of comparison for the first subject in one paragraph, do the same

for the second subject. If you apply a single point of comparison to both subjects in one paragraph, do the same for the next point of comparison.

This way of drafting will help you achieve balance in your comparison and see where you may need more information to flesh out your subjects and your points. If the finished draft seems to march too rigidly in its pattern, you can always loosen things up when revising (see below).

Revising and Editing

When you are revising and editing your draft, use the following questions and the box on the next page to be certain that your essay meets the principal requirements of the comparative method.

- *Are your subjects drawn from the same class?* The subjects must have notable differences *and* notable similarities to make comparison worthwhile—though, of course, you may stress one group over the other.
- *Does your essay have a clear purpose and say something significant about the subject?* Your purpose of explaining or evaluating and the point you are making should be evident in your thesis *and* throughout the essay. A vague, pointless comparison will quickly bore readers.
- *Do you apply all points of comparison to both subjects?* Even if you emphasize one subject, the two subjects must match feature for feature. An unmatched comparison may leave readers with unanswered questions or weaken their confidence in your authority.
- *Does the pattern of comparison suit readers' needs and the complexity of the material?* Although readers will appreciate a clear organization and roughly equal treatment of your subjects and points of comparison, they will also appreciate some variety in the way you move back and forth. You needn't devote a sentence to each point, first for one subject and then for the other, or alternate subjects sentence by sentence through several paragraphs. Instead, you might write a single sentence on one point or subject but four sentences on the other—if that's what your information requires.

FOCUS ON PARAGRAPH COHERENCE

With several points of comparison and alternating subjects, a comparison will be easy for your readers to follow only if you frequently clarify what subject and what point you are discussing. To help readers keep your comparison straight, you can rely on the techniques of paragraph coherence discussed on pages 35–36, especially on transitions and on repetition or restatement:

- Transitions like those listed on page 372 act as signposts to tell readers where you, and they, are headed. Some transitions indicate that you are shifting between subjects, either finding resemblances between them (*also, like, likewise, similarly*) or finding differences (*but, however, in contrast, instead, unlike, whereas, yet*). Other transitions indicate that you are moving on to a new point (*in addition, also, furthermore, moreover*).

  Traditional public schools depend for financing, of course, on tax receipts and on other public money like bonds, and as a result they generally open enrollment to all students without regard to background, skills, or special needs. Magnet schools are *similarly* funded by public money. *But* they often require prospective students to pass a test or other hurdle for admission. *In addition, whereas* traditional public schools usually offer a general curriculum, magnet schools often focus on a specialized program emphasizing an area of knowledge or competence, such as science and technology or performing arts.

- Repetition or restatement of labels for your subjects or for your points of comparison makes clear the topic of each sentence. In the passage above, the repetitions of *traditional public schools* and *magnet schools* and the substitution of *they* for each clarify the subjects of the comparison. The restatements of *financing/public money/funded, enrollment/admission,* and *curriculum/program* clarify the points of comparison.

See the sample paragraphs on pages 225–27 for additional examples of these two techniques.

A NOTE ON THEMATIC CONNECTIONS

When writers see something amiss in the way people conventionally regard a subject—person, object, group, social problem, trend—they often choose comparison and contrast to show the mistaken and the corrected views side by side. Each writer represented in this chapter uses comparison for just such a goal. The paragraph by Michael Dorris contrasts the media's image of Native Americans with the group's reality (p. 225). The paragraph by Gretel Ehrlich sets the myth of the Marlboro man against the life and character of true working cowboys (p. 226). The essay by Stephen Manes questions whether the book is really threatened by its supposed substitute, the CD-ROM (next page). The essay by Bryan Garvey argues the similarities between substances usually considered quite different: legal prescription drugs and illegal recreational drugs (p. 238). And the essay by Leanita McClain distinguishes the reality of being a middle-class African American from the misperceptions of both blacks and whites (p. 243).

Stephen Manes

Stephen Manes has a dual career as a well-known computer journalist and an award-winning writer for children and young adults. He was born in 1949 and received a B.A. degree in cinema from the University of Southern California. Since 1982 he has written about computers and the computer industry for PC Magazine *and other periodicals, and he currently writes regular columns for* Information Week, PC World, *and the* New York Times. *He has also contributed to television and radio, either as a writer or as a commentator. His more than thirty books for young people include* Be a Perfect Person in Just Three Days! *(1982) and* Make Four Million Dollars by Next Thursday *(1992). Manes lives in Seattle.*

The Endangered Book?

Computer hype has it that we'll soon be reading computers instead of books. Taking a close comparative look at one book that's also available on CD-ROM, Manes disputes this notion. "The Endangered Book?" (editor's title) first appeared in the New York Times *in 1995.*

Material World: A Global Family Portrait (Sierra Club Books) is a fascinating volume of photographs, essays and statistics about the way people live around the globe. Conceived by the photographer Peter Menzel, the book portrays the worldly goods and daily life of thirty representative families, along with statistics and commentaries about the countries they inhabit. 1

Material World from Starpress Multimedia, phone (800) 782-7944, is also a CD-ROM that, according to the book's jacket flap, "brings even greater life to the subject with spectacular video, breathtaking photography, and stereo sound." If these claims were true, books in general, and this book in particular, would seem to be endangered species. A comparison between bound volume and CD-ROM should help reveal whether reports of the death of the book are greatly exaggerated. 2

The CD-ROM requires a 25-megahertz 386DX or faster IBM-compatible computer (486 is recommended), Microsoft Windows 3.1 or higher, DOS 5.0 or higher, four megabytes of random access 3 memory (eight is recommended), VGA/SVGA or better display quality with 640 by 480 dots and 256 colors, a mouse, a hard drive, a CD-ROM drive with at least 150 kilobit/second transfer rate and a Sound-Blaster-compatible, Sound Blaster Pro, or Roland sound card. (Macintosh requirements differ.) The book requires only a source of light.

Installing the CD-ROM is an interactive process requiring minutes of pointing, clicking, and waiting in front of a keyboard and computer screen. The book can be installed instantaneously in one's hands or lap indoors or out. 4

On a seventeen-inch monitor, the CD-ROM can display fifty dots per inch and 256 colors at a time. On pages slightly smaller than a typical seventeen-inch screen, the book displays millions of colors at a resolution of more than 130 dots per inch. The book's photos are therefore immensely sharper and richer than their electronic counterparts. 5

Details that leap out in ink on paper are unrecognizable in phosphor under glass. The quality of light, almost palpable on the page, is absent on the screen. And the book's double-page "big pictures" of families with their possessions dwarf all but the biggest computer displays. 6

The book is organized geographically. A standard information-retrieval device known as a table of contents provides quick access, as does a stunning map based on satellite photographs of the earth. Moving from the table to the actual contents is fast and easy even though some of the pages lack numbers. Digital placeholders commonly known as "fingers" are not supplied, but using those typically at hand lets you compare two sections with ease. 7

Navigating through the CD-ROM can be infuriating. The disk is organized along four pathways: questionnaire, countries, lifestyles and families. Sometimes you can jump easily from one place to another; often you cannot. To figure out whether a photograph is supplemented by a video clip (grainy, tiny and decidedly unspectacular), you must move the cursor over the photo and see if the arrow changes to a camera. To reveal additional information, you may have to click on an icon of a camera, a clipboard or a collection of maps. A "Roadmap" chart and a "Backtrack" button offer modest navigational assistance. 8

The publisher says the disk contains about 1,400 photos, the book about 360. The CD-ROM also includes other information missing from the book, like responses to the questionnaires that the fami- 9 lies answered, slide shows narrated by Charles Kuralt, overview maps of each country and the opening bars of national anthems.

But the book can display far more information at once, and uses this advantage to create a much stronger editorial viewpoint. In the book, each "big picture" is displayed alongside a caption describing the family and its possessions. The CD-ROM uses tiny "pages" of short captions that identify only three or four items at a time and even then obscure part of the picture. However, the CD-ROM's lists do include possessions not included in the photos; in the book, these are inconveniently noted on a page at the back. 10

What takes a couple of glances in the book can require many mouse clicks with the CD. The book's double-page "material world at a glance" table brings together a wealth of statistical and factual information. The disk omits some of these data entirely and takes thirty-six separate screens to display the rest. Although the CD-ROM can show the data as bar graphs, only one-third of the countries can be displayed at once, and then only alphabetically, so statistics for Albania and Vietnam cannot appear simultaneously. Enlightening and amusing two-page spreads of sixteen small photos of meals, televisions and toilets around the world appear as interludes in the book. Their equivalent in the CD-ROM includes additional photos as well as sections on toys, music, recreation, animals, transportation, homes, markets, kitchens, schools and most valuable possessions. Unfortunately, the small format, low resolution and lack of captions make these photos tantalizing rather than useful. 11

The book lacks the simplistic introduction narrated by Mr. Kuralt. The disk lacks the book's detailed source notes and three introductory articles, including a comment on methodology in which Mr. Menzel cheerfully admits that the selection process included countries "I wanted to see" and an essay in which the historian Paul Kennedy points out the importance of understanding the project's findings "especially on a *comparative* basis," an aspect in which the CD-ROM comes up particularly short. 12

The CD-ROM costs about $40, the book about $30. The book does not come with a number you can call for technical help. 13

Meaning

1. What does Manes think about "reports of the death of the book"? In what way is his essay a response to those reports?

2. What advantages of the book over the CD-ROM does Manes identify? What are the advantages of the CD-ROM over the book?
3. What does Manes refer to with the phrase "phosphor under glass" (paragraph 6)?
4. If any of the following words are new to you, try to guess their meanings from the context of Manes's essay. Check your guesses in a dictionary, and then use each new word in a sentence or two of your own.

resolution (5)	icon (8)	tantalizing (11)
phosphor (6)	interludes (11)	methodology (12)
palpable (6)		

Purpose and Audience

1. What is Manes's stated purpose?
2. Is this an explanatory or an evaluative comparison? Does Manes have an agenda beyond objectively comparing and contrasting the merits of the book and CD-ROM versions of *Material World*?
3. Manes uses technical terms, especially in paragraph 3, without any explanation for the uninitiated. Do you think he is writing only for computer-literate readers? Why, or why not?

Method and Structure

1. Why do you think Manes chose the method of comparison and contrast to accomplish his purpose? How might the effect of the essay have been different if he had written a personal, narrative essay on the enduring pleasure of reading books in the computer age?
2. What does Manes gain by comparing a specific book to a specific CD-ROM, rather than comparing books and CD-ROMs in general?
3. Manes's organization is point-by-point, alternating between book and CD-ROM. What are the points of comparison he focuses on?
4. What is the effect of the last paragraph? Why do you think Manes chose to end this way?
5. **Other Methods** Manes uses description (Chapter 4), example (Chapter 6), and analysis (Chapter 7) in the service of his comparison. Is the description mostly objective or mostly subjective? What does it contribute to the essay?

Language

1. What is the overall tone of this essay? What do you make of the occasional moments of strong opinion and irony? (If necessary, see *irony* in the Glossary.)

2. Manes reveals his pro-book bias in paragraphs 1–2 before he even begins the comparison. Point out some words in these two paragraphs that tip readers off to Manes's opinion.

Writing Topics

1. **Journal Response** Think of a book you have read that was made into a movie, or vice versa. Write down as many points of comparison between the two as you can think of. Did one form leave out anything important? How were the characters the same or different? Which form did you like more, and why?
   Journal to Essay Write an essay in which you compare and contrast the relative advantages of books and movies, using the specific book and movie chosen above as an extended example. Choose three or four well-defined points of comparison that you think apply generally to book-movie adaptations.
2. Write a tongue-in-cheek essay in which you compare and contrast a traditional way of doing something with a supposedly "new and improved" way that's actually more of a hassle—for example, traditional datebooks versus electronic ones, or telephone operators versus voice mail systems. Use paragraphs 3, 4, and 7 of Manes's essay as a guide to style and tone.
3. What was your reaction to Manes's essay? Do you agree or disagree with Manes's belief that the book is superior to its computer cousin? Manes writes about a certain kind of book, but are there other kinds that might be more effective in electronic form—perhaps reference books such as dictionaries, encyclopedias, and atlases. Write an essay comparing the advantages and disadvantages of the two media.
4. **Cultural Considerations** The book and CD-ROM Manes writes about show the "worldly goods and daily life" of families around the world. In many of these families, such as those living in Albania and Vietnam, it's likely that computers do not appear among the family's possessions or figure significantly in the family's daily life. In the United States, in contrast, computers enter almost every facet of daily life (health, education, business, government, even our cars), and nearly 50 percent of American homes have personal computers. What do those in less-developed countries perhaps gain or lose from not having such access to computers? Write an essay that develops your opinion of the effects of widespread computer use in our culture. To keep the subject manageable, you may want to focus on the effects you deal with in your own life.
5. **Connections** Compare this essay to Bryan Garvey's "Drugs vs. Drugs" (next page). How objectively does each author view the subjects of his comparison? How effectively does each one support his opinion? Focusing on language and evidence, which essay do you find more convincing, and why?

Bryan Garvey

Born in 1975 in Jacksonville, Florida, Bryan Garvey grew up in Kentucky and Tennessee. He attended the University of Tennessee at Knoxville, where he majored in journalism and contributed to the newspaper, the Daily Beacon. *Garvey graduated in 1998 with a B.S. in communications. He plays in a band in the Knoxville area and says he "wouldn't mind" a career as a writer.*

Drugs vs. Drugs

Illegal drugs like marijuana and cocaine are poles apart from legal drugs like Prozac and codeine—right? Not according to Garvey, who finds similarities where conventional wisdom finds only differences. Garvey wrote this essay for the Daily Beacon *and revised it especially for* The Compact Reader.

What are drugs? Heroin and cocaine are drugs, as is marijuana. 1
Alcohol is also a drug, and who can forget about nicotine? But what about aspirin, codeine, caffeine, and Prozac? These are drugs, too, but not, in our society, the big, bad "Drugs." So what is the difference between drugs and Drugs? It can be misleading to make the distinction, because both drugs and Drugs can be harmful and helpful.

I grew up hearing the ubiquitous "Just Say No to Drugs." Yet my 2
mother stuffed me with every kind of pill she could find at the drop of a mucous blob. I can't open a box of Lemonheads or Red Hots or even go into a public restroom without being exposed to an anti-Drug message. (For you women out there, makers of rubber mats that lie inside urinals often print such messages on their products.) But when I open an issue of *Newsweek* magazine, half the ads are for pharmaceuticals.

Now, the basic definition of a *drug* is "any foreign substance that 3
elicits a change in the body." That means any foreign substance, from the illegal opiates in poppy flowers to over-the-counter pain relievers. It seems then that both drugs and Drugs are on the same level by definition.

So why do pharmaceuticals, even the abused Valium and Xanax, 4
meet with little disdain, while marijuana and narcotics are considered

the scourge of our youth and of society as a whole? I have several friends who had bad car accidents because they were on Valium or Xanax, yet no one seems to acknowledge this dangerous side of these commonly abused pills. I don't understand. We must say "no" to Drugs but "yes" to drugs?

Well, actually, I do understand. 5

We have been brought up to believe that Mom needs Valium to sleep and Dad needs codeine to feel better. Nowadays, Brother needs Ritalin for hyperactivity and Sister must have Prozac for depression—while their real problems go unaddressed and their energies are quelled instead of redirected. But the family's drugs are legal—and as American as red, white, and blue. Narcotics and other Drugs, however, are illegal—and usually associated with society's outsiders. 6

Consider the case of marijuana, a plant cultivated legally until earlier in the twentieth century. Political unrest in Mexico, culminating in the revolution of 1910, sent a flood of immigration into the United States. The immigrants brought with them their preferred form of intoxication, marijuana, which eventually suffered the same prejudices directed at Mexicans themselves. Other immigrant and outcast groups were also associated with the Drug, further stigmatizing the "evil weed." By 1937 Congress had criminalized possession. The laws and sentiments regarding marijuana have changed little since then, despite medical evidence that the Drug can help people with glaucoma and debilitating nausea. 7

Contrast this path with that of a legal pharmaceutical drug. The Food and Drug Administration, a federal agency whose head is appointed by the president, is responsible for approving drugs for sale. The FDA often receives pressure from lobbyists for pharmaceutical companies to push through the companies' own drugs or hold back approval of competitors' drugs. This political environment can be double-edged. AIDS and cancer patients awaiting new drugs may benefit, but harmful drugs may also be rushed to market. For instance, the weight-loss drugs Fenfluramine and Phenteramine were approved separately by the FDA, but no study was made of their effects in combination, which is how they were often sold. Fen-Phen proved a great reducing aid—that is, until many users began experiencing liver and heart valve problems and Fenfluramine was taken off the market. 8

The different routes of marijuana and Fenfluramine are the result of prejudices, political pressures, and social definitions of "bad" and 9 "good"—not absolute harmfulness. In fact, any medical or nursing student will tell you that just about any drug, legal or not, prescription or over-the-counter, has negative effects on the liver and kidneys, which filter the body's toxins. (Substantial liver damage is the main reason for removing drugs from the market that were formerly approved by the FDA.) We hear about the harmful effects of Drugs all the time, even exaggerations. But we rarely hear about the harmful effects of pharmaceutical drugs, and they become that much more open to abuse. A research professional is paid handsomely to invent and study a drug that will take the place of daily exercise but is prohibited from researching marijuana's alleviation of nausea.

It's not that marijuana and cocaine are "good" and should be 10
legal while Ritalin, codeine, and aspirin are "bad" and should not be. It's just that the scales are unbalanced; both can have good or bad effects, and money and politics and prejudice should not distort our understanding of this fact. Know that drugs are Drugs are drugs, and respect them all accordingly.

Meaning

1. Where does Garvey state his thesis?
2. How does Garvey answer the two questions with which he begins the essay: "What are drugs?" and "So what is the difference between drugs and Drugs?"
3. How does politics influence which drugs are legalized?
4. Based on their context in Garvey's essay, try to guess the meanings of any of the following words you don't already know. Test your guesses in a dictionary, and then use each new word in a sentence or two of your own.

ubiquitous (2)	narcotics (4)	glaucoma (7)
pharmaceuticals (2)	quelled (6)	lobbyists (8)
elicits (3)	cultivated (7)	toxins (9)
opiates (3)	stigmatizing (7)	alleviation (9)
disdain (4)		

Purpose and Audience

1. Where does Garvey explicitly state his purpose?
2. What does Garvey seem to assume about his readers' attitudes toward legal and illegal drugs? What information does he provide to bring readers around to this view? Does he persuade you? Why, or why not?

Method and Structure

1. How is the method of comparison and contrast central to Garvey's purpose in writing this essay? Does he emphasize the differences or the similarities between drugs and Drugs? Why?
2. Point out places where Garvey brings his personal experience into the essay. What purpose does each of these passages serve?
3. **Other Methods** Many other methods besides comparison are woven into this complex essay, including narration (Chapter 5), example (Chapter 6), classification (Chapter 8), definition (Chapter 11), cause-and-effect analysis (Chapter 12), and argument and persuasion (Chapter 13). What does the cause-and-effect analysis in paragraph 7 contribute to the essay? How does it help Garvey achieve his purpose?

Language

1. How would you describe Garvey's tone? Is it appropriate for the subject? What are some words that reveal Garvey's attitude?
2. What is the effect of the one-sentence paragraph 5?
3. What does Garvey mean when he compares the "political environment" of the FDA to a double-edged sword (paragraph 8)?

Writing Topics

1. **Journal Response** Is there any illegal drug that you think should be legalized? Is there any legal drug you think should not be? What would be the effects, both positive and negative, of changing the legislation on this drug? Consider for example whether a change in status would increase or decrease use of the drug, whether it would hurt or harm users, and what the social and economic repercussions might be.
   Journal to Essay Starting from your journal notes, write an argument in favor of changing the existing laws on the drug you have chosen. Make sure to present both sides of the argument and demonstrate why your side makes more sense. (See Chapter 13 for help with argument and persuasion.)
2. At your library or video store, try to find *Reefer Madness,* a film made in 1936 that shows middle-class teenagers descending from uncontrollable laughter to murder after smoking marijuana. What tactics does the film use to persuade viewers of the dangers of marijuana? What assumptions does it make? Write an essay analyzing the film as a work of propaganda. (See Chapter 7 for help with analysis.)
3. **Cultural Considerations** Think of a substance that is or was illegal in the United States but legal in another country. An example is hashish,

which is legal in the Netherlands but not in this country, or RU-486, the French pharmaceutical for terminating pregnancy that has not yet received final approval for use here. Do some research on the substance and the debates surrounding it. Can the differences in acceptance be accounted for by different cultural contexts in the two countries? Did scientific studies in the two countries yield different results? Is there a historical explanation, such as the one Garvey gives for marijuana's criminalization? Write an essay in which you compare and contrast attitudes toward the substance in the two countries and try to explain why the authorities in those countries came to different conclusions about its legality.

4. **Connections** Like Garvey, Charles Krauthammer, in "Of Headless Mice . . . and Men" (p. 329), questions whether scientific "progress" is always for the good. Write an essay in which you compare and contrast the issues involved in cloning and drug approval, drawing on both the two essays and your own knowledge of the debates.

Leanita McClain

An African American journalist, Leanita McClain earned a reputation for honest, if sometimes bitter, reporting on racism in America. She was born in 1952 on Chicago's South Side and grew up in a housing project there. She attended Chicago State University and the Medill School of Journalism at Northwestern University. Immediately after graduate school she began working as a reporter at the Chicago Tribune, *and over the next decade she advanced to writing a twice-weekly column and serving as the first African American member of the paper's editorial board. In 1983 she published an essay in the* Washington Post, *"How Chicago Taught Me to Hate Whites," that expressed her anguish over a racially divisive election in Chicago. The essay caused a furious controversy that probably undermined McClain's already fragile psychological condition. Long suffering from severe depression, she committed suicide in 1984, at the age of thirty-two. In the words of her former husband, Clarence Page, she could no longer "distinguish between the world's problems and her own."*

The Middle-Class Black's Burden

McClain wrote this essay for the "My Turn" column in Newsweek *magazine in October 1980, and it was reprinted in a collection of her essays,* A Foot in Each World *(1986). As her comparison makes disturbingly clear, McClain's position as an economically successful African American subjected her to mistaken judgments by both blacks and whites.*

I am a member of the black middle class who has had it with being patted on the head by white hands and slapped in the face by black hands for my success. 1

Here's a discovery that too many people still find startling: when given equal opportunities at white-collar pencil pushing, blacks want the same things from life that everyone else wants. These include the proverbial dream house, two cars, an above-average school, and a vacation for the kids at Disneyland. We may, in fact, want these things more than other Americans because most of us have been denied them so long. 2

Meanwhile, a considerable number of the folks we left behind in the "old country," commonly called the ghetto, and the militants we left behind in their antiquated ideology can't berate middle-class blacks enough for "forgetting where we came from." We have forsaken the revolution, we are told, we have sold out. We are Oreos, they say, black on the outside, white within. 3

The truth is, we have not forgotten; we would not dare. We are simply fighting on different fronts and are no less war weary, and possibly more heartbroken, for we know the black and white worlds can meld, that there can be a better world. 4

It is impossible for me to forget where I came from as long as I am prey to the jive hustler who does not hesitate to exploit my childhood friendship. I am reminded, too, when I go back to the old neighborhood in fear—and have my purse snatched—and when I sit down to a business lunch and have an old classmate wait on my table. I recall the girl I played dolls with who now rears five children on welfare, the boy from church who is in prison for murder, the pal found dead of a drug overdose in the alley where we once played tag. 5

My life abounds in incongruities. Fresh from a vacation in Paris, I may, a week later, be on the milk-run Trailways bus in Deep South back-country attending the funeral of an ancient uncle whose world stretched only 50 miles and who never learned to read. Sometimes when I wait at the bus stop with my attaché case, I meet my aunt getting off the bus with other cleaning ladies on their way to do my neighbors' floors. 6

But I am not ashamed. Black progress has surpassed our greatest expectations; we never even saw much hope for it, and the achievement has taken us by surprise. 7

In my heart, however, there is no safe distance from the wretched past of my ancestors or the purposeless present of some of my contemporaries; I fear such a fate can reclaim me. I am not comfortably middle class; I am uncomfortably middle class. 8

I have made it, but where? Racism still dogs my people. There are still communities in which crosses are burned on the lawns of black families who have the money and grit to move in. 9

What a hollow victory we have won when my sister, dressed in her designer everything, is driven to the rear door of the luxury high rise in which she lives because the cab driver, noting only her skin color, assumes she is the maid, or the nanny, or the cook, but certainly not the lady of any house at this address. 10

I have heard the immigrants' bootstrap tales, the simplistic reproach of "why can't you people be like us." I have fulfilled the entry requirements of the American middle class, yet I am left, at times, feeling unwelcome and stereotyped. I have overcome the problems of food, clothing and shelter, but I have not overcome my old nemesis, prejudice. Life is easier, being black is not. 11

I am burdened daily with showing whites that blacks are people. I am, in the old vernacular, a credit to my race. I am my brothers' keeper, and my sisters', though many of them have abandoned me because they think that I have abandoned them. 12

I run a gauntlet between two worlds, and I am cursed and blessed by both. I travel, observe, and take part in both; I can also be used by both. I am a rope in a tug of war. If I am a token in my downtown office, so am I at my cousin's church tea. I assuage white guilt. I disprove black inadequacy and prove to my parents' generation that their patience was indeed a virtue. 13

I have a foot in each world, but I cannot fool myself about either. I can see the transparent deceptions of some whites and the bitter hopelessness of some blacks. I know how tenuous my grip on one way of life is, and how strangling the grip of the other way of life can be. 14

Many whites have lulled themselves into thinking that race relations are just grand because they were the first on their block to discuss crab grass with the new black family. Yet too few blacks and whites in this country send their children to school together, entertain each other, or call each other friend. Blacks and whites dining out together draw stares. Many of my coworkers see no black faces from the time the train pulls out Friday evening until they meet me at the coffee machine Monday morning. I remain a novelty. 15

Some of my "liberal" white acquaintances pat me on the head, hinting that I am a freak, that my success is less a matter of talent than of luck and affirmative action. I may live among them, but it is difficult to live with them. How can they be sincere about respecting me, yet hold my fellows in contempt? And if I am silent when they attempt to sever me from my own, how can I live with myself? 16

Whites won't believe I remain culturally different; blacks won't believe I remain culturally the same. 17

I need only look in a mirror to know my true allegiance, and I am painfully aware that, even with my off-white trappings, I am prejudged by my color. 18

As for the envy of my own people, am I to give up my career, my standard of living, to pacify them and set my conscience at ease? No. 19

I have worked for these amenities and deserve them, though I can never enjoy them without feeling guilty.

These comforts do not make me less black, nor oblivious to the woe in which many of my people are drowning. As long as we are denigrated as a group, no one of us has made it. Inasmuch as we all suffer for every one left behind, we all gain for every one who conquers the hurdle. 20

Meaning

1. McClain states, "My life abounds in incongruities" (paragraph 6). What does the word *incongruities* mean? How does it apply to McClain's life?
2. What is the "middle-class black's burden" to which the title refers? What is McClain's main idea?
3. McClain writes that "there is no safe distance from the wretched past of my ancestors or the purposeless present of some of my contemporaries" (paragraph 8). What do you think she means by this statement?
4. If any of the words below are new to you, try to guess their meanings from their context in McClain's essay. Check your guesses against a dictionary's definitions, and then try to use each word in a sentence or two of your own.

proverbial (2)	nemesis (11)	tenuous (14)
antiquated (3)	vernacular (12)	amenities (19)
ideology (3)	gauntlet (13)	oblivious (20)
berate (3)	assuage (13)	denigrated (20)
reproach (11)		

Purpose and Audience

1. What seems to be McClain's primary purpose in this piece? Does she simply want to express her frustration at whites and blacks, or is she trying to do something else here?
2. Is McClain writing primarily to whites or to blacks or to both? What feelings do you think she might evoke in white readers? in black readers? What is *your* reaction to this essay?
3. McClain's essay poses several questions, including "I have made it, but where?" (paragraph 9) and "How can they be sincere about respecting me, yet hold my fellows in contempt?" (16). What is the purpose of such questions?

Method and Structure

1. What exactly is McClain comparing here? What are her main points of comparison?
2. Paragraph 6 on "incongruities" represents a turning point in McClain's essay. What does she discuss before this paragraph? What does she discuss after?
3. McClain uses many expressions to make her comparison clear, such as "Meanwhile" (paragraph 3) and "different fronts" (4). Locate three more such expressions, and explain what relationship each one establishes.
4. **Other Methods** McClain relies on many other methods to develop her comparison. Locate one instance each of description (Chapter 4), narration (Chapter 5), example (Chapter 6), and cause-and-effect analysis (Chapter 12). What does each contribute to the essay?

Language

1. McClain sets the tone for this essay in the very first sentence. How would you describe this tone? Is it appropriate, do you think?
2. In her opening sentence, does McClain use the words *patted* and *slapped* literally? How would you explain her use of these words in the context of her essay?
3. Notice McClain's use of parallelism in paragraph 8: "I am not comfortably middle class; I am uncomfortably middle class." Locate two or three other uses of parallelism. How does this technique serve McClain's comparison? (For more on parallelism, see p. 48 and *parallelism* in the Glossary.)
4. In paragraph 16, McClain uses quotation marks around the term "liberal" in reference to her white acquaintances. Why do you think she uses the quotation marks here? What effect does this achieve?

Writing Topics

1. **Journal Response** Think of a time when you were stereotyped because of your membership in a group (as an ethnic, religious, or sexual minority, a jock, a "nerd," a "homeboy," and so on). How were you perceived and by whom? What about this perception was accurate? What was unfair? How did the experience affect you?

   Journal to Essay Write a narrative in which you recount the experience of being stereotyped. Write for a reader who is not a member of the stereotyped group, being sure to include enough detail to bring the experience to life.

2. McClain's essay reports in part her experience of conflict resulting from her growth beyond the boundaries of her childhood and community. Think of a time when you outgrew a particular group or community. What conflicts and satisfactions did you experience? Write an essay comparing your experience with McClain's.
3. **Cultural Considerations** Are there any ways in which you feel, like McClain, that you have "a foot in each world"? These worlds might be related to race and affluence, as McClain's worlds are, or they might be aligned by gender, social class, religion, or some other characteristic. Write an essay describing your own experience in balancing these two worlds. Are there ways in which you appreciate having a dual membership, or is it only a burden? What have you learned from your experience?
4. **Connections** Like McClain, Gloria Naylor (p. 266) also speaks of existing in two worlds: home and school, black and white, public and private. What similarities and differences do you notice in these two writers' experiences? Use evidence from both essays to support your comparison.

Writing with the Method

Comparison and Contrast

Choose one of the following topics, or any other topic they suggest, for an essay developed by comparison and contrast. The topic you decide on should be something you care about so that the comparison and contrast is a means of communicating an idea, not an end in itself.

EXPERIENCE

1. Two jobs you have held
2. Two experiences with discrimination
3. Your own version of an event you witnessed or participated in and someone else's view of the same event (perhaps a friend's or a newspaper account's)
4. A good and a bad job interview

PEOPLE

5. Your relationships with two friends
6. Someone before and after marriage or the birth of a child
7. Two or more candidates for public office
8. Two relatives

PLACES AND THINGS

9. A place as it is now and as it was years ago
10. Two cars
11. Contact lenses and glasses
12. Two towns or cities
13. Nature in the city and in the country

ART AND ENTERTAINMENT

14. The work of two artists or writers, or two works by the same artist or writer
15. Two or more forms of jazz, classical music, or rock music
16. Movies or television today and when you were a child
17. A novel and a movie or television show on which it's based
18. A high school or college football, baseball, or basketball game and a professional game in the same sport
19. The advertisements during two very different television programs, or in two very different magazines

EDUCATION AND IDEAS

20. Talent and skill
21. Learning and teaching
22. Two styles of teaching
23. Two religions
24. Humanities courses and science or mathematics courses
25. A passive student and an active student

Writing About the Theme

Challenging Misconceptions

1. All the writers in this chapter try to correct what they see as mistaken notions: about the reality of life for members of a racial minority (Dorris, p. 225, and McClain, p. 243), about the character of working cowboys (Ehrlich, p. 226), about the precarious position of books (Manes, p. 233), and about the relative risks of legal and illegal drugs (Garvey, p. 238). All five authors rely on comparison and contrast, but otherwise they go about their tasks very differently. Most notably, perhaps, their tones vary widely, from light irony to serious anger. Choose the two works that seem most different in this respect and analyze how the tone of each does or doesn't help the author achieve his or her purpose. Give specific examples to support your ideas. Does your analysis lead you to conclude that one tone is likely to be more effective than another in challenging misconceptions? (For more on tone, see pp. 39–40 and 327.)
2. Michael Dorris and Leanita McClain both refer to misperceptions of their minority group on the part of the dominant white society. Think of a minority group to which you belong: it could be based on race, ethnicity, language, sexual orientation, religion, physical disability, or any other characteristic. How is your minority perceived in the dominant culture, and how does this perception resemble or differ from the reality as you know it? Write an essay comparing perception and reality.
3. Gretel Ehrlich contrasts the true cowboy character with the image conveyed by the "strong and silent" cowboy in Marlboro ads, while Michael Dorris contrasts the reality of Native American life with the "white noise" of Indian images in the media. To what extent, if at all, are the misconceptions addressed by Manes, Garvey, and McClain also the result of media hype or distortion, whether in advertising, news stories, television programming, movies, or elsewhere? What else might contribute to the misconceptions in each case? Write an essay explaining how such notions arise in the first place. You could use the misconceptions identified by Manes, Garvey, and McClain for your examples or you could supply examples of your own.

Chapter 11

DEFINITION

Clarifying Our Relationships

USING THE METHOD

Definition sets the boundaries of a thing, a concept, an emotion, or a value. In answering "What is it?" and also "What is it *not*?" definition specifies the main qualities of the subject and its essential nature. Since words are only symbols, pinning down their precise meanings is essential for us to understand ourselves and one another. Thus we use definition constantly, whether we are explaining a slang word like *dis* to someone who has never heard it or explaining what *culture* means on an essay examination.

There are several kinds of definition, each with different uses. One is the **formal definition**, usually a statement of the general class of things to which the word belongs, followed by the distinction(s) between it and other members of the class. For example:

	General class	*Distinction(s)*
A submarine is	a seagoing vessel	that operates underwater.
A parable is	a brief, simple story	that illustrates a moral or religious principle.
Pressure is	the force	applied to a given surface.
Insanity is	a mental condition	in which a defendant does not know right from wrong.

A formal definition usually gives a standard dictionary meaning of the word (as in the first two examples) or a specialized meaning agreed to by the members of a profession or discipline (as in the last two examples, from physics and criminal law, respectively). It is most useful to explain the basic meaning of a term that readers need to know in order to understand the rest of a discussion. Occasionally, you might also use a formal definition as a springboard to a more elaborate, detailed exploration of a word. For instance, you might define *pride* simply as "a sense of self-respect" before probing the varied meanings of the word as people actually understand it and then settling on a fuller and more precise meaning of your own devising.

This more detailed definition of *pride* could fall into one of two other types of definition: stipulative and extended. A **stipulative definition** clarifies the particular way you are using a word: you stipulate, or specify, a meaning to suit a larger purpose; the definition is part of a larger whole. For example, if you wanted to show how pride can destroy personal relationships, you might first stipulate a meaning of *pride* that ties in with that purpose. Though a stipulative definition may sometimes take the form of a brief formal definition, most require several sentences or even paragraphs. In a physics textbook, for instance, the physicist's definition of *pressure* quoted above probably would not suffice to give readers a good sense of the term and eliminate all the other possible meanings they may have in mind.

Whereas you use a formal or stipulative definition for some larger purpose, you write an **extended definition** for the sake of defining—that is, for the purpose of exploring a thing, quality, or idea in its full complexity and drawing boundaries around it until its meaning is complete and precise. Extended definitions usually treat subjects so complex, vague, or laden with emotions or values that people misunderstand or disagree over their meanings. The subject may be an abstract concept like *patriotism,* a controversial phrase like *beginnings of life,* a colloquial or slang expression like *hype,* a thing like *microcomputer,* a scientific idea like *natural selection,* even an everyday expression like *nagging.* Besides defining, your purpose may be to persuade readers to accept a definition (for instance, that life begins at conception, or at birth), to explain (what is natural selection?), or to amuse (nagging as exemplified by great nags).

As the variety of possible subjects and purposes may suggest, an extended definition may draw on whatever methods will best accomplish the goal of specifying what the subject encompasses and distinguishing it from similar things, qualities, or concepts. Several strategies are unique to definition:

- **Synonyms,** or words of similar meaning, can convey the range of the word's meanings. For example, you could equate *misery* with *wretchedness* and *distress.*
- **Negation,** or saying what a word does not mean, can limit the meaning, particularly when you want to focus on only one sense of an abstract term, such as *pride,* that is open to diverse interpretations.
- The **etymology** of a word—its history—may illuminate its meaning, perhaps by showing the direction and extent of its change (*pride,* for instance, comes from a Latin word meaning "to be beneficial or useful") or by uncovering buried origins that remain implicit in the modern meaning (*patriotism* comes from the Greek word for "father"; *happy* comes from the Old Norse word for "good luck").

You may use these strategies of definition alone or together, and they may occupy whole paragraphs in an essay-length definition; but they rarely provide enough range to surround the subject completely. To do that, you'll need to draw on the other methods discussed in this book. One or two methods may predominate: an essay on nagging, for instance, might be developed with brief narratives. Or several methods may be combined: a definition of *patriotism* could compare it with *nationalism,* analyze its effects (such as the actions people take on its behalf), and give examples of patriotic individuals. The goal is not to employ every method in a sort of catalog of methods but to use those which best illuminate the subject. By drawing on the appropriate methods, you define and clarify your perspective on the subject so that the reader understands the meaning exactly.

ANALYZING DEFINITION IN PARAGRAPHS

Alice Walker (born 1944) is a teacher, essayist, poet, and fiction writer, the winner of a Pulitzer Prize for her novel *The Color Purple* (1982). The following paragraph comes from Walker's essay "The Black Writer and the Southern Experience," which appears in a collection of her essays, *In Search of Our Mothers' Gardens* (1983).

What the black Southern writer inherits as a natural right is a sense of *community,* something simple but surprisingly hard, especially these days, to come by. My mother, who is a walking history of our community, tells me that when each of her children was born the midwife accepted as payment such home-grown or home-made items as a pig, a quilt, jars of canned fruits and vegetables. But there was never any question that the midwife would come when she was needed, whatever the eventual payment for her services. I consider this each time I hear of a hospital that refuses to admit a woman in labor unless she can hand over a substantial sum of money, cash.

> *Introduction of the word to be defined (topic sentence underlined)*
>
> *Definition by example:*
> *Continuity*
> *Barter economy*
> *Reliability*
> *Flexibility*
>
> *Contrasting example:*
> *Unreliability*
> *Coldness*
> *Cash economy*

Wendell Berry (born 1934) is a poet, a fiction writer, an essayist, and a farmer. The following paragraph is a stipulative definition within a larger essay, "Higher Education and Home Defense," published in Berry's collection *Home Economics* (1987).

Education in the true sense, of course, is an enablement to *serve*—both the living human community in its natural household or neighborhood and the precious cultural possessions that the living community inherits or should inherit. To educate is, literally, to "bring up," to bring young people to a responsible maturity, to help them to be good caretakers of what they have been given, to help them to be charitable toward fellow creatures. Such an education is obviously pleasant and useful to have; that a sizable number of humans should have it is probably also one of the necessities of human life in this world. And if this education is to be used well, it is obvious that it must be used some *where;* it must be used where one lives, where one intends to continue to live; it must be brought home.

> *The author's definition, using* enablement *as a synonym (topic sentence underlined)*
>
> *The literal meaning, based on etymology*
>
> *The implications of the definition*

DEVELOPING AN ESSAY BY DEFINITION

Getting Started

You'll sometimes be asked to write definition essays, as when a psychology exam asks for a discussion of *schizophrenia* or a political science assignment calls for an explanation of the term *totalitarianism.* To come up with a subject on your own, consider words that have complex meanings and are either unfamiliar to readers or open to varied interpretations. The subject should be something you know and care enough about to explore in great detail and surround completely. An idea for a subject may come from an overheard conversation (for instance, a reference to someone as "too patriotic"), a personal experience (a broken marriage you think attributable to one spouse's pride), or something you've seen or read (another writer's definition of *jazz*).

Begin exploring your subject by examining and listing its conventional meanings (consulting an unabridged dictionary may help here, and the dictionary will also give you synonyms and etymology). Also examine the differences of opinion about the word's meanings—the different ways, wrong or right, that you have heard or seen it used. Run through the other methods to see what fresh approaches to the subject they open up:

- How can the subject be described?
- What are some examples?
- Can the subject be divided into qualities or characteristics?
- Can its functions help define it?
- Will comparing and contrasting it with something else help sharpen its meaning?
- Do its causes or effects help clarify its sense?

Some of the questions may turn up nothing, but others may open your eyes to meanings you had not seen.

When you have generated a good list of ideas about your subject, settle on the purpose of your definition. Do you mostly want to explain a word that is unfamiliar to readers? Do you want to express your own view so that readers see a familiar subject from a new angle? Do you want to argue in favor of a particular definition or perhaps persuade readers to look more critically at themselves or their surroundings? Try to work your purpose into a tentative thesis sentence that asserts something about the subject. For example:

Though generally considered entirely positive in meaning, *patriotism* in fact reflects selfish, childish emotions that have no place in a global society.

With a thesis sentence formulated, reevaluate your ideas in light of it and pause to consider the needs of your readers:

- What do readers already know about your subject, and what do they need to be told in order to understand it as you do?
- Are your readers likely to be biased for or against your subject? If you were defining *patriotism,* for example, you might assume that your readers see the word as representing a constructive, even essential value that contributes to the strength of the country. If your purpose were to contest this view, as implied by the thesis above, you would have to build your case carefully to win readers to your side.

Organizing

The introduction to a definition essay should provide a base from which to expand and at the same time explain to readers why the forthcoming definition is useful, significant, or necessary. You may want to report the incident that prompted you to define, say why the subject itself is important, or specify the common understandings, or misunderstandings, about its meaning. Several devices can serve as effective beginnings: the etymology of the word; a quotation from another writer supporting or contradicting your definition; or an explanation of what the word does *not* mean (negation). (Try to avoid the overused opening that cites a dictionary: "According to *The American Heritage Dictionary,* _______ means. . . ." Your readers have probably seen this opening many times before.) If it is not implied in the rest of your introduction, you may want to state your thesis so that readers know precisely what your purpose and point are.

The body of the essay should then proceed, paragraph by paragraph, to refine the characteristics or qualities of the subject, using the arrangement and methods that will distinguish it from anything similar and provide your perspective. For instance:

- You might draw increasingly tight boundaries around the subject, moving from broader, more familiar meanings to the one you have in mind.
- You might arrange your points in order of increasing drama.

- You might begin with your own experience of the subject and then show how you see it operating in your surroundings.

The conclusion to a definition essay is equally a matter of choice. You might summarize your definition, indicate its superiority to other definitions of the same subject, quote another writer whose view supports your own, or recommend that readers make some use of the information you have provided. The choice depends—as it does in any kind of essay—on your purpose and the impression you want to leave with readers.

Drafting

While drafting your extended definition, keep your subject vividly in mind. Say too much rather than too little about it to ensure that you capture its essence; you can always cut when you revise. And be sure to provide plenty of details and examples to support your view. Such evidence is particularly important when, as in the earlier example of patriotism, you seek to change readers' perceptions of your subject.

In definition the words you use are especially important. Abstractions and generalities cannot draw precise boundaries around a subject, so your words must be as concrete and specific as you can make them. You'll have chances during revising and editing to work on your words, but try during drafting to pin down your meanings. Use words and phrases that appeal directly to the senses and experiences of readers. When appropriate, use figures of speech to make meaning inescapably clear; instead of "Patriotism is childish," for example, write "The blindly patriotic person is like a small child who sees his or her parents as gods, all-knowing, always right." The connotations of words—the associations called up in readers' minds by words like *home, ambitious,* and *generous*—can contribute to your definition as well. But be sure that connotative words trigger associations suited to your purpose. And when you are trying to explain something precisely, rely most heavily on words with generally neutral meanings. (See pp. 50–52 for more on concrete and specific language and figures of speech. See p. 50 for more on connotation.)

Revising and Editing

When you are satisfied that your draft is complete, revise and edit it against the following questions and the information in the box.

- *Have you surrounded your subject completely and tightly?* Your definition should not leave gaps, nor should the boundaries be so broadly drawn that the subject overlaps something else. For instance, a definition of *hype* that focused on exaggerated and deliberately misleading claims should include all such claims (some political speeches, say, as well as some advertisements), and it

FOCUS ON PARAGRAPH AND ESSAY UNITY

When drafting a definition, you may find yourself being pulled away from your subject by the descriptions, examples, comparisons, and other methods you use to specify meaning. Let yourself explore byways of your subject—doing so will help you discover what you think. But in revising you'll need to direct all paragraphs to your thesis and, within paragraphs, to direct all sentences to the paragraph topic. In other words, you'll need to ensure that your essay and its paragraphs are unified.

One way to achieve unity is to focus each paragraph on some part of your definition and then to focus each sentence within the paragraph on that part. Judy Brady's "I Want a Wife" (p. 261) proceeds in just such a pattern, as the following outline shows. The sentences from paragraphs 3–9 specify the paragraph topics. A look at Brady's essay will show you that each of the paragraphs elaborates on its topic.

THESIS (PARAGRAPH 2) I . . . would like to have a wife.

PARAGRAPH 3 I want a wife who will work and send me to school . . . [and] take care of my children.

PARAGRAPH 4 I want a wife who will take care of *my* physical needs.

PARAGRAPH 5 I want a wife who will not bother me with rambling complaints . . . [and] will listen to me.

PARAGRAPH 6 I want a wife who will take care of the details of my social life.

PARAGRAPH 7 I want a wife who is sensitive to my sexual needs.

PARAGRAPH 8 I want the liberty to replace my present wife with another one.

PARAGRAPH 9 When I am through with school and have a job, I want my wife to quit working and remain at home.

If some part of your definition requires more than a single paragraph, by all means expand it. But keep the group of paragraphs focused on a single idea.

For more on unity in essays and paragraphs, see pages 33–35.

should exclude appeals that do not fit the basic definition (some public-service advertising, for instance).

- *Does your definition reflect the conventional meanings of the word?* Even if you are providing a fresh slant on your subject, you can't change its meaning entirely or you will confuse your readers and perhaps undermine your own credibility. *Patriotism,* for example, could not be defined from the first as "hatred of foreigners," for that definition strays into an entirely different realm. The conventional meaning of "love of country" would have to serve as the starting point, though your essay might interpret the meaning in an original way.

A NOTE ON THEMATIC CONNECTIONS

In our relationships with family, friends, colleagues, neighbors, or even the larger society, the words we use can help smooth communication and interaction or can impede them. The authors represented in this chapter all define terms that reflect and affect how we live together. In paragraphs, both Alice Walker and Wendell Berry consider the community: Walker defines the word (p. 255), and Berry shows how education, properly conceived, can hold the community together (p. 255). Judy Brady's concern is more particular: in defining a wife, she characterizes the marital relationship (next page). Gloria Naylor remembers the special vocabulary used within the extended family of her childhood (p. 266). And Allison Amend explores how calling our difficulties *issues* rather than *problems* allows us to blame others for them (p. 273).

Judy Brady

Judy Brady was born in 1937 in San Francisco. She attended the University of Iowa and graduated with a bachelor's degree in painting in 1962. Married in 1960, by the mid-1960s she was raising two daughters. She began working in the women's movement in 1969 and through it developed an ongoing concern with political and social issues, especially women's rights. She believes that "as long as women continue to tolerate a society which places profits above the needs of people, we will continue to be exploited as workers and as wives." Besides the essay reprinted here, Brady has written articles for various magazines and edited 1 in 3: Women with Cancer Confront an Epidemic *(1991), motivated by her own struggle with the disease. Divorced from her husband and with, as she says, "little in the way of saleable skills," she works as a secretary in San Francisco.*

I Want a Wife

Writing after eleven years of marriage, and before separating from her husband, Brady here pins down the meaning of the word wife *from the perspective of one person who lives the role. This essay was published in the first issue of* Ms. *magazine in December 1971, and it has since been reprinted widely. Is its harsh portrayal still relevant today?*

I belong to that classification of people known as wives. I am A Wife. And, not altogether incidentally, I am a mother. 1

Not too long ago a male friend of mine appeared on the scene fresh from a recent divorce. He had one child, who is, of course, with his ex-wife. He is looking for another wife. As I thought about him while I was ironing one evening, it suddenly occurred to me that I, too, would like to have a wife. Why do I want a wife? 2

I would like to go back to school so that I can become economically independent, support myself, and, if need be, support those dependent upon me. I want a wife who will work and send me to school. And while I am going to school I want a wife to take care of my children. I want a wife to keep track of the children's doctor and dentist appointments. And to keep track of mine, too. I want a wife to make sure my children eat properly and are kept clean. I want a 3 wife who will wash the children's clothes and keep them mended. I want a wife who is a good nurturant attendant to my children, who arranges for their schooling, makes sure that they have an adequate social life with their peers, takes them to the park, the zoo, etc. I want a wife who takes care of the children when they are sick, a wife who arranges to be around when the children need special care, because, of course, I cannot miss classes at school. My wife must arrange to lose time at work and not lose the job. It may mean a small cut in my wife's income from time to time, but I guess I can tolerate that. Needless to say, my wife will arrange and pay for the care of the children while my wife is working.

I want a wife who will take care of *my* physical needs. I want a wife who will keep my house clean. A wife who will pick up after my children, a wife who will pick up after me. I want a wife who will keep my clothes clean, ironed, mended, replaced when need be, and who will see to it that my personal things are kept in their proper place so that I can find what I need the minute I need it. I want a wife who cooks the meals, a wife who is a *good* cook. I want a wife who will plan the menus, do the necessary grocery shopping, prepare the meals, serve them pleasantly, and then do the cleaning up while I do my studying. I want a wife who will care for me when I am sick and sympathize with my pain and loss of time from school. I want a wife to go along when our family takes a vacation so that someone can continue to care for me and my children when I need a rest and change of scene. 4

I want a wife who will not bother me with rambling complaints about a wife's duties. But I want a wife who will listen to me when I feel the need to explain a rather difficult point I have come across in my course of studies. And I want a wife who will type my papers for me when I have written them. 5

I want a wife who will take care of the details of my social life. When my wife and I are invited out by friends, I want a wife who will take care of the babysitting arrangements. When I meet people at school that I like and want to entertain, I want a wife who will have the house clean, will prepare a special meal, serve it to me and my friends, and not interrupt when I talk about things that interest me and my friends. I want a wife who will have arranged that the children are fed and ready for bed before my guests arrive so that the children do not bother us. I want a wife who takes care of the needs of my guests so that they feel comfortable, who makes sure that they 6 have an ashtray, that they are passed the hors d'oeuvres, that they are offered a second helping of the food, that their wine glasses are replenished when necessary, that their coffee is served to them as they like it. And I want a wife who knows that sometimes I need a night out by myself.

I want a wife who is sensitive to my sexual needs, a wife who makes love passionately and eagerly when I feel like it, a wife who makes sure that I am satisfied. And, of course, I want a wife who will not demand sexual attention when I am not in the mood for it. I want a wife who assumes the complete responsibility for birth control, because I do not want more children. I want a wife who will remain sexually faithful to me so that I do not have to clutter up my intellectual life with jealousies. And I want a wife who understands that *my* sexual needs may entail more than strict adherence to monogamy. I must, after all, be able to relate to people as fully as possible. 7

If, by chance, I find another person more suitable as a wife than the wife I already have, I want the liberty to replace my present wife with another one. Naturally, I will expect a fresh, new life; my wife will take the children and be solely responsible for them so that I am left free. 8

When I am through with school and have a job, I want my wife to quit working and remain at home so that my wife can more fully and completely take care of a wife's duties. 9

My God, who *wouldn't* want a wife? 10

Meaning

1. In one or two sentences, summarize Brady's definition of a wife. Consider not only the functions she mentions but also the relationship she portrays.
2. Brady provides many instances of a double standard of behavior and responsibility for the wife and the wife's spouse. What are the wife's chief responsibilities and expected behaviors? What are the spouse's?
3. If any of the words below are unfamiliar, try to guess what they mean from the context of Brady's essay. Look the words up in a dictionary to check your guesses, and then use each one in a sentence or two of your own.

nurturant (3)	replenished (6)	monogamy (7)
hors d'oeuvres (6)	adherence (7)	

Purpose and Audience

1. Why do you think Brady wrote this essay? Was her purpose to explain a wife's duties, to complain about her own situation, to poke fun at men, to attack men, to attack society's attitudes toward women, or what? Was she trying to provide a realistic and fair definition of *wife?* What passages in the essay support your answers?
2. What does Brady seem to assume about her readers' gender (male or female) and their attitudes toward women's roles in society, relations between the sexes, and work inside and outside the home? Does she seem to write from the perspective of a particular age group or social and economic background? In answering these questions, cite specific passages from the essay.
3. Brady clearly intended to provoke a reaction from readers. What is *your* reaction to this essay: do you think it is realistic or exaggerated, fair or unfair to men, relevant or irrelevant to the present time? Why?

Method and Structure

1. Why would anybody need to write an essay defining a term like *wife?* Don't we know what a wife is already? How does Brady use definition in an original way to achieve her purpose?
2. Analyze Brady's essay as a piece of definition, considering its thoroughness, its specificity, and its effectiveness in distinguishing the subject from anything similar.
3. Analyze the introduction to Brady's essay. What function does paragraph 1 serve? In what way does paragraph 2 confirm Brady's definition? How does the question at the end of the introduction relate to the question at the end of the essay?
4. **Other Methods** Brady develops her definition primarily by classification (Chapter 8). What does she classify, and what categories does she form? What determines her arrangement of these categories? What does the classification contribute to the essay?

Language

1. How would you characterize Brady's tone: whining, amused, angry, contemptuous, or what? What phrases in the essay support your answer? (If necessary, see pp. 39–40 and 327 on tone.)
2. Why does Brady repeat "I want a wife" in almost every sentence, often at the beginning of the sentence? What does this stylistic device convey about the person who wants a wife? How does it fit in with Brady's main idea and purpose?

3. Why does Brady never substitute the personal pronoun "she" for "my wife"? Does the effect gained by repeating "my wife" justify the occasionally awkward sentences, such as the last one in paragraph 3?
4. What effect does Brady achieve with the expressions "of course" (paragraphs 3, 7), "Needless to say" (3), "after all" (7), and "Naturally" (8)?

Writing Topics

1. **Journal Response** Think of a role you now fill—friend, son, daughter, brother, sister, student, secretary, short-order cook. Write down the responsibilities, activities, and relationships that define that role.
   Journal to Essay From your journal notes, write an essay defining your role as you see it. You could, if appropriate, follow Brady's model by showing how your role makes you essential to the other person or people involved.
2. Combine the methods of definition and comparison (Chapter 10) in an essay that compares a wife or a husband you know with Brady's definition of either role. Be sure that the point of your comparison is clear and that you use specific examples to illustrate the similarities or differences you see.
3. **Cultural Considerations** Brady's essay was written in the specific cultural context of 1971. Undoubtedly, many cultural changes have taken place since then, particularly changes in gender roles. However, one could also argue that much remains the same. Write an essay in which you compare the stereotypical role of a wife now with the role Brady defines. In addition to your own observations and experiences, consider contemporary images of wives that the media present—for instance, in television advertising or sitcoms.
4. **Connections** Wendell Berry (p. 255) writes of the importance of raising young people to "be good caretakers of what they have been given." What is the difference between the way Berry uses the word *caretaker* and the way Brady uses the words *care* and *take care* (both of which appear repeatedly in paragraphs 3, 4, and 6 of her essay)? Write a brief essay comparing what these two writers mean by the word *care,* using examples from your own experience to illustrate the definitions.

Gloria Naylor

An American novelist and essayist, Gloria Naylor was born in 1950 in New York City. She served as a missionary for Jehovah's Witnesses from 1967 to 1975 and then worked as a hotel telephone operator until 1981. That year she graduated from Brooklyn College of the City of New York with a B.A. and went on to do graduate work in African American studies at Yale University. Since receiving an M.A. from Yale, Naylor has published five novels dealing with the varied histories and life-styles often lumped together as "the black experience": The Women of Brewster Place *(1982), about the lives of eight black women, which won the American Book Award for fiction and was made into a television movie;* Linden Hills *(1985), about a black middle-class neighborhood;* Mama Day *(1988), about a Georgian woman with visionary powers;* Bailey's Cafe *(1992), about a group of people whose lives are at crossroads; and* The Men of Brewster Place *(1997), about the men whose lives intersect those of the women of Brewster Place.*

The Meanings of a Word

Recalling an experience as a third-grader leads Naylor to probe the meanings of a highly sensitive word. At the same time she explores how words acquire their meanings from use. This essay first appeared in the New York Times *in 1986.*

Language is the subject. It is the written form with which I've managed to keep the wolf away from the door and, in diaries, to keep my sanity. In spite of this, I consider the written word inferior to the spoken, and much of the frustration experienced by novelists is the awareness that whatever we manage to capture in even the most transcendent passages falls far short of the richness of life. Dialogue achieves its power in the dynamics of a fleeting moment of sight, sound, smell, and touch. 1

I'm not going to enter the debate here about whether it is language that shapes reality or vice versa. The battle is doomed to be waged whenever we seek intermittent reprieve from the chicken and 2 egg dispute. I will simply take the position that the spoken word, like the written word, amounts to a nonsensical arrangement of sounds or letters without a consensus that assigns "meaning." And building from the meanings of what we hear, we order reality. Words themselves are innocuous; it is the consensus that gives them true power.

I remember the first time I heard the word *nigger.* In my third-grade class, our math tests were being passed down the rows, and as I handed the papers to a little boy in back of me, I remarked that once again he had received a much lower mark than I did. He snatched his test from me and spit out that word. Had he called me a nymphomaniac or a necrophiliac, I couldn't have been more puzzled. I didn't know what a nigger was, but I knew that whatever it meant, it was something he shouldn't have called me. This was verified when I raised my hand, and in a loud voice repeated what he had said and watched the teacher scold him for using a "bad" word. I was later to go home and ask the inevitable question that every black parent must face—"Mommy, what does *nigger* mean?" 3

And what exactly did it mean? Thinking back, I realize that this could not have been the first time the word was used in my presence. I was part of a large extended family that had migrated from the rural South after World War II and formed a close-knit network that gravitated around my maternal grandparents. Their ground-floor apartment in one of the buildings they owned in Harlem was a weekend mecca for my immediate family, along with countless aunts, uncles, and cousins who brought along assorted friends. It was a bustling and open house with assorted neighbors and tenants popping in and out to exchange bits of gossip, pick up an old quarrel, or referee the ongoing checkers game in which my grandmother cheated shamelessly. They were all there to let down their hair and put up their feet after a week of labor in the factories, laundries, and shipyards of New York. 4

Amid the clamor, which could reach deafening proportions—two or three conversations going on simultaneously, punctuated by the sound of a baby's crying somewhere in the back rooms or out on the street—there was still a rigid set of rules about what was said and how. Older children were sent out of the living room when it was time to get into the juicy details about "you-know-who" up on the third floor who had gone and gotten herself "p-r-e-g-n-a-n-t!" But my parents, knowing that I could spell well beyond my years, always demanded that I follow the others out to play. Beyond sexual 5 misconduct and death, everything else was considered harmless for our young ears. And so among the anecdotes of the triumphs and disappointments in the various workings of their lives, the word *nigger* was used in my presence, but it was set within contexts and inflections that caused it to register in my mind as something else.

In the singular, the word was always applied to a man who had 6
distinguished himself in some situation that brought their approval for his strength, intelligence, or drive:

"Did Johnny *really* do that?" 7

"I'm telling you, that nigger pulled in $6,000 of overtime last 8
year. Said he got enough for a down payment on a house."

When used with a possessive adjective by a woman—"my nig- 9
ger"—it became a term of endearment for her husband or boyfriend. But it could be more than just a term applied to a man. In their mouths it became the pure essence of manhood—a disembodied force that channeled their past history of struggle and present survival against the odds into a victorious statement of being: "Yeah, that old foreman found out quick enough—you don't mess with a nigger."

In the plural, it became a description of some group within the 10
community that had overstepped the bounds of decency as my family defined it. Parents who neglected their children, a drunken couple who fought in public, people who simply refused to look for work, those with excessively dirty mouths or unkempt households were all "trifling niggers." This particular circle could forgive hard times, unemployment, the occasional bout of depression—they had gone through all of that themselves—but the unforgivable sin was a lack of self-respect.

A woman could never be a "nigger" in the singular, with its con- 11
notation of confirming worth. The noun *girl* was its closest equivalent in that sense, but only when used in direct address and regardless of the gender doing the addressing. *Girl* was a token of respect for a woman. The one-syllable word was drawn out to sound like three in recognition of the extra ounce of wit, nerve, or daring that the woman had shown in the situation under discussion.

"G-i-r-l, stop. You mean you said that to his face?" 12

But if the word was used in a third-person reference or shortened 13
so that it almost snapped out of the mouth, it always involved some element of communal disapproval. And age became an important factor in these exchanges. It was only between individuals of the same

generation, or from any older person to a younger (but never the other way around), that *girl* would be considered a compliment.

I don't agree with the argument that use of the word *nigger* at this social stratum of the black community was an internalization of racism. The dynamics were the exact opposite: the people in my grandmother's living room took a word that whites used to signify worthlessness or degradation and rendered it impotent. Gathering there together, they transformed *nigger* to signify the varied and complex human beings they knew themselves to be. If the word was to disappear totally from the mouths of even the most liberal of white society, no one in that room was naive enough to believe it would disappear from white minds. Meeting the word head-on, they proved it had absolutely nothing to do with the way they were determined to live their lives. 14

So there must have been dozens of times that *nigger* was spoken in front of me before I reached the third grade. But I didn't "hear" it until it was said by a small pair of lips that had already learned it could be a way to humiliate me. That was the word I went home and asked my mother about. And since she knew that I had to grow up in America, she took me in her lap and explained. 15

Meaning

1. Naylor writes that "the spoken word, like the written word, amounts to a nonsensical arrangement of sounds or letters without a consensus that assigns 'meaning'" (paragraph 2). Explain this statement in your own words. How did this statement apply to the word *nigger* for the young Naylor?
2. What is Naylor's main idea? Where does she express it?
3. In paragraph 14 Naylor disagrees with those who claim that the African American community's use of the term *nigger* constitutes "an internalization of racism." What alternative explanation does she offer? Do you agree with her interpretation? Why, or why not?
4. At the beginning of paragraph 15 Naylor says that although the word *nigger* had been spoken in her presence many times, she didn't "hear" it until her classmate called her that name. What does she mean by this statement? Why had she not "heard" the word before?
5. This essay contains some difficult vocabulary. Don't be discouraged if many of the words below are new to you. Try to guess what they mean from their context in Naylor's essay, and then test your guesses in a dictionary. Use each new word in sentences of your own.

transcendent (1)
dynamics (1)
intermittent (2)
consensus (2)
innocuous (2)
nymphomaniac (3)
necrophiliac (3)
verified (3)
inevitable (3)
gravitated (4)
mecca (4)
clamor (5)
anecdotes (5)
inflections (5)
disembodied (9)
unkempt (10)
trifling (10)
communal (13)
stratum (14)
internalization (14)
rendered (14)
impotent (14)
naive (14)

Purpose and Audience

1. What is Naylor's purpose or purposes in writing this essay: to express herself? to explain something? to convince readers of something? Support your answer by referring to passages from the essay.
2. Naylor's essay first appeared in the *New York Times,* a daily newspaper whose readers are largely middle-class whites. In what ways does she seem to consider and address this audience?

Method and Structure

1. Why is Naylor's choice of the method of definition especially appropriate given the point she is trying to make about language?
2. Naylor supports her main idea by defining two words, *nigger* and *girl.* What factors influence the various meanings of each word?
3. Naylor's essay is divided into sections, each contributing something different to the whole. Identify the sections and their functions.
4. **Other Methods** Like many writers of definition, Naylor employs a number of other methods of development: for instance, in paragraphs 4 and 5 she describes the atmosphere of her grandparents' apartment (Chapter 4); in 8, 9, and 12 she cites examples of speech (Chapter 6); and in 11–13 she compares and contrasts the two uses of *girl* (Chapter 10). At two points in the essay Naylor relies on a narrative of the same incident (Chapter 5). Where, and for what purpose?

Language

1. How would you describe the tone of Naylor's essay? Steady and reasoned, or impassioned? Is the style more academic or more informal? Do you find Naylor's tone and style appropriate given her subject matter? Why?
2. In paragraph 3 Naylor uses language to convey a child's perspective. For example, she seems to become the arrogant little girl who "remarked

that once again he had received a much lower mark than I did." Locate three or four other uses of language in the essay that emphasize her separation from the world of adults. How does this perspective contribute to the effect of the essay?

3. In paragraph 14 Naylor concludes that her family used *nigger* "to signify the varied and complex human beings they knew themselves to be." This variety and complexity is demonstrated through the words and expressions she uses to describe life in her grandparents' home—"a weekend mecca," "a bustling and open house" (4). Cite five or six other examples of concrete, vivid language in this description.
4. Occasionally Naylor uses bits of dialogue to support her definitions. In paragraphs 7–8, for example, she demonstrates the approval that accompanies *nigger* by quoting an anonymous conversation. She does the same thing in paragraphs 9 and 12. Do you think the dialogue interferes with Naylor's definitions? Enhances them? Explain your response.

Writing Topics

1. **Journal Response** As Naylor shows, the language of stereotypes can be powerful and painful to encounter. Have you ever experienced or witnessed this kind of labeling? What were your reactions? (Keep in mind that race is just one possible object of stereotypes. Consider ethnic group, gender, income, marital status, sexual preference, weight, or height as possible objects.)

   Journal to Essay Using your own experiences for examples, write an essay modeled on Naylor's in which you define "the meanings of a word" (or words). Have you found, too, that meaning varies with context? If so, make the variations clear.
2. Choose another word whose meanings vary depending on who says it and when (for example, *marriage, ambition, home, loyalty*). Using Naylor's essay as a model, write an essay exploring the various meanings of the word. If you choose a word with strong meaning for you, you can use personal experience and dialogue, as Naylor does, to support your analysis.
3. A recent grassroots movement tried but failed to have the word *nigger* removed from dictionaries. Are there some words so hateful that they should be banned from the language? Or is such an attempt to control language even more objectionable? Write an essay that states and supports your answers, giving plenty of examples.
4. **Cultural Considerations** About African Americans' use of the word *nigger,* Naylor writes that "the people in my grandmother's living room took a word that whites used to signify worthlessness or degradation and rendered it impotent" (paragraph 14). Write an essay in which you

discuss a symbol, a trait, or another word that has been used negatively by one group toward another but has been transformed by the targeted group into a positive meaning. Examples include the gay community's use of the word *queer* and the Jewish community's reclaiming of the Star of David after the Nazis used the symbol to stigmatize Jews. How did the definition of the symbol, trait, or word change from one community to another? Like Naylor, provide readers with examples that clarify your definitions.

5. **Connections** Naylor's essay concludes "And since she knew that I had to grow up in America, she took me in her lap and explained." Is this an optimistic or a pessimistic statement? Compare Naylor's vision of America to that given by Martin Luther King, Jr., in "I Have a Dream" (p. 349). Whom do Naylor and King hold responsible for improving race relations in this country?

Allison Amend

Born in 1974, Allison Amend grew up in Chicago and graduated from Stanford University with a B.A. in comparative literature. She has traveled widely, living in Europe as an exchange student and a Fulbright teaching fellow. At the University of Iowa, she is currently pursuing an M.F.A. and teaching creative writing. Her short stories have won prizes from Story *magazine and* The Atlantic, *and she is at work on a novel.*

Taking Issue with Problems

What does it matter if these days we talk about our personal difficulties not as problems *but as* issues? *Amend believes that the change could affect us and those around us quite a bit. She wrote this essay for the* Stanford Daily *in 1996 while she was a student at the university.*

Issues. Everyone's got 'em. Issues with food, issues with politics, issues with other people. I can take issue with you. I can bring an issue to a head. I can buy an issue. I could even issue you a ticket if I had the proper authority. 1

But what are *issues?* If you strip the word down, determine what we really mean, an issue is a problem. But what's the problem with the word *problem?* 2

If you have intimacy issues or alcohol issues, the truth is that you have a problem with intimacy or alcohol. The dictionary defines a *problem* as "a question or situation that presents uncertainty, perplexity or difficulty. . . . A source of trouble or annoyance." A problem is defined by its precarious state between the action that causes uncertainty and its resolution. A problem is forever; once it's solved, it ceases to be a problem. 3

An *issue,* on the other hand, the dictionary calls "an act or instance of flowing, passing or giving out . . . something produced . . . the result of an action . . . a point of discussion . . . an outlet." Wow, an issue is all that? The difference, then, is that an issue has an 4 ontology of its own. That is to say that an issue requires the agency of an act or instance, whereas a problem has origins as hazy as a morning by the bay.

5 *Issue* seems to be an end in itself. The flowing, outlet imagery recalls a dam, a wealth of emotions that are set loose by the issue in a tirade leaving the issuer spent and pleasantly empty. Where have ulceric uncertainty and painful perplexity gone?

6 Truth be told, we have replaced *problem* with *issue* in our vocabulary. And *issue* is a euphemism. It seems healthier to find the cause of our malaise, identify it as an issue and therefore assign it a cause and expiate it through its appellation. Doesn't *issue* provide a Freudian field-day of realizing causes, earmarking the individuals or situations that are responsible and effecting magical cures from that knowledge? How can a word, a name, perform that function, and why is it comforting to name a disease, even if we have no methods of treating it?

7 The issue (I'm using it here myself) becomes symptomatic of a larger cultural phenomenon, that of blame. We throw around blame like confetti on New Year's, claiming our parents culpable, our genes, our friends, our lovers, stress, jobs. By allowing ourselves to give the problem an agent, we can remove the onus from ourselves.

8 Dealing with an issue is like dealing with an old car whose insurance is worth more than its chassis. You drive into a collision, hoping to collect, praying you won't get hurt in the process. Honesty functions as the weapon, the shield, as well as the flag under which we march to battle. Honesty at all costs.

9 But honesty, while traditionally the best policy, has also been given the epithet *brutal.* Honesty can injure. And yet honesty is what issues forth when a problem becomes an issue. The confronter is comforted by the sensation that he or she has "dealt with the issue." But has he or she "resolved the problem"?

10 Conflict resolution requires the satisfied acquiescence of both parties involved, whereas issues demand only the release of pressure from one side. The river only flows one way. An issue is selfish; a problem is shared.

11 It's easy to see why we've taken to calling a problem an issue these days. A problem is so superficial, so mental. It's uncertainty and discomfort, annoyance. An issue, even in its vague definition, seems tied to the synthesis between mind and body. It's visceral, corporeal, pervasive. We think a problem is weakness, mental laziness, intellec-

tual inflation, but an issue is deep-rooted, interior and personal. We'll excuse someone's issues, but sneer at their problems.

This discrimination against problems is also due to their confinement to the realm of personal dialogue. A problem begs resolution; you think about it, you solve your own spiritual discomfort. An issue, on the other hand, is defined by action. You find the person or people who are the source of your anxiety and you vent. And this venting is taking place entirely too often and is offered as an excuse for impolite behavior. *12*

There is often a fine line between honesty and rudeness, and issues are served up as the reason behind its blurring. I've heard myself explain away blasting tirades with "Well, you know, he has issues." We all nod knowingly. Everyone has problems, but unvented issues are inexcusable in our society: "She hasn't dealt with that issue." *13*

It becomes, of course, an issue of personal responsibility, for aren't "issue-probs" (if I may coin the term) yours, first of all? We need to use good judgment, then, in finding the proper balance between healing our own uncertainty and blowing our tops. We must search for the resolution to the situation before digging for its cause, and then empty ourselves of it slowly, peacefully. *14*

Meaning

1. Summarize in your own words the distinction Amend makes between the words *issue* and *problem.* What is the difference between "dealing with an issue" and "solving a problem" (paragraph 9)?
2. What does Amend mean by "A problem is forever; once it's solved, it ceases to be a problem" (paragraph 3)? How is a problem different from an issue in this regard?
3. Some of the words Amend uses may be new to you. If so, try to guess what they mean from their context in the essay. See how close your definitions were to the dictionary's, and then use the new words in sentences of your own.

perplexity (3)
ontology (4)
agency (4)
ulceric (5)
euphemism (6)
malaise (6)
expiate (6)
appellation (6)
culpable (7)
onus (7)
chassis (8)
acquiescence (10)
synthesis (11)
visceral (11)
corporeal (11)
tirades (13)

Purpose and Audience

1. Why do you think Amend wrote this essay: to point out the different meanings of *issue* and *problem?* to challenge people who use *issue* instead of *problem?* to point out risks in using *issue* instead of *problem?* for some other reason?
2. Amend wrote this essay for her fellow students at Stanford University. How do you think her original readers may have responded to her ideas? How do *you* respond? Why?

Method and Structure

1. Was definition the only method Amend could have chosen for an essay urging people to take responsibility for their problems? Was it even the most obvious choice? How does the method help her achieve her purpose?
2. Amend opens the essay with examples of uses of the word *issue.* Are all of these uses accounted for by the definition she gives in the essay? If not, is the incompleteness of her definition a "problem"?
3. What function is served by the quotations of formal definitions in paragraphs 3 and 4? How does Amend build on them to structure the rest of her essay?
4. **Other Methods** Amend's essay is as much a comparison and contrast (Chapter 10) as it is a definition. How do the two methods work together?

Language

1. Comment on Amend's style. What does it say about her and her intended audience? Is it consistent throughout?
2. Explain the water metaphor Amend uses in paragraph 5. How does it help her define *issue?* (See p. 52 if you need a definition of *metaphor.*)

Writing Topics

1. **Journal Response** Listen for the word *issue* wherever people are talking—in your conversations with friends, in conversations you overhear, on television or radio talk shows, and so on. Record the uses of the word in your journal, making sure to include enough context so that you can remember just how the word was used.
   Journal to Essay What can you learn about the way people use *issue* from the examples in your journal? Do they use the word in the way

Amend describes? Write your own definition of *issue*. If you like, compare and contrast your definition with Amend's.

2. Think of another popular word like *issue* that people substitute for a word they would rather avoid, or think of a word that is so overused that it has become diluted or meaningless. Examples might be *situation* ("We've got a situation here"), *special* ("a child with special needs"), or *victim* ("a victim of her own success"). Write an essay like Amend's in which you give a formal definition of the word and examples of the way it is misused. Analyze why people use the word the way they do, and explain why you see this use as wrong or harmful.
3. **Cultural Considerations** Does our culture encourage people to take responsibility for their own "problems"? Or does it foster an environment in which people wallow happily in their "issues"? Have we gone too far, as Amend suggests, in our attempts to be honest, preferring "venting" about difficulties to solving them? Write an essay about our culture of complaint.
4. **Connections** In "Blah Blah Blah" (p. 119), Kim Kessler criticizes the laziness and dishonesty involved when people overuse the title expression. Is the same thing at work with *issue?* Write an essay exploring the similarities and differences in the way these two expressions function, drawing on both essays as well as your own experience.

Writing with the Method

Definition

Choose one of the following topics, or any other topic they suggest, for an essay developed by definition. The topic you decide on should be something you care about so that definition is a means of communicating an idea, not an end in itself.

PERSONAL QUALITIES

1. Ignorance
2. Sophistication
3. Spirituality or worldliness
4. Selflessness or selfishness
5. Loyalty or disloyalty
6. Responsibility
7. A good sport
8. Hypocrisy

EXPERIENCES AND FEELINGS

9. A nightmare
10. A good teacher, coach, parent, or friend
11. A good joke or a tasteless joke
12. Religious faith

ASPIRATIONS

13. The Good Life
14. Success or failure
15. A good job

SOCIAL CONCERNS

16. Poverty
17. Education
18. Domestic violence
19. Substance abuse
20. Prejudice
21. An American ethnic group such as Italians, WASPs, Japanese, Norwegians, or Chinese

ART AND ENTERTAINMENT

22. Jazz or some other kind of music
23. A good novel, movie, or television program
24. Impressionist painting or some other school of art

IDEAS

25. Freedom
26. Nostalgia
27. Feminism
28. A key concept in a course you're taking

Writing About the Theme

Clarifying Our Relationships

1. Alice Walker (p. 255), Wendell Berry (p. 255), and Gloria Naylor (p. 266) all write of the importance of community in our lives. Does each of these writers use the word in the same way? Write an essay discussing each one's definition of *community*. Where do they overlap? Where do they differ? Can you come up with a definition that comfortably includes the beliefs of all three writers?
2. Allison Amend (p. 273) observes, "Conflict resolution demands the satisfied acquiescence of both parties involved, whereas issues demand only the release of pressure from one side. . . . An issue is selfish; a problem is shared." Alice Walker, Wendell Berry, and Judy Brady (p. 261) also discuss situations when shared conflict resolution—or compromise—does or could benefit human relationships. Write an essay in which you define the word *compromise* and then apply it to Walker's, Berry's, Brady's, and Amend's pieces. (It's fine to use the dictionary definition of *compromise,* but you should move beyond it to your own ideas of the word.) How does compromise work in each author's conception, or how *could* it work if it is absent now?
3. The essays by Judy Brady, Gloria Naylor, and Allison Amend all define words that cause or reflect difficulties among people. What does each writer contribute to resolving those difficulties? Which writer do you think contributes the most, and why? Write an essay that supports your opinion with examples from all three essays.

Chapter 12

CAUSE-AND-EFFECT ANALYSIS

Exploring the Influence of Gender

USING THE METHOD

Why did free agency become so important in professional baseball, and how has it affected the sport? What caused the recent warming of the Pacific Ocean, and how did the warming affect the earth's weather? We answer questions like these with **cause-and-effect analysis,** the method of dividing occurrences into their elements to find relationships among them. Cause-and-effect analysis is a specific kind of analysis, the method discussed in Chapter 7.

When we analyze **causes,** we discover which of the events preceding a specified outcome actually made it happen:

> What caused Adolf Hitler's rise in Germany?
>
> Why have herbal medicines become so popular?

When we analyze **effects,** we discover which of the events following a specified occurrence actually resulted from it:

> What do we do for (or to) drug addicts when we imprison them?
>
> What happens to our foreign policy when the president's advisers disagree over its conduct?

These are existing effects of past or current situations, but effects are often predicted for the future:

> How would a cure for cancer affect the average life expectancy of men and women?
>
> How might your decision to major in history affect your job prospects?

Causes and effects can also be analyzed together, as the questions opening this chapter illustrate.

Cause-and-effect analysis is found in just about every discipline and occupation, including history, social science, natural science, engineering, medicine, law, business, and sports. In any of these fields, as well as in writing done for college courses, your purpose in analyzing may be to explain or to persuade. In explaining why something happened or what its outcome was or will be, you try to order experience and pin down the connections in it. In arguing with cause-and-effect analysis, you try to demonstrate why one explanation of causes is more accurate than another or how a proposed action will produce desirable or undesirable consequences.

The possibility of arguing about causes and effects points to the main challenge of this method. Related events sometimes overlap, sometimes follow one another immediately, and sometimes connect over gaps in time. They vary in their duration and complexity. They vary in their importance. Analyzing causes and effects thus requires not only identifying them but also discerning their relationships accurately and weighing their significance fairly.

Causes and effects often do occur in a sequence, each contributing to the next in what is called a **causal chain.** For instance, an unlucky man named Jones ends up in prison, and the causal chain leading to his imprisonment can be outlined as follows: Jones's neighbor, Smith, dumped trash on Jones's lawn. In reprisal, Jones set a small brushfire in Smith's yard. A spark from the fire accidentally ignited Smith's house. Jones was prosecuted for the fire and sent to jail. In this chain each event is the cause of an effect, which in turn is the cause of another effect, and so on to the unhappy conclusion.

Identifying a causal chain partly involves sorting out events in time:

- **Immediate** causes or effects occur nearest an event. For instance, the immediate cause of a town's high unemployment rate may be the closing of a large manufacturing plant where many townspeople work.
- **Remote** causes or effects occur further away in time. The remote cause of the town's unemployment rate may be a drastic decline in the company's sales or (more remote) a weak regional or national economy.

Analyzing causes also requires distinguishing their relative importance in the sequence:

- **Major** causes are directly and primarily responsible for the outcome. For instance, if a weak economy is responsible for low sales, it is a major cause of the manufacturing plant's closing.
- **Minor** causes (also called **contributory** causes) merely contribute to the outcome. The manufacturing plant may have closed for the additional reason that the owners could not afford to make repairs to its machines.

As these examples illustrate, time and significance can overlap in cause-and-effect analysis: a weak economy, for instance, is both a remote and a major cause; the lack of funds for repairs is both an immediate and a minor cause.

Since most cause-and-effect relationships are complex, you should take care to avoid several pitfalls in analyzing and presenting them. One is a confusion of coincidence and cause—that is, an assumption that because one event preceded another, it must have caused the other. This error is nicknamed **post hoc,** from the Latin *post hoc, ergo propter hoc,* meaning "after this, therefore because of this." Superstitions often illustrate post hoc: a basketball player believes that a charm once ended her shooting slump, so she now wears the charm whenever she plays. But post hoc also occurs in more serious matters. For instance, the office of a school administrator is vandalized, and he blames the incident on a recent speech by the student-government president criticizing the administration. But the administrator has no grounds for his accusation unless he can prove that the speech incited the vandals. In the absence of proof, the administrator commits the error of post hoc by asserting that the speech caused the vandalism simply because the speech preceded the vandalism.

Another potential problem in cause-and-effect writing is **oversimplification.** You must consider not just the causes and effects that seem obvious or important but all the possibilities: remote as well as immediate, minor as well as major. One form of oversimplification confuses a necessary cause with a sufficient cause:

- A **necessary** cause, as the term implies, is one that must happen in order for an effect to come about; an effect can have more than one necessary cause. For example, if emissions from a factory cause a high rate of illness in a neighborhood, the emissions are a necessary cause.
- A **sufficient** cause, in contrast, is one that brings about the effect *by itself.* The emissions are not a sufficient cause of the illness rate unless all other possible causes—such as water pollution or infection—can be eliminated.

Oversimplification can also occur if you allow opinions or emotions to cloud the interpretation of evidence. Suppose that you are examining the reasons why a gun-control bill you opposed was passed by the state legislature. Some of your evidence strongly suggests that a member of the legislature, a vocal supporter of the bill, was unduly influenced by lobbyists. But if you attributed the passage of the bill solely to this legislator, you would be exaggerating the significance of a single legislator and you would be ignoring the opinions of the many others who also voted for the bill. To achieve a balanced analysis, you would have to put aside your own feelings and consider all possible causes for the bill's passage.

ANALYZING CAUSES AND EFFECTS IN PARAGRAPHS

Mark Gerzon (born 1949) is a writer and administrator with an interest in global issues and human development. This paragraph comes from Gerzon's second book, *A Choice of Heroes: The Changing Faces of American Manhood* (1983).

Many movies are made as surrogate rites of passage for young men. They are designed for the guy who, in actor Clint Eastwood's words, "sits alone in the theater. He's young and he's scared. He doesn't know what he's going to do with his life. He wishes he could be self-

Causes:

Young men are insecure.

sufficient, like the man he sees up there on the screen, somebody who can look out for himself, solve his own problems." The heroes of these films are men who are tough and hard, quick to use violence, wary of women. Whether cowboys, cops, or superheroes, they dominate everything—women, nature, and other men. Young men cannot outmaneuver the Nazis as Indiana Jones did in *Raiders of the Lost Ark*, or battle Darth Vader, or outsmart Dr. No with James Bond's derring-do. To feel like heroes they turn to the other sex. They ask young women for more than companionship, or sex, or marriage. They ask women to give them what their culture could not—their manhood.

Movies represent heroic masculinity.

This kind of masculinity is unattainable.

Effect (topic sentence underlined): Young men seek their manhood in young women.

Elizabeth Janeway (born 1913) is a novelist and a social critic. The paragraph below is from one of her books on women's changing roles in society, *Man's World, Woman's Place: A Study in Social Mythology* (1971).

Urbanization and industrialization have changed everyone's way of living, not only that of women; but, as in so many other matters, the changes for men and the changes for women are different. To put it at its simplest, men work in the labor market and they therefore work outside the home—with a very few special exceptions, mostly in the arts. Their work and their homes are separate. Women's lives are divided, too, if they work outside the home, but the division falls in a different place. In their homes they work for the welfare and well-being of their immediate families as their great-grandmother used to do. But if they have to work for money, they can't make it at home. They must turn to the labor market and, like men, work as part of an industrial or commercial enterprise. Whether it is large or small, they work with people to whom they are not related, at a schedule they do not control and usually at a job that bears no relation to what they do in the rest of their working time at home. This experience can be very valuable indeed, if only because it keeps women in touch with the way the world runs. But it means that while

Causes (topic sentence underlined): urbanization and industrialization

Effects on men: They work outside the home.

Effects on women:

They work in the home (as in the past) . . .

. . . and outside the home (like men).

The two kinds of women's work are unrelated.

men almost all work in just one way, women who work work in two ways. The change from one sort of work to the other may often be stimulating, but it contributes to the part-timeness that is so characteristic of women's lives. They are the original moonlighters.

Women lead fragmented lives.

DEVELOPING AN ESSAY BY CAUSE-AND-EFFECT ANALYSIS

Getting Started

Assignments in almost any course or line of work ask for cause-and-effect analysis: What caused the Vietnam War? In the theory of sociobiology, what are the effects of altruism on the survival of the group? Why did costs exceed the budget last month? You can find your own subject for cause-and-effect analysis from your experiences, from observation of others, from your course work, or from your reading outside school. Anytime you find yourself wondering what happened or why or what if, you may be onto an appropriate subject.

Remember that your treatment of causes or effects or both must be thorough; thus your subject must be manageable within the constraints of time and space imposed on you. Broad subjects like those below must be narrowed to something whose complexities you can cover adequately.

BROAD SUBJECT	Causes of the decline in American industrial productivity
NARROWER SUBJECT	Causes of decreasing productivity on one assembly line
BROAD SUBJECT	Effects of cigarette smoke
NARROWER SUBJECT	Effects of parents' secondhand smoke on small children

Whether your subject suggests a focus on causes or effects, or both, list as many of them as you can from memory or from further reading. If the subject does not suggest a focus, then ask yourself questions to begin exploring it:

- Why did it happen?
- What contributed to it?
- What were or are its results?
- What might its consequences be?

One or more of these questions should lead you to a focus and, as you explore further, to a more complete list of ideas.

But you cannot stop with a simple list, for you must arrange the causes or effects in sequence and weigh their relative importance: Do the events sort out into a causal chain? Besides the immediate causes and effects, are there also less obvious, more remote ones? Besides the major causes or effects, are there also minor ones? At this stage, you may find that diagramming relationships helps you see them more clearly. The diagram below illustrates the earlier example of the plant closing (see p. 283):

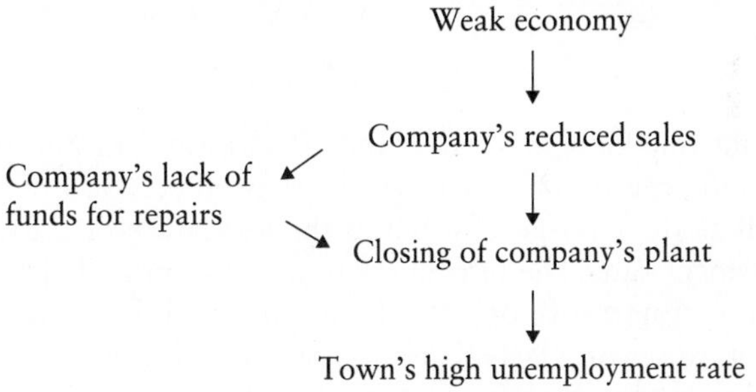

Though uncomplicated, the diagram does sort out the causes and effects and show their relationships and sequence.

While you are developing a clear picture of your subject, you should also be anticipating the expectations and needs of your readers. As with the other methods of essay development, consider especially what your readers already know about your subject and what they need to be told:

- Do readers require background information?
- Are they likely to be familiar with some of the causes or effects you are analyzing, or should you explain every one completely?
- Which causes or effects might readers already accept?
- Which ones might they disagree with? If, for instance, the plant closing affected many of your readers—putting them or their relatives out of work—they might blame the company's owners rather than economic forces beyond the owners' control. You would have to address these preconceptions and provide plenty of evidence for your own interpretation.

To help manage your ideas and information, try to develop a thesis sentence that states your subject, your perspective on it, and your purpose. The thesis sentence should reflect your judgments about the relative significance of possible causes or effects. For instance:

> EXPLANATORY THESIS SENTENCE Being caught in the middle of a family quarrel has affected not only my feelings about my family but also my relations with friends.
>
> PERSUASIVE THESIS SENTENCE Contrary to local opinion, the many people put out of work by the closing of Windsor Manufacturing were victims not of the owners' incompetence but of the nation's weak economy.

Organizing

The introduction to a cause-and-effect essay can pull readers in by describing the situation whose causes or effects you plan to analyze, such as the passage of a bill in the legislature or a town's high unemployment rate. The introduction may also provide background, such as a brief narrative of a family quarrel; or it may summarize the analysis of causes or effects that the essay disputes, such as the townspeople's blaming the owners for a plant's closing. If your thesis is not already apparent in the introduction, stating it explicitly can tell readers exactly what your purpose is and which causes or effects or both you plan to highlight. But if you anticipate that readers will oppose your thesis, you may want to delay stating it until the end of the essay, after you have provided the evidence to support it.

The arrangement of the body of the essay depends primarily on your material and your emphasis. If events unfold in a causal chain with each effect becoming the cause of another effect, and if stressing these links coincides with your purpose, then a simple chronological sequence will probably be clearest. But if events overlap and vary in significance, their organization will require more planning. Probably the most effective way to arrange either causes or effects is in order of increasing importance. Such an arrangement helps readers see which causes or effects you consider minor and which major, while it also reserves your most significant (and probably most detailed) point for last. The groups of minor or major events may then fit into a chronological framework.

To avoid being preoccupied with organization while you are drafting your essay, prepare some sort of outline before you start writing. The outline need not be detailed so long as you have written the details elsewhere or can retrieve them easily from your mind. But it should show all the causes or effects you want to discuss and the order in which you will cover them.

To conclude your essay, you may want to restate your thesis—or state it, if you deliberately withheld it for the end—so that readers are left with the point of your analysis. If your analysis is complex, readers may also benefit from a summary of the relationships you have identified. And depending on your purpose, you may want to specify why your analysis is significant, what use your readers can make of it, or what action you hope they will take.

Drafting

While drafting your essay, strive primarily for clarity—sharp details, strong examples, concrete explanations. To make readers see not only *what* you see but also *why* you see it, you can draw on just about any method of writing discussed in this book. For instance, you might narrate the effect of a situation on one person, analyze a process, or compare and contrast two interpretations of cause. Particularly if your thesis is debatable (like the earlier example asserting the owners' blamelessness for the plant's closing), you will need accurate, representative facts to back up your interpretation, and you may also need quotations from experts such as witnesses and scholars. If you do not support your assertions specifically, your readers will have no reason to believe them. (For more on evidence in persuasive writing, see pp. 316 and 323–24.)

Revising and Editing

While revising and editing your draft, consider the following questions and the box on the next page to be sure your analysis is sound and clear.

- *Have you explained causes or effects clearly and specifically?* Readers will need to see the pattern of causes or effects—their sequence and relative importance. And readers will need facts, examples, and other evidence to understand and accept your analysis.
- *Have you demonstrated that causes are not merely coincidences?* Avoid the error of post hoc, of assuming that one event caused

another just because it preceded the other. To be convincing, a claim that one event caused another must be supported with ample evidence.

- *Have you considered all the possible causes or effects?* Your analysis should go beyond what is most immediate or obvious so that you do not oversimplify the cause-and-effect relationships. Your readers will expect you to present the relationships in all their complexity.

FOCUS ON CLARITY AND CONCISENESS

While drafting a cause-and-effect analysis, you may need to grope a bit to discover just what you think about the sequence and relative importance of reasons and consequences. As a result, your sentences may grope a bit, too, reflecting your initial confusion or your need to circle around your ideas in order to find them. The following draft passage reveals such difficulties:

> WORDY AND UNCLEAR Employees often worry about suggestive comments from others. The employee may not only worry but feel the need to discuss the situation with co-workers. One thing that is an effect of sexual harassment, even verbal harassment, in the workplace is that productivity is lost. Plans also need to be made to figure out how to deal with future comments. Engaging in these activities is sure to take time and concentration from work.

Drafting this passage, the writer seems to have built up to the idea about lost productivity (third sentence) after providing support for it in the first two sentences. The fourth sentence then adds more support. And sentences 2–4 all show a writer working out his ideas: sentence subjects and verbs do not focus on the main actors and actions of the sentences, words repeat unnecessarily, and word groups run longer than needed for clarity.

These problems disappear from the edited version below, which moves the main ideas up front, uses subjects and verbs to state what the sentences are about, and cuts unneeded words.

> CONCISE AND CLEAR Even verbal sexual harassment in the workplace causes a loss of productivity. Worrying about suggestive comments from others, discussing those comments with co-workers, planning how to deal with future comments—all these activities take time and concentration that a harassed employee could spend on work.

For more on editing for conciseness and clarity, see pages 45–49.

- *Have you represented the cause-and-effect relationships honestly?* Don't deliberately ignore or exaggerate causes or effects in a misguided effort to strengthen your essay. If a cause fails to support your thesis but still does not invalidate it, mention the cause and explain why you believe it to be unimportant. If a change you are proposing will have bad effects as well as good, mention the bad effects and explain how they are outweighed by the good. As long as your reasoning and evidence are sound, such admissions will not weaken your essay; on the contrary, readers will appreciate your fairness.
- *Have you used transitions to signal the sequence and relative importance of events?* Transitions between sentences can help you pinpoint causes or effects (*for this reason, as a result*), show the steps in a sequence (*first, second, third*), link events in time (*in the same month*), specify duration (*a year later*), and indicate the weights you assign events (*equally important, even more crucial*). (See also *transitions* in the Glossary.)

A NOTE ON THEMATIC CONNECTIONS

The differences between men and women continually engage writers in a search for causes and effects. In this chapter the authors try to explain how men's and women's environments affect their lives. In paragraphs, Mark Gerzon suggests reasons why young men seek out young women (p. 284) and Elizabeth Janeway explains why women's lives are often fragmented (p. 285). Deborah Tannen's essay probes the differing attitudes of men and women toward computers (next page). Jon Katz's essay considers how boys push each other to become tough men (p. 298). And Amy Beck's essay views the media images of women as a significant cause of their eating disorders and their abuse by men (p. 303).

Deborah Tannen

Well known for her books on how men and women communicate, Deborah Tannen is a linguist with a knack for popular writing. She was born in 1945 in Brooklyn, New York, and attended Hunter College High School in Manhattan. She received a B.A. in 1966 from Harpur College (now the State University of New York at Binghamton), M.A. degrees in 1970 from Wayne State University and in 1976 from the University of California at Berkeley, and a linguistics Ph.D. in 1979 from Berkeley. Tannen attributes her interest in linguistics partly to a childhood hearing impairment that, she says, schooled her in "tone of voice, attitude, and all the other conversational signals" in addition to the words themselves. She has been teaching linguistics since 1979 at Georgetown University, has published extensively in scholarly and popular periodicals, and has lectured widely. Her best-selling books, all concerning communication breakdowns and how to repair them, are That's Not What I Meant! *(1986),* You Just Don't Understand *(1990),* Talking 9 to 5 *(1994), and* The Argument Culture *(1998).*

Gender Gap in Cyberspace

Tannen's most popular books examine differences in the ways men and women talk to each other. Here she branches out to probe another gender difference, in the ways men and women use computers. Why is it, she asks, that men seek to dominate the machines while women just want the things to work properly? This essay first appeared in Newsweek *in 1994.*

I was a computer pioneer, but I'm still something of a novice. That paradox is telling. 1

I was the second person on my block to get a computer. The first was my colleague Ralph. It was 1980. Ralph got a Radio Shack TRS-80; I got a used Apple II+. He helped me get started and went on to become a maven, reading computer magazines, hungering for the new technology he read about, and buying and mastering it as quickly as he could afford. I hung on to old equipment far too long because I dislike giving up what I'm used to, fear making the wrong decision about what to buy, and resent the time it takes to install and learn a new system. 2

My first Apple came with videogames; I gave them away. Playing 3
games on the computer didn't interest me. If I had free time I'd spend it talking on the telephone to friends.

Ralph got hooked. His wife was often annoyed by the hours he 4
spent at his computer and the money he spent upgrading it. My marriage had no such strains—until I discovered e-mail. Then I got hooked. E-mail draws me the same way the phone does: it's a souped-up conversation.

E-mail deepened my friendship with Ralph. Though his office 5
was next to mine, we rarely had extended conversations because he is shy. Face to face he mumbled so, I could barely tell he was speaking. But when we both got on e-mail, I started receiving long, self-revealing messages; we poured our hearts out to each other. A friend discovered that e-mail opened up that kind of communication with her father. He would never talk much on the phone (as her mother would), but they have become close since they both got online.

Why, I wondered, would some men find it easier to open up on 6
e-mail? It's a combination of the technology (which they enjoy) and the obliqueness of the written word, just as many men will reveal feelings in dribs and drabs while riding in the car or doing something, which they'd never talk about sitting face to face. It's too intense, too bearing-down on them, and once you start you have to keep going. With a computer in between, it's safer.

It was on e-mail, in fact, that I described to Ralph how boys in 7
groups often struggle to get the upper hand whereas girls tend to maintain an appearance of cooperation. And he pointed out that this explained why boys are more likely to be captivated by computers than girls are. Boys are typically motivated by a social structure that says if you don't dominate you will be dominated. Computers, by their nature, balk; you type a perfectly appropriate command and it refuses to do what it should. Many boys and men are incited by this defiance: "I'm going to whip this into line and teach it who's boss! I'll get it to do what I say!" (and if they work hard enough, they always can). Girls and women are more likely to respond, "This thing won't cooperate. Get it away from me!"

Although no one wants to think of herself as "typical"—how 8
much nicer to be *sui generis*[1]—my relationship to my computer is —gulp—fairly typical for a woman. Most women (with plenty of

[1] *Sui generis* is Latin meaning "of its own kind," "unique." [Editor's note.]

exceptions) aren't excited by tinkering with the technology, grappling with the challenge of eliminating bugs or getting the biggest and best computer. These dynamics appeal to many men's interest in making sure they're on the top side of the inevitable who's-up-who's-down struggle that life is for them. E-mail appeals to my view of life as a contest for connections to others. When I see that I have fifteen messages, I feel loved.

I once posted a technical question on a computer network for linguists and was flooded with long dispositions, some pages long. I was staggered by the generosity and the expertise, but wondered where these guys found the time—and why all the answers I got were from men. 9

Like coed classrooms and meetings, discussions on e-mail networks tend to be dominated by male voices, unless they're specifically women-only, like single-sex schools. Online, women don't have to worry about getting the floor (you just send a message when you feel like it), but, according to linguists Susan Herring and Laurel Sutton, who have studied this, they have the usual problems of having their messages ignored or attacked. The anonymity of public networks frees a small number of men to send long, vituperative, sarcastic messages that many other men either can tolerate or actually enjoy, but that turn most women off. 10

The anonymity of networks leads to another sad part of the e-mail story: there are men who deluge women with questions about their appearance and invitations to sex. On college campuses, as soon as women students log on, they are bombarded by references to sex, like going to work and finding pornographic posters adorning the walls. 11

Most women want one thing from a computer—to work. This is significant counterevidence to the claim that men want to focus on information while women are interested in rapport. That claim I found was often true in casual conversation, in which there is no particular information to be conveyed. But with computers, it is often women who are more focused on information, because they don't respond to the challenge of getting equipment to submit. 12

Once I had learned the basics, my interest in computers waned. I use it to write books (though I never mastered having it do bibliographies or tables of contents) and write checks (but not balance my checkbook). Much as I'd like to use it to do more, I begrudge the time it would take to learn. 13

Ralph's computer expertise costs him a lot of time. Chivalry requires that he rescue novices in need, and he is called upon by damsel 14 novices far more often than knaves. More men would rather study the instruction booklet than ask directions, as it were, from another person. "When I do help men," Ralph wrote (on e-mail, of course), "they want to be more involved. I once installed a hard drive for a guy, and he wanted to be there with me, wielding the screwdriver and giving his own advice where he could." Women, he finds, usually are not interested in what he's doing; they just want him to get the computer to the point where they can do what they want.

Which pretty much explains how I managed to be a pioneer 15
without becoming an expert.

Meaning

1. How do Tannen and her colleague Ralph relate to computers differently? What larger point is Tannen trying to make through this example?
2. What is the "paradox" Tannen identifies in paragraph 1? (A *paradox* is a statement or situation that seems contradictory.) How does she explain the paradox?
3. Tannen writes, "Most women want one thing from a computer—to work. This is significant counterevidence to the claim that men want to focus on information while women are interested in rapport" (paragraph 12). What does *counterevidence* mean? What point is Tannen making in this paragraph?
4. What is Tannen's explanation for why, when she posted a technical question on a computer network, she received responses only from men?
5. If any of the following words are new to you, try to guess their meanings from the context of Tannen's essay. Look up the words in a dictionary to check your guesses, and then try to use each word in a sentence or two of your own.

novice (1)	linguists (9)	begrudge (13)
maven (2)	dispositions (9)	chivalry (14)
obliqueness (6)	vituperative (10)	damsel (14)
balk (7)	rapport (12)	knaves (14)
incited (7)	waned (13)	

Purpose and Audience

1. In paragraph 5 Tannen says, "E-mail deepened my friendship with Ralph." Why does she tell us this? What purpose does it serve in her discussion?

2. What can you assume about Tannen's original readers? What assumptions does she make about them?

Method and Structure

1. What prompted Tannen to seek out the causes for why women and men respond differently to computers? What causes does she identify?
2. Tannen concludes with a paragraph that is not even a complete sentence. What effect does this last paragraph have, and how does it connect to her essay as a whole?
3. **Other Methods** What does Tannen gain by using the example (Chapter 6) of her relationship with Ralph?

Language

1. What do you notice about Tannen's use of language? Is it technical? formal? conversational? Give examples from the essay to support your answer. How effective do you find this style? (If necessary, consult *style* in the Glossary.)
2. "Computers, by their nature, balk: you type a perfectly appropriate command and it refuses to do what it should" (paragraph 7). How would you characterize Tannen's tone in this passage, and what effect does it have? What figure of speech is she using? (See pp. 51–52 on figures of speech.)

Writing Topics

1. **Journal Response** Tannen details her personal experience with computers as partial evidence for her conclusions about a much larger issue: the "gender gap in cyberspace." Think of a question you'd like answered, one that you have some personal experience with. For example: Why do men seem to like sports more than women? Or why do so many children of doctors become doctors themselves? Write down your experiences and opinions on the question you choose.
   Journal to Essay Write a cause-and-effect essay in which you use your own experiences as partial support for the answer to your question. In the essay, identify the effect you want to explain, and then detail the causes as you understand them.
2. Tannen claims that in casual conversation, "men want to focus on information while women are interested in rapport" (paragraph 12). Write an essay in which you rely on your experiences and observations to agree or disagree with this claim.

3. **Cultural Considerations** Tannen asserts that the differences between girls and boys translate into differences between women and men. Spend some time researching the differences between the culture of girls and the culture of boys. (An encyclopedia of psychology or sociology can get you started, as can a periodical index such as the *Readers' Guide to Periodical Literature* or the *Social Sciences Index*.) Select a conclusion about a difference that you find especially interesting and write an essay that details your findings and relates them to your personal experience. Be sure the essay has a central, controlling idea about gender difference.
4. **Connections** Elizabeth Janeway writes that "while men almost all work in just one way, women who work work in two ways" (pp. 285–86). To what extent do you think the division of labor discussed by Janeway influences the different responses to computers discussed by Tannen? Write an essay in which you analyze Tannen's essay in relation to Janeway's paragraph. Use specific examples from both pieces and from your own experience to support your ideas.

Jon Katz

Born in 1947, Jon Katz is a journalist and critic. He has worked as a reporter and editor at a number of American newspapers—the Washington Post, *the* Boston Globe, *the* Dallas Times-Herald, *and the* Philadelphia Inquirer *—and in television as executive producer of the* CBS Morning News. *In magazines he has been the media critic for* New York *and* Rolling Stone, *and he is now a contributing editor at* Wired *magazine. Katz has written a book about values and the media,* Virtual Reality, *and five novels:* Sign Off, Death by Station Wagon, The Family Stalker, The Last Housewife, *and* Death Row: A Suburban Detective Mystery. *He lives in New Jersey with his wife and daughter.*

How Boys Become Men

In this essay Katz veers from hard news and media criticism, drawing on personal experience to explain why many men seem insensitive. The essay was published in January 1993 in Glamour, *a magazine for young women.*

Two nine-year-old boys, neighbors and friends, were walking home from school. The one in the bright blue windbreaker was laughing and swinging a heavy-looking book bag toward the head of his friend, who kept ducking and stepping back. "What's the matter?" asked the kid with the bag, whooshing it over his head. "You chicken?" 1

His friend stopped, stood still and braced himself. The bag slammed into the side of his face, the thump audible all the way across the street where I stood watching. The impact knocked him to the ground, where he lay mildly stunned for a second. Then he struggled up, rubbing the side of his head. "See?" he said proudly. "I'm no chicken." 2

No. A chicken would probably have had the sense to get out of the way. This boy was already well on the road to becoming a *man*, having learned one of the central ethics of his gender: Experience pain rather than show fear. 3

Women tend to see men as a giant problem in need of solution. They tell us that we're remote and uncommunicative, that we need to 4 demonstrate less machismo and more commitment, more humanity. But if you don't understand something about boys, you can't understand why men are the way we are, why we find it so difficult to make friends or to acknowledge our fears and problems.

Boys live in a world with its own Code of Conduct, a set of ruthless, unspoken, and unyielding rules: 5

> Don't be a goody-goody.
>
> Never rat. If your parents ask about bruises, shrug.
>
> Never admit fear. Ride the roller coaster, join the fistfight, do what you have to do. Asking for help is for sissies.
>
> Empathy is for nerds. You can help your best buddy, under certain circumstances. Everyone else is on his own.
>
> Never discuss anything of substance with anybody. Grunt, shrug, dump on teachers, laugh at wimps, talk about comic books. Anything else is risky.

Boys are rewarded for throwing hard. Most other activities—reading, befriending girls, or just thinking—are considered weird. And if there's one thing boys don't want to be, it's weird. 6

More than anything else, boys are supposed to learn how to handle themselves. I remember the bitter fifth-grade conflict I touched off by elbowing aside a bigger boy named Barry and seizing the cafeteria's last carton of chocolate milk. Teased for getting aced out by a wimp, he had to reclaim his place in the pack. Our fistfight, at recess, ended with my knees buckling and my lip bleeding while my friends, sympathetic but out of range, watched resignedly. 7

When I got home, my mother took one look at my swollen face and screamed. I wouldn't tell her anything, but when my father got home I cracked and confessed, pleading with them to do nothing. Instead, they called Barry's parents, who restricted his television for a week. 8

The following morning, Barry and six of his pals stepped out from behind a stand of trees. "It's the rat," said Barry. 9

I bled a little more. *Rat* was scrawled in crayon across my desk. 10

They were waiting for me after school for a number of afternoons to follow. I tried varying my routes and avoiding bushes and hedges. It usually didn't work. 11

I was as ashamed for telling as I was frightened. "You did ask for it," said my best friend. Frontier Justice has nothing on Boy Justice. 12

In panic, I appealed to a cousin who was several years older. He followed me home from school, and when Barry's gang surrounded 13 me, he came barreling toward us. "Stay away from my cousin," he shouted, "or I'll kill you."

After they were gone, however, my cousin could barely stop laughing. "You were afraid of *them?*" he howled. "They barely came up to my waist." 14

Men remember receiving little mercy as boys; maybe that's why it's sometimes difficult for them to show any. 15

"I know lots of men who had happy childhoods, but none who have happy memories of the way other boys treated them," says a friend. "It's a macho marathon from third grade up, when you start butting each other in the stomach." 16

"The thing is," adds another friend, "you learn early on to hide what you feel. It's never safe to say, 'I'm scared.' My girlfriend asks me why I don't talk more about what I'm feeling. I've gotten better at it, but it will *never* come naturally." 17

You don't need to be a shrink to see how the lessons boys learn affect their behavior as men. Men are being asked, more and more, to show sensitivity, but they dread the very word. They struggle to build their increasingly uncertain work lives but will deny they're in trouble. They want love, affection, and support but don't know how to ask for them. They hide their weaknesses and fears from all, even those they care for. They've learned to be wary of intervening when they see others in trouble. They often still balk at being stigmatized as weird. 18

Some men get shocked into sensitivity—when they lose their jobs, their wives, or their lovers. Others learn it through a strong marriage, or through their own children. 19

It may be a long while, however, before male culture evolves to the point that boys can learn more from one another than how to hit curve balls. Last month, walking my dog past the playground near my house, I saw three boys encircling a fourth, laughing and pushing him. He was skinny and rumpled, and he looked frightened. One boy knelt behind him while another pushed him from the front, a trick familiar to any former boy. He fell backward. 20

When the others ran off, he brushed the dirt off his elbows and walked toward the swings. His eyes were moist and he was struggling for control. 21

"Hi," I said through the chain-link fence. "How ya doing?" 22

"Fine," he said quickly, kicking his legs out and beginning his swing. 23

Meaning

1. Katz lists five unspoken rules of what he calls boys' Code of Conduct. What are these rules, and how do they affect the behavior of men?
2. What is Katz's main idea?
3. Katz says "Frontier Justice has nothing on Boy Justice" (paragraph 12). What do you think he means?
4. Try to guess the meanings of any word below that you don't already know, using the context of Katz's essay as a guide. Test your guesses in a dictionary, and then use the words in sentences of your own.

audible (2)	empathy (5)	intervening (18)
ethics (3)	resignedly (7)	stigmatized (18)
machismo (4)		

Purpose and Audience

1. Do you think Katz wrote this piece to entertain with boyhood stories, or did he have some larger purpose in mind? If so, what was it? How do you know?
2. Who do you think Katz's intended audience is? (Consider the magazine in which this column appeared.) What in the text specifically acknowledges this audience?
3. What do you think of Katz's characterizations of boys and men? Do you know people like those he describes? Does he overgeneralize, and if so, where? Does your own gender influence your responses?

Method and Structure

1. Where does Katz explicitly defend his use of cause-and-effect analysis to explain why men are remote and uncommunicative?
2. Katz opens and closes his essay with brief stories about boyhood behavior he has recently witnessed. What is the effect of these stories?
3. Katz's evidence for causes and effects consists of observations of boys (paragraphs 1–2, 20–23), the comments of some friends (16, 17), and an extended story about his own boyhood (7–14). How convincing do you find this evidence? Why do you think Katz doesn't offer expert opinions, statistics, and other more formal evidence for his analysis?
4. **Other Methods** Besides cause-and-effect analysis, Katz uses narration (Chapter 5) and example (Chapter 6). Locate instances of each, and consider how they contribute to the essay as a whole.

Language

1. How would you describe Katz's tone? Is it the same throughout?
2. In paragraph 4 Katz addresses his audience as *you* and includes himself in the category of men with *we*. In paragraph 18 he refers to men as *they*. Why do you suppose Katz shifts pronouns in this way? What happens in between?
3. Katz capitalizes words that do not normally require capitals: "Code of Conduct" (paragraph 5) and "Frontier Justice" and "Boy Justice" (12). What effect do the capitals have?

Writing Topics

1. **Journal Response** Katz quotes a friend as saying, "I know lots of men who had happy childhoods, but none who have happy memories of the way other boys treated them" (paragraph 16). If you are a man, do you agree or disagree with this statement, based on your own experiences of boyhood? If you are a woman, to what extent would this statement, if said of women, describe your experiences and observations of girlhood? Write down your responses.
   Journal to Essay Starting with your journal notes, write an essay in which you explain how relationships with other children colored your own boyhood or girlhood. Did other children help or hurt you, or both? What have been the lasting effects of these experiences?
2. Katz claims that the ruthlessness of boys shapes their remote, insensitive behavior as men. Write an essay that proposes a new Code of Conduct for children—both males and females—that might lead to healthier interactions as adults. Discuss what changes would need to occur in the existing social structure, outline the code, and explain what effects it would have.
3. **Cultural Considerations** However true Katz's observations may be for his culture, they surely don't apply to all boys and men everywhere. In an essay explain the Code of Conduct for boys in a culture you know well. It could be in another country, in an extended family, in a religion, in a club or other organization. How does this code influence the way boys become men? Be specific, offering narrative examples, as Katz does, or more formal expert opinions and statistics.
4. **Connections** Deborah Tannen (p. 292) writes, "Boys are typically motivated by a social structure that says if you don't dominate you will be dominated" (paragraph 7). Do you think Katz would agree with this? Write a brief essay in which you analyze Katz's essay in relation to Tannen's observation. What examples does Katz provide to support Tannen's claim? What comments does he make that might counter her claim?

Amy L. Beck

Born in 1979, Amy L. Beck graduated from Greenwich, Connecticut, High School in 1996, after spending her junior year as an exchange student in Venezuela. She now attends Harvard University, class of 2000, as a history and science major. At Harvard she founded a dance troupe, is a member of a theatrical group that performs educational shows about eating disorders, and tutors high school students. She spent a summer as an intern at a large hospital, another summer in France as a researcher for the travel guide Let's Go France, *and a semester as an intern with the French Public Health Administration.*

Struggling for Perfection

In this essay published in the Harvard Crimson *in 1998, Beck draws on her experiences working in a hospital to show how media images of women contribute both to their self-abuse and to their abuse by others.*

Sex sells. This truth is a boon for marketing gurus and the pornography industry but a rather unfortunate situation for women. Every issue of *Playboy,* every lewd poster and even the Victoria's Secret catalogue transform real women into ornaments, valued exclusively for their outward appearance. These publications are responsible for defining what is sexy and reinforce the belief that aesthetic appeal is a woman's highest virtue. 1

Some argue that the proliferation of pornography and other sexually explicit images of women is both harmless for society and inevitable. Just this point was made in a recent *Crimson* column titled "In Defense of Hooters and the St. Pauli Girl." In the tone of an expert, the author boldly claims that the objectification of women in the media does not affect the way men treat the real women in their lives, nor does it give those with pathological tendencies "the decisive nudge into misogyny." Furthermore, the author says, those women who feel pressure to conform to beauty standards set by the media are suffering from a classic psychosis in which they "confuse fiction with reality." 2

My first reaction was to ask how anyone could possibly believe that the pervasiveness of pornography and sexually explicit de- 3 pictions of women could fail to have any sort of effect on society. Having spent twelve weeks working in a psychiatric hospital last summer, I am writing from a starkly different perspective.

During my first eight weeks at the hospital, I worked on an eat- 4
ing disorder unit in constant contact with anorexics and bulimics. Many patients on the unit were so emaciated that I could never accustom myself to their appearance; every time I saw them I experienced the same shock. Most had been in and out of countless other hospitals and treatment programs, improving slightly each time but always sliding back into eating-disordered behavior when released.

These people were truly at rock bottom, considered by many to 5
be incurable. Their eating disorders had consumed them entirely, leaving no trace of the vibrant, intelligent people that once inhabited their now skeletal bodies. Certainly, these people also had family problems, alcoholic parents, histories of abuse and clinical depression, to name a few, all of which contribute to feelings of worthlessness and extremely low self-esteem—cited by experts as a major cause of eating disorders. What I find significant, however, is not the root of their problems but that these women (there were a few men, but never more than five percent of the patient population) turned to their bodies as a means of expression and self-healing. Profoundly influenced by the depiction of women by the fashion industry, they had been convinced that the only way to attain love, respect, and personal fulfillment was through a relentless pursuit of physical perfection. Most were perfectly aware that they would never look like a supermodel, but it was inconceivable not to try to do so. They found that they were good at dieting and that they were praised and rewarded for their success. And by the time things had gone too far, they had lost all sense of perspective.

Convinced by the media and popular culture to believe that, as 6
women, they should look a certain way and that only if they looked that way would they be loved and respected, they turned to dieting as a means of personal fulfillment and self-definition. While cases as extreme as those I saw at the hospital are rare, many women experience milder but still debilitating forms of eating disorders. They may never get sick enough to require hospitalization, but they nonetheless devote excessive mental and physical energy to diet and exercise, often jeopardizing their health in the process.

For my last four weeks at the hospital I transferred from eating 7
disorders to a general psychology unit. The diagnoses varied, but the number of patients with histories of abuse was astounding. After lis-

tening to and reading countless case histories, I began to recognize the patterns. In many cases, domestic battering was chronic, occurring weekly or daily whenever the victim broke some sort of household rule, such as serving dinner late or dressing "too sexy." The majority of the sexual abuse victims had been raped by people close to them: relatives, ex-boyfriends, or family friends. In one particularly striking case, a patient's boyfriend made her have sex with five of his friends on a frequent basis.

The men who committed these heinous crimes were rarely pathological rapists or batterers. Few would even be deemed mentally ill or classically misogynistic. Rather, they are men who view the real women in their lives in the same manner that they would view a *Playboy* model, a waitress at Hooters or a prostitute—as objects that exist solely for their pleasure and convenience. These men are not genetically predisposed to disrespect and abuse women. Their attitudes towards women were societally conditioned. 8

Some would argue that pornography did not contribute to these men's behavior towards women. I disagree. Rape and battery are not new problems, and objectification of women by the media reinforces historically entrenched beliefs that a woman's main reason for existence is procreation and the sexual pleasure of her mate. Pornographic magazines and lewd posters reduce women to a commodity that can be purchased and owned, divorcing the physical manifestation from the person within. The power of popular culture to affect how we eat, how we dress and how we behave is enormous. Conceptions of gender are in no way immune to this phenomenon. 9

Certainly some of us are more affected by the media than others. Not all teenage girls develop anorexia, nor do all men who read *Playboy* abuse their wives. Nonetheless, the prevalence of both eating disorders and various forms of domestic and sexual abuse indicate major societal trends. The American Anorexia/Bulimia Association reports that 5 percent of women will develop a full-fledged eating disorder, while 15 percent have "substantially disordered eating." The Family Violence Prevention Program documents that 4 million American women were battered last year. And, yes, I am absolutely convinced that the objectification of women by the media is an integral part of both of these problems, presenting women with unrealistic role models while encouraging men to think of women solely in terms of their sexuality. 10

Women are up against a long history of devaluation and oppression, and, unfortunately, the feminist movements have been only 11 partially successful in purging those legacies. Sexually charged images of women in the media are not the only cause of this continuing problem, but they certainly play a central role.

Meaning

1. What is Beck's thesis? Is it persuasive or explanatory?
2. What are the two causes and two effects that Beck identifies in this essay?
3. Why does Beck stress that men who abuse women are "rarely pathological rapists or batterers" (paragraph 8)? Is she seeking to excuse these men?
4. Try to guess the meanings of any of the following words you don't already know by studying their context in Beck's essay. Check your guesses in a dictionary, and then use the words in sentences of your own.

gurus (1)	psychosis (2)	procreation (9)
aesthetic (1)	emaciated (4)	commodity (9)
proliferation (2)	debilitating (6)	manifestation (9)
objectification (2)	chronic (7)	devaluation (11)
pathological (2)	heinous (8)	purging (11)
misogyny (2)	predisposed (8)	legacies (11)

Purpose and Audience

1. Beck wrote this article in part as a response to another article in the *Harvard Crimson,* which she refers to in paragraph 2. What else do you think may have motivated her to write this piece? What do you think she wanted the essay to accomplish?
2. What assumptions does Beck make about her audience? Does she assume her readers' agreement with her ideas, or is she also writing for people who might disagree? How can you tell?

Method and Structure

1. Why do you think Beck chose cause-and-effect analysis to write about eating disorders and abuse? Does this method provide an effective means of achieving her purpose?
2. Summarize the causal chain Beck identifies in paragraph 5.
3. Why does Beck grant that media images of women only partly account for abuse and eating disorders? Do the qualifications weaken Beck's argument?

4. **Other Methods** What does Beck accomplish by describing (Chapter 4) and narrating (Chapter 5) her experience at the psychiatric hospital (paragraphs 4–8)? How persuasive do you find this evidence?

Language

1. What is Beck's overall tone? Impassioned? Angry? Cool? Solemn? Is the tone appropriate for the subject?
2. What effect does Beck achieve with her opening sentence?
3. Beck criticizes the other *Crimson* writer for taking the "tone of an expert" without being one (paragraph 2). But Beck is not an expert either. How does she avoid the same problem?

Writing Topics

1. **Journal Response** Think of a problem that you have a strong interest in whose causes are multiple and complex. The problem could be as serious or as unserious as you like—the appeal of radio talk shows, the sorry state of prime-time television, bad food in the cafeteria, the lack of community at your school, or anything you feel strongly about. Spend some time thinking of and writing down as many causes as you can for this problem.

   Journal to Essay Out of all the causes you generated in your journal, choose one or two that seem to be the most important or the most interesting. Write an essay in which you demonstrate how these causes helped to produce the problem. Be careful to admit the full complexity of the problem by acknowledging the other possible causes as well.
2. Write a response to Beck's essay. Do you see any weaknesses in her analysis of cause and effect? Do you find that she backs up her points with convincing and sufficient examples? Are there certain parts of her argument you agree with and not others? Does she overstate causes or fail to mention important causes?
3. **Cultural Considerations** Not all cultures permit as much exposure of and emphasis on women's bodies as American culture does; for instance, in some other cultures women cover their bodies, heads, and faces in public. What do you think of American attitudes toward the female body? Are they healthy? unhealthy? Are they an appropriate expression of women's freedom, or the result of too much freedom? What role do the media play: do they simply reflect people's behavior and attitudes, or do they lead them? From what you know of other cultures, are Americans unusual or unique in their attitudes toward women's bodies? After considering these questions (and others that may occur to you), write an essay explaining what you see as American attitudes toward the female body and what the major causes of those attitudes are.

4. **Connections** In the paragraph on pages 284–85, Mark Gerzon argues that young men, unable to find ways of living up to the movies' heroic images of masculinity in their own lives, turn to the other sex to make them feel like men. Write an essay in which you compare the effects of the media on young men and young women. What are the most important differences? You may want to draw on both Beck's and Gerzon's pieces as well as your own experiences and observations.

Writing with the Method

Cause-and-Effect Analysis

Choose one of the following questions, or any other question they suggest, and answer it in an essay developed by analyzing causes or effects. The question you decide on should concern a topic you care about so that your analysis of causes or effects is a means of communicating an idea, not an end in itself.

PEOPLE AND THEIR BEHAVIOR

1. Why is a past or present politician, athlete, or actor considered a hero?
2. Why did one couple you know marry or divorce?
3. What does a sound body contribute to a sound mind?
4. Why is a particular friend or relative always getting into trouble?
5. Why do people root for the underdog?
6. How does a person's alcohol or drug dependency affect others in his or her family?

WORK

7. At what age should a person start working for pay, and why?
8. What effects do you expect your education to have on your career?
9. Why would a man or woman enter a field that has traditionally been filled by the opposite sex, such as nursing or engineering?
10. What effect has the job market had on you and your friends?

ART AND ENTERTAINMENT

11. Why do teenagers like rock music?
12. Why have art museums become so popular?
13. What makes a professional sports team succeed in a new city?
14. Why is (or was) a particular television show or movie so popular?

CONTEMPORARY ISSUES

15. Why does the United States spend so much money on defense?
16. What are the possible effects of rising college tuitions?
17. How can a long period of involuntary unemployment affect a person?
18. Why is a college education important?
19. Why do marriages between teenagers fail more often than marriages between people in other age groups?

20. What are the possible effects of widespread adult illiteracy on American society?
21. Why might someone resort to a public act of violence, such as bombing a building?

Writing About the Theme

Exploring the Influence of Gender

1. Each of the authors in this chapter attempts to explain how gender influences the lives of women and men. Mark Gerzon (p. 284) explains how men turn to women to "feel like heroes"; Elizabeth Janeway (p. 285) asserts that women's lives are more fragmented than men's; Deborah Tannen (p. 292) looks at the differing ways men and women respond to computers; Jon Katz (p. 298) explains how the interactions between boys shape adult male behavior; and Amy Beck (p. 303) finds that media images of women contribute to their eating disorders and abuse by men. Select a gender influence not addressed in these works and write an essay that explores the influence. For example, you might examine why many of the care-giving professions, such as nursing and teaching, tend to be dominated by women; or you might research the salary differentials between men and women; or you might consider why women in public may go to the restroom in pairs, but men in public never seem to. In other words, your range of topics is wide open. Regardless of topic, you should review the cause-and-effect guidelines on pages 281–84 before beginning your analysis.
2. Mark Gerzon asserts that young men "ask women for more than companionship, or sex, or marriage. They ask women to give them what their culture could not—their manhood." Write an essay in which you explain what you think Gerzon means by this, and then discuss whether Jon Katz would agree with Gerzon. Be sure to provide evidence from both works to support your ideas.
3. Is sex destiny? That is, are our lives determined by our genes and by the social roles assigned to us as boys and girls, men and women? Write an essay that addresses this question. You could write a narrative about someone you know who broke through traditional gender roles or someone you know who tried but failed to break through. You could compare and contrast two people, one who was raised to flaunt traditional gender roles and one who was raised to flout them. You could analyze a book, movie, television show, or other media product that deals with gender: for instance, one that strongly reinforces traditional roles, one that undermines them, or one that pretends to undermine them while actually reinforcing them. Just be sure that your essay has a clear, limited thesis and plenty of details to support it.

Chapter 13

ARGUMENT AND PERSUASION

Debating Cloning

USING THE METHOD

Since we argue all the time—with relatives, with friends, with the auto mechanic or the shop clerk—a chapter devoted to argument and persuasion may at first seem unnecessary. But arguing with an auto mechanic over the cost of repairs is quite a different process from arguing with readers over a complex issue. In both cases we are trying to find common ground with our audience, perhaps to change its views or even to compel it to act as we wish. But the mechanic is in front of us; we can shift our tactics in response to his or her gestures, expressions, and words. The reader, in contrast, is "out there"; we have to anticipate those gestures, expressions, and words in the way we structure the argument, the kinds of evidence we use to support it, even the way we conceive of the subject.

A great many assertions that are worth making are debatable at some level—whether over the facts on which the assertions are based or over the values they imply. Two witnesses to an accident cannot agree on what they saw; two scientists cannot agree on what an experiment shows; two economists cannot agree on what measures will reduce unemployment; two doctors cannot agree on what constitutes life or death. Making an effective case for our opinions requires upholding certain responsibilities and attending to several established techniques of argumentation, most of them dating back to ancient Greece.

Technically, argument and persuasion are two different processes:

- **Argument** appeals mainly to an audience's sense of reason in order to negotiate a common understanding or to win agreement with a claim. It is the method of a columnist who defends a president's foreign policy on the grounds of economics and defense strategy.
- **Persuasion** appeals mainly to an audience's feelings and values in order to compel some action, or at least to win support for an action. It is the method of a mayoral candidate who urges voters to support her because she is sensitive to the poor.

But argument and persuasion so often mingle that we will use the one term *argument* to mean a deliberate appeal to an audience's reason and emotions in order to create compromise, win agreement, or compel action.

The Elements of Argument

All arguments share certain elements:

- The core of the argument is an **assertion** or **proposition,** a debatable claim about the subject. Generally, you express this assertion as your thesis statement. It may defend or attack a position, suggest a solution to a problem, recommend a change in policy, or challenge a value or belief. Here are a few examples:

  > The college should give first priority for on-campus jobs to students who need financial aid.
  >
  > School prayer has been rightly declared unconstitutional and should not be reinstituted in any form.
  >
  > Smokers who wish to poison themselves should be allowed to do so, but not in any place where their smoke will poison others.

- You break down the central assertion into subclaims, each one supported by evidence.

- You raise significant opposing arguments and dispense with them, again with the support of evidence.
- You organize the parts of the argument into a clear, logical structure that pushes steadily toward the conclusion.

You may draw on classification, comparison, or any other rhetorical method to develop the entire argument or to introduce evidence or strengthen your conclusion. For instance, in a paper arguing for raising a college's standards of admission, you might contrast the existing standards with the proposed standards, analyze a process for raising the standards over a period of years, and predict the effects of the new standards on future students' preparedness for college work.

Appeals to Readers

In arguing you are appealing to readers: you want them to listen to what you have to say, judge your words fairly, and, as much as they can, agree with you. Most arguments combine three kinds of appeals to readers: ethical, emotional, and rational.

Ethical Appeal

The **ethical appeal** is often not explicit in an argument, yet it pervades the whole. It is the sense you convey of your expertise and character, projected by the reasonableness of the argument, by the use of evidence, and by tone. A rational argument shows readers that you are thinking logically and fairly (see pp. 316–18). Strong evidence establishes your credibility (see pp. 316, 323–24). And a sincere, reasonable tone demonstrates your balance and goodwill (see p. 327).

Emotional Appeal

The **emotional appeal** in argument aims directly for readers' hearts—for the complex of beliefs, values, and feelings deeply embedded in all of us. We are just as often motivated by these ingrained ideas and emotions as by our intellects. Even scientists, who stress the rational interpretation of facts above all else, are sometimes influenced in their interpretations by emotions deriving from, say, competition with other scientists. And the willingness of a nation's citizens to go to war may result more from their fear and pride than from their reasoned considerations of risks and gains. An emotional appeal in argument attempts to tap such feelings for any of several reasons:

- To heighten the responsiveness of readers
- To inspire readers to new beliefs
- To compel readers to act
- To assure readers that their values remain unchallenged

An emotional appeal may be explicit, as when an argument against capital punishment appeals to readers' religious values by citing the Bible's Sixth Commandment, "Thou shalt not kill." But an emotional appeal may also be less obvious, because individual words may have connotations that elicit emotional responses from readers. For instance, one writer may characterize an environmental group as "a well-organized team representing diverse interests," while another may call the same group "a hodgepodge of nature lovers and irresponsible businesspeople." The first appeals to readers' preference for order and balance, the second to readers' fear of extremism and disdain for unsound business practices. (See pp. 50 and 327 for more on connotation.)

The use of emotional appeals requires care:

- The appeal must be directed at the audience's actual beliefs and feelings.
- The appeal must be presented dispassionately enough so that readers have no reason to doubt your fairness in the rest of the argument.
- The appeal must be appropriate to the subject and to the argument. For instance, in arguing against a pay raise for city councilors, you might be tempted to appeal to readers' resentment and distrust of wealthy people by pointing out that two of the councilors are rich enough to work for nothing. But such an appeal would divert attention from the issue of whether the pay raise is justified for all councilors on the basis of the work they do and the city's ability to pay the extra cost.

Carefully used, emotional appeals have great force, particularly when they contribute to an argument based largely on sound reasoning and evidence. The appropriate mix of emotion and reason in a given essay is entirely dependent on the subject, your purpose, and the audience. Emotional appeals are out of place in most arguments in the natural and social sciences, where rational interpretations of factual evidence are all that will convince readers of the truth of an assertion. But emotional appeals may be essential when you want an audience to support or take an action, for emotion is a stronger motivator than reason.

Rational Appeal

A **rational appeal** is one that, as the name implies, addresses the rational faculties of readers—their capacity to reason logically about a problem. You establish the truth of a proposition or claim by moving through a series of related subclaims, each supported by evidence. In doing so, you follow processes of reasoning that are natural to all of us and thus are expected by readers. These processes are induction and deduction.

Inductive reasoning moves from the particular to the general, from evidence to a generalization or conclusion about the evidence. It is a process we begin learning in infancy and use daily throughout our lives: a child burns herself the three times she touches a stove, so she concludes that stoves burn; we have liked four movies directed by Oliver Stone, so we form the generalization that Oliver Stone makes good movies. Inductive reasoning is also very common in argument: you might offer facts showing that chronic patients in the state's mental hospitals receive only drugs as treatment, and then you conclude that the state's hospitals rely exclusively on drugs to treat chronic patients.

The movement from particular to general is called an **inductive leap** because you must make something of a jump to conclude that what is true of some instances (the chronic patients whose records were available) is also true of all other instances in the class (the rest of the chronic patients). In an ideal world we could perhaps avoid the inductive leap by pinning down every conceivable instance, but in the real world such thoroughness is usually impractical and often impossible. Instead, we gather enough evidence to make our generalizations probable.

The evidence for induction may be of several kinds:

- Facts: statistics or other hard data that are verifiable or, failing that, attested to by reliable sources (for instance, the number of drug doses per chronic patient, derived from hospital records).
- The opinions of recognized experts on the subject, opinions that are themselves conclusions based on research and observation (for instance, the testimony of an experienced hospital doctor).
- Examples illustrating the evidence (for instance, the treatment history of one patient).

A sound inductive generalization can form the basis for the second reasoning process, **deductive reasoning.** Working from the general to the particular, you start with such a generalization and apply it to a new situation in order to draw a conclusion about that situation. Like induction, deduction is a process we use constantly to order our experience. The child who learns from three experiences that all stoves burn then sees a new stove and concludes that this stove also will burn. The child's thought process can be written in the form of a **syllogism,** a three-step outline of deductive reasoning:

All stoves burn me.
This is a stove.
Therefore, this stove will burn me.

The first statement, the generalization derived from induction, is called the **major premise.** The second statement, a more specific assertion about some element of the major premise, is called the **minor premise.** And the third statement, an assertion of the logical connection between premises, is called the **conclusion.** The following syllogism takes the earlier example about mental hospitals one step further:

MAJOR PREMISE The state hospitals' treatment of chronic patients relies exclusively on drugs.

MINOR PREMISE Drugs do not cure chronic patients.

CONCLUSION Therefore, the state hospitals' treatment of chronic patients will not cure them.

Unlike an inductive conclusion, which requires a leap, the deductive conclusion derives necessarily from the premises: as long as the reasoning process is valid and the premises are accepted as true, then the conclusion must also be true. To be valid, the reasoning must conform to the process outlined above. The following syllogism is *not* valid, even though the premises are true:

All radicals want to change the system.
Georgia Allport wants to change the system.
Therefore, Georgia Allport is a radical.

The flaw in this syllogism is that not *only* radicals want to change the system, so Allport does not *necessarily* fall within the class of radicals just because she wants to change the system. The conclusion, then, is invalid.

A syllogism can be valid without being true if either of the premises is untrue. For example:

> All people who want political change are radicals.
> Georgia Allport wants political change.
> Therefore, Georgia Allport is a radical.

The conclusion here is valid because Allport falls within the class of people who want political change. But the conclusion is untrue because the major premise is untrue. As commonly defined, a radical seeks extreme change, often by revolutionary means. But other forms and means of change are also possible; Allport, for instance, may be interested in improving the delivery of services to the poor and in achieving passage of tougher environmental-protection laws—both political changes, to be sure, but neither radical.

In arguments, syllogisms are rarely spelled out as neatly as in these examples. Sometimes the order of the statements is reversed, as in this sentence paraphrasing a Supreme Court decision:

> The state may not imprison a man just because he is too poor to pay a fine; the only justification for imprisonment is a certain danger to society, and poverty does not constitute certain danger.

The buried syllogism can be stated thus:

> MAJOR PREMISE The state may imprison only those who are a certain danger to society.
>
> MINOR PREMISE A man who is too poor to pay a fine is not a certain danger to society.
>
> CONCLUSION Therefore, the state cannot imprison a man just because he is too poor to pay a fine.

Often, one of a syllogism's premises or even its conclusion is implied but not expressed. Each of the following sentences omits one part of the same syllogism:

> All five students cheated, so they should be expelled. [Implied major premise: cheaters should be expelled.]
>
> Cheaters should be punished by expulsion, so all five students should be expelled. [Implied minor premise: all five students cheated.]
>
> Cheaters should be punished by expulsion, and all five students cheated. [Implied conclusion: all five students should be expelled.]

Fallacies

Inappropriate emotional appeals and flaws in reasoning—called **fallacies**—can trap you as you construct an argument. Watch out for the following, which your readers will find if you don't:

- **Hasty generalization:** an inductive conclusion that leaps to include *all* instances when at best only *some* instances provide any evidence. Hasty generalizations form some of our worst stereotypes:

  Physically challenged people are mentally challenged, too.
  African Americans are good athletes.
  Italian Americans are volatile.

- **Oversimplification:** an inductive conclusion that ignores complexities in the evidence that, if heeded, would weaken the conclusion or suggest an entirely different one. For example:

  The newspaper folded because it couldn't compete with television.

  Although television may have taken some business from the paper, hundreds of other papers continue to thrive; thus television could not be the only cause of the paper's failure.

- **Begging the question:** assuming a conclusion in the statement of a premise, and thus begging readers to accept the conclusion—the question—before it is proved. For example:

  We can trust the president not to neglect the needy, because he is a compassionate man.

  This sentence asserts in a circular fashion that the president is not uncompassionate because he is compassionate. He may indeed be compassionate, but this is the question that needs addressing.

- **Ignoring the question:** introducing an issue or consideration that shifts the argument away from the real issue. Offering an emotional appeal as a premise in a logical argument is a form of ignoring the question. The following sentence, for instance, appeals to pity, not to logic:

  The mayor was badly used by people he loved and trusted, so we should not blame him for the corruption in his administration.

- **Ad hominem** (Latin for "to the man"): a form of ignoring the question by attacking the opponents instead of the opponents' arguments. For example:

  O'Brien is married to a convict, so her proposals for prison reform should not be taken seriously.

- **Either-or:** requiring that readers choose between two interpretations or actions when in fact the choices are more numerous.

  > Either we imprison all drug users, or we will become their prisoners.

  The factors contributing to drug addiction, and the choices for dealing with it, are obviously more complex than this statement suggests. Not all either-or arguments are invalid, for sometimes the alternatives encompass all the possibilities. But when they do not, the argument is false.
- **Non sequitur** (Latin for "it does not follow"): a conclusion derived illogically or erroneously from stated or implied premises. For instance:

  > Young children are too immature to engage in sex, so they should not be taught about it.

  This sentence implies one of two meanings, both of them questionable: only the sexually active can learn anything about sex, or teaching young children about sex will cause them to engage in it.
- **Post hoc** (from the Latin *post hoc, ergo propter hoc,* "after this, therefore because of this"): assuming that because one thing preceded another, it must have caused the other. For example:

  > After the town banned smoking in closed public places, the incidence of vandalism went up.

  Many things may have caused the rise in vandalism, including improved weather and a climbing unemployment rate. It does not follow that the ban on smoking, and that alone, caused the rise.

ANALYZING ARGUMENT AND PERSUASION IN PARAGRAPHS

Jean Bethke Elshtain (born 1941) is a professor of ethics at the University of Chicago and the author of many articles and books on political philosophy. This paragraph comes from "Ewegenics," an essay on the possibilities of cloning human beings that was published in *The New Republic* in 1997. Just before this paragraph, Elshtain worries about "our yearning to create without pausing to reflect on what we are simultaneously destroying." The paragraph itself is deductive, with the minor premise coming before the major premise.

A few nights ago, I watched the Chicago Bulls clobber the San Antonio Spurs. Michael Jordan performed one of his typically superhuman feats, an assist that suggested he had eyes in the back of his head and two sets of arms. To one citizen who called a local program, the prospect of "more Michael Jordans" made the whole "cloning thing" not only palatable but desirable. "Can you imagine a whole basketball team of Michael Jordans?" he asked giddily. Unfortunately, I can. It's a nightmare. If there were basketball teams fielding Jordans against Jordans, we wouldn't be able to recognize the one, the only, Michael Jordan. It's like suggesting that forty Mozarts are better than one. There would be no Mozart if there were forty Mozarts. We know the singularity of the one, the extraordinary genius—a Jordan, a Mozart—because they stand apart from and above the rest. Absent that irreducible singularity, their gifts and glorious accomplishments would mean nothing. They would be the norm, commonplace: another dunk, another concerto.

Minor premise: Cloning could destroy singularity or uniqueness.

Major premise: Genius is unique.

Conclusion (and topic sentence, underlined): Cloning could destroy genius.

Lianna Chu (born 1978) is a student at Louisiana Technical College. The following paragraph appeared in her essay "Weighing the Arguments Against Cloning," written for a course in science and human values. Chu's paragraph is inductive, showing evidence for a conclusion that she states early on.

One frequent claim about potential cloning of human beings is that it would reduce our individuality, making us all alike. But an important challenge to this fear already exists: identical twins, born with the same genes. Identical twins who are raised apart (for instance, in separate adoptive families) often differ significantly in IQ, temperament, sociability, adjustment, and other factors. Even when they are raised together in the same family, identical twins grow up as unique individuals. My cousins are identical twins who were raised together until they were eighteen. At age twenty-nine, one is now a hot-tempered basketball coach and a loner, while the

Generalization (and topic sentence, underlined): Identical twins challenge fears that cloning would make us all alike.

Evidence:

Differences among identical twins raised apart

Differences among identical twins raised together

An example of identical twins raised together

other is a shy doctoral student in linguistics, happily married with a child. Except for both being men, they could hardly be more different.

DEVELOPING AN ARGUMENTATIVE AND PERSUASIVE ESSAY

Getting Started

You will have many chances to write arguments, from defending or opposing a policy such as progressive taxation in an economics course to justifying a new procedure at work to persuading a company to refund your money for a bad product. To choose a subject for an argumentative essay, consider a behavior or policy that irks you, an opinion you want to defend, a change you would like to see implemented, a way to solve a problem. The subject you pick should meet certain criteria:

- It should be something you have some knowledge of from your own experience or observations, from class discussions, or from reading, although you may need to do further research as well.
- It should be limited to a topic you can treat thoroughly in the space and time available to you—for instance, the quality of computer instruction at your school rather than in the whole nation.
- It should be something that you feel strongly about so that you can make a convincing case. (However, it's best to avoid subjects that you cannot view with some objectivity, seeing the opposite side as well as your own; otherwise, you may not be open to flaws in your argument, and you may not be able to represent the opposition fairly.)

With your subject in hand, you should develop a tentative thesis. Since the thesis is essentially a conclusion from evidence, you may have to do some preliminary reading to be sure the evidence exists. This step is especially important with an issue like welfare cheating or tax advantages for the wealthy that we all tend to have opinions about whether we know the facts or not. But don't feel you have to prove your thesis at this early stage; fixing it too firmly may make you unwilling to reshape it if further evidence, your audience, or the structure of your argument so demands.

Stating your thesis in a preliminary thesis sentence can help you form your idea. Make this sentence as clear and specific as possible. Don't resort to a vague generality or a nondebatable statement of fact. Instead, state the precise opinion you want readers to accept or the precise action you want them to take or support. For instance:

VAGUE Computer instruction is important.

NONDEBATABLE The school's investment in computer instruction is less than the average investment of the nation's colleges and universities.

PRECISE Money designated for new dormitories and athletic facilities should be diverted to constructing computer facilities and hiring a first-rate computer faculty.

VAGUE Cloning research is promising.

NONDEBATABLE Scientists have been experimenting with cloning procedures for many years.

PRECISE Those who oppose cloning research should consider the potentially valuable applications of the research for human health and development.

Once you have framed a tentative thesis sentence, the next step is to begin gathering evidence in earnest. You should consult as broad a range of sources as necessary to uncover the facts and opinions supporting not only your view but also any opposing views. Though it may be tempting to ignore your opposition in the hope that readers know nothing of it, it is dishonest and probably futile to do so. Acknowledging and, whenever possible, refuting significant opposing views will enhance your credibility with readers. If you find that some counterarguments damage your own argument too greatly, then you will have to revise your thesis.

Where to seek evidence depends on the nature of your thesis.

- For a thesis derived from your own experiences and observations, such as a recommendation that all students work part-time for the education if not for the money, gathering evidence will be primarily a matter of searching your own thoughts and also uncovering opposing views, perhaps by consulting others.
- Some arguments derived from personal experience can also be strengthened by the judicious use of facts and opinions from other sources. An essay arguing in favor of vegetarianism, for instance, could mix the benefits you have felt with those demonstrated by scientific data.

- Nonpersonal and controversial subjects require the evidence of other sources. Though you might strongly favor or oppose a massive federal investment in solar-energy research, your opinions would count little if they were not supported with facts and the opinions of experts.

As you generate or collect evidence, it should suggest the reasons that will support the claim of your thesis—essentially the minor arguments that bolster the main argument. In an essay favoring federal investment in solar-energy research, for instance, the minor arguments might include the need for solar power, the feasibility of its widespread use, and its cost and safety compared with the cost and safety of other energy sources. It is in developing these minor arguments that you are most likely to use induction and deduction consciously—generalizing from specifics or applying generalizations to new information. Thus the minor arguments provide the entry points for your evidence, and together they should encompass all the relevant evidence you find.

As we have already seen, knowledge of readers' needs and expectations is absolutely crucial in argument. In explanatory writing, detail and clarity alone may accomplish your purpose; but you cannot hope to move readers in a certain direction unless you have some idea of where they stand. You need a sense of their background in your subject, of course. But even more, you need a good idea of their values and beliefs, their attitudes toward your subject—in short, their willingness to be convinced by your argument. In a composition class, your readers will probably be your instructor and your classmates, a small but diverse group. A good target when you are addressing a diverse audience is the reader who is neutral or mildly biased one way or the other toward your thesis. This person you can hope to influence as long as your argument is reasonable, your evidence is thorough and convincing, your treatment of opposing views is fair, and your appeals to readers' emotions are appropriate to your purpose, your subject, and especially your readers' values and feelings.

Organizing

Once you have formulated your thesis, gathered reasons and the evidence to support them, and evaluated these against the needs and expectations of your audience, you should plan how you will arrange your argument. The introduction to your essay should draw readers into your framework, making them see how the subject affects them and predisposing them to consider your argument. Sometimes, a forthright approach works best, but an eye-opening anecdote or quotation can also be effective. Your thesis sentence may end your introduction. But if you think readers will not even entertain your thesis until they have seen some or all of your evidence, then withhold your thesis for later.

The main part of the essay consists of your minor arguments or reasons and your evidence for them. Unless the minor arguments form a chain, with each growing out of the one before, their order should be determined by their potential effects on readers. In general, it is most effective to arrange the reasons in order of increasing importance or strength so as to finish powerfully. But to engage readers in the argument from the start, try to begin with a reason that they will find compelling or that they already know and accept; that way, the weaker reasons will be sandwiched between a strong beginning and an even stronger ending.

The views opposing yours can be raised and dispensed with wherever it seems most appropriate to do so. If a counterargument pertains to just one of your minor arguments, then dispose of it at that point. But if the counterarguments are more basic, pertaining to your whole thesis, you should dispose of them either after the introduction or shortly before the conclusion. Use the former strategy if the opposition is particularly strong and you fear that readers will be disinclined to listen unless you address their concerns first. Use the latter strategy when the counterarguments are generally weak or easily dispensed with once you've presented your case.

In the conclusion to your essay, you may summarize the main point of your argument and state your thesis for the first time, if you have saved it for the end, or restate it from your introduction. An effective quotation, an appropriate emotional appeal, or a call for support or action can often provide a strong finish to an argument.

Drafting

While you are drafting the essay, work to make your reasoning clear by showing how each bit of evidence relates to the reason or minor argument being discussed, and how each minor argument relates to the main argument contained in the thesis. In working through the reasons and evidence, you may find it helpful to state each reason as the first sentence in a paragraph and then support it in the following sentences. If this scheme seems too rigid or creates overlong paragraphs, you can always make changes after you have got the draft down on paper. Draw on a range of methods to clarify your points. For instance, define specialized terms or those you use in a special sense, compare and contrast one policy or piece of evidence with another, or carefully analyze causes or effects.

Revising and Editing

When your draft is complete, use the following questions and the box opposite to guide your revision and editing.

- *Is your thesis debatable, precise, and clear?* Readers must know what you are trying to convince them of, at least by the end of the essay if not up front.
- *Is your argument unified?* Does each minor claim support the thesis? Do all opinions, facts, and examples provide evidence for a minor claim? In behalf of your readers, question every sentence you have written to be sure it contributes to the point you are making and to the argument as a whole.
- *Is the structure of your argument clear and compelling?* Readers should be able to follow easily, seeing when and why you move from one idea to the next.
- *Is the evidence specific, representative, and adequate?* Facts, examples, and expert opinions should be well detailed, should fairly represent the available information, and should be sufficient to support your claim.
- *Have you slipped into any logical fallacies?* Detecting fallacies in your own work can be difficult, but your readers will find them if you don't. Look for the following fallacies discussed earlier (pp. 319–20): hasty generalization, oversimplification, begging the question, ignoring the question, ad hominem, either-or, non sequitur, and post hoc. (All of these are also listed in the Glossary under *fallacies*.)

A NOTE ON THEMATIC CONNECTIONS

In 1997 a team of Scottish scientists announced that it had cloned a sheep named Dolly from a single adult cell. The news sparked a tremendous public controversy over the ethics of cloning—or copying the genetic makeup of an individual to produce one or more genetically identical individuals. All five of the authors represented in this chapter address the potential of one day cloning human beings, each arguing a different position. In a paragraph Jean Bethke

FOCUS ON TONE

Readers are most likely to be persuaded by an argument when they sense a writer who is reasonable, trustworthy, and sincere. A rational appeal, strong evidence, and acknowledgment of opposing views do much to convey these attributes, but so does tone, the attitude implied by choice of words and sentence structures.

Generally, you should try for a tone of moderation in your view of your subject and respectfulness and goodwill toward readers and opponents.

- State opinions and facts calmly:

  OVEREXCITED One clueless administrator was quoted in the newspaper as saying she thought many students who claim learning disabilities are faking their difficulties to obtain special treatment! Has she never heard of dyslexia, attention deficit disorders, and other well-established disabilities?

  CALM Particularly worrisome was one administrator's statement, quoted in the newspaper, that many students who claim learning disabilities may be "faking" their difficulties to obtain special treatment.

- Replace arrogance with deference and sarcasm with plain speaking:

  ARROGANT I happen to know that many students would rather party or just bury their heads in the sand than get involved in a serious, worthy campaign against the school's unjust learning-disabled policies.

  DEFERENTIAL Time pressures and lack of information about the issues may be what prevents students from joining the campaign against the school's unjust learning-disabled policies.

  SARCASTIC Of course, the administration knows even without meeting students what is best for every one of them.

  PLAIN SPEAKING The administration should agree to meet with each learning-disabled student to learn about his or her needs.

- Choose words whose connotations convey reasonableness rather than anger, hostility, or another negative emotion:

  HOSTILE The administration *coerced* some students into dropping their lawsuits. [*Coerced* implies the use of threats or even violence.]

  REASONABLE The administration *convinced* some students to drop their lawsuits. [*Convinced* implies the use of reason.]

See pages 39–40 for more on tone and page 50 for more on connotation.

Elshtain maintains that cloning humans would destroy the individuality of human genius (p. 321). In another paragraph Lianna Chu takes the contrary view that individuality is due more to a person's environment than to his or her genes (p. 321). In an essay Charles Krauthammer takes up a potential use of cloning, the creation of headless creatures with fully functioning organs, and calls for an outright ban on any human cloning and capital punishment for this type (next page). In an opposing essay Kenneth Hamner holds that creating headless humans, beings without consciousness, would be equivalent to making useful machines (p. 334). And in the final essay Timothy Backous takes a middle ground, arguing that we need to know much more about the science and ourselves before we can accept or reject the possible human benefits of cloning (p. 339).

Charles Krauthammer

Born in 1950 in New York City, Charles Krauthammer was raised in Montreal, Canada, and attended McGill University (B.A., 1970), Oxford University, and Harvard Medical School (M.D., 1975). He worked as a psychiatrist at Massachusetts General Hospital until 1978 and then left medicine to serve as a science adviser to President Jimmy Carter and a speechwriter for Vice President Walter Mondale. Turning to journalism in 1981, Krauthammer wrote for The New Republic *and in 1985 began a weekly column for the* Washington Post *and a monthly column for* Time *magazine. In 1987 he won the Pulitzer Prize for distinguished commentary.* Cutting Edges, *a collection of his essays, was published in 1985. He lives in Chevy Chase, Maryland.*

Of Headless Mice . . . and Men

To Krauthammer, the cloning of human beings would be nothing more than vanity, nothing less than "high-tech barbarity." This essay was published in Time *in 1998.*

Last year Dolly the cloned sheep was received with wonder, titters and some vague apprehension. Last week the announcement by a Chicago physicist that he is assembling a team to produce the first human clone occasioned yet another wave of Brave New World anxiety. But the scariest news of all—and largely overlooked—comes from two obscure labs, at the University of Texas and at the University of Bath. During the past four years, one group created headless mice; the other, headless tadpoles. 1

For sheer Frankenstein wattage, the purposeful creation of these animal monsters has no equal. Take the mice. Researchers found the gene that tells the embryo to produce the head. They deleted it. They did this in a thousand mice embryos, four of which were born. I use the term loosely. Having no way to breathe, the mice died instantly. 2

Why then create them? The Texas researchers want to learn how genes determine embryo development. But you don't have to be a 3 genius to see the true utility of manufacturing headless creatures: for their organs—fully formed, perfectly useful, ripe for plundering.

Why should you be panicked? Because humans are next. "It would almost certainly be possible to produce human bodies without a forebrain," Princeton biologist Lee Silver told the London *Sunday Times*. "These human bodies without any semblance of consciousness would not be considered persons, and thus it would be perfectly legal to keep them 'alive' as a future source of organs." 4

"Alive." Never have a pair of quotation marks loomed so ominously. Take the mouse-frog technology, apply it to humans, combine it with cloning, and you are become a god: with a single cell taken from, say, your finger, you produce a headless replica of yourself, a mutant twin, arguably lifeless, that becomes your own personal, precisely tissue-matched organ farm. 5

There are, of course, technical hurdles along the way. Suppressing the equivalent "head" gene in man. Incubating tiny infant organs to grow into larger ones that adults could use. And creating artificial wombs (as per Aldous Huxley),[1] given that it might be difficult to recruit sane women to carry headless fetuses to their birth/death. 6

It won't be long, however, before these technical barriers are breached. The ethical barriers are already cracking. Lewis Wolpert, professor of biology at University College, London, finds producing headless humans "personally distasteful" but, given the shortage of organs, does not think distaste is sufficient reason not to go ahead with something that would save lives. And Professor Silver not only sees "nothing wrong, philosophically or rationally," with producing headless humans for organ harvesting, he wants to convince a skeptical public that it is perfectly O.K. 7

When prominent scientists are prepared to acquiesce in—or indeed encourage—the deliberate creation of deformed and dying quasi-human life, you know we are facing a bioethical abyss. Human beings are ends, not means. There is no grosser corruption of biotechnology than creating a human mutant and disemboweling it at our pleasure for spare parts. 8

[1] Aldous Huxley (1894–1963) was an English novelist and essayist. His novel *Brave New World* (1932) offers a dark satire of a technological society in which human embryos are developed in bottles. (Krauthammer refers to the title of the book in his opening paragraph.) [Editor's note.]

The prospect of headless human clones should put the whole debate about "normal" cloning in a new light. Normal cloning is less a treatment for infertility than a treatment for vanity. It is a way to produce an exact genetic replica of yourself that will walk the earth years after you're gone. *9*

But there is a problem with a clone. It is not really you. It is but a twin, a perfect John Doe Jr., but still a junior. With its own independent consciousness, it is, alas, just a facsimile of you. *10*

The headless clone solves the facsimile problem. It is a gateway to the ultimate vanity: immortality. If you create a real clone, you cannot transfer your consciousness into it to truly live on. But if you create a headless clone of just your body, you have created a ready source of replacement parts to keep you—your consciousness—going indefinitely. *11*

Which is why one form of cloning will inevitably lead to the other. Cloning is the technology of narcissism, and nothing satisfies narcissism like immortality. Headlessness will be cloning's crowning achievement. *12*

The time to put a stop to this is now. Dolly moved President Clinton to create a commission that recommended a temporary ban on human cloning. But with physicist Richard Seed threatening to clone humans, and with headless animals already here, we are past the time for toothless commissions and meaningless bans. *13*

Clinton banned federal funding of human-cloning research, of which there is none anyway. He then proposed a five-year ban on cloning. This is not enough. Congress should ban human cloning now. Totally. And regarding one particular form, it should be draconian: the deliberate creation of headless humans must be made a crime, indeed a capital crime. If we flinch in the face of this high-tech barbarity, we'll deserve to live in the hell it heralds. *14*

Meaning

1. In what two separate statements does Krauthammer most forcefully state his position on the issue of cloning?
2. Does Krauthammer see any benefit to cloning? What is his objection to the use of clones for replacement body parts?
3. Some of the following words may be new to you. Try to guess their meanings from the context of Krauthammer's essay. Test your guesses in a dictionary, and then use each new word in a sentence or two of your own.

wattage (2)
plundering (3)
semblance (4)
ominously (5)
suppressing (6)
incubating (6)
breached (7)
acquiesce (8)
quasi- (8)
abyss (8)
mutant (8)
disemboweling (8)
facsimile (10)
narcissism (12)
draconian (14)
capital (14)
heralds (14)

Purpose and Audience

1. Krauthammer makes his purpose quite clear in the last paragraph: he wants Congress to ban human cloning immediately and entirely. Can an essay like this one, published in a magazine with a circulation in the millions, have an effect on national legislation? What would the intermediary steps have to be?
2. Who would Krauthammer's ideal readers be? Geneticists? Members of Congress? Average Joes and Janes?

Method and Structure

1. Is Krauthammer's appeal mostly emotional or mostly rational? How so?
2. Which part of the essay is more explanatory than argumentative? Is this part entirely objective? Why, or why not?
3. How does Krauthammer present his opponents' side of the issue? What is the effect of the quotations from Lee Silver and Lewis Wolpert in paragraphs 4 and 7?
4. **Other Methods** In paragraphs 9–11, Krauthammer uses comparison and contrast (Chapter 10) to distinguish headless clones from so-called normal clones. What are the "advantages" of headless clones? How does this comparison further Krauthammer's anticloning argument?

Language

1. How would you describe Krauthammer's attitude toward his subject? What is the tone of the last paragraph?
2. What is the effect of "Because humans are next" (paragraph 4)?
3. What is the difference between "acquiescing in" and "encouraging" something (paragraph 8)?

Writing Topics

1. **Journal Response** Think of an issue you feel very strongly about, with no hesitation about your point of view being the right one. Take notes on why you feel the way you do and what you would like to see change with respect to this issue.

Journal to Essay Write an essay, based largely on emotional appeal, in which you argue your point of view on the issue you have chosen and state as your thesis the action you think should be taken. Remember that *emotional* does not mean *irrational:* your reasoning must be sound even when you rely on readers' feelings and beliefs, and your appeal must be appropriate to the subject and to the argument (see p. 315).

2. Find five or six articles on the subject of cloning, either in the periodicals collection at the library or on the World Wide Web. (The cloning of Dolly the sheep was announced in early 1997, and a great many articles appeared in that year and the next.) From these articles, list the actual and potential uses of cloning: Krauthammer mentions only two (to treat infertility and to replace body parts), but there are many other possibilities. Write a classification essay in which you sort the various uses of cloning into categories of your choosing—for example, "frivolous," "useful," and "dangerous." Be sure to explain the reasons for your categories and the uses you assign to each.
3. **Cultural Considerations** As Krauthammer's essay indicates, cloning is an issue that raises questions about basic human values: What makes us human? Is it ethical to tamper with our genetic coding? How far should we go in trying to cure human diseases or repair human bodies? To a great extent, the answers to such questions depend on one's moral framework—one's religious beliefs or philosophy of life. Write an essay of personal response to Krauthammer's essay, explaining how your moral framework colors or dictates your views. It may help you get started to consider Krauthammer's assertion that "[h]uman beings are ends, not means" (paragraph 8).
4. **Connections** Until recently, cloning was a topic for science fiction. Find a novel or film that takes cloning, or something like cloning, as its subject. (For novels, you could consider Aldous Huxley's *Brave New World,* mentioned by Krauthammer, or Ira Levin's *The Boys from Brazil,* Fay Weldon's *The Cloning of Joanna May,* or Mary Wollstonecraft Shelley's *Frankenstein.*) Write an essay comparing and contrasting the novel's or film's attitudes toward cloning with the contemporary views of Charles Krauthammer, Kenneth Hamner (next page), and Timothy Backous (p. 339). Are the hopes and fears the same? Has science fiction become reality?

Kenneth Hamner

Kenneth Hamner was born in 1976 in Alamosa, Colorado, and grew up in Salida and Glenwood Springs, Colorado. He was valedictorian of his Glenwood Springs High School graduating class. At Colorado State University, Hamner majored in microbiology and biology, graduating Phi Beta Kappa with honors in 1998. He intends to do graduate work in immunology but is also interested in "juggling torches, playing drums, and droning a didgeridoo"—the last a long bamboo pipe used by Australian aborigines.

Move Over, Ichabod Crane

Hamner's title refers to the main character in "The Legend of Sleepy Hollow," a story by the American Washington Irving (1783–1859) about a man who is frightened out of town by a horseman who appears to be headless. Hamner confronts a contemporary fear of headlessness—concern over the possibility that scientists will create headless people by cloning. His essay appeared in 1997 in the Collegian, *the student newspaper of Colorado State.*

All Hallow's Eve approaches. The bizarre Celtic fairies will rise again for yet another night of evil and mischief. Besides glorious bonfires, we will see the twisted forms of vampires, wrinkled witches, hideous reincarnated Nixons and maybe a headless horseman or two. Of course, we all know these creatures could never haunt us in real life. Not yet, anyway. Though science oftentimes makes fiction a reality, the technology to create blood-sucking fiends of the night or to reincarnate dead presidents (blood-sucking fiends of the day) is decades, or perhaps centuries, away. 1

Except for headless people, perhaps. One would say that decapitating a man is relatively simple, though highly immoral and illegal. However, it is the quest of many scientists now to genetically create headless people. Is this possible? More important, would this be immoral? 2

As one who wishes to become a biologist, the most frequent question I am asked is what I think about cloning. "Cloning what?" I 3 ask. "Bacterial genomes, friendly yeast or fuzzy sheep?" "Fuzzy sheep," they respond, referring to Dolly, the world's first cloned mammal. I respond by saying it is a great achievement, that it is a major advancement both for the livestock industries and for our understanding of how genes work. Of course, there are the few dangers inherent with all genetically undiversified populations that need to be accounted for, but as long as the scientists and technicians of this technology are responsible, I only see good things coming from this field of research. "When are scientists ever responsible?" I commonly hear. "What if they start doing this stuff on people?" The fear here is not in creating thousands of Adolf Hitlers or Rush Limbaughs, but rather in creating a race of slave clones, people who are made specifically to be tissue and organ banks. If scientists were stupid enough to make nuclear bombs and Olestra, what's to prevent them from making a race of slaves?

Well, there is the issue of natural rights. Without going into the debate of where natural rights come from or exactly what they are, it is safe to assume that all creatures have the right to live their lives as nature intended—birds to fly, rabbits to hop, and tree sloths to be lazy. To prevent or inhibit these rights (cutting a bird's wings off, forcing a sloth to run on a treadmill) would be a violation of this right and thus be immoral. 4

Of course, these rights are violated all the time against animals, particularly those that are domesticated (cramming a pig inside a small box from birth to slaughter is not exactly what a pig wants to do), but these issues seldom cause riots. However, being the masters of hypocrisy that we are, when the rights of humans are violated, the trumpet of righteousness blares, particularly when the right in question is the right to choose your destiny. Slavery was abolished because it violated the free will of the slave. Abortion is a hot issue because the fetus is not asked if it wants to live. Its right to survive—to become a living, thinking human—is destroyed against its choice. Euthanasia likewise is frowned upon in situations where the person cannot communicate his/her own feelings on whether to live or die. The same issues apply towards a clone—nobody asks what it thinks about being created nor how it would feel about being an organ storage tank. 5

However, what if the clone cannot think? Scientists in Britain recently learned how to make headless frog embryos. By toying with the transcription factors that allow fetal cells to differentiate, they suppressed the formation of the head. Because these factors are 6 similar in humans, it would be quite simple to make a headless human embryo, one that can make hearts, lungs and kidneys but not a brain and therefore no consciousness. (Say goodbye to long organ-waiting lists; make your own lung or heart with this fun and easy technology. Operators are standing by.)

Many are attacking this foreseeable procedure. Professor Andrew Linzey of Oxford calls it scientific fascism to create servants and says "it is morally regressive to create a mutant form of life." Others like Lewis Wolpert of University College of London say there is no ethical issue at all "because you are not doing harm to anyone." It would be easy to counter Linzey's statement if mere animals were at issue—humans have been creating mutant animal servants under the guise of domestication for thousands of years. In regard to humans, though, the matter is much different, largely due to the fear many have of tinkering with the human genome. For me, the issue centers on consciousness and thus the ability to perceive harm, and like Wolpert I see no moral dilemma. The result of this procedure would have no brain and thus no consciousness to violate. Rather, the creation of a headless embryo is like making a bridge, a toaster or a computer. The end product cannot think, but it is incredibly useful. 7

So what is different about creating a headless embryo and aborting a fetus? In the case of abortion, the natural progression from fertilization to embryo to fetus to living creatures is unjustifiably interrupted. The process of cloning, however, is completely artificial. Nobody's natural rights are being compromised. No natural fetuses are being killed, nor will thinking slaves be made. We would instead be making machines like toasters, incredibly useful machines such as hearts and lungs that will save lives. Is that morally wrong? 8

Meaning

1. Where does Hamner state the problem he is about to address? Where does he state his thesis?
2. What hypocrisy does Hamner see in the argument that cloning human beings would violate the clones' natural rights?
3. Explain Hamner's view that abortion is wrong while cloning headless humans is justifiable.
4. You may be unfamiliar with some of the words in this essay. If so, try to guess their meanings from Hamner's context. Check your guesses

against a dictionary's definitions. Using each new word in a sentence or two will help you learn it.

genomes (3)	righteousness (5)	fascism (7)
inherent (3)	euthanasia (5)	regressive (7)
undiversified (3)	fetal (6)	mutant (7)
domesticated (5)	differentiate (6)	guise (7)

Purpose and Audience

1. Why do you think Hamner wrote this essay? To criticize people who think cloning is wrong? To bring cloning out of the realm of science fiction and horror films? Something else?
2. Whom is Hamner writing for? People who already favor cloning? People who think it is wrong? Both?

Method and Structure

1. Is the appeal of Hamner's argument mainly emotional or mainly rational? Explain your answer with examples from the essay.
2. In paragraph 3 Hamner first makes the argument for cloning sheep before asserting that it is acceptable to clone people. What persuasive tactic is he employing here?
3. Why do you think Hamner mentions his desire to become a biologist (paragraph 3)? What does this information contribute to his ethical appeal?
4. **Other Methods** Hamner uses several other methods to strengthen his argument, including examples (Chapter 6) of what he considers to be unacceptable violations of natural rights. What are these examples? How does defining what he doesn't accept help to further Hamner's argument in favor of headless clones? How does this strategy contribute to the persuasiveness of the essay?

Language

1. How would you describe Hamner's tone? Is it consistent throughout? Is it appropriate for his subject?
2. What is the effect of Hamner's introductory catalog of Halloween creatures? Why does he take such pains to describe "the twisted forms of vampires" and other characters?
3. What is the purpose of the question with which Hamner ends the essay?

Writing Topics

1. **Journal Response** Think of a controversial issue on which your opinion differs from that of other people you know: it could be a political issue such as affirmative action or bilingual education, a social issue such as date rape or violence in movies, even a less weighty issue like physical fitness or nutrition. Make a list of points that support your position. Next to each point, write down the objections that people who think differently from you might have. Talk to some of these people if you need help with your "objections" list.

   Journal to Essay Write an essay in which you attempt to persuade readers of your point of view on the issue you have selected. Make sure your essay not only presents your side of things but also details the other side. Refute all the objections you can, and acknowledge the validity of any you cannot refute, showing why their validity does not undermine your thesis.
2. What do you think about the idea of creating headless humans to serve as "organ banks"? Do you agree with Hamner that consciousness is what determines our humanity? Would headless clones really be comparable to toasters or computers? Write an essay either agreeing or disagreeing with Hamner's argument.
3. **Cultural Considerations** Hamner points out that our society has a double standard when it comes to natural rights for animals versus natural rights for humans. Yet according human rights to animals would dramatically change our lives. Consider all the ways we use animals—for instance, as pets, as sources of food, as sources of clothing, as exhibits in zoos. Write an essay in which you describe what life would be like in a society in which it was a crime to infringe on any animal's "natural rights."
4. **Connections** Charles Krauthammer, in his essay "Of Headless Mice . . . and Men" (p. 329), makes the opposite argument from Hamner's. How do the tones of the two essays compare? Which writer seems more convinced of being in the right? Which essay do you find more convincing, and why?

Timothy Backous

A Roman Catholic monk and ordained priest, Timothy Backous teaches morality at the College of St. Benedict and St. John's University in Collegeville, Minnesota. He was born in Aberdeen, South Dakota, and graduated from O'Gorman High School in Sioux Falls. In 1978 he became a monk at St. John's Abbey, a Benedictine community in Collegeville, and in 1986 he was ordained a priest. In 1989 he received a doctorate in sacred theology from the Alphonsianum, a pontifical university in Rome. Backous has edited one book on moral theology, Common Good: Uncommon Questions, *and contributed to a reference book on the teachings of the Catholic church,* Exploring the New Cathechism.

Making Sheep: Possible, but Right?

Weighing the potential benefits of cloning against the morality of "toying with the essence of creation," Backous calls for education and reflection to help us make complex and risky decisions about the new technology. This essay appeared in the Record *of St. John's University in 1997.*

OK. So now we can clone sheep. The papers and TV are full of all kinds of doomsday responses that express outrage and fear. Once again, we seem to have a situation where technology is out ahead of ethics. We must ask ourselves yet again, "Just because we can do it, should we?" The proponents say this is breakthrough technology which will change the face of human existence. We may be able to genetically engineer a whole parallel species for our exclusive use. A child who is dying could be "rebuilt," thus circumventing the great tragedy of infant death. We could each have a clone that would provide replacement parts in case of need. The whole problem of world hunger would take an astonishing turn if animals could be engineered to provide milk, meat and labor. 1

The critics, on the other hand, ask the question "How far do we go?" Without a guide book or even a set of universally accepted principles, do we as a race simply allow scientific experiments of this 2 nature to be left to chance? It would appear that the only limitations are the skill and the scientific talent of those doing the laboratory work. Something feels wrong with that scenario.

From the perspective of morality, we have a very complex situation here. We are hesitant whenever something right out of the pages of science fiction becomes a reality. Suddenly, what was only fodder for late night arguments about humanity and its place in the universe becomes frighteningly critical to the future. And while we like to say that we shouldn't play God with this kind of technology, who among us wouldn't rush to employ any technique that would save our own flesh and blood? Looking into the eyes of a dying child does not help one reflect on the principles of ethics. Knowing that genetic manipulation could help feed people makes it more difficult to say no on the basis of moral guidelines. 3

Perhaps the only thing we can do at this point is recognize that what was only a fantasy is now real and that education might be our first step in helping to shape the future of genetic engineering. To say that we can stop the proliferation of experiments and research altogether seems naive. One article insists that last year alone, there were more than 80,000 animals manufactured in Britain. One such animal is a sheep which goes by the name Tracy and has human genes in every one of her cells. This "transgenic" breed is a step toward production of similar species who will provide "human substances" for medical treatments. With those kinds of numbers and results, putting on the brakes seems a bit unrealistic. Besides, when one ethicist was asked to explain why such mass production of genetically manipulated animals is such a surprise to us, he explained that the secrecy has more to do with protecting a veritable gold mine. If the market is cornered, this technology is going to make someone very rich. 4

No matter where you stand on this issue, there is a nagging question left unanswered: where does God fit into all of this? Up to this point, the magnificent and awesome scientific discoveries we've made lead us to ask deeper questions about the origin of life and its destiny. Even though we are not authors of creation, are we still not called to use our God-given intelligence to help perfect it? What is the problem with using technology to ease suffering and pain? If bionics help paralytics walk again, is that not unnatural but still good? What about changing the direction of a river to help avert natural disasters? What about building pipelines that carry water to arid regions of the world? Most of us would be forced to agree that in those cases, our human ingenuity crosses boundaries but for good reason. Even so, it 5 is hard to make that giant leap of faith to issues involving genetic manipulation. For there we are toying with the very essence of creation itself. True, God still had to create the cells that we use to clone others, but we can't ignore the fact that we upset the apple cart of existence just a bit. Perhaps the best way to stifle the march toward technological wonders is to ponder the consequences of our actions and realize that we know neither what those are nor what it means to accept responsibility for them.

Meaning

1. Backous twice states what he thinks should be done now about cloning. Where? What does he recommend?
2. What is the moral dilemma Backous sees at the heart of the issue of cloning?
3. If any of the following words are unfamiliar to you, try to guess their meanings based on their context in Backous's essay. Check your guesses in a dictionary, and then use each new word in a sentence or two.

proponents (1)	veritable (4)	arid (5)
circumventing (1)	bionics (5)	ingenuity (5)
fodder (3)	paralytics (5)	stifle (5)
proliferation (4)	avert (5)	

Purpose and Audience

1. How strong an argument does Backous make about cloning? Does he seek to win readers over to his point of view on the issue? Or does he have another purpose in mind?
2. Does Backous seem to have written for readers who know a lot about cloning and have strong opinions on the subject? Would such readers be likely to change their minds after reading this essay? Why, or why not?
3. What assumptions about readers does Backous make in the last paragraph? How does this assumption affect your reading of the essay?

Method and Structure

1. How does Backous use ethical appeal to convince readers to think about the consequences of cloning? How does the way he presents his own ambivalence (or possession of opposing views) encourage readers to feel the same way?

2. What effect does Backous achieve in paragraph 3 by appealing directly to readers ("who among us wouldn't rush to employ any technique that would save our own flesh and blood?")?
3. Show how Backous employs inductive reasoning in paragraph 4. What is his generalization? What is his evidence?
4. **Other Methods** In paragraph 5 Backous cites several examples of human ingenuity triumphing over nature. How do these examples fit into the argument he is making?

Language

1. How do the words Backous uses in paragraph 3 to describe the cloning question support his view of it as a dilemma?
2. What is the tone of this essay? Is it mainly impassioned or mainly reasoned?
3. Why does Backous begin his essay "OK. So now we can clone sheep"? What does this opening immediately communicate about his attitude toward cloning?

Writing Topics

1. **Journal Response** Think of a debate on which your personal position is ambivalent: you see the merit of both or all sides. Determine what the possible positions on the issue are. For example, on the issue of the First Amendment to the Constitution, you might see two sides: those who favor free speech with no qualifications, and those who think certain forms of discourse, such as hate speech, should be excluded from protection. Form as many columns in your journal as there are sides to the issue. In each column, write down the arguments for that side, as well as that side's responses to its opposition.

   Journal to Essay Write an essay using Backous's as a model, in which you present the various sides of the debate you have chosen. Your essay could be explanatory, focusing just on articulating the various positions. Or, if you can take the issue further, you could develop a persuasive thesis that proposes a solution or compromise to the debate.
2. Backous is concerned about cloning because it marks uncharted moral territory, with humans playing the role of God. But he doesn't mention any of his specific fears. Why should we be concerned about a future in which cloning has become commonplace? Even if you are generally in favor of cloning, write an essay in which you give three or four reasons why we should "ponder the consequences" of genetic engineering.
3. **Cultural Considerations** Backous argues that the best approach to cloning at this point is to learn as much as we can and to reflect deeply about its moral implications. How can these aims best be achieved, in

your opinion? Through incorporation of the subject into high-school and college courses? Through public forums? Through advertisements or public-service announcements? Take Backous's essay one step further by writing a process analysis in which you develop a program of concrete steps toward educating the public about this difficult issue.

4. **Connections** Backous's position on cloning can in some ways be seen as a compromise between the more fixed opinions expressed by Charles Krauthammer in "Of Headless Mice . . . and Men" (p. 329) and Kenneth Hamner in "Move Over, Ichabod Crane" (p. 334). Write an essay in which you examine how Backous creates a synthesis of the two other arguments.

Writing with the Method

Argument and Persuasion

Choose one of the following statements, or any other statement they suggest, and support *or* refute it in an argumentative essay. The statement you decide on should concern a topic you care about so that argument is a means of convincing readers to accept an idea, not an end in itself.

MEDIA

1. Pornographic magazines and films should be banned.
2. Violence and sex should be prohibited from television.
3. Advertisements for consumer products (or political candidates) should be recognized as serving useful purposes.
4. Recordings of popular music should be specially labeled if their lyrics contain violent or sexual images.

SPORTS

5. Professional athletes should not be allowed to compete in the Olympics.
6. Professional athletes are overpaid for their work.
7. The school's costly athletic programs should be eliminated in favor of improving the academic curriculum.

HEALTH AND TECHNOLOGY

8. People should have the right to choose when to die without interference from the government or medical community.
9. Private automobiles should be restricted in cities.
10. Laboratory experiments on dogs, cats, and primates should be banned.
11. Smoking should be banned in all public places, including outdoors in congested places.

EDUCATION

12. Students caught in any form of academic cheating should be expelled.
13. Students should not be granted high-school diplomas until they can demonstrate reasonable competence in writing and mathematics.
14. Like high-school textbooks, college textbooks should be purchased by the school and loaned to students for the duration of a course.

SOCIAL AND POLITICAL ISSUES

15. The elderly are entitled to unlimited free medical care.
16. Private institutions should have the right to make rules that would be unconstitutional outside those institutions.
17. Children should be able to sue their parents for negligence or abuse.
18. A citizen should be able to buy and keep a handgun for protection without having to register it.
19. When they turn eighteen, adopted children should have free access to information about their birth parents.

Writing About the Theme

Debating Cloning

1. Based on the arguments of Jean Bethke Elshtain (p. 320), Lianna Chu (p. 321), Charles Krauthammer (p. 329), Kenneth Hamner (p. 334), and Timothy Backous (p. 339), what do you think about the possibility of cloning human beings? Are you for or against it, or do you see merits to both sides? How do your religious or ethical beliefs shape your opinion? If you favor cloning only for some purposes or under certain circumstances, what are they? Write an argumentative essay in which you state your opinion and the reasons for it, trying to persuade readers to accept or agree with your view.
2. Turn the previous writing topic into a research project by seeking sources beyond this chapter's selections to support and extend your own view. Either at the library or online, seek sources published since early 1997, when the announcement of a cloned mammal, a sheep named Dolly, ignited wide debate on cloning. *The Readers' Guide to Periodical Literature* is an index that will lead you to nonspecialist periodicals; more specialized sources can be found through the *General Science Index* or, online, through the *WWW Virtual Library: Biosciences* at http://golgi.harvard.edu/biopages.
3. The essays by Charles Krauthammer, Kenneth Hamner, and Timothy Backous each convey a strong sense of the author's character and personality. Write an essay in which you compare and contrast the different ethical appeals these writers make. (See p. 314 for more on ethical appeal.) Try to look at each author's appeal apart from his opinion—you may find you agree with what one says but dislike the way he says it, or vice versa. Which writer's ethical appeal do you find the most appropriate? The least? Why?

Chapter 14

COMBINING METHODS OF DEVELOPMENT

Articulating a Vision

Though each essay in the preceding chapters illustrates one overall method of development, all the essays also illustrate other methods at the level of passages or paragraphs. (Follow-up questions labeled "Other Methods" highlight these varied strategies.) In fact, an essay is rarely developed by a single method alone. Even when you are purposefully comparing or classifying, you may also describe, narrate, define, or employ other methods. And often you may use no dominant method at all but select whatever methods you need, in whatever sequence, to achieve your purpose.

Combining methods usually adds texture and substance to an essay, for the methods provide different approaches to a subject, different ways to introduce the details and other evidence needed to interest and convince readers. Sometimes the appropriate methods may suggest themselves, but at other times it can help to explore them deliberately. The introductory discussion of the writing process shows how a set of questions derived from the methods of development can aid such a deliberate search (see pp. 21–25). Say you are writing a paper on owls. Right off several methods suggest themselves: a classification of kinds of owls, a description of each kind of owl, a process analysis of an owl's life cycle or hunting behavior. But you want your paper to go beyond the facts to convey your fascination with owls. Running through the list of questions, you find that "What is the story in the subject?" suggests a narrative of your first encounter with a barn owl, when your own awe and fear recalled the owl's reputation for wisdom and bad luck. Other questions then lead you further along this path: for instance, "How can the subject be illustrated?" calls forth examples of myths and superstitions involving owls; and "Why did the subject happen?" leads you to consider why people see owls as symbols and omens. In the course of asking the questions, you have moved from a straightforward look at owls to a more imaginative and complex examination of their meaning and significance for human beings.

The more you use the methods of development—alone or in combination—the more comfortable you will be with them and the better they will serve you. The two essays in this chapter illustrate how the methods may be combined in any way the author chooses to express ideas and achieve a purpose. (Brief annotations accompany each essay to point out some of the methods.) Both essays demonstrate how much the authors gain from having a battery of techniques and strategies to employ at will.

A NOTE ON THEMATIC CONNECTIONS

The authors of the essays in this chapter combine methods of development to articulate, or spell out, a vision of a future in which a person's race can no longer impede his or her freedom and opportunity. In a 1963 speech that has become a classic of American prose, Martin Luther King, Jr., gives voice to the frustrations and aspirations of African Americans (next page). And in an essay written for his college newspaper, Brian Kaufman considers how communication by computer could make American society race-blind (p. 355).

Martin Luther King, Jr.

Born in 1929 in Atlanta, Georgia, the son of a Baptist minister, Martin Luther King, Jr., was a revered and powerful leader of the African American civil rights movement during the 1950s and 1960s. He was ordained in his father's church before he was twenty and went on to earn degrees at Morehouse College (B.A. in 1948), Crozer Theological Seminary (B.D. in 1951), and Boston University (Ph.D. in 1955). In 1955 and 1956, while he was pastor of a church in Montgomery, Alabama, King attracted national attention to the plight of Southern blacks by leading a boycott that succeeded in desegregating the city's buses. He was elected the first president of the Southern Christian Leadership Conference and continued to organize demonstrations for equal rights in other cities. By the early 1960s his efforts had helped raise the national consciousness so that the landmark Civil Rights Act of 1964 and Voting Rights Act of 1965 could be passed by Congress. In 1964 King was awarded the Nobel Peace Prize. When leading sit-ins, boycotts, and marches, King always insisted on nonviolent resistance "because our end is a community at peace with itself." But his nonviolence often met with violent opposition. Over the years he was jailed, stoned, and stabbed. His house in Montgomery was bombed. And on April 4, 1968, at a motel in Memphis, Tennessee, he was assassinated. He was not yet forty years old.

I Have a Dream

On August 28, 1963, one hundred years after Abraham Lincoln's Emancipation Proclamation had freed the slaves, 200,000 black and white Americans marched on Washington, D.C., to demand equal rights for blacks. It was the largest crowd ever to assemble in the capital in behalf of a cause, and the high point of the day was this speech delivered by King on the steps of the Lincoln Memorial. Always an eloquent and inspirational speaker, King succeeded in giving hope to the oppressed and opening the eyes of many oppressors.

King's speech is an argument: a persuasive appeal for racial justice. It is especially notable for its use of repetition and parallelism, two devices common to inspirational speech. (See pp. 35–36 and 48.) But King also uses several of the methods of development discussed in this book, such as narrative, example, and cause-and-effect analysis. He uses description to convey the situation and feelings of African Americans, relying heavily on figures of speech to make these qualities concrete. Some (but not all) of these descriptive figures are noted. (See the discussion of figures of speech on pp. 51–52.)

Five score years ago, a great American, in whose sym- 1
bolic shadow we stand, signed the Emancipation Proclamation. This momentous decree came as a great beacon light of hope to millions of Negro slaves who had been seared in the flames of withering injustice. It came as a joyous daybreak to end the long night of captivity.

Description

But one hundred years later, we must face the tragic 2
fact that the Negro is still not free. One hundred years later, the life of the Negro is still sadly crippled by the manacles of segregation and the chains of discrimination. One hundred years later, the Negro lives on a lonely island of poverty in the midst of a vast ocean of material prosperity. One hundred years later, the Negro is still languishing in the corners of American society and finds himself an exile in his own land. So we have come here today to dramatize an appalling condition.

Narration

Description

In a sense we have come to our nation's capital to 3
cash a check. When the architects of our republic wrote the magnificent words of the Constitution and the Declaration of Independence, they were signing a promissory note to which every American was to fall heir. This note was a promise that all men—yes, black men as well as white men—would be guaranteed the unalienable rights of life, liberty, and the pursuit of happiness.

Comparison

It is obvious today that America has defaulted on this 4
promissory note insofar as her citizens of color are concerned. Instead of honoring this sacred obligation, America has given the Negro people a bad check, a check which has come back marked "insufficient funds." But we refuse to believe that there are insufficient funds in the great vaults of opportunity of this nation. So we have come to cash this check—a check that will give us upon demand the riches of freedom and the security of justice. We have also come to this hallowed spot to remind America of the fierce urgency of *now*. This is no time to engage in the luxury of cooling off or to take the tranquilizing drugs of gradualism. *Now* is the time to make real the promises of Democracy. *Now* is the time to rise from the dark and desolate valley of segregation to the sunlit path of racial justice. *Now* is the time to open the doors of opportunity to all of God's children. *Now* is the time to lift our nation

Description

from the quicksands of racial injustice to the solid rock of brotherhood.

5 It would be fatal for the nation to overlook the urgency of the moment and to underestimate the determination of the Negro. This sweltering summer of the Negro's legitimate discontent will not pass until there is an invigorating autumn of freedom and equality; 1963 is not an end, but a beginning. Those who hope that the Negro needed to blow off steam and will now be content will have a rude awakening if the nation returns to business as usual. There will be neither rest nor tranquility in America until the Negro is granted his citizenship rights. The whirlwinds of revolt will continue to shake the foundations of our nation until the bright day of justice emerges.

Cause and effect

6 But there is something that I must say to my people who stand on the warm threshold which leads into the palace of justice. In the process of gaining our rightful place we must not be guilty of wrongful deeds. Let us not seek to satisfy our thirst for freedom by drinking from the cup of bitterness and hatred. We must forever conduct our struggle on the high plane of dignity and discipline. We must not allow our creative protest to degenerate into physical violence. Again and again we must rise to the majestic heights of meeting physical force with soul force. The marvelous new militancy which has engulfed the Negro community must not lead us to a distrust of all white people, for many of our white brothers, as evidenced by their presence here today, have come to realize that their destiny is tied up with our destiny and their freedom is inextricably bound to our freedom. We cannot walk alone.

Example and comparison

7 And as we walk, we must make the pledge that we shall march ahead. We cannot turn back. There are those who are asking the devotees of civil rights, "When will you be satisfied?" We can never be satisfied as long as the Negro is the victim of the unspeakable horrors of police brutality. We can never be satisfied as long as our bodies, heavy with the fatigue of travel, cannot gain lodging in the motels of the highways and the hotels of the cities. We cannot be satisfied as long as the Negro's basic mobility is from a smaller ghetto to a larger one. We can never be satisfied as long as a Negro in Mississippi cannot vote and a

Example and cause and effect

Negro in New York believes he has nothing for which to vote. No, no, we are not satisfied, and we will not be satisfied until justice rolls down like waters and righteousness like a mighty stream.

Example and cause and effect

I am not unmindful that some of you have come here 8
out of great trials and tribulations. Some of you have come fresh from narrow jail cells. Some of you have come from areas where your quest for freedom left you battered by the storms of persecution and staggered by the winds of police brutality. You have been the veterans of creative suffering. Continue to work with the faith that unearned suffering is redemptive.

Description

Example

Go back to Mississippi, go back to Alabama, go back to 9
South Carolina, go back to Georgia, go back to Louisiana, go back to the slums and ghettos of our northern cities, knowing that somehow this situation can and will be changed. Let us not wallow in the valley of despair.

I say to you today, my friends, that in spite of the dif- 10
ficulties and frustrations of the moment I still have a dream. It is a dream deeply rooted in the American dream.

I have a dream that one day this nation will rise up 11
and live out the true meaning of its creed: "We hold these truths to be self-evident, that all men are created equal."

I have a dream that one day on the red hills of Geor- 12
gia the sons of former slaves and the sons of former slaveowners will be able to sit down together at the table of brotherhood.

I have a dream that one day even the state of Missis- 13
sippi, a desert state sweltering with the heat of injustice and oppression, will be transformed into an oasis of freedom and justice.

Description

I have a dream that my four little children will one 14
day live in a nation where they will not be judged by the color of their skin but by the content of their character.

Example

I have a dream today. 15

I have a dream that one day the state of Alabama, 16
whose governor's lips are presently dripping with the words of interposition and nullification, will be transformed into a situation where little black boys and black girls will be able to join hands with little white boys and white girls and walk together as sisters and brothers.

I have a dream today. 17

I have a dream that one day every valley shall be 18
exalted, every hill and mountain shall be made low, the rough places will be made plain, and the crooked places will be made straight, and the glory of the Lord shall be revealed, and all flesh shall see it together.[1]

This is our hope. This is the faith with which I return to 19
the South. With this faith we will be able to hew out of the mountain of despair a stone of hope. With this faith we will
be able to transform the jangling discords of our nation into *Cause and effect*
a beautiful symphony of brotherhood. With this faith we will be able to work together, to pray together, to struggle together, to go to jail together, to stand up for freedom together, knowing that we will be free one day.

This will be the day when all of God's children will be 20
able to sing with new meaning

> My country, 'tis of thee,
> Sweet land of liberty,
>   Of thee I sing:
> Land where my fathers died,
> Land of the pilgrims' pride,
> From every mountainside,
>   Let freedom ring.

So let freedom ring from the prodigious hilltops of 21
New Hampshire. Let freedom ring from the mighty mountains of New York. Let freedom ring from the heightening Alleghenies of Pennsylvania. Let freedom ring from the
snowcapped Rockies of Colorado. Let freedom ring from *Example*
the curvaceous peaks of California.

But not only that. Let freedom ring from Stone Moun- 22
tain of Georgia. Let freedom ring from Lookout Mountain of Tennessee. Let freedom ring from every hill and molehill of Mississippi. From every mountainside, let freedom ring.

When we let freedom ring, when we let it ring from 23
every village and every hamlet, from every state and every city, we will be able to speed up that day when all of

[1] This paragraph alludes to the Bible, Isaiah 40:4–5. [Editor's note.]

God's children, black men and white men, Jews and Gentiles, Protestants and Catholics, will be able to join hands and sing in the words of the old Negro spiritual, "Free at last! Free at last! Thank God almighty, we are free at last!"

Brian Kaufman

Brian Kaufman was born in 1952 in Cleveland, Ohio, and grew up in Berea, a Cleveland suburb. He moved to Fort Collins, Colorado, in high school. He currently attends Colorado State University there, "resuming," he says, "an education that I abandoned twenty-five years ago." Kaufman cooks for a living and in his free time lifts weights, plays blues guitar, and enjoys the company of his wife and three children. He also writes fiction and has completed a historical novel, The Breach.

Can Technology Make Us Colorblind?

Many writers have predicted bold changes in our lives and society resulting from communication by computer. Kaufman foresees an especially positive change, the achievement of the vision articulated by Martin Luther King, Jr., in "I Have a Dream." This essay appeared in 1998 in the Collegian, *Colorado State's student newspaper.*

My wife plays in computer chat rooms. Recently, she 1
told me about a twenty-nine-year-old artist, single, who turned out to be a forty-five-year-old married salesman. I had a hard time mustering the proper amount of sympathetic outrage. "You don't ever really know who you're talking to," she complained.

Narration and example

Exactly. The Internet lets us go beyond ordinary role- 2
play, to the extent that we can ignore the limitations of who and what we are. Chat rooms are a testing ground for the lives you've never led. Men can go online as women and discover what it's like to be (virtually) drooled on by every slob with whom they come in contact. Women can go online as men and find out how clever they have to be—as in trained-dog-through-hoops clever—in order to attract attention.

Cause and effect

Example

Most chat programs have picture access, but the user 3
decides what snapshot to scan. Heavy people can be thin,

angry people can put on a smile, and old people can be young again. Nor is the potential for identity-liberation limited to chat-room conversation. *Example*

4 *Time* magazine estimates that within the decade, over half of the jobs in the United States will be done at home. With so many people doing their primary commercial work over a keyboard and monitor, we have a chance to do something no other culture has done. Simply put, we can go colorblind. *Cause and effect*

5 In his landmark "I Have a Dream" speech, Dr. Martin Luther King, Jr., wished for a day when children will "live in a nation where they will not be judged by the color of their skin but by the content of their character."

6 Thanks to technology and a changing workplace, that day no longer seems impossible. Without a visual label, how can we continue to discriminate on a consistent basis? If we don't know what the people at the other end of the terminal look like, how can we judge them on the basis of their appearance? *Cause and effect*

7 Yet at the moment when technology offers a chance at an old dream, we seem to wish to separate and alienate. Most people (you know, Toyota's "everyday people") don't believe in what used to be called "melting pot" equality. In the 90s, personal identities are based on differences and similarities are viewed with suspicion, as if every shared moment is a potential shackle.

8 Even the form our language takes becomes a separatist's battleground. For example, one side of the ebonics controversy[1] is the contention that ebonics is a legitimate, rule-driven language in its own right and, as such, is a legitimate primary language and genuine voice for black America. (This line of reasoning is discrete from a second argument that educational approaches that attend properly to vernacular dialects, comparing and contrasting *Example and division or analysis*

[1] *Ebonics* is a name given to the African American vernacular (or everyday language), generally considered a dialect of English with a distinct grammar, vocabulary, and pronunciation. In late 1996 the school board of Oakland, California, decided to recognize ebonics as a language whose speakers can use help learning to translate between ebonics and standard English. The school board's decision ignited a nationwide debate. [Editor's note.]

rather than ignoring the vernacular, are more successful in
teaching commercial English.)

I respect these arguments, but in the context of our 9
new technology, I can't help wondering if ebonics
amounts to a lingual uniform. Does our sense of self depend on providing language clues to our genetic heritage
through the one medium that shields visual clues? We
have a common language of commerce and a technology *Cause and*
with the potential for a certain kind of equality. Must we *effect*
sacrifice this opportunity in the name of personal identity
through collective identifications?

I am not arguing that ebonics is the sole impediment 10
to freedom on the information highway. I am arguing that
it is a symptom of an America that has splintered, perhaps
irreparably.

It may be that we no longer share King's dream of 11
transforming "the jangling discords of our nation into
a beautiful symphony of brotherhood." Perhaps I am being nostalgic for a romantic vision with no relevance to
today's world. King's importance may lie in the symbol,
not the substance, of his discourse.

Or maybe the change is already underway, like it 12
or not. Watch any politician speak on television. His or
her cadence is cued by a TelePrompTer. The width of the *Example*
screen dictates sentence breaks.

The fact is that technology alters communication. Per- 13
haps the computer and its blind-eye monitor have already *Cause and*
become too large a part of our lives to avoid the influence. *effect*
In the near future, the way we do business may drag us,
kicking and screaming, into King's dream.

ACKNOWLEDGMENTS (continued from page vi)

Allison Amend, "Taking Issue with Problems," from *The Stanford Daily Online*, April 12, 1996. Copyright © 1996 The Stanford Daily. Reprinted by permission.

Barbara Lazear Ascher, "The Box Man," from *Playing After Dark* by Barbara Lazear Ascher. Copyright © 1982, 1983, 1984, 1985, 1986 by Barbara Lazear Ascher. Used by permission of Doubleday, a division of Bantam Doubleday Dell Publishing Group, Inc.

Timothy Backous, "Making Sheep," *The Record*, March 6, 1997. Reprinted by permission of *The Record* and the author.

Russell Baker, "The Plot Against People," from *The New York Times*, June 18, 1968. Copyright © 1968 by The New York Times Co. Reprinted by permission.

Amy L. Beck, "Struggling for Perfection," *The Harvard Crimson*, March 19, 1998. Copyright © 1998 The Harvard Crimson. Reprinted with permission.

Wendell Berry, excerpt from "Higher Education and Home Defense," from *Home Economics* by Wendell Berry. Copyright © 1987 by Wendell Berry. Reprinted by permission of North Point Press, a division of Farrar, Straus & Giroux, Inc.

Judy Brady, "I Want a Wife," *Ms.*, Vol.1, No.1, December 31, 1971. Reprinted by permission of the author.

Leo Buscaglia, excerpt from *Papa, My Father: A Celebration of Dads* by Leo Buscaglia. Copyright © 1989. Reprinted with permission of the Leo F. Buscaglia Trust. Published by Slack, Inc.

Joan Didion, excerpt from "Los Angeles Notebook," in *Slouching Towards Bethlehem* by Joan Didion. Copyright © 1966, 1968 and copyright renewed © 1996 by Joan Didion. Reprinted by permission of Farrar, Straus & Giroux, Inc.

Annie Dillard, excerpt from *An American Childhood* by Annie Dillard. Copyright © 1987 by Annie Dillard. Reprinted by permission of HarperCollins Publishers, Inc.

Michael Dorris, excerpt from "Noble Savages? We'll Drink to That," from *The New York Times*, April 21, 1992. Copyright © 1992 by The New York Times Co. Reprinted by permission.

Andre Dubus, excerpt from *Broken Vessels* by Andre Dubus. Copyright © 1991 by Andre Dubus. Reprinted by permission of David R. Godine, Publisher, Inc.

Max Eastman, excerpt from *The Enjoyment of Poetry* by Max Eastman. Copyright © 1913 by Charles Scribner's Sons, renewed 1941 by Max Eastman. Reprinted with the permission of Scribner, a division of Simon & Schuster.

Gretel Ehrlich, excerpt from "About Men," in *The Solace of Open Spaces* by Greta Ehrlich. Copyright © 1985 by Gretel Ehrlich. Used by permission of Viking Penguin, a division of Penguin Putnam Inc.

Jean Bethke Elshtain, excerpt from "Ewegenics," *The New Republic*, March 31, 1997. Reprinted by permission of *The New Republic*. Copyright © 1997 The New Republic, Inc.

Bryan Garvey, "Drugs vs. Drugs." Reprinted by permission of the author.

Mark Gerzon, excerpt from *A Choice of Heroes* by Mark Gerzon. Copyright © 1982 by Mark Gerzon. Reprinted by permission of Houghton Mifflin Company. All rights reserved.

Daniel Goleman, excerpt from "As Addiction Medicine Gains, Experts Debate What It Should Cover," from *The New York Times*, March 31, 1992. Copyright © 1992 by The New York Times Co. Reprinted by permission.

Jonathan R. Gould, Jr., "The People Next Door." Reprinted by permission of the author.

Monica Haena, excerpt from "Scented," *Delta Winds*, Vol. 4, Spring 1993. Reprinted by permission of the author.

Kenneth Hamner, "Move Over, Ichabod Crane," *The Collegian*, October 29, 1997. Reprinted by permission of *The Collegian* and the author.

L. Rust Hills, excerpt from *How to Do Things Right* by L. Rust Hills. Reprinted by permission of David R. Godine, Publisher, Inc. Copyright © 1972 by L. Rust Hills.

Langston Hughes, "Salvation," from *The Big Sea* by Langston Hughes. Copyright © 1940 by Langston Hughes. Copyright renewed © 1968 by Arna Bontemps and George Houston Bass. Reprinted by permission of Hill and Wang, a division of Farrar, Straus & Giroux, Inc.

Elizabeth Janeway, excerpt from *Man's World, Woman's Place* by Elizabeth Janeway. Copyright © 1971 by Elizabeth Janeway. Reprinted by permission of William Morrow & Company, Inc.

Jon Katz, "How Boys Become Men," *Glamour*, January 1993. Reprinted by permission of Sterling Lord Literistic, Inc. Copyright © 1993 by Jon Katz.

Brian Kaufman, "Can Technology Make Us Colorblind?" *The Collegian*, January 30, 1998. Reprinted by permission of *The Collegian* and the author.

Cortney Keim, "Making the Bed." Printed by permission of the author.

Kim Kessler, "Blah, Blah, Blah," from *The Brown Daily Herald*, April 8, 1996. Reprinted by permission of The Brown Daily Herald, Inc. and the author.

Martin Luther King, Jr., "I Have a Dream." Copyright © 1963 by Martin Luther King, Jr., copyright renewed 1991 by Coretta Scott King. Reprinted by arrangement with the Heirs to the Estate of Martin Luther King, Jr., c/o Writers House, Inc., as agent for proprietor.

Perri Klass, "She's Your Basic L.O.L. in N.A.D.," from *A Not Entirely Benign Procedure* by Perri Klass. Copyright © 1987 by Perri Klass. Reprinted by permission of The Putnam Publishing Group.

Charles Krauthammer, "Of Headless Mice . . . and Men," *Time*, January 19, 1998. Copyright © 1998 Time Inc. Reprinted by permission.

William Lutz, excerpt from *Doublespeak* by William Lutz. Copyright © 1989 by Blonde Bear, Inc. Reprinted by permission of HarperCollins Publishers, Inc.

Stephen Manes, "The Endangered Book?" from *The New York Times*, April 25, 1995. Originally titled "User-Friendliness: Book vs. Disk." Copyright © 1995 by The New York Times Co. Reprinted by permission.

Leanita McClain, "The Middle-Class Black's Burden," from *A Foot In Each World: Essays and Articles* by Leanita McClain. Copyright © 1986 by the Estate of Leanita McClain. Reprinted by permission of Northwestern University Press.

Michael W. Miller, "The Type That Turns Head in Computer Circles," *The Wall Street Journal*, September 15, 1992. Reprinted by permission of *The Wall Street Journal*. Copyright © 1992 Dow Jones & Company, Inc. All rights reserved worldwide.

Jessica Mitford, "Embalming Mr. Jones," from *The American Way of Death* by Jessica Mitford. Copyright © 1963, 1978 by Jessica Mitford, all rights reserved. Reprinted by permission of Jessica Mitford.

David Mura, excerpt from *Turning Japanese* by David Mura. Copyright © 1991 by David Mura. Used by permission of Grove/Atlantic, Inc.

Gloria Naylor, "The Meanings of a Word," "Hers" column, *The New York Times*, February 20, 1986. Reprinted by permission of Sterling Lord Literistic, Inc. Copyright © 1986 by Gloria Naylor.

Michael Ondaatje, excerpt from *Running in the Family* by Michael Ondaatje. Copyright © 1982 by Michael Ondaatje. Reprinted by permission of W. W. Norton & Company, Inc.

Jon Pareles, excerpt from "Gather No Moss, Take No Prisoners . . .," from *The New York Times*, Feb. 22, 1993. Copyright © 1993 by The New York Times Co. Reprinted by permission.

Emily Prager, "Our Barbies, Ourselves." Originally published in INTERVIEW, Brant Publications, Inc., December, 1991. Reprinted by permission of INTERVIEW Magazine.

Lionel L. Prokop, "In the Eyes of a Little Boy." Reprinted by permission of the author.

Shafeeq Sadiq, "Racism and Sexism in Advertising." Originally published in *Delta Winds,* 1997, Vol. 10. Reprinted by permission of *Delta Winds* and the author.

Deborah Tannen, "Gender Gap in Cyberspace," *Newsweek*, May 16, 1994. Copyright © Deborah Tannen. Reprinted by permission. This article is based in part on material in the author's book *You Just Don't Understand* (Ballantine, 1990).

Luci Tapahonso, excerpt from "The Way It Is," in *Sign Language*. Copyright © 1989 by Luci Tapahonso. Reprinted by permission of Aperture, New York, NY, 1989.

Marta K. Taylor, "Desert Dance," *Exposé*, 1988–1989. Reprinted by permission of the author.

Lewis Thomas, from *The Fragile Species* by Lewis Thomas. Copyright © 1992 by Lewis Thomas. Reprinted with the permission of Scribner, a division of Simon & Schuster.

Margaret Visser, "The Ritual of Fast Food," from *The Rituals of Dinner* by Margaret Visser. Copyright © 1991 by Margaret Visser. Used by permission of Grove/Atlantic, Inc., and by HarperCollins Publishers Ltd.

Alice Walker, excerpt from "The Black Writer and the Southern Experience," from *In Search of Our Mothers' Gardens: Womanist Prose*. Copyright © 1983 by Alice Walker. Reprinted by permission of Harcourt Brace & Company.

Larry Woiwode, "Ode to an Orange." Reprinted by permission of Donadio & Ashworth, Inc. Copyright © 1986.

Franklin E. Zimring, "Confessions of a Former Smoker," *Newsweek*, April 20, 1987. Originally titled "Hot Boxes for Ex-Smokers." Reprinted by permission of the author.

Glossary

abstract and concrete words An **abstract** word refers to an idea, quality, attitude, or state that we cannot perceive with our senses: *democracy, generosity, love, grief.* It conveys a general concept or impression. A **concrete** word, in contrast, refers to an object, person, place, or state that we can perceive with our senses: *lawnmower, teacher, Chicago, moaning.* Concrete words make writing specific and vivid. See also pp. 50–51, p. 63, and *general and specific words.*

allusion A brief reference to a real or fictitious person, place, object, or event. An allusion can convey considerable meaning with few words, as when a writer describes a movie as "potentially this decade's *Star Wars*" to imply both that the movie is a space adventure and that it may be a blockbuster. But to be effective, the allusion must refer to something readers know well.

analysis (also called **division**) The method of development in which a subject is separated into its elements or parts and then reassembled into a new whole. See Chapter 7 on division or analysis, p. 139.

anecdote A brief narrative that recounts an episode from a person's experience. See, for instance, Naylor, paragraph 3, p. 267. See also Chapter 5 on narration, p. 84.

argument The form of writing that appeals to readers' reason and emotions in order to win agreement with a claim or to compel some action. This definition encompasses both argument in a narrower sense—the appeal to reason to win agreement—and persuasion—the appeal to emotion to compel action. See Chapter 13 on argument and persuasion, p. 312.

assertion A debatable claim about a subject; the central idea of an argument.

audience A writer's audience is the group of readers for whom a particular work is intended. To communicate effectively, the writer should estimate readers' knowledge of the subject, their interests in it, and their biases toward it and should then consider these needs and expectations in choosing what to say and how to say it. For further discussion of audience, see pp. 2, 11–12, 19.

body The part of an essay that develops the main idea. See also pp. 26–27.

cause-and-effect analysis The method of development in which occurrences are divided into their elements to find what made an event happen (its causes) and what the consequences were (its effects). See Chapter 12 on cause-and-effect analysis, p. 281.

chronological order A pattern of organization in which events are arranged as they occurred over time, earliest to latest. Narratives usually follow a chronological order; see Chapter 5, p. 84.

classification The method of development in which the members of a group are sorted into classes or subgroups according to shared characteristics. See Chapter 8 on classification, p. 165.

cliché An expression that has become tired from overuse and that therefore deadens rather than enlivens writing. Examples: *in over their heads, turn over a new leaf, march to a different drummer, as heavy as lead, as clear as a bell.* See also p. 52.

climactic order A pattern of organization in which elements—words, sentences, examples, ideas—are arranged in order of increasing importance or drama. See also p. 38.

coherence The quality of effective writing that comes from clear, logical connections among all the parts, so that the reader can follow the writer's thought process without difficulty. See also pp. 35–38 and 231.

colloquial language The language of conversation, including contractions *(don't, can't)* and informal words and expressions (*hot* for new or popular, *boss* for employer, *ad* for advertisement, *get away with it, flunk the exam*). Most dictionaries label such words and expressions *colloquial* or *informal.* Colloquial language is inappropriate when the writing situation demands precision and formality, as a college term paper or a business report usually does. But in other situations it can be used selectively to relax a piece of writing and reduce the distance between writer and reader. (See, for instance, Hughes, p. 93, and Prager, p. 147.) See also *diction.*

comparison and contrast The method of development in which the similarities and differences between subjects are examined. Comparison examines similarities and contrast examines differences, but the two are generally used together. See Chapter 10 on comparison and contrast, p. 222.

conclusions The endings of written works—the sentences that bring the writing to a close. A conclusion provides readers with a sense of completion, with a sense that the writer has finished. Sometimes the final point in the body of an essay may accomplish this purpose, especially if it is very important or dramatic (for instance, see Manes, p. 235). But usually a separate conclusion is needed to achieve completion. It may be a single sentence or several paragraphs, depending on the length and complexity of the piece of writing. And it may include one of the following, or a combination, depending on your subject and purpose:

- A summary of the main points of the essay (see Visser, p. 159)
- A statement of the main idea of the essay, if it has not been stated before (see Klass, p. 133), or a restatement of the main idea incorporating information from the body of the essay (see Naylor, p. 269)

- A comment on the significance or implications of the subject (see Woiwode, p. 72, Dillard, pp. 105–6)
- A call for reflection, support, or action (see Sadiq. p. 154; Amend, p. 275; Krauthammer, p. 331; Backous, pp. 340–41)
- A prediction for the future (see King, pp. 353–54)
- An example, anecdote, question, or quotation that reinforces the point of the essay (see Miller, p. 127; Brady, p. 263; Katz, p. 300)

Excluded from this list are several endings that should be avoided because they tend to weaken the overall effect of an essay: (1) an example, fact, or quotation that pertains to only part of the essay; (2) an apology for your ideas, for the quality of the writing, or for omissions; (3) an attempt to enhance the significance of the essay by overgeneralizing from its ideas and evidence; (4) a new idea that requires the support of an entirely different essay.

concrete words See *abstract and concrete words.*

connotation and denotation A word's **denotation** is its literal meaning: *famous* denotes the quality of being well known. A word's **connotations** are the associations or suggestions that go beyond its literal meaning: *notorious* denotes fame but also connotes sensational, even unfavorable, recognition. See also pp. 49–50.

contrast See *comparison and contrast.*

critical reading Reading that looks beneath the surface of a work, seeking to uncover both its substance and the writer's interpretation of the substance.

deductive reasoning The method of reasoning that moves from the general to the specific. See Chapter 13 on argument and persuasion, especially pp. 317–18.

definition An explanation of the meaning of a word. An extended definition may serve as the primary method of developing an essay. See Chapter 11 on definition, p. 252.

denotation See *connotation and denotation.*

description The form of writing that conveys the perceptions of the senses—sight, hearing, smell, taste, touch—to make a person, place, object, or state of mind vivid and concrete. See Chapter 4 on description, p. 57.

diction The choice of words you make to achieve a purpose and make meaning clear. Effective diction conveys your meaning exactly, emphatically, and concisely, and it is appropriate to your intentions and audience. **Standard English,** the written language of educated native speakers, is expected in all writing for college, business and the professions, and publication. The vocabulary of standard English is large and varied, encompassing, for instance, both *comestibles* and *food* for edible things, both *paroxysm* and *fit* for a sudden seizure. In some writing situations, standard English may also include words and expressions typical of conversation (see *colloquial language*). But it excludes other levels of diction that only certain groups understand or find acceptable. Most dictionaries label expressions at these levels as follows:

- **Nonstandard:** words spoken among particular social groups, such as *ain't, them guys, hisself,* and *nowheres.*
- **Slang:** words that are usually short-lived and that may not be understood by all readers, such as *tanked* for drunk, *bread* for money, and *honcho* for one in charge.
- **Regional** or **dialect:** words spoken in a particular region but not in the country as a whole, such as *poke* for a sack or bag, *holler* for a hollow or small valley.
- **Obsolete:** words that have passed out of use, such as *cleam* for smear.

See also *connotation and denotation* and *style.*

division or analysis See *analysis.*

dominant impression The central ideal or feeling conveyed by a description of a person, place, object, or state of mind. See Chapter 4 on description, especially p. 58.

effect See *cause-and-effect analysis.*

emotional appeal In argumentative and persuasive writing, the appeal to readers' values, beliefs, or feelings in order to win agreement or compel action. See pp. 314–16.

essay A prose composition on a single nonfictional topic or idea. An essay usually reflects the personal experiences and opinions of the writer.

ethical appeal In argumentative and persuasive writing, the sense of the writer's expertise and character projected by the reasonableness of the argument, the use and quality of evidence, and tone. See p. 314.

evidence The details, examples, facts, statistics, or expert opinions that support any general statement or claim. See pp. 316 and 323–24 on the use of evidence in argumentative writing.

example An instance or representative of a general group or an abstract concept or quality. One or more examples may serve as the primary method of developing an essay. See Chapter 6 on example, p. 112.

exposition The form of writing that explains or informs. Most of the essays in this book are primarily expository, and some essays whose primary purpose is self-expression or persuasion employ exposition to clarify ideas.

fallacies Flaws in reasoning that weaken or invalidate an argument. Some of the most common fallacies are listed below (the page numbers refer to further discussion in the text).

- **Oversimplification,** overlooking or ignoring inconsistencies or complexities in evidence: *If the United States banned immigration, our unemployment problems would be solved* (pp. 284, 319).
- **Hasty generalization,** leaping to a conclusion on the basis of inadequate or unrepresentative evidence: *Every one of the twelve students*

polled supports the change in the grading system, so the administration should implement it (p. 319).

- **Begging the question,** assuming the truth of a conclusion that has not been proved: *Acid rain does not do serious damage, so it is not a serious problem* (p. 319).
- **Ignoring the question,** shifting the argument away from the real issue: *A fine, churchgoing man like Charles Harold would make an excellent mayor* (p. 319).
- **Ad hominem** ("to the man") **argument,** attacking an opponent instead of the opponent's argument: *She is just a student, so we need not listen to her criticisms of foreign policy* (p. 319).
- **Either-or,** presenting only two alternatives when the choices are more numerous: *If you want to do well in college, you have to cheat a little* (p. 320).
- **Non sequitur** ("It does not follow"), deriving a wrong or illogical conclusion from stated premises: *Because students are actually in school, they should be the ones to determine our educational policies* (p. 320).
- **Post hoc** (from *post hoc, ergo propter hoc,* "after this, therefore because of this"), assuming that one thing caused another simply because it preceded the other: *Two students left school in the week after the new policies were announced, proving that the policies will eventually cause a reduction in enrollments* (pp. 283, 320).

figures of speech Expressions that imply meanings beyond or different from their literal meanings in order to achieve vividness or force. See pp. 51–52 for discussion and examples of specific figures.

formal style See *style.*

freewriting A technique for discovering ideas for writing: writing for a fixed amount of time without stopping to reread or edit. See pp. 20–21.

general and specific words A **general** word refers to a group or class: *car, mood, book.* A **specific** word refers to a particular member of a group or class: *Toyota, irritation, dictionary.* Usually, the more specific a word is, the more interesting and informative it will be for readers. See also pp. 50–51, p. 63, and *abstract and concrete words.*

generalization A statement about a group or a class derived from knowledge of some or all of its members: for instance, *Dolphins can be trained to count* or *Television news rarely penetrates beneath the headlines.* The more instances the generalization is based on, the more accurate it is likely to be. A generalization is the result of inductive reasoning; see p. 316.

hasty generalization See *fallacies.*

hyperbole Deliberate overstatement or exaggeration: *The desk provided an acre of work surface.* See also p. 52. (The opposite of hyperbole is understatement, discussed under *irony.*)

image A verbal representation of sensory experience—that is, of something seen, heard, felt, tasted, or smelled. Images may be literal: *Snow stuck to her eyelashes; The red car sped past us.* Or they may be figures of speech: *Her eyelashes were snowy feathers; The car rocketed past us like a red missile.* (See pp. 51–52.) Through images, a writer touches the readers' experiences, thus sharpening meaning and adding immediacy. See also *abstract and concrete words.*

inductive reasoning The method of reasoning that moves from the particular to the general. See Chapter 13 on argument and persuasion, especially p. 316.

informal style See *style.*

introductions The openings of written works, the sentences that set the stage for what follows. An introduction to an essay identifies and restricts the subject while establishing your attitude toward it. Accomplishing these purposes may require anything from a single sentence to several paragraphs, depending on your purpose and how much readers need to know before they can begin to grasp the ideas in the essay. The introduction often includes a thesis sentence stating the main idea of the essay (see pp. 17–18). To set up the thesis sentence, or as a substitute for it, any of the following openings, or a combination, may be effective:

- Background on the subject that establishes a time or place or that provides essential information (see Prager, pp. 146–47; Gould, p. 178; Manes, p. 233; Krauthammer, p. 329)
- An anecdote or other reference to the writer's experience that forecasts or illustrates the main idea or that explains what prompted the essay (see Dillard, pp. 102–3; Keim, p. 199; McClain, p. 243; Brady, p. 261; Kaufman, pp. 355–56)
- An explanation of the significance of the subject (see Naylor, pp. 266–67)
- An outline of the situation or problem that the essay will address, perhaps using interesting facts or statistics (see Sadiq, p. 152; Zimring, pp. 182–83; King, p. 350)
- A statement or quotation of an opinion that the writer will modify or disagree with (see Beck, p. 303)
- An example, quotation, or question that reinforces the main idea (see Klass, pp. 130–31; Garvey, p. 238)

A good introduction does not mislead readers by exaggerating the significance of the subject or the essay, and it does not bore readers by saying more than is necessary. In addition, a good introduction avoids three openings that are always clumsy: (1) beginning with *The purpose of this essay is . . .* or something similar; (2) referring to the title of the essay in the first sentence, as in *This is not as hard as it looks* or *This is a serious problem;* and (3) starting too broadly or vaguely, as in *Ever since humans walked upright . . .* or *In today's world. . . .*

irony In writing, irony is the use of words to suggest a meaning different from their literal meaning. Mitford's "Embalming Mr. Jones" contains considerable irony, as when she notes that making a corpse "presentable for viewing in an attitude of healthy repose . . . is rather a large order [for the undertaker] since few people die in the full bloom of health, unravaged by illness or unmarked by some disfigurement" (paragraph 14, p. 213). Mitford is not sympathizing with the undertaker's difficult job but pointing out the absurdity of trying to restore a corpse at all, much less to "an attitude of healthy repose." Mitford's irony derives from **understatement,** from saying less than is meant. But irony can also derive from **hyperbole,** or exaggerating meaning, and from **reversal,** or saying the opposite of the actual meaning. Irony can be witty, teasing, biting, or cruel. At its most humorless and heavily contemptuous, it becomes **sarcasm:** *Thanks a lot for telling Dad we stayed out all night; that was really bright of you.*

metaphor A figure of speech that compares two unlike things by saying that one is the other: *Bright circles of ebony, her eyes smiled back at me.* See also p. 52.

narration The form of writing that tells a story, relating a sequence of events. See Chapter 5 on narration, p. 84.

nonstandard English See *diction.*

oversimplification See *fallacies.*

paragraph A group of related sentences, set off by an initial indentation, that develops an idea. By breaking continuous text into units, paragraphing helps the writer manage ideas and helps the reader follow those ideas. Each paragraph makes a distinct contribution to the main idea governing the entire piece of writing. The idea of the paragraph itself is often stated in a topic sentence (see pp. 33–34), and it is supported with sentences containing specific details, examples, and reasons. Like the larger piece of writing to which it contributes, the paragraph should be unified, coherent, and well developed. For examples of successful paragraphs, see the paragraph analyses in the introduction to each method of development (Chapters 4–13). See also pp. 33–34 and 259 (unity), 35–36 and 231 (coherence), and 38–39 and 171 (development).

parallelism The use of similar grammatical form for ideas of equal importance. Parallelism occurs within sentences: *The doctor recommends swimming, bicycling, or walking.* It also occurs among sentences: *Strumming her guitar, she made listeners feel her anger. Singing lines, she made listeners believe her pain.* See also p. 48.

personification A figure of speech that gives human qualities to things or abstractions: *The bright day smirked at my bad mood.* See also p. 52.

persuasion See *argument.*

point of view The position of the writer in relation to the subject. In description, point of view depends on the writer's physical and psychological relation to the subject (see pp. 58–59). In narration, point of view depends on the writer's place in the story and on his or her relation to it in time (see pp. 85–86). More broadly, point of view can also mean the writer's particular mental stance or attitude. For instance, an employee and employer might have different points of view toward the employee's absenteeism or the employer's sick-leave policies.

premise The generalization or assumption on which an argument is based. See *syllogism.*

process analysis The method of development in which a sequence of actions with a specified result is divided into its component steps. See Chapter 9 on process analysis, p. 191.

pronoun A word that refers to a noun or other pronoun: *Six days after King picked up his Nobel Peace Prize in Norway, he was jailed in Alabama.* The personal pronouns, the most common, are *I, you, he, she, it, we,* and *they.* See also pp. 35–36 (pronouns and coherence), 59 and 85–86 (pronouns and point of view), and 197 (consistency in pronouns).

proposition A debatable claim about a subject; the central idea of an argument.

purpose The reason for writing, the goal the writer wants to achieve. The purpose may be primarily to explain the subject so that readers understand it or see it in a new light; to convince readers to accept or reject an opinion or to take a certain action; to entertain readers with a humorous or exciting story; or to express the thoughts and emotions triggered by a revealing or instructive experience. The writer's purpose overlaps the main idea—the particular point being made about the subject. In effective writing, the two together direct and control every choice the writer makes. See also p. 17 and *thesis* and *unity.*

rational appeal In argumentative and persuasive writing, the appeal to readers' rational faculties—to their ability to reason logically—in order to win agreement or compel action. See pp. 316–18.

repetition and restatement The careful use of the same words or close parallels to clarify meaning and tie sentences together. See also pp. 35–36 and 231.

revision The stage of the writing process devoted to "re-seeing" a draft, divided into fundamental changes in content and structure (revision) and more superficial changes in grammar, word choice, and the like (editing). See Chapter 3, pp. 31–56.

rhetoric The art of using words effectively to communicate with an audience, or the study of that art. To the ancient Greeks, rhetoric was the art of the *rhetor*—orator, or public speaker—and included the art of persuasion. Later the word shifted to mean elegant language, and a version of that meaning persists in today's occasional use of *rhetoric* to mean pretentious or hollow language, as in *Their argument was mere rhetoric.*

sarcasm See *irony.*

satire The combination of wit and criticism to mock or condemn human foolishness or evil. The intent of satire is to arouse readers to contempt or action, and thus it differs from comedy, which seeks simply to amuse. Much satire relies on irony—saying one thing but meaning another (see *irony*).

simile A figure of speech that equates two unlike things with *like* or *as*: *The crowd was restless, like bees in a hive.* See also p. 51.

slang See *diction.*

spatial organization A pattern of organization that views an object, scene, or person by paralleling the way we normally scan things—for instance, top to bottom or near to far. See also pp. 37 and 62.

specific words See *general and specific words.*

Standard English See *diction.*

style The *way* something is said, as opposed to *what* is said. Style results primarily from a writer's characteristic word choices and sentence structures. A person's writing style, like his or her voice or manner of speaking, is distinctive. Style can also be viewed more broadly as ranging from formal to informal. A very formal style adheres strictly to the conventions of Standard English (see *diction*); tends toward long sentences with sophisticated structures; and relies on learned words, such as *malodorous* and *psychopathic.* A very informal style, in contrast, is more conversational (see *colloquial language*); tends toward short, uncomplicated sentences; and relies on words typical of casual speech, such as *smelly* or *crazy.* Among the writers represented in this book, King (p. 349) writes quite formally, Hughes (p. 93) quite informally. The formality of style may often be modified to suit a particular audience or occasion: a college term paper, for instance, demands a more formal style than an essay narrating a personal experience. See also *tone.*

syllogism The basic form of deductive reasoning, in which a conclusion derives necessarily from proven or accepted premises. For example: *The roof always leaks when it rains* (the major premise). *It is raining* (the minor premise). *Therefore, the roof will leak* (the conclusion). See Chapter 13 on argument and persuasion, especially pp. 317–18.

symbol A person, place, or thing that represents an abstract quality or concept. A red heart symbolizes love; the Golden Gate Bridge symbolizes San Francisco's dramatic beauty; a cross symbolizes Christianity.

thesis The main idea of a piece of writing, to which all other ideas and details relate. The main idea is often stated in a **thesis sentence** (or sentences), which asserts something about the subject and conveys the writer's purpose. The thesis sentence is often included near the beginning of an essay. Even when the writer does not state the main idea and purpose, however, they govern all the ideas and details in the essay. See also p. 17, p. 33, and *unity.*

tone The attitude toward the subject, and sometimes toward the audience and the writer's own self, expressed in choice of words and sentence structures as well as in what is said. Tone in writing is similar to tone of voice in speaking, from warm to serious, amused to angry, joyful to sorrowful, sympathetic to contemptuous. For examples of strong tone in writing, see Woiwode (p. 69), Mitford (p. 209), McClain (p. 243), Brady (p. 261), and King (p. 349). See also pp. 39–40 and 327.

transitions Links between sentences and paragraphs that relate ideas and thus contribute to clarity and smoothness. Transitions may be sentences beginning paragraphs or brief paragraphs that shift the focus or introduce new ideas. They may also be words and phrases that signal and specify relationships. Some of these words and phrases—by no means all—are listed below:

- **Space:** above, below, beyond, farther away, here, nearby, opposite, there, to the right
- **Time:** afterward, at last, earlier, later, meanwhile, simultaneously, soon, then
- **Illustration:** for example, for instance, specifically, that is
- **Comparison:** also, in the same way, likewise, similarly
- **Contrast:** but, even so, however, in contrast, on the contrary, still, yet
- **Addition or repetition:** again, also, finally, furthermore, in addition, moreover, next, that is
- **Cause or effect:** as a result, consequently, equally important, hence, then, therefore, thus
- **Summary or conclusion:** all in all, in brief, in conclusion, in short, in summary, therefore, thus
- **Intensification:** indeed, in fact, of course, truly

understatement See *irony.*

unity The quality of effective writing that occurs when all the parts relate to the main idea and contribute to the writer's purpose. See also pp. 33–35 and 259.

Index of Authors and Titles

Sixth Edition

Resources for Teaching

THE COMPACT READER

Short Essays by Method and Theme

JANE E. AARON

Resources for Teaching

THE COMPACT READER

Short Essays by Method and Theme

Sixth Edition

Jane E. Aaron
David Gibbs

BEDFORD/ST. MARTIN'S
Boston *New York*

Manufactured in the United States of America.

3 2 1 0 9 8
f e d c b a

For information, write: Bedford/St. Martin's, 75 Arlington Street, Boston, MA 02116 (617-426-7440)

ISBN: 0–312–19664–4

Preface

This manual has three parts, all intended to help you take maximum advantage of *The Compact Reader* as a classroom text. Part I discusses the content and possible classroom uses of the three new introductory chapters and each element of the editorial apparatus in *The Compact Reader.* Part II discusses the kinds of course materials with which *The Compact Reader* may be combined. And Part III offers teaching suggestions, a content quiz, and a vocabulary quiz for each essay in the book as well as possible answers to the discussion questions following each essay. Further, this edition of the manual offers annotations for one essay from each of the book's chapters. These annotations, resembling those in the text's Chapter 14, "Combining Methods of Development," highlight the essay's thesis and show how the author draws on diverse methods to develop the thesis.

Contents

Resources for Teaching

THE COMPACT READER
Short Essays by Method and Theme

I
USING *THE COMPACT READER*

The Compact Reader's structure is uncomplicated: three introductory chapters coach students on reading and writing, ten chapters explain and illustrate ten rhetorical methods of development, an eleventh chapter shows how the methods combine in works of writing, and a glossary defines key writing terms.

THREE INTRODUCTORY CHAPTERS ON READING AND WRITING

The former introduction is now three full chapters on reading and writing. You may wish to discuss these chapters explicitly in class, adapting all or parts of them to your syllabus; or you may find the chapters self-explanatory enough simply to ask students to read them on their own. Either way, these chapters lay useful groundwork for a reading and writing course. They explain and illustrate how critical reading is linked to good writing, how to read a text critically, how to work productively through the initial stages of writing, and how to revise and edit one's own drafts.

Reading (Chapter 1)

The introduction to critical reading is organized as follows:

A highlight of the chapter is the discussion of Barbara Lazear Ascher's essay "The Box Man," showing how a critical reader might approach an essay and what conclusions might result. This discussion is organized around generalized versions of the questions that appear after each essay in Chapters 4–13. These questions — divided into the four categories of meaning, purpose and audience, method and structure, and language — invite students to consider the elements an author calls upon in constructing an essay. By observing how a critical reader might answer these questions for Ascher's essay, students have an opportunity to see what kinds of answers they might provide to the questions following the other essays in the book — and, more significant, to begin honing their own skills as critical readers.

Ascher's essay combines many of the methods of development (definition, example, description, etc.), thus providing an overview of the methods treated separately in the subsequent chapters. At the same time, the discussion of Ascher's essay introduces a point assumed throughout *The Compact Reader* and made explicit in Chapter 14: writers rarely use a single method alone, but rather gain shape, texture, and clarity for their writing by applying whatever method is best suited to a particular point or purpose.

To engage students actively in writing during the first or second class period, you might ask them to do some prewriting as preparation for reading the Ascher essay. Possible questions: What's the difference between solitude and loneliness? What kind of people would you describe as lonely? solitary? Or, to move in another direction: What is your impression of the homeless? Do you think some people choose to be homeless? Can one find dignity in such a situation? After reading Ascher's essay, students could compare their responses with hers and with one another's. They may see Ascher's as more complete and insightful than their own, and they will probably note that she presents her characters quite vividly, perhaps even prompting some students to recall similar characters in their experience. This comparison would provide a useful springboard to a discussion of the writer's task — and to new Chapters 2 and 3.

Writing: Getting Started Through Drafting (Chapter 2)

This chapter and the next provide an overview and illustrations of the writing process, detailing the basic concepts, terms, and stages that are then used in the introductions to the rhetorical methods. Chapter 2 divides into the following sections:

The new material here includes more detailed discussion of the thesis, sections on journal writing and brainstorming, guidance on using the methods of development to prompt ideas for particular purposes, and advice on thinking in paragraphs.

The two-chapter introduction to the writing process focuses on the work-in-progress of a student, Grace Patterson, as she develops a response to Ascher's "The Box Man." Chapter 2 includes Patterson's journal writing (p. 20) and freewriting (p. 21), along with her complete first draft (p. 28). If your class does peer editing, you might ask students to comment on the draft as a beginning exercise: in discussing their own and their classmates' comments, they will come to see what kinds of responses are appropoiate and how best to phrase responses.

Writing: Revising and Editing (Chapter 3)

Continuing the two-chapter introduction to the writing process, this chapter covers the crucial stages of revising and editing. The material here is almost entirely new to this edition:

These new sections are part of a broader change in *The Compact Reader* that aims to help students with questions they may have while revising and editing. In Chapter 3 concise text and specific examples explain each element of writing, and two boxed checklists guide students through rethinking and correcting their own work. Then, in the introduction to each rhetorical method, a more specific revision and editing checklist appears with a new "Focus" box that treats an element of writing especially relevant to the method — for instance, verbs in narration, transitions in process analysis, and tone in argument. All discussions of the elements — both in Chapters 2 and 3 and in the method introductions — are indexed inside the book's front cover, so that students know just where to go for help.

ELEVEN CHAPTERS ON THE METHODS OF DEVELOPMENT

Chapter Introductions

The introductions to Chapters 4–13 all proceed in the same way. The opening section, "Using the Method," discusses the purposes for which the method is suited and provides essential concepts and definitions. The next section, "Analyzing ______ in Paragraphs," annotates two paragraphs that illustrate the method. Then the section "Developing an Essay by ______" suggests strategies for starting, organizing, drafting, and revising and editing an essay using the method. As noted above, a new "Focus" box in each chapter emphasizes a particular element that students should be aware of when revising or editing, whether it be concrete and specific language in description or paragraph coherence in comparison and contrast. Finally, "A Note on Thematic Connections" highlights the common topic of the chapter's two paragraphs and three essays.

The two paragraphs in each introduction allow students to study the method in brief, uncomplicated examples before moving on to complete essays. If you discuss the methods of development in class, the annotated paragraphs can serve as concrete illustrations of each method's special concerns. In addition, the paragraphs can serve as models for students to follow in writing paragraphs of their own (perhaps drawing on the list of topics at the end of each chapter) before they move on to more complex, essay-length applications of the method.

Chapter 14, "Combining Methods of Development," is different from the thirteen chapters before it. The introduction discusses explicitly how and why authors use the battery of rhetorical methods to accomplish their purpose in writing. Then, in place of questions about each of the two essays, brief annotations point toward the various methods used by the author. You may find it a useful exercise to ask students to formulate their own questions about these essays and even, perhaps, their own writing topics. (This manual provides both on pp. 120–25.)

The Essays

The Compact Reader's thirty-four essays satisfy several criteria. Most important, they plainly illustrate the rhetorical methods, and they are interesting. The essays are also short, averaging under three pages, so a student will find them imitable; yet they are substantial enough for sharpening reading skills and encouraging lively discussion. A few longer essays provide transition to more challenging academic work.

While mainly a rhetorical reader, *The Compact Reader* offers an alternative, thematic approach because the paragraphs and essays in each chapter relate in subject as well as form. Thus, for example, Chapter 5's narrative selections all deal with the subject of growing up, and Chapter 13's argument selections all address the controversy of cloning. You might have students read two or three of a chapter's essays and then in class discuss their theme as an entry to their rhetorical approach. Or you could of course focus discussion just on the theme. As noted on the following page, a "Connections" writing topic for each essay and a set of thematic topics for each chapter help students perceive and write about the thematic links both within and among chapters.

Biographical and Essay Headnotes

These prefaces to the essays establish a context for each essay, offering background on the writer's interests and expertise in his or her subject and providing information about his or her intended audience. Students are often inclined to skip sections like these, so it may be worthwhile to point out how helpful the headnotes can be for analyzing the essays with the discussion questions.

Discussion Questions

The questions following each essay help students analyze and evaluate the essay, either on their own or in class discussions. The questions are organized in four groups — meaning, purpose and audience, method and structure, and language — that lead students to examine the essay with an increasingly sharp focus. As mentioned earlier, the four groups of questions correspond to those following Ascher's essay in the general introduction. Possible answers to the questions are provided in this manual.

Writing Topics

At least four writing topics follow each essay. Some relate to the essay's content; some suggest a subject compatible with the method introduced in the chapter; several ask students to do research on a subject raised by the essay. A new topic for each essay, divided into "Journal Response" and "Journal to Essay," offers a prompt for students' journal writing and then guidance on developing that response into a work for readers. A topic labeled "Cultural Considerations," leads students to examine the differences and likenesses between cultures and subcultures. And a final topic, labeled "Connections," encourages students to tease out thematic or rhetorical links between the essay and either a paragraph or another essay in the book.

In addition to the topics following each essay, every chapter ends with two sets of supplementary writing suggestions. The first set, "Writing with the Method," includes many possibilities for applying the chapter's method of development. The second set, "Writing About the Theme," includes several detailed ideas for drawing on the chapter's resources to explore its topic.

GLOSSARY

This section provides definitions of the terms used in the text. Because most entries include page references to longer text discussions, the glossary can serve as an index as well as a freestanding quick reference. In some cases the glossary offers specific aids — such as options for essay introductions and conclusions, with cross-references to the book's essays — that could serve as the basis of class discussion.

II
COMBINING *THE COMPACT READER* WITH OTHER MATERIALS

Because of its brevity, *The Compact Reader* can easily be combined with other classroom materials and approaches. Teachers using previous editions report that they have successfully integrated the reader with other textbooks, library research, current newspaper and magazine articles, and the writing of their own students.

OTHER TEXTBOOKS

Though brief, *The Compact Reader* anticipates many student questions about the use of the methods of development; hence you can ask students to read the chapter introductions independently, reserving class time to discuss the chapter's theme or the application of the writing principles.

Given its coverage of the writing process, *The Compact Reader* can complement a handbook or a sentence-combining textbook. The reader can inspire writing assignments and guide students through the stages of drafting, revising, and editing. For more detailed discussion of their specific problems — such as paragraph coherence, clear sentences, or word choice — and for help with grammar and punctuation, students can consult the other textbook. A class that meets three days a week could spend one day discussing an essay from the reader, one day discussing and planning the students' own essays, and one day covering sentence-level issues.

Or you may want to pair *The Compact Reader* with a literature anthology, using the chapter introductions and the essay models to guide students as they construct their own essays in response to literature. The discussions of description (Chapter 4) and narration (Chapter 5) may help students analyze the descriptive and narrative passages they encounter in short stories or novels; and you may want to discuss the similarities and differences between fictional and nonfictional description and narration. Using these methods, students could experiment with either fiction or nonfiction (or both, contrasting in a class discussion the problems they encountered with each). You can also emphasize that much writing about literature relies heavily on example (Chapter 6), comparison and contrast (Chapter 10), cause-and-effect analysis (Chapter 12), and argument and persuasion (Chapter 13); and you can tailor assignments in which students use these methods to explain, analyze, or evaluate the readings in the literature anthology.

RESEARCH TOOLS

You may wish to help prepare students for academic writing by asking them to use outside sources in at least some of their writing. Many of the essays and themes in *The Compact Reader* invite further investigation — for example, Miller, p. 124; Sadiq, p. 152; Mitford, p. 209; Tannen, p. 292; and the whole issue of cloning in Chapter 13. Occasional suggestions for research writing ask students to consult a dictionary, an encyclopedia, *The New York Times Index,* or a book or article found through the card catalog, *The Readers' Guide,* or the Internet. The assignments are specific and limited so that students can quickly find and read the other sources, using most of their time to construct their essays.

If you incorporate research into the course you may wish to spend a class period or two introducing students to the library and its basic reference tools. You may also teach formats for documentation of sources, such as those in the *MLA Handbook for Writers of Research Papers* or almost any handbook on writing.

READING FROM CURRENT SOURCES

One advantage of a brief collection like *The Compact Reader* is that you can supplement the paragraphs and essays with topical articles on the book's themes or examples of the methods of development, or both. Op-ed pieces, essays in *Time* and *Newsweek,* articles in the school paper or the local paper, letters to the editor — all of these are good sources. Students are often surprised to see how the "textbook" methods abound in current periodicals, and at the same time they often respond well to the immediacy of last week's or yesterday's news items. In small groups or in the class as a whole, students can analyze the structure of these samples using questions like those first presented in Chapter 1 on reading. Outside readings can also serve as the basis for in-class writing topics. For instance, Stephen Manes's "The Endangered Book?" might be compared with another article on the virtues or defects of printed and electronic texts.

You can also encourage students to look for thematic connections or applications of the methods and bring them into class. For instance, students may watch for ways they use the methods in their own lives: comparing and contrasting in order to buy a new car; analyzing causes and effects in order to uncover the reasons for an unexpectedly high or low grade. Or students may examine television programs, films, magazines, and other sources for ideas to support the readings' or the class's approach to a chapter topic such as cloning or the influences of gender. And, of course, students can watch for the methods in the readings, lectures, and exams of their other courses: the descriptive lab report in chemistry, the cause-and-effect analysis in history, and so on.

STUDENT WRITING

Like many instructors you may rely on students' own writing to provide the substance of some class discussion. Given drafts of student papers to read, students may work in small groups or in pairs, using the method of careful reading and analysis recommended in Chapter 1. Then, using as a model the comments on Grace Patterson's drafts in Chapters 2 and 3, students can evaluate their peers' writing, making specific recommendations for improving each draft. When the paper employs a particular method of development, students may tailor their recommendations by referring to the chapter introduction to the method. To instruct students in this kind of peer-editing procedure — or instead of the small-group work — you may want to go over a sample student essay with the whole class.

In addition to responding to the essays in the reader, students may respond, in writing, to one another's essays. Especially for topics in argument and persuasion (Chapter 13), you can circulate one or two provocative student essays and ask the class to write arguments countering (or reinforcing) the arguments in those essays. Or students can exchange their own argumentative essays blindly, and then write an essay in response to the one they receive. Knowing that someone will be responding to their essays invites students to formulate their arguments specifically and persuasively — perhaps more so than if they were writing just for you.

III
TEACHING THE ESSAYS IN *THE COMPACT READER*

Chapter 4

DESCRIPTION

Sensing the Natural World

Marta K. Taylor

Desert Dance *(p. 65)*

Taylor's piece provides an excellent example of description and, as a student essay, is most inspiring. Her images are strong and fresh, relying on figures of speech throughout, so you might focus discussion on how Taylor's use of figures contributes to the emotion of her description. (See question 4 under "Language.") As noted in question 2 under "Method and Structure," the essay builds to a climax and effectively juxtaposes the two components of her piece: safety and violence.

Taylor's essay may remind students of significant places from their childhood, and the first writing topic has them explore their memories in a subjective description. You might have students do some freewriting to recall as much detail as possible from their memories, exploring each of their senses in relation to the place.

Content Quiz

1. Why does Taylor's family drive through the night?
   [The hotels are filled because of the rodeo.]

2. Where did Taylor grow up?
   [Los Angeles.]

3. What phenomenon was seldom seen in Taylor's childhood?
   [Rain.]

4. What looks like old men to Taylor?
   [The twisted forms of the Joshua trees.]

5. What tells Taylor that she is not dreaming?
   [The cramp in her neck and the pain in her elbow.]

Vocabulary Quiz

1. *Paragon* (paragraph 3) is closest in meaning to
   a. tower b. model c. protection
   [b. model]

2. *Silhouette* (5) is closest in meaning to
   a. figure b. outline c. frame
   [b. outline]

3. *Gnarled* (6) is closest in meaning to
   a. contorted b. mangled c. extended
   [a. contorted]

4. *Frolicked* (6) is closest in meaning to
   a. played b. zigzagged c. lit
   [a. played]

5. *Gaudy* (7) is closest in meaning to
   a. magnificent b. costly c. showy
   [c. showy]

ANSWERS

Meaning

1. "State of grace" (paragraph 7) does seem to capture Taylor's dominant impression. For her, this state consists of feeling safe (e.g., "motionless, soundless, protective paragon," [3]) while witnessing a violent, God-created lightning storm (5–6). Taylor's trip through the desert resembles a religious experience: besides "state of grace," she refers to "sacred silence" (2), draws an image of her father's haloed head (3), notes the timelessness of the experience (4), and alludes to God (6).

Purpose and Audience

1. Taylor's opening sentence explains why she and her family are traveling at night and at the same time pulls the reader quickly into the story. By using the pronoun *we* without any initial explanation of who "we" is, she captures her reader's interest.

2. Students' answers will vary, perhaps depending on whether they're familiar with the desert. Some especially vivid images: the Joshua trees like old men, God taking a photograph, the flashing fireworks of the lightning (all paragraph 6).

Method and Structure

1. Taylor is trying to convey a contrast between the interior peace of the car and the exterior chaos of the storm. The "violent, gaudy display" (paragraph 7) going on outside makes her feel even safer and more cocooned in the car, where her father, the "protective paragon of security and strength" (3) is in control, there is no noise, her sleeping brother's chest rises and falls, and the "gentle heat of the engine" (5) keeps her warm.

2. The structure builds to a climax and evenly juxtaposes safety and violence, the components of Taylor's "state of grace."

3. Taylor's emotions appear, for example, in "wicked" and "cleverly" (paragraph 1), "sacred silence" (2), "protective paragon" (3), "violent sucking rush of air" (4), "gentle heat of the engine" (5), the "empty and lonely" road (6).

4. Since the narrative framework builds to a climax at Taylor's "state of grace" (paragraph 7), it rivets attention on that impression.

Language

1. Taylor's language creates an atmosphere of peace, stillness, and protection: "Sacred silence" (paragraph 2), "protective paragon of security and strength" (3); "gentle heat of the engine" (3); "still in silence, still in darkness" (6).

2. The title refers to the "dance" of the lightning, and several phrases in paragraphs 6–7 support the notion of movement: the "natural strobe" of the lightning, the "hobble" of the trees, the fireworks that "frolicked," the "movements of a marionette," the "gaudy display."

3. The Joshua trees are "twisted" and look like "old men" with a "feeble hobble" (paragraph 6). This is a vivid if economical description of the trees, which are thought to have been named after Joshua, the biblical leader of Israel, because their limbs angle upward like arms. On the desert, they stand taller than their surroundings and do resemble gnarled humans.

4. Similes: hair playing with light "like tinsel" (paragraph 3), the lightning "like a rapidly growing twig" (5), a flash "as if God were taking a photograph" (6), the road that "shone like a dagger," (6), the trees that "looked like old men" (6).

5. The final long sentence intensifies the sense that Taylor is coming out of the spell of the storm. The rush of words parallels the rush of feeling in her neck and elbow.

Larry Woiwode

Ode to an Orange *(p. 69)*

Woiwode's essay is perhaps the most accessible of the descriptive essays in this chapter, dealing with a subject familiar to all. But Woiwode's knowledge of the orange is unusually intimate: he comes up with a wealth of detail that no ordinary orange consumer could match, at least not on a conscious level. To appreciate this, students could, before reading the essay, list everything they know about oranges and then compare their lists with the multitude of points Woiwode makes.

Despite its reverie-like quality, Woiwode's essay is meticulously organized; paragraphs 12 through 14 provide a particularly ingenious example of spatially organized description as Woiwode's attention moves from the peel of the orange to the "nubbin, like half of a tiny orange, tucked into its bottom" (see question 2 under "Method and Structure"). Students with a scientific bent may enjoy mimicking Woiwode's powers of observation and his organizational strategy to describe, say, a flower — but with the objectivity of the botanist.

You could point out that Woiwode is not the first to pay tribute to the orange. Oranges relieved winter doldrums in much the same way for Laura Ingalls Wilder in *Little House on the Prairie,* for example, and kept the hero of *Shogun* alive when his ship was lost at sea.

Content Quiz

1. Where did Larry Woiwode grow up?
   [North Dakota.]

2. When did the oranges arrive every year?
   [Usually by Thanksgiving but always before Christmas.]

3. Where did Woiwode and his brother find oranges on Christmas day?
   [At the tip of their Christmas stockings.]

4. What was Woiwode's indirect way of asking for an orange?
   ["Mom, we think we're getting a cold."]

5. According to Woiwode, what happens if you bite at the peel of an orange too much?
   ["Your front teeth will feel scraped, like dry bone, and your lips will begin to burn from the bitter oil."]

Vocabulary Quiz

1. *Degradation* (paragraph 10) is closest in meaning to
   a. lowering b. humiliation c. dejection
   [b. humiliation]

2. *Elixir* (10) is closest in meaning to
   a. cleanser   b. cure-all   c. vitamin
   [b. cure-all]

3. *Heft* (12) is closest in meaning to
   a. weight   b. thickness   c. peel
   [a. weight]

4. *Feat* (13) is closest in meaning to
   a. appendage   b. accomplishment   c. challenge
   [b. accomplishment]

5. *Abrade* (15) is closest in meaning to
   a. scrape   b. numb   c. excite
   [a. scrape]

ANSWERS

Meaning

1. The boys' longing encompassed much more than simply a desire to eat an orange, but they had neither the desire nor the ability to articulate all that the orange represented to them. Woiwode as an adult can (and does, in this essay) articulate its significance: it is complex, perfect, and a vehicle for the imagination to play upon.

2. The orange is everything that winters in North Dakota are not: warm, full of light, colorful, round and whole, sensually appealing. This impression, begun in the first paragraph ("the mere color of them"), is sustained throughout the essay.

Purpose and Audience

1. The shift into the present tense suggests that the orange gives the adult the same pleasure and relief from the "wintry world" as it brought the child (paragraphs 11–12). The North Dakota winters were literally cold, harsh, and "hard-edged yet insubstantial"; "this . . . wintry world" possesses those same qualities, but metaphorically (44).

2. Woiwode's description of the orange's unpleasantness actually strengthens his praise, for several reasons: it reflects a small boy's relish for nastiness as well as niceness; it injects a feeling of clear-eyed realism, mitigating sentimentality; and it intensifies, through contrast, the more pleasurable sensations the orange produces (as, for example, in the last two sentences of paragraph 14).

3. The essay succeeds precisely because Woiwode evokes everyone's familiar feelings about the orange so completely — what's fresh (and extraordinarily successful) is the wealth of detailed description and the significance attached to the orange (see question 1 under "Meaning"). The sensory details will probably be the most familiar to students: the

"springtime acidity" of oranges "filling that musty place" (10), "the packed heft and texture . . . of an orange in your hand" (12), and "the gaseous spray" that "can form a mist" when the orange is sliced (12), among many other examples. Surprising details might include the way this spray "can be lit with a match to create actual fireworks" (12) or the hand grenade imagery (13).

Method and Structure

1. Objective description (for example, the first three sentences of paragraph 14) tempers the passion and sentimentality of the subjective description, suggesting, too, a small boy playing scientist. The subjective description (the last sentence of paragraph 14, or most of paragraph 16) lends exuberance, ingenuousness, the authenticity of personal experience. The two kinds together encircle the subject completely, giving both an accurate and an emotional impression.

2. Paragraphs 10–12 describe the arrival of the oranges, Woiwode's lens zooming from the crates stacked in the depot to the oranges stacked in a crate to a single orange in the toe of a Christmas stocking, and — finally — in hand. He then focuses on the orange itself: paragraphs 13–14 analyze one way to eat an orange, describing at the same time its composition, from peel to interior; 15–16 analyze two other ways to eat an orange, in decreasing order of popularity but (perhaps) in increasing order of intimacy — by paragraph 16 we're inside the orange looking out. The sequence, then, is quite logical.

3. Woiwode's painstaking explanations suggest the deliberate probing and playing of a boy, whose endless examination uncovers the complexities of the fruit.

Language

1. Examples of poetic language abound; they include "Oh, those oranges . . . the mere color of them" (paragraph 1); "wended," "elixir" (10); "lovely spheres," "nestled positions" (11); and finally, "Oh, oranges, solid *o*'s, light from afar in the midst of the freeze, and not unlike that unspherical fruit . . ." (16). The language is hyperbolic, and, though tongue-in-cheek, suggests the ultimate seriousness with which Woiwode regards his subject.

2. The shift in pronouns is effective, for its purpose is clear: to include Woiwode's audience in his experience.

3. Woiwode appeals to all five senses: sight ("each orange . . . as vivid in your vision as a pebbled sun," paragraph 11); smell ("the resinous smell of fresh wood in addition to the already orangy atmosphere," 10); touch ("the packed heft and texture, finally, of an orange in your hand," 12); taste ("the eruption in your mouth of the slivers of watery meat . . . the essence of orange," 15); and even hearing ("sputtery ignitions," 12).

4. Other words evoking heat and light: "pebbled sun," (paragraph 11); "match," "fireworks," "sputtery ignitions," "candle," "stove top" (12), "burn" (13 and 15); "daylight" (15); "the light from the windows (shining through an empty glass bowl)" and "light from afar" (16). This imagery helps create Woiwode's dominant impression of the orange (see question 2 under "Meaning"), and vividly illustrates how the oranges brightened the "white winter landscape" of North Dakota (1).

ANNOTATED ESSAY

Oh, those oranges arriving in the midst of the North Da- 1
kota winters of the forties — the mere color of them, carried
through the door in a net bag or a crate from out of the white
winter landscape. Their appearance was enough to set my
brother and me to thinking that it might be about time to
develop an illness, which was the surest way of receiving a
steady supply of them.

"Mom, we think we're getting a cold." 2

"*We?* You mean, you two want an orange?" 3

This was difficult for us to answer or dispute; the matter 4
seemed moved beyond our mere wanting.

"If you want an orange," she would say, "why don't you 5
ask for one?"

"We want an orange." 6

"'We' again. '*We want an orange.*'" 7

"May we have an orange, please." 8

"That's the way you know I like you to ask for one. Now, 9
why don't each of you ask for one in that same way, but separately?" *Narration*

"Mom . . ." And so on. There was no depth of degrada- 10
tion that we wouldn't descend to in order to get one. If the
oranges hadn't wended their way northward by Thanksgiving, they were sure to arrive before the Christmas season,
stacked first in crates at the depot, filling that musty place,
where pews sat back to back, with a springtime acidity, as if
the building had been rinsed with a renewing elixir that set
it right for yet another year. Then the crates would appear at
the local grocery store, often with the top slats pried back on
a few of them, so that we were aware of a resinous smell of
fresh wood in addition to the already orangy atmosphere that
foretold the season more explicitly than any calendar.

And in the broken-open crates (as if burst by the power 11 *Description*
of the oranges themselves), one or two of the lovely spheres
would lie free of the tissue they came wrapped in — always
purple tissue, as if that were the only color that could contain the populations of them in their nestled positions. The
crates bore paper labels at one end — of an orange against a
blue background, or of a blue goose against an orange background — signifying the colorful otherworld (unlike our wintry one) that these phenomena had arisen from. Each orange,

stripped of its protective wrapping, as vivid in your vision as a pebbled sun, encouraged you to picture a whole pyramid of them in a bowl on your dining room table, glowing in the light, as if giving off the warmth that came through the windows from the real winter sun. And all of them came stamped with a blue-purple name as foreign as the otherworld that you might imagine as their place of origin, so that on Christmas day you would find yourself digging past everything else in your Christmas stocking, as if tunneling down to the country of China, in order to reach the rounded bulge at the tip of the toe which meant that you had received a personal reminder of another state of existence, wholly separate from your own.

Description

12 The packed heft and texture, finally, of an orange in your hand — this is it! — and the eruption of smell and the watery fireworks as a knife, in the hand of someone skilled, like our mother, goes slicing through the skin so perfect for slicing. This gaseous spray can form a mist like smoke, which can then be lit with a match to create actual fireworks if there is a chance to hide alone with a match (matches being forbidden) and the peel from one. Sputtery ignitions can also be produced by squeezing a peel near a candle (at least one candle is generally always going at Christmastime), and the leftover peels are set on the stove top to scent the house.

13 And the ingenious way in which oranges come packed into their globes! The green nib at the top, like a detonator, can be bitten off, as if disarming the orange, in order to clear a place for you to sink a tooth under the peel. This is the best way to start. If you bite at the peel too much, your front teeth will feel scraped, like dry bone, and your lips will begin to burn from the bitter oil. Better to sink a tooth into this greenish or creamy depression, and then pick at that point with the nail of your thumb, removing a little piece of the peel at a time. Later, you might want to practice to see how large a piece you can remove intact. The peel can also be undone in one continuous ribbon, a feat which maybe your father is able to perform, so that after the orange is freed, looking yellowish, the peel, rewound, will stand in its original shape, although empty.

Description and process analysis

Division or analysis

14 The yellowish whole of the orange can now be divided into sections, usually about a dozen, by beginning with a division down the middle; after this, each section, enclosed in its papery skin, will be able to be lifted and torn loose more easily. There is a stem up the center of the sections like a mushroom stalk, but tougher; this can be eaten. A special variety of orange, without any pits, has an extra growth, or nubbin, like half of a tiny orange, tucked into its bottom. This nubbin is nearly as bitter as the peel, but it can be eaten, too; don't worry. Some of the sections will have miniature sec-

tions embedded in them and clinging as if for life, giving the impression that babies are being hatched, and should you happen to find some of these you've found the sweetest morsels of any.

Description and process analysis

If you prefer to have your orange sliced in half, as some 15
people do, the edges of the peel will abrade the corners of your mouth, making them feel raw, as you eat down into the white of the rind (which is the only way to do it) until you can see daylight through the orangy bubbles composing its outside. Your eyes might burn; there is no proper way to eat an orange. If there are pits, they can get in the way, and the slower you eat an orange, the more you'll find your fingers sticking together. And no matter how carefully you eat one, or bite into a quarter, juice can always fly or slip from a corner of your mouth; this happens to everyone. Close your eyes to be on the safe side, and for the eruption in your mouth of the slivers of watery meat, which should be broken and rolled fine over your tongue for the essence of orange. And if indeed you have sensed yourself coming down with a cold, there is a chance that you will feel it driven from your head — your nose and sinuses suddenly opening — in the midst of the scent of a peel and eating an orange.

And oranges can also be eaten whole — rolled into a 16
spongy mass and punctured with a pencil (if you don't find this offensive) or a knife, and then sucked upon. Then, once the juice is gone, you can disembowel the orange as you wish and eat away its pulpy remains, and eat once more into the whitish interior of the peel, which scours the coating from your teeth and makes your numbing lips and tip of your tongue start to tingle and swell up from behind, until, in the light from the windows (shining through an empty glass bowl), you see orange again from the inside. Oh, oranges, solid *o*'s, light from afar in the midst of the freeze, and not unlike that unspherical fruit which first went from Eve to Adam and from there (to abbreviate matters) to my brother and me.

"Mom, we think we're getting a cold." 17

"You mean, you want an orange?" 18

This is difficult to answer or dispute or even to acknowl- 19
edge, finally, with the fullness that the subject deserves, and that each orange bears, within its own makeup, into this hard-edged yet insubstantial, incomplete, cold, wintry world.

DOMINANT IMPRESSION (THESIS)

Joan Didion

The Santa Ana *(p. 75)*

Joan Didion's piece is an excellent example of descriptive writing. Her colorful yet unsettling images appeal to the senses — sight, sound, taste, and touch. Didion's precision permits the reader to share her sensual impressions of and experiences with the "persistent [and] malevolent" (paragraph 3) Santa Ana wind. Perhaps the most interesting question to begin discussion with your students is whether Didion admires the destructive force she writes about. (See question 4 under "Writing Topics.") Because it may remind them of one, Didion's essay could start a discussion about a "phenomenon" that drives students crazy where they live, leading into questions 1 and 2 under "Writing Topics."

Content Quiz

1. Where does the Santa Ana come from?
   [From the northeast, down mountains and through canyons.]

2. Has Didion lived in Los Angeles all her life?
   [No: "when I first moved to Los Angeles . . . ."]

3. What color is the sky right before the Santa Ana comes?
   [Yellow.]

4. What are the two extremes of weather in Southern California?
   [The rainy season and the dry season of the Santa Ana.]

5. How long does the Santa Ana usually last?
   [Three or four days.]

Vocabulary Quiz

1. *Mechanistic* (paragraph 1) is closest in meaning to
   a. conniving b. determined c. complex
   [b. determined]

2. *Malevolent* (3) is closest in meaning to
   a. evil b. powerful c. dangerous
   [a. evil]

3. *Mitigating* (3) is closest in meaning to
   a. aggravating b. circumstantial c. excusing
   [c. excusing]

4. *Incendiary* (4) is closest in meaning to
   a. inflammatory b. insensitive c. windy
   [a. inflammatory]

5. *Apocalypse* (6) is closest in meaning to
   a. draught b. end of the world c. winter
   [b. end of the world]

ANSWERS

Meaning

1. Didion's statement of thesis is found in paragraph 6: "[T]he violence and the unpredictability of the Santa Ana affect the entire quality of life in Los Angeles, accentuate its impermanence, its unreliability. The wind shows us how close to the edge we are."

2. The wind leaves the city dry, hot, and still. It makes people a little crazy, "drying the hills and the nerves to the flash point" (paragraph 1). "The baby frets. The maid sulks" (1). It makes Didion testy and argumentative, causing her to "rekindle a waning argument with the telephone company" (1). Indians used to throw themselves into the sea when the Santa Ana came. Didion's neighbor holes up inside, and the neighbor's husband runs around with a machete. People go to their doctors complaining of "headaches and nausea and allergies, about 'nervousness,' about 'depression'" (3). Schoolchildren become unmanageable. People have even committed murder.

3. A mechanistic view holds that human behavior is entirely controlled by outside forces (in this case, a force of nature). The opposite view would be that humans act of their own accord, that they have free will.

4. The last sentence could be read both literally (Los Angeles is on the edge of the continent) and figuratively (life in Los Angeles pushes residents to the edge of sanity).

Purpose and Audience

1. The essay uses the Santa Ana to make a larger point about the craziness of life in Los Angeles. Didion seems to be responding to the problem she states in paragraph 6: "It is hard for people who have not lived in Los Angeles to realize how radically the Santa Ana figures in the local imagination." At the same time there is a self-expressive element to the essay: such a potent force begs to be written about and affords Didion the opportunity to explore its dramatic effects on herself and her surroundings.

2. Didion is writing for the outsider as well: "It is hard for people who have not lived in Los Angeles to realize how radically the Santa Ana figures in the local imagination" (paragraph 6). We know she is from the city because the essay is written from a personal, insider's point of view, and she uses the first person: "when I first moved to Los Angeles" (2); "just as we had always known it would be in the end" (6).

Method and Structure

1. Because the wind itself is nearly intangible, Didion is limited to describing its physical and psychological effects: on nature (the Pacific, peacocks, the sky [paragraph 2]), on property (the fires and property damage described in paragraph 4), and on people (see the second question under "Meaning"). By describing these effects so vividly and thoroughly, she brings to life a phenomenon that people who have not lived in Los Angeles would otherwise have trouble understanding.

2. Paragraphs 1 and 2 are mostly subjective: Didion describes the first signs of a Santa Ana coming on as she is writing, then goes on to describe its effects on herself and on her neighbors. Paragraphs 3–5 are mostly objective, based on literary and journalistic sources: Didion situates the Santa Ana in the context of other malevolent winds throughout the world, attempts a scientific explanation for its effects, discusses the two violent seasons in Los Angeles, and recounts a particularly devastating Santa Ana in 1957. Paragraph 6 returns to a subjective point of view: Didion suggests that the Santa Ana is emblematic of life in southern California.

3. The quotation helps move the essay from examples based on Didion's personal experience to examples she has heard or read about.

4. Didion's description relies on concrete examples because what she's trying to describe is essentially intangible. Her examples are colorful and memorable and paint a vivid portrait for the outsider of what it's like to live with such a malign phenomenon.

Language

1. The first person makes the description more personal and intimate, helping us feel the effects of the Santa Ana as though we were there. The present tense gives a sense of immediacy to the essay, creating the impression that Didion is spontaneously recording her thoughts.

2. The colorful images (the glossy ocean, screaming peacocks in trees, the yellow sky) bring the effects of the Santa Ana to life and make them memorable. The imagery is surreal because it's jarring, otherworldly.

Chapter 5

NARRATION

Growing Up

Langston Hughes

Salvation *(p. 93)*

Students usually understand and identify with Hughes's childhood emotions, for nearly everyone can recall an early experience of disappointed expectations. That point of connection can provide a starting place for discussion of the essay.

Though Hughes does provide informative details on the revival, students who are unfamiliar with the ideas of sin, salvation, and the like may participate in discussion more actively if they are given some brief background information. In contrast, students whose own religious experiences parallel those of Hughes's aunt, rather than of Hughes himself, may bring to the essay their own strong convictions and may therefore have difficulty understanding (and accepting, even as a different opinion) Hughes's point.

Content Quiz

1. What is Hughes "not really" saved from?
   [Sin.]

2. Where is "Salvation" mainly set?
   [In Hughes's Auntie Reed's church.]

3. What is the "mourner's bench"?
   [The place in church for those who had not yet been "saved."]

4. Who is Westley?
   [The last boy to be saved besides Hughes.]

5. What did Hughes do the night of the day he was saved?
   [Cried in bed.]

Vocabulary Quiz

1. *Dire* (paragraph 3) is closest in meaning to
   a. dreadful b. angry c. sacrilegious
   [a. dreadful]

2. *Fold* (3) is closest in meaning to
   a. class   b. bevy   c. flock
   [c. flock]

3. *Rounder* (6) is closest in meaning to
   a. minister   b. watchman   c. mortician
   [b. watchman]

4. *Deacons* (6) is closest in meaning to
   a. fathers   b. minister's assistants   c. singers
   [b. minister's assistants]

5. *Rejoicing* (13) is closest in meaning to
   a. singing   b. praying   c. expressing joy
   [c. expressing joy]

ANSWERS

Meaning

1. Hughes's point seems to be that his faith was shattered because he was not saved and because his lie passed for salvation. Whereas at first he is naively faithful, in the end he feels shameful and betrayed.

2. Hughes decides to get up because of the pressure he feels and because Westley has lied without suffering for it. Afterward, however, he feels betrayed that Jesus did not save him from the pressure or from lying.

3. Hughes plays on the word *salvation*. In saying that he "was saved from sin. . . . But not really saved" (first two sentences), he means that he performed the ritual convincingly yet felt no spiritual change. He pretended to be saved and in doing so lost his faith. For Hughes, at least, salvation seems a sham. (It is also possible that the adult Hughes felt he *had* in a sense been saved — from hypocrisy.)

Purpose and Audience

1. Clearly, the experience was a significant one for Hughes (paragraph 15), and that fact alone could explain his including the essay in his autobiography. He does not seem critical of his aunt and the other adults in the congregation; as an adult he seems to understand that they would "see" Jesus in other than the literal way he expected to "see" (15). But this play on *see* itself may point up another purpose of the essay: to underscore the literal-mindedness of children, their inability to comprehend the abstractions by which adults live. Hughes may also have wanted to illustrate the point at which a child learns to rely on himself or herself, not on others, for truth.

2. Hughes does not assume that his readers are familiar with the kind of service he describes. Particularly in paragraphs 1, 3, 4, 11, 13, and 14, he provides details that clarify the procedure, such as the purpose and activity of a revival (1), the appeals made to the children (3, 4), and the blessing of the children (14).

3. The dialogue, lines from hymns, and descriptions of the noise level in the church (e.g., paragraphs 3 and 7) re-create the pressure Hughes felt in a way that simple assertions such as "Everyone was after me to get up" could not possibly do. Besides sound, the details contributing to the sense of pressure include heat (6), loneliness (6, 11), time (6, 11), the aunt's presence (7), and Westley's proud grin (11).

Method and Structure

1. The autobiographical narrative form makes this more personal, and probably more memorable, than an argumentative essay would be. A title of an argumentative essay on the same subject might be "Hypocrisy in Organized Religion." Such an essay would probably also be more objective, presenting both sides of the subjct, and possibly more objectionable to those who disagreed with the author's opinion.

2. Examples of explanation in Hughes's narrative: what he expected salvation to be like (paragraph 2); who Westley is (6). Examples of compression of time: several weeks of the revival retold in just a few sentences (1); the procession of children to the altar (6). Example of omitted events: the gap between the end of the meeting (14) and Hughes in bed that night (15). Example of expanded time: the moments before Hughes decides to be saved (7–12).

   By condensing or omitting some events, Hughes keeps the narrative moving and emphasizes the crucial moments of pressure leading to his decision. These moments are drawn out in a way that makes us sympathize with Hughes's predicament, understand his reason for lying, and share his sense of shame and betrayal.

3. Examples of transitions: "then" (paragraph 3); "still" (5); "finally," "now" (6); "then," "while" (7); "now" (11); "suddenly" (13); "when," "then" (14); "that night," "now," "any more" (15).

4. The process analysis is important because many readers will not have been to a revival meeting or will not understand how one works. It also puts us inside the process, allowing us to see it through Hughes's eyes.

Language

1. Hughes as an adult seems both amused and sorrowful. His use of "young sinners" (paragraph 1) is ironic, and a similar wryness runs through his descriptions of Westley (6, 11) and even of his predicament (7, 11). But there is no amusement in the last paragraph, where Hughes conveys his pain and a sense of loss. Here the juxtaposition of Hughes's wish not to cry (because it is childish and he does not want his aunt to hear) with his inability to keep from crying (some form of *cry* appears four times) intensifies the sense of sorrow.

2. Hughes achieves the breathless pattern of a child reporting an overwhelming experience, thus leading us to see the experience from a child's view rather than an adult's.

3. The young Hughes seems to expect a literal physical experience (paragraphs 5, 7, 15); he will "see" something that "comes to" him from the outside. Hughes's aunt, in contrast, believes that one can "see" Jesus in one's soul (2); the seeing is not literal but spiritual. Hughes's understanding of *see* makes his disappointment and sense of betrayal inevitable.

ANNOTATED ESSAY

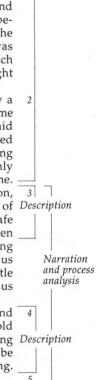

I was saved from sin when I was going on thirteen. But 1
not really saved. It happened like this. There was a big revival at my Auntie Reed's church. Every night for weeks there had been much preaching, singing, praying, and shouting, *Narration*
and some very hardened sinners had been brought to Christ, and the membership of the church had grown by leaps and bounds. Then just before the revival ended, they held a special meeting for children, "to bring the young lambs to the fold." My aunt spoke of it for days ahead. That night, I was escorted to the front row and placed on the mourner's bench with all other young sinners, who had not yet been brought to Jesus.

My aunt told me that when you were saved you saw a 2
light, and something happened to you inside! And Jesus came into your life! And God was with you from then on! She said you could see and hear and feel Jesus in your soul. I believed her. I have heard a great many old people say the same thing and it seemed to me they ought to know. So I sat there calmly in the hot, crowded church, waiting for Jesus to come to me.

The preacher preached a wonderful rhythmical sermon, 3
all moans and shouts and lonely cries and dire pictures of *Description*
hell, and then he sang a song about the ninety and nine safe in the fold, but one little lamb was left out in the cold. Then he said: "Won't you come? Won't you come to Jesus? Young lambs, won't you come?" And he held out his arms to all us young sinners, there on the mourner's bench. And the little girls cried. And some of them jumped up and went to Jesus right away. But most of us just sat there. *Narration and process analysis*

A great many old people came and knelt around us and 4
prayed, old women with jet-black faces and braided hair, old men with work-gnarled hands. And the church sang a song *Description*
about the lower lights are burning, some poor sinners to be saved. And the whole building rocked with prayer and song.

Still I kept waiting to *see* Jesus. 5

Finally all the young people had gone to the altar and 6
were saved, but one boy and me. He was a rounder's son named Westley. Westley and I were surrounded by sisters and deacons praying. It was very hot in the church, and getting late now. Finally Westley said to me in a whisper: " God damn! I'm tired o' sitting here. Let's get up and be saved." So he got up and was saved.

Then I was left all alone on the mourner's bench. My aunt 7
came and knelt at my knees and cried, while prayers and *Narration*
songs swirled all around me in the little church. The whole *and process*
congregation prayed for me alone, in a mighty wail of moans *analysis*
and voices. And I kept waiting serenely for Jesus, waiting, *Description*
waiting — but he didn't come. I wanted to see him, but nothing happened to me. Nothing! I wanted something to happen to me, but nothing happened.

I heard the songs and the minister saying: "Why don't 8
you come? My dear child, why don't you come to Jesus? Jesus
is waiting for you. He wants you. Why don't you come? Sister Reed, what is this child's name?"

"Langston," my aunt sobbed. 9

"Langston, why don't you come and be saved? Oh, Lamb 10
of God! Why don't you come?"

Now it was really getting late. I began to be ashamed of 11
myself, holding everything up so long. I began to wonder
what God thought about Westley, who certainly hadn't seen
Jesus either, but who was now sitting proudly on the plat- *Description*
form, swinging his knickerbockered legs and grinning down
at me, surrounded by deacons and old women on their knees
praying. God had not struck Westley dead for taking his name
in vain or for lying in the temple. So I decided that maybe to
save further trouble, I'd better lie, too, and say that Jesus had
come, and get up and be saved.

So I got up. 12

Suddenly the whole room broke into a sea of shouting, as 13
they saw me rise. Waves of rejoicing swept the place. Women
leaped in the air. My aunt threw her arms around me. The *Description*
minister took me by the hand and led me to the platform.

When things quieted down, in a hushed silence, punctu- 14
ated by a few ecstatic "Amens," all the new young lambs were
blessed in the name of God. Then joyous singing filled the
room.

That night, for the last time in my life but one — for I 15
was a big boy twelve years old—I cried. I cried, in bed alone,
and couldn't stop. I buried my head under the quilts, but my *Narration*
aunt heard me. She woke up and told my uncle I was crying
because the Holy Ghost had come into my life, and because I
had seen Jesus. But I was really crying because I couldn't bear
to tell her that I had lied, that I had deceived everybody in *THESIS*
the church, that I hadn't seen Jesus, and that now I didn't
believe there was a Jesus any more, since he didn't come to
help me.

Lionel L. Prokop

In the Eyes of a Little Boy *(p. 98)*

Students should be able to relate to this essay (written in Prokop's freshman composition course) because of the narrator's innocence. Most students will be able to connect to the story in some way, perhaps recalling the first time they had to deal with the loss of a loved one. You may want to explain to students the importance that a chronological sequence plays when writing a narrative, using Prokop's essay as an example.

One opening for class discussion is to look at the role Prokop's questions play in the narrative form. (See question 1 under "Language.")

Content Quiz

1. What event takes place in the church?
   [The narrator's father's funeral.]

2. Who are the last people to leave the church?
   [The narrator's family.]

3. How many siblings does the narrator have?
   [One brother and at least two sisters.]

4. What does the narrator compare to statues on the hill?
   [Big bones — that is, tombstones.]

5. What seems to have been the father's occupation?
   [He seems to have worked the land: "that he helped them build their barns, that he could pick the most corn."]

Vocabulary Quiz

Told from the perspective of a little boy, this essay presents fewer uncommon words than other selections in *The Compact Reader.* Subsequently, the vocabulary quiz has been omitted.

ANSWERS

Meaning

1. Prokop's unstated thesis is that children are often incapable of understanding death.

2. It's never explicitly stated that the father is dead, and the word *death* is never used. This helps show that the narrator didn't understand that his father was dead and forces the reader to identify with his point of view.

3. Prokop doesn't use its name because the young narrator doesn't know it: he needs to keep the point of view consistent and keep us wondering as he does.

4. The community is rural and close-knit. We learn in paragraph 6 that the father worked the land and was a well-liked member of the community: he helped his neighbors build their barns, was their friend, shared his home brew with them, and enjoyed playing pranks on them.

Purpose and Audience

1. Prokop doesn't state his purpose. One possibility is that he wrote the essay as a form of catharsis to help him deal with his father's death or to better remember the distant event (assuming the essay is autobiographical). Or he may have wanted to make an observation about the innocence of childhood.

2. The essay requires little of readers except a willingness to accept the narrator's innocence and ingenuousness. Students who find the voice unconvincing may not like the piece.

Method and Structure

1. Narration allows Prokop to show the effects of the death as he experienced them at the time. The result is startling, perhaps more so than if Prokop had used another method — for instance, explaining the effects or contrasting life before and after the death.

2. The present tense gives the essay a sense of immediacy, as if the reader were experiencing the funeral and burial at the same time as the boy.

3. The events in paragraphs 3 and 4 are narrated with no compression of time, and Prokop lingers on the crying. In paragraph 5 the "long ride" is glossed over (it is a mere pause in the ceremony), putting the coffin in the ground is given full attention, and the priest's speech (which the narrator presumably wouldn't understand) is glossed over. Whereas an adult rendering of the event would be influenced by preconceived notions about what a funeral is, the narrator — who has no label for the event — is more impressed by sensual details (the tears, the flowers).

4. The first hints that this is a funeral are people crying in a church (halfway through paragraph 1) and the flowers (toward the end of paragraph 1). As the ambiguous opening gradually comes into focus, readers will likely feel both relieved that they finally understand what's going on and shocked that the boy is at his father's funeral. The disjunction between he reader's new knowledge and the child's continued ignorance creates a sense of pathos.

5. Prokop appeals to all five senses. The richest descriptions are in the first half of the essay: sight (five colors), smell ("Sweet aroma"), and sound (organ music) are all evoked in paragraph 1. In paragraph 2 the

narrator mentions the "funny odor" and the sting in his eyes from the lantern and the "sunlight coming through the stained-glass windows," which makes "red, blue, and yellow colors" on the coffin. Paragraph 3 brings back the "sad music" and the feel and taste of the tear.

Language

1. These are questions the child narrator is asking himself, or possibly asking the adults around him at the funeral. The reader knows the answers all too well, which creates dramatic irony and increases the poignancy of the essay — especially with the questions placed at the ends of paragraphs and at the end of the essay.

2. The tone is detached, objective, reportorial. The reader is all the more moved because the child doesn't understand what's happening.

Annie Dillard

The Chase *(p. 102)*

Students should enjoy Dillard's dramatic rendering of a childhood thrill, which is likely to inspire them to write their own tales of glories past. Dillard is at her narrative and descriptive best here, capturing the feeling of childhood and the rhythm of the chase. Vivid, convincing detail is, of course, the key to making a story compelling, and only through careful word choice will students be able to recreate their excitement as effectively as Dillard does hers. The narrative provides rich opportunity to discuss how such description operates: see question 4 under "Method and Structure" and question 3 under "Language."

Content Quiz

1. How old was Dillard when the snowball event took place?
   [Seven years old.]

2. What kind of car did Dillard and her friends throw snowballs at?
   [A black Buick.]

3. Who got chased by the driver?
   [Dillard and Mike Fahey.]

4. What did the driver say when he finally caught them?
   ["You stupid kids."]

5. How would Dillard have reacted if the driver "cut off [their] heads"?
   [She would have "died happy."]

Vocabulary Quiz

1. *Translucent* (paragraph 6) is closest in meaning to
   a. clear b. frozen c. solid
   [a. clear]

2. *Impelled* (14) is closest in meaning to
   a. chased b. drove c. knocked
   [b. drove]

3. *Compelled* (14) is closest in meaning to
   a. forced b. teased c. chased
   [a. forced]

4. *Obscure* (16) is closest in meaning to
   a. mountainous b. hidden c. empty
   [b. hidden]

5. *Exalting* (20) is closest in meaning to
   a. furious b. close c. glorious
   [c. glorious]

ANSWERS

Meaning

1. "That you have to fling yourself at what you're doing, you have to point yourself, forget yourself, aim, dive" (paragraph 13); that the unbridled, unfettered enthusiasm of childhood comes from wholehearted concentration on whatever you're doing; that the courage to do it is simultaneously the catalyst for and reward of childhood enthusiasms, enthusiasms most adults (though not the driver of the Buick) abandon.

2. Getting in trouble is not per se a means to happiness — total concentration and courage and commitment, to the point of forgetting yourself, is. Being open to this kind of abandon may well get you into trouble, but it's the *abandon* rather than the trouble that leads to happiness.

Purpose and Audience

1. To recapture the glories of childhood, to recreate its adrenaline rush, and possibly to remind adults what they are missing — getting the most out of life.

2. Dillard's shift to *you* moves the spotlight from herself, the narrator, to the reader. The reader becomes an active participant in the football plays described, thus increasing the immediacy and intensity of the scene Dillard is trying to create.

Method and Structure

1. Dillard could have chosen to illustrate the enthusiasm of youth and its loss in adulthood through example, which would have brought concreteness to a general observation (much as the narration, a kind of extended example, does here), or comparison and contrast, which would have placed the change at the center of the essay. But the vivid narration brings with it an immediacy and a memorableness that might be hard to achieve through these other methods.

2. The elaborate detail in paragraph 12 — including specific homes, a woodpile, and an intersection — gives a feel for the intricacy and length of the chase. But to go on in this way, mentioning every feature of the landscape, would probably try readers' patience. Thus in succeeding paragraphs Dillard summarizes: the chase runs "block after block" (13, 14).

3. This sentence entices readers to read on and also lets readers know that whatever "trouble" Dillard got into was not serious. Hence, readers can relax, become fully engaged in the story, and vicariously enjoy the chase.

4. Description contributes specific concrete details that bring the scene to life. Some are "up to our boot tops in snow" (paragraph 3), "tire chains came clanking from afar" (7), "a smashed star with a hump in the middle" (8), "every breath tore my throat" (14), "there was a prow of snow beneath [the man's cuffs] on his shoes and socks" (16).

Language

1. Dillard seamlessly interweaves the straightforward, declarative language and limited experience of a child ("Some boys taught me to play football" [paragraph 1]; "we all popped it one" [5]; "this time, the only time in all of life" [9]) with the greater powers of observation and more sophisticated perspective of an adult ("complex trail of beige chunks like crenellated castle walls" [5]; "we reverted to the natural solitude of children" [5]).

2. Dillard feels admiration and approval because the man throws himself into the chase with the same verve she and her friends do. Some evidence: "a man got out of it [the car], running. He didn't even close the car door" (9); "incredibly, he was still after us" (10); "Any normal adult would have quit. . . . He was a thin man, all action. All of a sudden, we were running for our lives" (10); all of paragraph 13; "He impelled us forward" (14); "he would never give up, this man" (14); "The point was that he had chased us passionately without giving up, and so he had caught us" (19).

3. Both images suggest presents, gifts, magic, enchantment, a childhood fantasy world.

Chapter 6

EXAMPLE

Using Language

Kim Kessler

Blah Blah Blah *(p. 119)*

Kessler wrote this essay as a student to comment on a seemingly meaningless phrase common among her peers. Using examples, she shows that the phrase "blah blah blah" does have meaning — "generic rhetoric" (paragraph 2), "an intimacy that transcends . . . language" (4), and finally a "coverup" (5). For this last meaning Kessler provides a narrative example whose concrete, specific details are particularly effective.

One way to initiate class discussion may be to ask students who Kessler's audience is. Building on this question, have students discuss the various audiences they write to when they create compositions. Their instructors? Their friends? The free world? How do their examples change according to their audience?

Content Quiz

1. What are two other versions of "blah blah blah" used by Kessler's friends?
   ["yadda yadda" and "etc., etc."]

2. What are some of the "good reasons" why people use "blah blah blah"?
   [What one is about to say is so trite that it's not worth repeating; one wants to cut to the chase; the speakers are intimates who understand each other without words.]

3. Whom does Kessler bump into while walking across campus?
   [An acquaintance.]

4. What caused Kessler to have a mini-breakdown?
   [She was caught in the rain, lonely, wet, and carrying a heavy trombone.]

5. What solution does Kessler offer to "this 'blah blah' thing"?
   ["Put on your Walkman and avoid it all."]

Vocabulary Quiz

1. *Articulate* (paragraph 2) is closest in meaning to
   a. intelligent b. well-spoken c. interesting
   [b. well-spoken]

2. *Transcends* (4) is closest in meaning to
   a. rises above b. eliminates c. climbs
   [a. rises above]

3. *Accosted* (6) is closest in meaning to
   a. molested b. priced c. approached
   [c. approached]

4. *Gratuitous* (6) is closest in meaning to
   a. pointless b. typical c. tedious
   [a. pointless]

5. *Repercussions* (9) is closest in meaning to
   a. reasons b. consequences c. drumbeats
   [b. consequences]

ANSWERS

Meaning

1. Kessler feels she's being deceptive by using the phrase to avoid a subject she doesn't want to talk about. She uses it "in place of the atypical" rather than to "impl[y] the typical" (paragraph 7).

2. The "symbol of generic rhetoric" (paragraph 2) is "blah blah blah." The phrase is symbolic in that it stands in the place of something else — it has no meaning of its own. It's generic because it can mean anything. This captures Kessler's main idea: that the phrase is deceptive because it is open to almost any interpretation the listener chooses to assign to it. The speaker can use this ambiguity to avoid speaking the truth without actually lying.

Purpose and Audience

1. Both: although Kessler says she is on the fence about "blah blah blah," most of her examples imply criticism of the phrase. She disparagingly refers to her "oh-so-articulate friends" (paragraph 1) who use it, and she feels dismissed and rejected when its use implies that "it is not worth their time or their energy to actually recount a story for my sake" (4). Equally, she feels guilty when she finds herself using the phrase to cover up something she doesn't want to talk about. Kessler may also be trying to amuse, as is indicated by her ironic tone: "Oh-so-articulate friends" (1), "yeah, it's a verb" (4), "it's not very often that I share like that" (6).

2. Kessler is writing for an audience of her fellow college students. The subject is current slang among young adults, her peers; the evidence consists of anecdotes from campus life; and the tone is ironic and informal (see question 1 under "Language").

Method and Structure

1. It's hard to talk about language in the abstract; it's a subject that calls for examples. The long example in paragraph 6 shows us exactly how Kessler uses "blah blah blah" to avoid subjects she doesn't want to talk about. Without it we'd have no idea what she means.

2. In paragraph 4 the examples illustrate the "couple of good reasons" for the prevalence of the phrase: many conversations are trite, and intimates do not always require language. The extended example in paragraph 6 shows that for the author the expression "is a refuge, a wall of meaningless words with which to protect myself" (7).

3. The introduction consists of paragraphs 1–3: these provide the background of the phenomenon and Kessler's main idea. In the body of the essay (paragraphs 4–8) Kessler gives examples that illustrate her main idea, showing how the phrase is used and misused. Paragraph 9 serves as the conclusion, offering a "solution" to the problem.

4. Kessler not only shows how "blah blah blah" is used but also explains what it may mean in these uses. "Blah blah blah" can be a shortcut for something trite or obvious; it can suggest that the person speaking doesn't want to waste his or her time; it can indicate intimacy between the speakers; and it can mean that the speaker doesn't wish to tell the whole truth. This use of definition helps Kessler demonstrate her thesis from paragraph 2.

Language

1. Kessler's tone is partly serious, partly ironic. Her style is at times very informal, almost like spoken language: "The thing about it is . . ." (paragraph 2); "Well, maybe *lie* isn't the best word" (5); "But, hey . . ." (9); and all of her parenthetical remarks. This informality is appropriate for an audience of college peers: she writes as if she were talking to a group of friends. At other times she takes on a mock serious tone, imitating an earnest academic analysis: "It has come to my attention," "symbol of general rhetoric" (2); "recently noticed phenomenon" (3); much of paragraph 4. Kessler means everything she says (until the last paragraph), but she seems to realize that there are more important problems than this one.

2. "Oh-so-articulate friends" (paragraph 2); "I hope you can all handle that open display of vulnerability. It's not very often that I share like that" (6); the "modest proposal" at the end of paragraph 9.

3. Kessler gives the piece an informal, chatty feel and makes it clear that she is writing for her peers.

Michael W. Miller

The Type That Turns Heads in Computer Circles *(p. 124)*

With the popularity of electronic mail, Miller's essay should be intriguing to students. The essay addresses smileys, or emoticons, such as the "odd little punctuation sequence :-) or one of its many variants" (paragraph 3). Miller provides examples of the symbols and of testimony for and against them.

You might want to build class discussion around the two sides of the smiley controversy: Do the symbols enrich e-mail messages, or are they poor substitutes for words? You might also ask students to question the author's purpose: Does Miller want the reader to draw his or her own conclusion, or is he leading the reader to his own opinion?

Miller's essay also provides a good occasion to point out an appropriate structure for an example essay: the thesis is supported by generalizations that are in turn supported by examples. Does Miller's supporting evidence persuade students to believe what he concludes? (See question 2 under "Method and Structure.")

Content Quiz

1. What does 7:^] mean in smiley language?
   ["I resemble Ronald Reagan."]

2. According to "smiley scholars," is e-mail more like an exchange of letters or a telephone conversation?
   [A telephone conversation.]

3. When did smileys first appear?
   [More than a decade before the essay was written, or around 1980.]

4. What are *Spaceship* and *Rhodomagnetic Digest*?
   [Science fiction fanzines from the 40s and 50s.]

5. What do Roger Ebert and Penn Jillette think about smileys?
   [Ebert cringes when he sees them but thinks they may be useful for dimwitted people. Jillette hates them even more; he thinks they ruin the joke.]

Vocabulary Quiz

1. *Etiquette* (paragraph 2) is closest in meaning to
   a. letter writing b. society c. manners
   [c. manners]

2. *Posterity* (6) is closest in meaning to
   a. wealth b. history c. future generations
   [c. future generations]

3. *De rigueur* (7) is closest in meaning to
   a. fashionable b. rigorous c. risky
   [a. fashionable]

4. *Ubiquitous* (7) is closest in meaning to
   a. useless b. widespread c. happy
   [b. widespread]

5. *Habitué* (16) is closest in meaning to
   a. habit b. creature of habit c. one who frequents
   [c. one who frequents]

ANSWERS

Meaning

1. Miller's thesis is that the electronic smiley and its variants serve as a form of "emotional punctuation" (paragraph 5) that helps reduce potential misunderstandings in electronic communication (10).

2. *Turns heads* means (figuratively) "attracts attention" and (literally) causes people to tilt their heads to the side, as they must when reading smileys because the smileys themselves are tilted to the side.

3. Like other punctuation marks, emotional punctuation marks tell the reader how to read or interpret a sentence.

Purpose and Audience

1. Miller wrote the essay primarily to chronicle and explain a current phenomenon. But, judging by the tone of the essay, he may also have wanted to amuse readers with his anecdotes about creative uses of the smiley.

2. Miller assumes familiarity with certain rudimentary computer terms: "bulletin board," "online" (paragraph 1); "electronic mail" (3); "e-mail" (5); "Hacker's" (6); "CompuServe," "network" (7). The ideal reader will have first-hand experience with electronic mail and the phenomenon discussed here, but such experience is not necessary to understand or appreciate the essay.

Method and Structure

1. Examples allow Miller to show the various uses of smileys and explain how they serve the function of "emotional punctuation" (paragraph 5). The general subject of e-mail conversation is a natural source of amusing examples, which helps Miller achieve his secondary purpose — to entertain.

2. Paragraphs 1 and 2 support the generalization in paragraph 3. The examples in paragraph 6 support the last sentence in paragraph 5. Paragraph 7 begins with a generalization, followed by two examples (paragraphs 7 and 8). Paragraphs 10 and 11 contain a generalization, exemplified in paragraphs 12–14. Paragraph 15 offers a generalization about anti-smiley opinion, supported in paragraphs 16–18. The final paragraph takes issue with this opinion, offering a final example.

3. The first sentence and first two examples grab the reader's attention and establish the essay's humorous tone. This isn't a flaw in the organization of the essay, just an anecdotal way of introducing the subject.

4. Paragraph 4 defines what a smiley is. If you didn't know that you had to look at them sideways, you wouldn't understand any of the numerous examples.

Language

1. The tone is bemused, as fits Miller's purpose of entertaining while informing readers.

2. Miller's approach is evenhanded, giving the floor to those both pro- and anti-smiley. At times his language seems to criticize the phenomenon: "spreading like a virus" (paragraph 5, although this is a pun); "tripping over someone's electronic face" (7). But he seems to come down in favor of the devices in his last paragraph: "Flat and stereotyped? Hey, Sproull and Kiesler, do some real research!"

3. Emoticon = emotional + icon: it's a sign (icon) of one's emotion.

Perri Klass

She's Your Basic L.O.L. in N.A.D. *(p. 130)*

Klass's subject is inherently interesting to students: even if they don't hope or plan to go to medical school, they are at least intrigued by doctors. This essay addresses the issue of how language establishes the boundaries of groups. As such, it could initiate a discussion of special languages — in particular, technical terminology, jargon, and slang. Before or after reading the essay, students could discuss (in class or in writing) the purposes and effects of special language — is it alienating? mysterious? authoritative? Other sources of jargon worth examining: a sports broadcast, a conversation between computer specialists, or the writing class itself (e.g., what effects do expressions like *comma splice* and *relative clause* have on students?). The goal of any of these discussions: to arrive at an understanding of when jargon is useful, necessary, and effective, and when it is superfluous, distracting, or downright harmful.

Klass's essay beautifully surmounts a central difficulty in essays developed by example: how to weave together many examples without sounding monotonous. She avoids tedium through sentence variety (see the box on text p. 117) and also by varying the way she presents her examples: she explains some medical terms in parenthetical comments, others by anecdote; she treats some briefly, lingers over others; she groups those having to do with baseball into a separate class. Students often overlook the importance of variety — or, if they are aware that their writing lacks it, don't quite know how to remedy the problem. Klass's essay provides a useful model. (Question 2 under "Method and Structure" focuses their attention on this point.)

Content Quiz

1. What does the abbreviation "N.A.D." stand for in this essay?
   [No apparent distress.]

2. In medical jargon, what is a "no-hitter"?
   [A night without any new admissions.]

3. In medical jargon what is the accepted abbreviation for "nasogastric"?
   [NG.]

4. What nickname did the interns give the medical student who liked to cite syndromes named after researchers?
   [Mr. Eponym.]

5. In neurological research, what is a "brainstem preparation"?
   ["An animal whose higher brain functions have been destroyed."]

Vocabulary Quiz

1. *Primeval* (paragraph 2) is closest in meaning to
   a. mean b. blissful c. earliest
   [c. earliest]

2. *Terminal* (6) is closest in meaning to
   a. dead b. final c. calloused
   [b. final]

3. *Pompous* (15) is closest in meaning to
   a. pretentious b. important c. principled
   [a. pretentious]

4. *Locutions* (15) is closest in meaning to
   a. phrases b. exclamations c. jokes
   [a. phrases]

5. *Jurisdiction* (17) is closest in meaning to
   a. government b. authority c. guidance
   [b. authority]

ANSWERS

Meaning

1. Klass's point: learning medical jargon marks a rite of passage into doctorhood, a passage mitigated by her realization that the "new alien assumptions" (paragraph 18) of the language are not wholly positive or for the better. She reveals her full point in the final paragraph.

2. To Klass, medical jargon serves two useful purposes: the language builds "closeness and professional spirit" (8), and it creates distance between doctors and patients (17). Given Klass's evident distaste for the disrespectful and even inhumane jargon illustrated in paragraphs 10–16, those particular expressions seem unlikely to build her professional spirit. They certainly do create distance between doctor and patient.

Purpose and Audience

1. Klass implies that she lost something by becoming a doctor; that there was something idyllic about the lack of knowledge she had before and something corrupted about her now-complex life. The phrase suggests that she wants to explain a process that medical students must go through and also *why* they must go through it — in part, why the corrupted state is necessary for doctors.

2. Klass is halfway between a nondoctor and a doctor; she's looking ahead, gaining knowledge, but still clearly remembers that state of "primeval innocence" (paragraph 2). She expects her readers not to know about the doctor side, which she is at pains to explain for them in paragraphs 1, 2, 4, and many others, but she expects readers to identify with the nondoctor side: see, for example, "endless jargon and abbreviations" (2), terms that go "a little too far" (10), "I had resolved not to be shy" (11), jargon that makes "the beginning medical student nervous about the effects of medical training" (15).

3. Answers will vary. Klass does not define every term (e.g., "nasogastric," [paragraph 3]; "cardiac enzymes," [4]; "sickle-cell," [15]). But in most if not all cases her meaning is clear without definitions: we don't need to know exactly what's wrong with the patient to see the point being made about jargon.

Method and Structure

1. Klass begins with an example for the sake of interest — and to create a sense of mystery: What are these terms? Will they be defined? She immediately makes her audience feel befuddled, thus putting them in the position she was in when she started working in the hospital — and in the position of a patient. The opening example in effect gives readers a capsule version of Klass's experience, which is what she wants to explain.

2. Other examples: "This sort of construction probably reflects . . . profound irritation" (paragraph 4); "Baseball metaphor is pervasive" (6); "Some people seem to become enamored of the jargon for its own sake" (8); "Then there are the more pompous locutions" (15).

3. Effects: camaraderie (paragraph 8), excitement (8, 18), arrogance and pomposity (8–15), discomfort (15, 18), distance (17).

Language

1. Klass is deeply concerned about the desensitizing effects that medical jargon has had on her and her colleagues. This seriousness toward her subject is most evident in the last paragraph: the tone becomes graver as Klass makes her concerns explicit. The essay's black humor is cautionary, serving to expose a troubling phenomenon.

2. Answers will vary. The shifts between *we/us* and *they/them* may be seen as emphasizing that Klass's own role is shifting: she doesn't identify fully with the doctors. The shifts between *I* and *you* are more difficult to justify thematically, though Klass evidently uses *you* — especially in paragraph 18 — to extend her conclusions beyond herself.

3. Positive: "thrills," "communicate effectively," "professional speech," "closer and closer to being a doctor." Negative: "uncomfortably," "peculiarities and even atrocities," "avoid," "strange," "afraid," "alien."

ANNOTATED ESSAY

"Mrs. Tolstoy is your basic L.O.L. in N.A.D., admitted for 1
a soft rule-out M.I.," the intern announces. I scribble that on
my patient list. In other words Mrs. Tolstoy is a Little Old
Lady in No Apparent Distress who is in the hospital to make
sure she hasn't had a heart attack (rule out a myocardial infarction). And we think it's unlikely that she has had a heart
attack (a *soft* rule-out).

Definition

If I learned nothing else during my first three months of 2
working in the hospital as a medical student, I learned endless jargon and abbreviations. I started out in a state of primeval innocence, in which I didn't even know that "s̄ C.P.,
S.O.B., N/V" meant "without chest pain, shortness of breath,
or nausea and vomiting." By the end I took the abbreviations
so for granted that I would complain to my mother the English Professor, "And can you believe I had to put down *three*
NG tubes last night?"

Example and definition

"You'll have to tell me what an NG tube is if you want 3
me to sympathize properly," my mother said. NG,
nasogastric — isn't it obvious?

I picked up not only the specific expressions but also the 4
patterns of speech and the grammatical conventions; for example, you never say that a patient's blood pressure fell or
that his cardiac enzymes rose. Instead, the patient is always

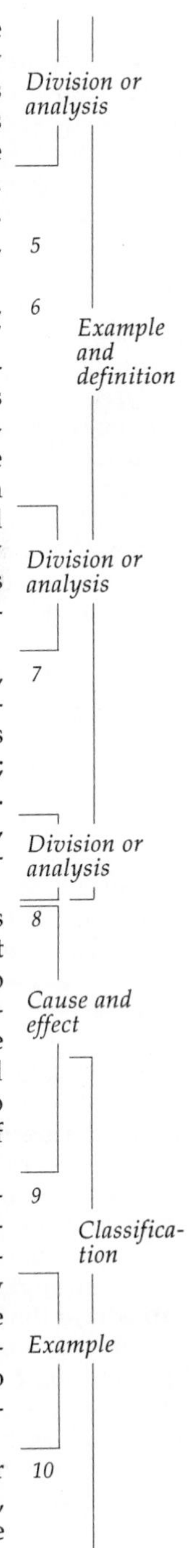

the subject of the verb: "He dropped his pressure." "He bumped his enzymes." This sort of construction probably reflects that profound irritation of the intern when the nurses come in the middle of the night to say that Mr. Dickinson has disturbingly low blood pressure. "Oh, he's gonna hurt me bad tonight," the intern may say, inevitably angry at Mr. Dickinson for dropping his pressure and creating a problem.

When chemotherapy fails to cure Mrs. Bacon's cancer, 5
what we say is, "Mrs. Bacon failed chemotherapy."

"Well, we've already had one hit today, and we're up next, 6
but at least we've got mostly stable players on our team." This means that our team (group of doctors and medical students) has already gotten one new admission today, and it is our turn again, so we'll get whoever is next admitted in emergency, but at least most of the patients we already have are fairly stable, that is, unlikely to drop their pressures or in any other way get suddenly sicker and hurt us bad. Baseball metaphor is pervasive: a no-hitter is a night without any new admissions. A player is always a patient — a nitrate player is a patient on nitrates, a unit player is a patient in the intensive-care unit and so on, until you reach the terminal player.

It is interesting to consider what it means to be winning, 7
or doing well, in this perennial baseball game. When the intern hangs up the phone and announces, "I got a hit," that is not cause for congratulations. The team is not scoring points; rather, it is getting hit, being bombarded with new patients. The object of the game from the point of view of the doctors, considering the players for whom they are already responsible, is to get as few new hits as possible.

These special languages contribute to a sense of closeness 8
and professional spirit among people who are under a great deal of stress. As a medical student, it was exciting for me to discover that I'd finally cracked the code, that I could understand what doctors said and wrote and could use the same formulations myself. Some people seem to become enamored of the jargon for its own sake, perhaps because they are so deeply thrilled with the idea of medicine, with the idea of themselves as doctors.

I knew a medical student who was referred to by the in- 9
terns on the team as Mr. Eponym because he was so infatuated with eponymous terminology, the more obscure the better. He never said "capillarypulsation" if he could say "Quincke's pulses." He would lovingly tell over the multinamed syndromes — Wolff-Parkinson-White, Lown-Ganong-Levine, Henoch-Schonlein — until the temptation to suggest Schleswig-Holstein or Stevenson-Kefauver or Baskin-Robbins became irresistible to his less reverent colleagues.

And there is the jargon that you don't ever want to hear 10
yourself using. You know that your training is changing you, but there are certain changes you think would be going a little too far.

11 The resident was describing a man with devastating terminal pancreatic cancer. "Basically he's C.T.D.," the resident concluded. I reminded myself that I had resolved not to be shy about asking when I didn't understand things. "C.T.D.?" I asked timidly.

Example and definition

12 The resident smirked at me. "Circling The Drain."

13 The images are vivid and terrible. "What happened to Mrs. Melville?"

14 "Oh, she boxed last night." To box is to die, of course.

15 Then there are the more pompous locutions that can make the beginning medical student nervous about the effects of medical training. A friend of mine was told by his resident, "A pregnant woman with sickle-cell represents a failure of genetic counseling."

Classification

16 Mr. Eponym, who tried hard to talk like the doctors, once explained to me, "An infant is basically a brainstem preparation." A brainstem preparation, as used in eurological research, is an animal whose higher brain functions have been destroyed so that only the most primitive reflexes remain, like the sucking reflex, the startle reflex, and the rooting reflex.

17 The more extreme forms aside, one most important function of medical jargon is to help doctors maintain some distance from their patients. By reformulating a patient's pain and problems into a language that the patient doesn't even speak, I suppose we are in some sense taking those pains and problems under our jurisdiction and also reducing their emotional impact. This linguistic separation between doctors and patients allows conversations to go on at the bedside that are unintelligible to the patient. "Naturally, we're worried about adeno-C.A.," the intern can say to the medical student, and lung cancer need never be mentioned.

Cause and effect

Example

18 I learned a new language this past summer. At times it thrills me to hear myself using it. It enables me to understand my colleagues, to communicate effectively in the hospital. Yet I am uncomfortably aware that I will never again notice the peculiarities and even atrocities of medical language as keenly as I did this summer. There may be specific expressions I manage to avoid, but even as I remark them, promising myself I will never use them, I find that this language is becoming my professional speech. It no longer sounds strange in my ears — or coming from my mouth. And I am afraid that as with any new language, to use it properly you must absorb not only the vocabulary but also the structure, the logic, the attitudes. At first you may notice these new alien assumptions every time you put together a sentence, but with time and increased fluency you stop being aware of them at all. And as you lose that awareness, for better or for worse, you move closer and closer to being a doctor instead of just talking like one.

THESIS

Chapter 7

DIVISION OR ANALYSIS

Looking at Popular Culture

Emily Prager

Our Barbies, Ourselves *(p. 147)*

Prager's essay is sure to promote a lively discussion about women's roles, women and power, and images of women in popular culture. While Prager's focus is on how Barbie helps perpetuate certain stereotypes of women, Prager opens her essay out at the end to claim that the damage done extends well beyond the arena of toys for children and into the world of mainstream movies and videos for adults. You might begin discussion by asking students whether they think girls and women today are still being stereotyped in similar ways. (Barbie, after all, is still being sold.) You might also have them read two other essays that address this theme: Judy Brady's "I Want a Wife" (p. 261) and Amy Beck's "Struggling for Perfection" (p. 303).

Content Quiz

1. Who is Jack Ryan?
   [The man who helped design Barbie, along with Sparrow and Hawk missiles.]

2. To whom was Jack Ryan once married?
   [Zsa Zsa Gabor.]

3. What kind of accessories are available for Barbie?
   [Condos, fashion plazas, beauty salons, a boyfriend (Ken).]

4. What does Barbie lack?
   ["A certain softness."]

5. What does Ken's lack of genitals signify?
   [Injustice.]

Vocabulary Quiz

1. *Eclectic* (paragraph 1) is closest in meaning to
   a. successful b. diverse c. artistic
   [b. diverse]

2. *Ameliorate* (3) is closest in meaning to
   a. improve b. bridge c. erase
   [a. improve]

3. *Epitome* (3) is closest in meaning to
   a. fragment b. representative c. quality
   [b. representative]

4. *Totemic* (6) is closest in meaning to
   a. related b. promiscuous c. symbolic
   [c. symbolic]

5. *Ineffably* (6) is closest in meaning to
   a. inexpressibly b. uncharacteristically c. positively
   [a. inexpressibly]

ANSWERS

Meaning

1. Prager's main idea is that Barbie is not a harmless, innocent toy for girls but is instead an artificial image constructed by a man to perpetuate stereotypes that he and many other men would like to see women embody. Barbie's extremely unrealistic figure, that "something indescribably masculine" (paragraph 5), and Ken's lack of genitals now make sense to Prager. Barbie was created to conform to men's concepts of what women should look like, but also what they should *be* like: "no matter how much sexuality Barbie possessed, she would never turn Ken on" (7). She would never have that power.

2. Prager's question is partly tongue-in-cheek; her essay opens with the "astounding" (paragraph 1) information that the man who designed Barbie was also a designer of military weapons. But the question has a serious meaning as well: perhaps Barbie was intended as a weapon against women.

Purpose and Audience

1. Prager's purpose is to show and convince readers that Barbie in particular and toys in general are not necessarily what they appear to be, and their messages can do profound and lasting damage. Prager believes Barbie encouraged millions of women to feel that they must have a thirty-nine-inch bust and a twenty-three-inch waist to be attractive. She also believes that Barbie helped make acceptable a standard that remains the status quo today: movies and videos "filled with topless women and covered men" (paragraph 7).

2. Prager believes movies "filled with topless women and covered men" (paragraph 7) foster inequality and injustice, and she assumes her readers share this view. While many of her readers probably do, there are

clearly enough filmmakers, consumers, and viewers who disagree with Prager to perpetuate an industry that thrives on these images.

Method and Structure

1. Prager analyzes Barbie's physical appearance (her huge breasts and tiny waist; see paragraphs 2, 3, 5, 6, 7); her accessories (high heels, condos, fashion plazas, pools, beauty salon, Ken; see paragraphs 4–6); her personality and attitude toward life ("into free love and fun colors," [6]); and her sexuality ("humongous breasts" but a "disturbing" "loneliness" because she could never make love [7]). All these elements transform Barbie from an ostensibly innocent toy to a dangerous cultural artifact intended to make girls both see themselves as Barbie and aspire to be her.

2. Claims about the sexism of Barbie need the support of the doll's particulars: her breasts are out of proportion to the rest of her body, she has high-heeled feet, she "lacks a certain softness" to the point of being "phallic" (paragraph 5). Even people who have seen the doll before (almost all readers) will not necessarily have thought about it from a perspective as critical as Prager's. The point of her analysis is to highlight the salient features of Barbie as she sees them in order to make a larger point about the effect the doll has on little girls.

3. Rather than opening her essay with a claim she would then systematically have to defend, Prager proceeds more informally, presenting evidence anecdotally and saving her claim for the end. By the time we reach her conclusion, the connection between Barbie and female nudity in the movies makes sense.

4. Before Barbie, American dolls looked like the children who played with them — prepubescent or even younger still, if they were baby dolls. They were sexless ("flatfooted and breastless," paragraph 6); refined (they looked like Elizabeth Taylor in *National Velvet,* 6); and had no apparent boyfriends, presumably so their owners couldn't imagine them doing anything they weren't supposed to. Dolls before Barbie promoted the stereotypes of women as "good little girls"; their message was that girls should grow up to be refined and "ineffably dignified"(6): perfect wives to important men. Barbie's message, in contrast, was primarily sexual: having huge breasts and flaunting them was desirable for girls, as was having material things associated with good looks.

Language

1. Prager's more casual language is always associated directly with Barbie; it describes either her or something she owns or feels. This language replicates Prager's (and presumably many women's) experience as girls playing with Barbie. Prager's more formal language helps to establish the seriousness of her purpose: to demonstrate that Barbie is no mere toy but a cultural artifact worth careful analysis.

2. Prager is being ironic. A woman defined by her condos, fashion plazas, pools, and beauty salons is definitely not liberated, at least not from male expectations of what she should be. She is not "on the move" to anything more important than improving her appearance, which is precisely what Barbie's manufacturers want women to be most concerned with. Other examples of irony include "I've never married, simply because I cannot find a man who looks as good in clam diggers as Ken" (paragraph 4) and Prager's statement that the dolls of the 1950s "grew up to be Jackie Kennedy — before she married Onassis" (6). (Good girls of the fifties wouldn't have remarried, especially if their deceased husbands were beloved national figures and especially not to foreign millionaires considerably older than themselves.)

Shafeeq Sadiq

Racism and Sexism in Advertising *(p. 152)*

This student essay provides a thought-provoking critique of advertising tactics and a good example of division or analysis. With the thesis that "minorities and women are constantly being exploited in everyday advertisements" (paragraph 1), the analysis may surprise students who do not view television commercials critically. Sadiq demonstrates the elements of advertisements that make them exploitative and then reassembles these elements to draw his conclusion that "there needs to be a public awakening, for racism and sexism should not be used in any situation. . . " (paragraph 7).

Sadiq's piece could open up class discussion about how minorities and women are exploited in the media. As an assignment, have students bring in magazines and newspaper articles or descriptions of television shows or commercials in order to analyze the stereotypes expressed. Students should feel free to explore other areas of American society where stereotypes may appear, such as the fashion industry or the music industry. (See question 1 under "Writing Topics.")

Content Quiz

1. What two products are frequently associated with sexist advertising?
[Beer and cars.]

2. Who is the target audience for the Geo Storm ad?
[Men.]

3. How does the ad for malt liquor perpetuate stereotypes of the African American community?
[It implies that blacks were happier in the past, singing and dancing in the streets, before they became responsible and had to get jobs.]

4. What is the implication of the ad for the computer company?
[That parts made in Arab countries must be inferior.]

5. Who does Sadiq suggest may be the most stereotyped group in advertising?
[Indian Americans.]

Vocabulary Quiz

1. *Notorious* (paragraph 3) is closest in meaning to
a. guilty b. irresponsible c. infamous
[c. infamous]

2. *Perpetuates* (4) is closest in meaning to
a. reinforces b. exaggerates c. endures
[a. reinforces]

3. *Monotony* (4) is closest in meaning to
a. fidelity b. tedium c. responsibility
[b. tedium]

4. *Insinuates* (5) is closest in meaning to
a. implies b. states forcefully c. imagines
[a. implies]

5. *Perpetrator* (6) is closest in meaning to
a. criminal b. sinner c. guilty party
[c. guilty party]

ANSWERS

Meaning

1. "Television, magazines, and billboards no longer show products, but rather show gimmicks in order to sell their product. In general, these gimmicks seem to enforce racial stereotypes and to view women in a negative way" (paragraph 1).

2. Advertisers attempt to associate their products with sexual success: they are selling the notion that buying their products will make their male customers more attractive to women. In doing so they exploit women, reducing them to objects to stimulate male fantasies.

3. Sadiq thinks the depiction plays into stereotypes of African Americans as not being responsible, implying that their true nature is carefree and fun-loving, while responsibility is something unnatural to them.

4. Sadiq opposes this example to an Indian American who wasn't born in the United States, whose foreignness is exaggerated for comic effect.

Purpose and Audience

1. Sadiq wants to convince readers that sexism and racism are alive and well in advertising today, despite the more "politically correct" atmosphere in other areas of life. But, as he indicates in the last paragraph he

also wants to encourage a grassroots movement to boycott companies that use racism and sexism to sell their products.

2. Sadiq is writing for a multiracial audience made up of both men and women. He seems to assume that his readers will be receptive to his message: he spends no time justifying why exploitation of women and minorities is undesirable or why advertisers should not engage in exploitation. At the same time, he seems to assume that his readers are not aware of the "gimmicks" that advertisers use to exploit women and minorities — his purpose is to bring them to light.

Method and Structure

1. Because the questionable aspects of ads may not be immediately apparent, Sadiq's analysis of the ads — revealing their elements — is necessary for him to show readers the offensive components.

2. The principle of analysis (the first, topic sentence) is the elements of the ad that cause it to exploit stereotypes of Arab Americans. These elements are the native garb, the camel, and the caption that insults the quality of Arab products.

3. Sadiq's first paragraph is a formal introduction that sets up the subject in a no-nonsense, right-to-the-point way. By contrast, Prager opens her essay with an anecdote. Sadiq's last paragraph is a formal conclusion calling for action that grows out of his thesis, while Prager's last paragraph continues building her thesis.

4. Sadiq probably doesn't think racism is a more serious problem. But he sees only one group of people — women — as exploited by sexism, whereas any number of racial or ethnic groups suffer from racism, each in a distinct way.

5. The description is necessary to translate a message from a visual medium into a written one. Viewers might not notice that the actors are attractive, that the women appear so quickly after the man opens the beer (paragraph 3), that the Arab was in native garb (5), or that the Indian spoke with an accent (6).

Language

1. Sadiq takes his subject very seriously; one might even accuse him of humorlessness. But this tone is in keeping with his high-minded purpose.

2. Answers will vary. Some students may find the irony inconsistent with Sadiq's otherwise serious tone. Others may appreciate the occasional lightness.

ANNOTATED ESSAY

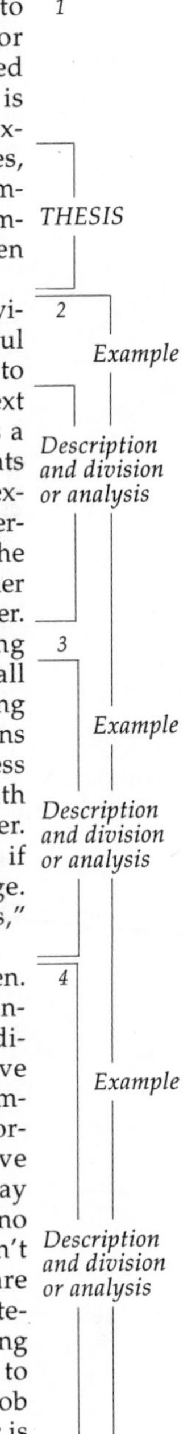

It seems as if everywhere you turn, someone is trying to 1
be politically correct. Whether it involves minorities or women, racist and sexist comments are no longer tolerated in places such as the school yard and the workplace. Why is it, then, that minorities and women are constantly being exploited in everyday advertisements? Television, magazines, and billboards no longer show products, but rather show gimmicks in order to sell their product. In general, these gimmicks seem to enforce racial stereotypes and to view women in a negative way.

It appears that on every channel, there is another televi- 2
sion commercial trying to sell its product with beautiful women. These commercials can range from selling beer to selling cars. Who can forget the gorgeous blonde standing next to the green Geo Storm, proudly exclaiming, "A man likes a woman who knows how to drive a stick!"? Advertisements like these, though seemingly aimed towards women, are exploiting them en route to the actual target: men. This commercial would routinely air during sporting events, when the majority of the viewers are male. It fits in well with the other commercials which, more often than not, have to do with beer.

Beer companies have been notorious for exploiting 3
women in their everyday promotions. Watching a football game, you can usually find an attractive young lady being swept off her feet by a less than attractive man after he opens the beer of his choice. Or, if you are lucky, you can witness several young women materializing on a desert island with the male drinker after, of course, he opens his can of beer. These advertisements present women as a goal, a trophy if you will, that can only be attained with the proper beverage. These women seldom have anything to say besides "Yes," making them seem like unintelligent sex objects.

Unfortunately, the exploitation does not stop with women. 4
Beer commercials exploit minorities as well. Black Entertainment Television frequently airs malt liquor commercials directed at African-American buyers. These ads usually involve a hip-hop rap artist who visits an unusually quiet ghetto community. When he brings the malt liquor, the entire neighborhood breaks into song and dance, with the very attractive African-American woman saying, "Things are back to the way they used to be." How did things used to be? Were there no peaceful afternoons in the 'hood? African-Americans can't be happy in a calm, serene environment? Though there are no racial slurs uttered, the entire commercial perpetuates stereotypes of the African-American community. They must sing and dance in the streets, trying to live life the way it used to be, before they were confined to the monotony of a good job and a quiet neighborhood. Perhaps the commercial maker is

trying to say that African-Americans, as a whole, have been subdued by society.

5 African-Americans are not the only minority group exploited in advertising; Arab-Americans are victims as well. On September 16, 1996, *Newsweek* magazine printed a two-page advertisement for a well-known computer company. This ad depicted an Arab man from an unknown Arab country, wearing his native garb and standing next to a camel. There are boxes of computer parts in the corner of the page. The ad reads, "Some computer companies don't make their own parts. Makes you wonder where they get them." This advertisement insinuates that if these parts were made in an Arab country, they would somehow be inferior. Though the country is not mentioned by name, the message is still very clear.

Example

Description and division or analysis

6 Perhaps the most stereotyped people, when it comes to advertising, are Indian-Americans, those whose family originated in India. To my recollection, there has never been a major commercial involving an Indian-American who didn't speak with a ridiculously exaggerated accent. The most recent perpetrator, MCI, promotes a dime-a-minute service featuring an Indian-American with a very thick and pronounced accent stereotypically driving a New York City taxicab. The actor will never be an American who happens to be of Indian descent. For the company, using Indian-Americans in this manner might add to the comic value of the commercial. But it is safe to say that to most Indian-Americans, it is no laughing matter.

Example

Description, division or analysis, and comparison

7 Racism and sexism are problems that go unnoticed in advertising today. Nevertheless, they must be dealt with. The only winners in these types of ads are the advertisers themselves, who make money when you buy the product. There needs to be a public awakening, for racism and sexism should not be used in any situation, especially not to sell products. Advertisers need to take responsibility for their own actions and to end this type of exploitation. If they do not, we the consumer can always force them. After all, we have the dollars and the sense.

Cause and effect

Margaret Visser

The Ritual of Fast Food *(p. 157)*

Visser's essay focuses on an experience many students probably take for granted: eating at a fast-food restaurant. Her assumption that most fast-food customers never stop to think about this ritual resembles the underlying assumptions of Prager (p. 147) and Sadiq (p. 152) that readers haven't really analyzed Barbie or advertisements. Students may wonder, Why *not* take fast-food meals for granted? Visser suggests some reasons in her last paragraph. Questions 2 and 3 under "Language" are intended to help students begin thinking about this issue, as are the second and fourth "Writing Topics."

Content Quiz

1. What is an "ordinary"?
   [A term referring both to a dinner served to the public at a fixed time and price and to the eating house or tavern in which it was served.]

2. Who are the customers the fast-food chains want?
   [Families.]

3. Who comes to fast-food restaurants craving the salt and fat in French fries?
   [Crack addicts.]

4. What does the formality of eating at a fast-food chain depend on?
   ["The fierce regularity of its product, its simple but carefully observed rituals, and its environment."]

5. When we buy a Big Mac, what more than the food are we purchasing?
   [The careful control expended on it.]

Vocabulary Quiz

1. *Precursor* (paragraph 1) is closest in meaning to
   a. example b. forerunner c. legacy
   [b. forerunner]

2. *Conglomerate* (1) is closest in meaning to
   a. diversified company b. monopoly c. restaurant
   [a. diversified company]

3. *Rubric* (3) is closest in meaning to
   a. philosophy b. training c. set of rules
   [c. set of rules]

4. *Ubiquitously* (5) is closest in meaning to
   a. everywhere b. mechanically c. worldwide
   [a. everywhere]

5. *Ramifications* (6) is closest in meaning to
   a. costs b. consequences c. faults
   [b. consequences]

ANSWERS

Meaning

1. This sentence provides a good illustration of Visser's main idea: that the apparently informal, comfortable, and predictable fast-food restaurant is actually the result of a tremendous amount of money, research, time, effort, and ingenuity. In short, it is not really quick or easy at all; it only appears that way to the patron.

2. A "cultural construct" is a concept created from elements of the culture. A Big Mac is not just a hamburger; when you buy one, you are also buying a whole set of cultural expectations about its appearance, size, shape, temperature, texture, taste, and how quickly it will be served. These expectations are unconscious and pervasive.

Purpose and Audience

1. Visser's purpose is explanatory: she wants to reveal how these chains and their customers thrive by following certain common rituals — rituals the chains are probably more aware of than their customers are. In paragraph 2 Visser writes that these rituals "inform the proceedings"; she then goes on to illustrate the rituals in paragraphs 2–5.

2. Visser seems to imagine a general audience rather than a professional one. Her essay includes little, if any, sociological terminology, and the people who run McDonald's chains already know the information Visser presents. (Since Visser mentions their handbooks and teaching sessions in paragraph 2, she has apparently had access to their inside information.) Visser assumes that her readers take fast-food establishments for granted, that they are oblivious to the "costs and complexities" (paragraph 6) of the fast-food experience, which is of course precisely what the restaurants themselves want their customers to be.

Method and Structure

1. Visser divides the restaurant into four elements: the environment, its rituals, its customers, and its products. The environment encompasses the restaurant's architecture (customers "know exactly what the building that houses the establishment should look like," [paragraph 2]); interior decor ("cottagy roofs, warm earth tones" or "glass walls, smooth surfaces, red trim," [3]); and a predictable ambience ("distinctive garments" and menus "in the same spot" and featuring the same content "in every outlet," [3]). Rituals include the employees' use of standard language and the "time off for [holiday] feasts" (4). The restaurant's ideal customers are families, who "maintain a clean, restrained, considerate, and competent demeanour" (5). Finally, the restaurant's product must adhere to standards of "fierce regularity" (6).

2. Although it is not, of course, true that all crack addicts necessarily look different from everyone else in a fast-food establishment, the restau-

rants can't afford to be tolerant. Filthy or crazy or violent crack addicts would violate the code of the "clean, restrained, considerate, and competent demeanour" (paragraph 5) expected of restaurant patrons. This, in turn, would drive "desirable" customers out the door.

Language

1. Visser seems to take her subject quite seriously. She writes with the formality and detached objectivity of the anthropologist: "rituals, in the sense of behaviour and expectations that conform to preordained rules, still inform the proceedings" (paragraph 2); "architectural variations merely ring changes on rigidly imposed themes" (2); "The staff wear distinctive garments" (3); "in groups of several at a time, the adults hovering over their children" (5). Nevertheless, she is writing for a general audience, and her language is not stuffy or academic.

2. The ostensible purpose of such questions is to be helpful — to remind customers of something they simply forgot to order. The real purpose, of course, is to get customers to buy something they had not originally intended to buy. Student responses to the last part of the question will vary. Some people regard these questions as harmless, but others resent their intrusion and manipulation.

3. Other instances: the company "knows that blunt and direct confrontation with a huge faceless corporation makes us suspicious, and even badly behaved" (paragraph 3); customers are "watching television, where carefully placed commercials will . . . re-imprint the image of the various chain stores for later" (4); "adults hovering over their children, teaching them the goodness of hamburgers, anxious to bring them up to behave typically and correctly. Customers usually maintain a clean, restrained, considerate, and competent demeanour" (5).

   The portrait that emerges is not flattering. Customers come off as childlike, susceptible, passive, malleable. This picture is an integral part of the "casual" eating experience Visser describes: if the customers did not play these roles (which most do not realize they're playing), the whole system would collapse.

Chapter 8

CLASSIFICATION

Sorting Thoughts and Behaviors

Russell Baker

The Plot Against People *(p. 173)*

Baker's humorous essay deals with a subject that every student can relate to: the "plot against people" in which all inanimate objects seem to be engaged. He uses the method of classification to help make sense of his bizarre experience with inanimate objects, trying to explain the phenomenon. Since Baker's piece tries to classify what every person experiences, you might begin class discussion by trying to elicit similar experiences from students.

Baker's essay provides a good chance to discuss how an author implements humor in essay writing. Taking off from question 1 under "Purpose and Audience" and question 1 under "Method and Structure," ask students if they were entertained by this essay and how they might use classification for comic effect. (See also the first "Writing Topic.")

Content Quiz

1. What do inanimate objects most want?
   [To "resist man and ultimately to defeat him."]

2. How is an automobile capable of reducing its owner's lifespan?
   [It breaks down at the most inconvenient of times, creating "maximum misery, inconvenience, frustration, and irritability among its human cargo."]

3. What does Baker see as an indication mat inanimate objects might not be entirely hostile to man?
   [The fact that objects that break down almost never get lost, and vice versa.]

4. What, according to one theory, is the highest state possible for an inanimate object?
   [Belonging to the category of things that don't work.]

5. How do things that don't work offer man "the only peace he receives from inanimate society?"
[Because we have no expectations of things that don't work, they don't upset us.]

Vocabulary Quiz

1. *Plausible* (paragraph 7) is closest in meaning to
a. obvious b. likely c. provable
[b. likely]

2. *Locomotion* (7) is closest in meaning to
a. boisterousness b. transportation c. movement
[c. movement]

3. *Invariably* (10) is closest in meaning to
a. probably b. always c. irritatingly
[b. always]

4. *Inherent* (10) is closest in meaning to
a. built-in b. inherited c. potential
[a. built-in]

5. *Conciliatory* (2) is closest in meaning to
a. defeatist b. weakened c. willing to make peace
[c. willing to make peace]

ANSWERS

Meaning

1. Baker's thesis is stated in paragraphs 1 and 2: "Inanimate objects are classified scientifically into three major categories . . . based on the method each object uses to achieve its purpose." The thesis is clearly facetious: Baker cannot really believe that all inanimate objects belong to one of these categories.

2. They have achieved this by "conditioning him never to expect anything of them" (paragraph 16)

Purpose and Audience

1. The entire essay is tongue-in-cheek. Baker's humor grows above all out of anthropomorphism, or ascribing human characteristics and motives to inanimate objects (cars that wait until the most inconvenient moment to break down, determined little stairclimbing pliers). To achieve comic effect, he also uses a consistently deadpan style, as well as hyperbole (see question 2 under "Language" for examples); mock invocations of science ("Science has still not solved the mystery of how they do it . . ." [paragraph 7], "Scientists have been struck by the fact . . ." [9]); and exaggerated fatalism and paranoia ("thereby reducing its owner's life span" [4], "all are in league . . . to take their turn at breaking down

whenever life threatens to flow smoothly for their human enemies" [5], "They have truly defeated man" [16]).

2. Baker assumes, probably rightly, that readers will all have first-hand experience with things breaking down, getting lost, and never working, and so will be able to identify with the frustration he feels.

Method and Structure

1. Baker uses classification in order to exaggerate: the claim that all inanimate objects fall into one of three categories is patently absurd. The humor also depends on recognition: Baker's categories are funny because, as farfetched as they are, we've all been frustrated enough with inanimate objects to believe him.

2. Baker states his principle in paragraph 2: each group uses a different method to thwart people's wishes.

3. Paragraphs 6–7, 9–10, 15, and 17 explicitly contrast the classes.

4. Paragraph 6 is transitional, explaining that objects that are incapable of breaking down evolved, acquiring the ability to get lost.

5. The examples make it clear how Baker forms his classes, provide a sense of recognition, and contribute to the essay's humor. Other examples of things that break down might be a computer or a photocopier; of things that get lost, socks or umbrellas; of things that don't work, three-way light bulbs, cheap watches.

Language

1. The essay is humorous not despite but because of Baker's tone, which is only mock-serious. It is the contrast between the earnest tone and the light subject matter that's funny.

2. "Any object capable of breaking down at the moment when it is most needed will do so" (paragraph 2); "thereby reducing its owner's life span" (4); "A furnace . . . will invariably break down . . ." (10); "Thereafter, they never work again" (13). (Students may, of course, find others.) Hyperbole establishes Baker's comic tone of exasperation.

3. *Cunning* means clever, malicious, plotting. This is where Baker begins anthropomorphizing objects as malicious enemies of people — a major element of the essay's humor.

Jonathan R. Gould, Jr.

The People Next Door *(p. 178)*

Writing for a composition course, Gould puts classification to good use in rendering of his experiences with neighbors. Students may be inspired to write their own classifications of the types of neighbors they've encountered. Gould's style is sometimes simple, sometimes humorous, but always direct and engaging — as reflected in his classification system. You might ask students what kind of neighbor Gould himself seems to be, based on his narratives, portrayals of his wife, and references to his family: too friendly, unsociable, irritable, or just right? You may then want to ask students what kind of neighbors they are: What category would their neighbors place them in?

Another way to prompt discussion is suggested by the first "Writing Topic": ask students to classify the members of a group they belong to, such as one centering on family background, ethnic groups, musical interest, or political belief. Gould's distinct classes and clear examples can provide a model for such a discussion.

Content Quiz

1. How often has Gould moved?
   [More often than he "care[s] to remember."]

2. How does Gould get rid of neighbors who are too friendly?
   [He opens the door and suggests they leave, or tells them their house is on fire.]

3. What is the rarest type of neighbor?
   [The irritable neighbor. ("Fortunately, I have only encountered this type of neighbor in a handful of settings.")]

4. Which neighbors like to cook?
   [Too-friendly neighbors and just-right neighbors. But too-friendly neighbors cook poorly.]

5. Can a neighbor change from one type to another?
   [Not according to Gould: "people do not really change."]

Vocabulary Quiz

1. *Culinary* (paragraph 2) is closest in meaning to
   a. social b. tasteful c. cooking-related
   [c. cooking-related]

2. *Disconcerting* (2) is closest in meaning to
   a. deceitful b. ironic c. disturbing
   [c. disturbing]

3. *Proximity* (4) is closest in meaning to
   a. approximateness b. nearness c. togetherness
   [b. nearness]

4. *Impoverished* (4) is closest in meaning to
   a. hungry b. poor c. dirty
   [b. poor]

5. *Pleasantries* (5) is closest in meaning to
   a. small talk b. advice c. niceties
   [a. small talk]

ANSWERS

Meaning

1. "Over time, I have begun putting my neighbors into one of four categories: too friendly, unsociable, irritable, and just right" (paragraph 1).

2. Unsociable neighbors try to pretend that Gould and his family don't exist, while irritable neighbors blame the Goulds for everything wrong in their lives.

Purpose and Audience

1. Gould's conclusion makes his purpose clear: identifying neighbors by type, he (and by extension his readers) will be better able to understand and deal with them. Gould wants to share his system so that others might use it, and at the same time, it seems, he wants to entertain readers with types they'll recognize.

2. Not really; his essay could register with anyone who has ever had a neighbor.

Method and Structure

1. Classification helps Gould arrange neighbors — an otherwise unmanageably diverse group — into recognizable and amusing categories.

2. His classification is based on levels of friendliness or hostility toward his family. The classification seems complete and consistent on its own terms. He could have chosen to classify neighbors by how well they kept up appearances, their level of activity, their wealth, or by any number of other criteria.

3. Gould wants to show that his categories are universal, not just based on his own limited or unrepresentative experience.

4. He restores the wholeness of the subject and suggests one reason for writing the essay: the ability to recognize the four types of neighbors makes for better relations with them.

5. The too-friendly neighbor doesn't seem to recognize boundaries (actual or psychological) between himself and Gould. The just-right neighbor has good instincts about Gould's needs for privacy and sociability.

Language

1. Gould's tone is deadpan: "For some strange reason these people become extremely attached to my family" (paragraph 2); "the only way I know that someone lives in their building is the presence of a name on the mailbox and the lights shining through the window at night" (3); "Interestingly, this fellow will eat anything my wife (bless her soul) might make in an attempt to be sociable" (4). In the final paragraph he shows that his true attitude toward bad neighbors is one of good-humored resignation: he sees them as unavoidable nuisances to be taken in stride.

2. "[S]top in as many as eight to ten times a day" (paragraph 2); Gould's pretending his neighbor's house is on fire (2); "no culinary skill whatsoever" (2); "the only way I know that someone lives in their building is the presence of a name on the mailbox and the lights shining through the window at night" (3); "I have to admire her courage" (3); "have them look at her as if she intended to poison them" (3); "will eat anything" (4); "not a crumb" (4); "starved and impoverished" (4). Students may make a case for other examples. The effect is to create humor by exaggerating the faults of the bad neighbors.

Franklin E. Zimring

Confessions of a Former Smoker *(p. 182)*

Zimring's essay, both serious and humorous, opens up a currently heated topic: cigarette smoking. As an ex-smoker himself, Zimring identifies the various types of reformed smokers. Former smokers are sure to find themselves in his categories, but so might smokers and even those who have never smoked. Although not specifically about the relative rights of nonsmokers and smokers, the essay does succeed in raising many issues and attitudes involved in that debate.

You might want to discuss the organization of this essay because Zimring's attention to each of the four categories appears to be imbalanced. Students should consider why Zimring varies the amount of space devoted to each category and whether his organization is effective or not. (See question 3 under "Method and Structure.")

Content Quiz

1. What links former smokers, ex-smokers, and reformed smokers?
[The experience of ceasing to smoke and the temptation of cigarettes.]

2. What do zealots believe will deter offensive behavior?
[Penalties.]

3. What is the hallmark of the evangelist?
   ["Insistence that he never misses tobacco."]

4. Who is resented more, the zealot or the evangelist?
   [The zealot.]

5. What does the serene person feel grateful for?
   ["The experience and memory of craving a cigarette."]

Vocabulary Quiz

1. *Watershed* (paragraph 1) is closest in meaning to
   a. unhappy b. intense c. critical
   [c. critical]

2. *Deter* (2) is closest in meaning to
   a. end b. promote c. discourage
   [c. discourage]

3. *Recidivist* (3) is closest in meaning to
   a. incessant smoker b. one who relapses c. outcast
   [b. one who relapses]

4. *Vitriolic* (4) is closest in meaning to
   a. caustic b. unpleasant c. indifferent
   [a. caustic]

5. *Excoriate* (10) is closest in meaning to
   a. bother b. blame c. denounce
   [c. denounce]

ANSWERS

Meaning

1. In the opening paragraph Zimring asserts that he has identified four kinds of ex-smokers: the zealot, the evangelist, the elect, the serene. Zimring's motive in classifying is that "it is vital that everyone understand the different emotional states cessation of smoking can cause" (paragraph 1) because the ranks of ex-smokers are growing.

2. In paragraph 10 Zimring seems to place himself among the serene. Serenity, he notes, "is a goal, an end stage in a process of development during which some former smokers progress through one or more of the less-than-positive psychological points en route" (paragraph 8).

Purpose and Audience

1. Zimring's primary purpose is to entertain, as evidenced by his humor throughout, but he may also want to generate sympathy for ex-smokers and even smokers. Ex-smokers (and, by implication, smokers) are shown to be more varied and more human than some readers might suppose.

2. Zimring's diction suggests that his audience is educated (as the readers of *Newsweek* would be). As noted above, he seems to address nonsmokers more than any other group in an attempt to win their understanding.

3. Answers will vary.

Method and Structure

1. For entertaining readers and also possibly generating sympathy for ex-smokers, classification serves Zimring well: he can draw out, even inflate, the differences between groups; show that not all ex-smokers are alike; and position himself among the preferred group, the serene.

2. Students should note the two categories, smokers and nonsmokers, mentioned in paragraph 1. The four categories Zimring discusses in detail are subgroups of reformed smokers (though zealots may also include nonsmokers). Zimring establishes a hierarchy of ex-smokers by the sequence he presents: zealot, evangelist, elect, and serene.

3. Zimring devotes three paragraphs to zealots, two to evangelists, one lengthy paragraph to the elect, and then three paragraphs (including his conclusion) to the serene. He devotes more space to his opening category because he is defining from scratch here, whereas for the two middle categories he relies heavily on contrast, defining each by what it is not in relation to preceding groups. The final category is lengthier because it is Zimring's ideal and also includes his conclusion.

4. Zimring uses description, example, division or analysis, and definition to explain each of his categories — see, for instance, the discussion of the evangelist (paragraphs 5–6). He uses cause-and-effect analysis when he notes, for example, the "zealot's fervor" as a direct result of "his own tenuous hold" on nonsmoking (3). Finally, he uses comparison and contrast to clarify his categories, notably in comparing the evangelist with the elect (7).

Language

1. All the labels have religious connotations, as do many of Zimring's other words, such as "predestination," "foreordained," and "proselytizing" (all paragraph 7). But Zimring's ideal group, the serene, has none of the negative connotations of the other three groups, "zealot," "evangelist," and "elect." The other three imply imbalance, meddling, arrogance, whereas serenity is self-contained, quiet, stable. The choice of such elevated words as labels for ex-smokers is typical of Zimring's exaggerated seriousness throughout the essay.

2. Zimring says in his opening paragraph that his classification is "in the interest of science," and his diction throughout, along with his third-

person point of view, suggests a more formal, mock-scientific type of writing. Examples include the following: "the different emotional states cessation of smoking can cause" (paragraph 1), "No systematic survey has been done yet" (4), "The hallmark of the evangelist" (6), "targets of his preachments" (6), "This classification is meant to encourage those who find the other psychic styles of ex-smokers disagreeable" (8), "This former smoker" (10).

ANNOTATED ESSAY

1 Americans can be divided into three groups — smokers, nonsmokers, and that expanding pack of us who have quit. Those who have never smoked don't know what they're missing, but former smokers, ex-smokers, reformed smokers can never forget. We are veterans of a personal war, linked by that watershed experience of ceasing to smoke and by the temptation to have just one more cigarette. For almost all of us ex-smokers, smoking continues to play an important part in our lives. And now that it is being restricted in restaurants around the country and will be banned in almost all indoor public places in New York state starting next month, it is vital that everyone understand the different emotional states cessation of smoking can cause. I have observed four of them; and in the interest of science I have classified them as those of the zealot, the evangelist, the elect, and the serene. Each day, each category gains new recruits.

Classification

THESIS

2 Not all antitobacco zealots are former smokers, but a substantial number of fire-and-brimstone opponents do come from the ranks of the reformed. Zealots believe that those who continue to smoke are degenerates who deserve scorn, not pity, and the penalties that will deter offensive behavior in public as well. Relations between these people and those who continue to smoke are strained.

Definition

Classification

3 One explanation for the zealot's fervor in seeking to outlaw tobacco consumption is his own tenuous hold on abstaining from smoking. But I think part of the emotional force arises from sheer envy as he watches and identifies with each lung-filling puff. By making smoking in public a crime, the zealot seeks reassurance that he will not revert to bad habits; give him strong social penalties and he won't become a recidivist.

Cause and effect

4 No systematic survey has been done yet, but anecdotal evidence suggests that a disproportionate number of doctors who have quit smoking can be found among the fanatics. Just as the most enthusiastic revolutionary tends to make the most enthusiastic counterrevolutionary, many of today's vitriolic zealots include those who had been deeply committed to tobacco habits.

Examples

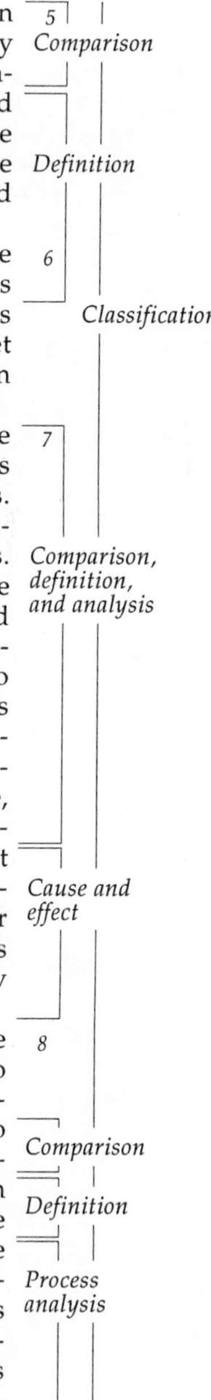

By contrast, the antismoking evangelist does not condemn 5
smokers. Unlike the zealot, he regards smoking as an easily curable condition, as social disease, and not a sin. The evangelist spends an enormous amount of time seeking and preaching to the unconverted. He argues that kicking the habit is not *that* difficult. After all, *he* did it; moreover, as he describes it, the benefits of quitting are beyond measure and the disadvantages are nil.

The hallmark of the evangelist is his insistence that he 6
never misses tobacco. Though he is less hostile to smokers than the zealot, he is resented more. Friends and loved ones who have been the targets of his preachments frequently greet the resumption of smoking by the evangelist as an occasion for unmitigated glee.

Among former smokers, the distinctions between the 7
evangelist and the elect are much the same as the differences between proselytizing and nonproselytizing religious sects. While the evangelists preach the ease and desirability of abstinence, the elect do not attempt to convert their friends. They think that virtue is its own reward and subscribe to the Puritan theory of predestination. Since they have proved themselves capable of abstaining from tobacco, they are therefore different from friends and relatives who continue to smoke. They feel superior, secure that their salvation was foreordained. These ex-smokers rarely give personal testimony on their conversion. They rarely speak about their tobacco habits, while evangelists talk about little else. Of course, active smokers find such bluenosed behavior far less offensive than that of the evangelist or the zealot, yet they resent the elect simply because they are smug. Their air of self-satisfaction rarely escapes the notice of those lighting up. For active smokers, life with a member of the ex-smoking elect is less stormy than with a zealot or evangelist, but it is subtly oppressive nonetheless.

I have labeled my final category of former smokers the 8
serene. This classification is meant to encourage those who find the other psychic styles of ex-smokers disagreeable. Serenity is quieter than zealotry and evangelism, and those who qualify are not as self-righteous as the elect. The serene ex-smoker accepts himself and also accepts those around him who continue to smoke. This kind of serenity does not come easily nor does it seem to be an immediate option for those who have stopped. Rather it is a goal, an end stage in a process of development during which some former smokers progress through one or more of the less-than-positive psychological points en route. For former smokers, serenity is thus a positive possibility that exists at the end of the rainbow. But all former smokers cannot reach that promised land.

What is it that permits some former smokers to become 9
serene? I think the key is self-acceptance and gratitude. The fully mature former smoker knows he has the soul of an addict and is grateful for the knowledge. He may sit up front in an airplane, but he knows he belongs in the smoking section in back. He doesn't regret that he quit smoking, nor any of his previous adventures with tobacco. As a former smoker, he is grateful for the experience and memory of craving a cigarette.

Classification

Serenity comes from accepting the lessons of one's life. 10
And ex-smokers who have reached this point in their world view have much to be grateful for. They have learned about the potential and limits of change. In becoming the right kind of former smoker, they developed a healthy sense of self. This former smoker, for one, believes that it is better to crave (one hopes only occasionally) and not to smoke than never to have craved at all. And by accepting that fact, the reformed smoker does not need to excoriate, envy, or disassociate himself from those who continue to smoke.

Cause and effect and definition

Chapter 9

PROCESS ANALYSIS

Explaining Customs

Cortney Keim

Making the Bed *(p. 199)*

Students will most likely identify with the ambivalence of fellow student Keim toward the daily chore of making the bed. Beginning with dialogue, Keim breathes life into a directive process analysis that meticulously outlines the steps in the bed-making process.

The conclusion of the essay may be the key to class discussion. Reflecting on her mundane task, Keim comments, "When I've finished making my bed, I actually feel good about starting this day" (paragraph 16). Ask students if any of their daily rituals give them a chance for reflection or a sense of accomplishment, or both. (The rituals could range from praying to showering.) What do students' experiences imply about ritual in general?

Content Quiz

1. Why does Keim make the bed?
   [Because she's a "good girl" and because it's a "beneficial ritual."]

2. What is the risk of bending at the waist while making the bed?
   [Back and joint strain.]

3. In what order should the bedding go on the floor?
   ["In the opposite order in which it will be placed on the bed."]

4. On which side of the bed should you stand?
   [Either.]

5. Why should you tuck in the sheet at the end of the bed?
   [So you will be held "still and secure" in bed.]

Vocabulary Quiz

1. *Regrouping* (paragraph 13) is closest in meaning to
   a. reinventing   b. reestablishing   c. reorganizing
   [c. reorganizing]

2. *Mandatory* (14) is closest in meaning to
   a. disciplinary b. required c. important
   [b. required]

ANSWERS

Meaning

1. Keim's point is that the ritual of making the bed is therapeutic: "I began to see that the routine offers a chance to pull myself together in the morning, to smooth my jumble of imperfections and unfinished business into defined layers. With just a little attention to detail, you too can turn this mundane task into a beneficial ritual" (paragraph 8).

Purpose and Audience

1. Keim probably does want to win more slovenly readers over to her careful bedmaking techniques. But her larger point is that seemingly mundane tasks, when carried out thoroughly and with a sense of pride in one's work, can actually help calm us down, create a sense of order in our lives, and give us a satisfaction that only comes with a job well done.

2. Keim's directive process analysis is so detailed that even someone who had never seen a bed could probably follow it. The ideal reader is probably someone who knows more or less how to make a bed but could use some guidance on the finer points. But even the most seasoned bed makers will appreciate Keim's amusing reflections on recalcitrant, vulnerable fitted sheets and pesky pillow tags.

Method and Structure

1. Keim wants to show readers that accomplishing a task with focus and industry can have an unexpectedly beneficial effect on other parts of their lives. To do this convincingly, she has to set an example, showing readers in her process analysis just how thoughtful and assiduous she is when it comes to making her bed.

2. The process analysis begins in paragraph 9. Keim switches into the imperative mood here — the mood of instructions — addressing the reader directly.

3. Examples of transitions include "At all times" (paragraph 9), "Then," "At this point" (10), "When" (11), "When," "later" (12), "when," "each time" (13), "then" (14), "For the final and most technical stage," "Then" (15).

4. Keim captures the reader's attention by starting her essay with dialogue. The scene in which we see her getting ready to start her day illustrates the hurried, chaotic nature of her life, which the bed ritual will help

allay. We also learn that even though making the bed has been imposed upon her, she's able to turn it into a positive force in her life.

Language

1. Keim's tone is lighthearted and occasionally ironic, as in paragraph 9 and in the personification of the sheets ("depressed comforter" [7], "sheets tend to pick up on frustration" [11], "vulnerable fitted sheet" [14]). Her deliberately overblown language (she writes as if she were describing a very complicated process) is self-mocking: "You may need several tries to master the difficult art of balanced distribution" (11); "This is one of the most important tasks, the finishing touch that makes the event special" (14); "the final and most technical stage" (15).

2. Metaphor: Keim describes the person making the bed as a "human iron" (paragraph 13) and compares turning down the top sheet to "the mandatory pumpkin pie after Thanksgiving dinner, no matter how full you are" (14). See the answer to the above question for examples of personification.

Leo Buscaglia

Alla Salute! (p. 204)

Buscaglia's essay deals specifically with the process of wine-making in his large Italian American family, but many students will find the author's experiences reminiscent of their own family customs. With an explanatory process analysis, ordered chronologically, Buscaglia provides an accessible model for students to follow in explaining such a custom. (The first "Writing Topic" offers some direction.)

Through his descriptions, Buscaglia leaves the reader with powerful impressions of the holiday atmosphere of the wine-making — and of its importance to him. Wine-making, to Buscaglia, is a labor of love. You might ask students what the difficulty of a ritual contributes to its effectiveness.

Content Quiz

1. What is Buscaglia's ethnic background?
   [Italian American.]

2. In what season was the new wine made?
   [In autumn.]

3. What was Buscaglia's favorite part of the wine-making process?
   [The grape stomping.]

4. What was the traditional meal eaten on the night the wine was made?
   [Gnocchi.]

5. At what point in the evening did Buscaglia's father make his speech about wine?
   [Right before dinner.]

Vocabulary Quiz

1. *Oenophile* (paragraph 2) is closest in meaning to
   a. cultured person   b. one who loves the good life
   c. one who loves wine
   [c. one who loves wine]

2. *Connoisseur* (2) is closest in meaning to
   a. discriminating judge   b. consumer   c. gourmet
   [a. discriminating judge]

3. *Prelude* (4) is closest in meaning to
   a. theme   b. introduction   c. symbol
   [b. introduction]

4. *Dissertation* (8) is closest in meaning to
   a. speech   b. disruption   c. distraction
   [a. speech]

5. *Nectar* (10) is closest in meaning to
   a. fruit   b. seed   c. juice
   [c. juice]

ANSWERS

Meaning

1. "[No festivity], except Christmas and Easter, topped the one night each year that we made the new wine" (paragraph 3). Readers will want to know why this night was so special and what was involved.

2. The phrase is a shorthand way of referring to the entire process of wine-making.

3. Buscaglia speaks of his father in the past tense in the first two paragraphs, which implies that he is no longer alive. This lends a certain poignancy to the essay and increases its nostalgic feel.

Purpose and Audience

1. Buscaglia's purpose is to record a family custom. The essay also seems intended as an admiring portrait of Buscaglia's father and a testament to the pleasure to be gained from hard work and making something from scratch.

2. Buscaglia makes the experience fresh and real for readers with specific details, such as the wine cellar (paragraph 2), preparing the equipment

(3), and crushing the grapes (5). Without such details, Buscaglia would be asking readers to take on faith the excitement of the tradition.

Method and Structure

1. Process analysis emphasizes the ritualized, ceremonial aspect of the day, making it seem almost a religious occasion. As Buscaglia says in paragraph 3, the festivity was second only to Christmas and Easter.

2. The process analysis takes up most of the essay, from "The anticipation and preparation began in July and August" (paragraph 3) to "the final, all-important swallow" (10). The process being analyzed is not just the wine-making but also the preparation and celebration that surround it.

3. They introduce the subject, establishing a context and showing how important wine was for the narrator's father.

4. Description is especially important in this essay because wine, as Buscaglia's father notes in paragraph 9, appeals to all the senses. Buscaglia wants to re-create all the sensory impressions he felt as a child while making the wine and enjoying it afterward. He appeals to all five senses in the essay: sight ("bodies glistening with perspiration" [4], "rich, deep color of Cabernet Sauvignon" [5], "from dark purple, like a bishop's robe, to the golden amber of an aspen leaf" [9]); smell ("sweet-smelling Cabernet grapes" [4], "heady fragrance of the crushed grapes, mingled with the savory aromas of dinner wafting from the house" [6]); touch ("cool, dark cellar . . . full of dusty bottles" [2], "small, touch-skinned . . . grapes" [4], "cool, dark moisture" [5], "grape residue gushing between my toes" [5]); sound ("grind noisily into the night" [4]); and taste ("growing appetites" [6], "cooked to perfection and topped with a wonderful sauce that had been simmering for hours" [6]).

Language

1. The tone is celebratory. Buscaglia's language conveys his youthful excitement and enthusiasm for the wine-making and the celebration that followed: "brimming" (paragraph 4), "most exciting part of the evening" (4), "sensual experience unlike any other" (5), "savory aromas of dinner wafting from the house" (6), "cooked to perfection" (6). The adult Buscaglia clearly has a deep appreciation for his family's tradition and his father's love of wine, and the language suggests a certain nostalgia: "He always made his own wine" (2), "hand-carried" (4), "hand-powered" (4), "traditional grape stomping" (5).

2. The phrase conveys Buscaglia's pride — in his father and his Italian American heritage.

3. *Would* reminds the reader of the predictable nature of the process, that this is something that happened in the exact same way every year.

ANNOTATED ESSAY

1 Like all good Italians, Papa loved his wine, although I never knew him to drink to excess. A glass or two of wine to accompany his dinner was his limit. He never touched hard liquor.

2 Papa's love of wine went far beyond the simple enjoyment of drinking it. He was truly an oenophile, a connoisseur. He always made his own wine, from ripened grapes to dated label. [*Description*] His cool, dark cellar was full of dusty bottles and cylindrical, wooden barrels of varying sizes, all carefully marked to indicate the type of grape and the year of the harvest.

3 [*THESIS*] When I was growing up, we had many festivities in our home. None, except Christmas and Easter, topped the one night each year that we made the new wine. [*Process analysis*] The anticipation and preparation began in July and August, long before the eventful September evening when the truckload of grapes was delivered. By then Papa had made several visits to his friends — grape growers in Cucamonga, about forty miles from our home — to observe the progress of his grapes. He had spent hours scouring the barrels in which the wine would be made and stored, and applying antitrust varnish on every visible metal part of the wine-making equipment. The fermenting vat had been filled with water to swell the wood.

4 On the appointed evening, the truck would arrive after nightfall, brimming with small, tough-skinned, sweet-smelling Cabernet grapes. The boxes of grapes were hand-carried about two hundred feet to the garage, where a giant empty vat awaited. [*Description*] A hand-powered crusher was positioned precariously on top of the vat, ready to grind noisily into the night, as thousands of grapes were poured into it. It was an all-male operation that included Papa, his relatives, and friends. Dressed in their undershirts, bodies glistening with perspiration, they took turns cranking the crusher handle. My job was to stack the empty crates neatly out of the way as a prelude to what for me was the most exciting part of the evening.

5 After all the grapes had been mashed and the empty boxes stacked, it was time for us to remove our shoes, socks, and pants and slip into the cool, dark moisture for the traditional grape stomping. This was done, of course, to break up the skins, but I couldn't have cared less why it was necessary. [*Description*] For me it was a sensual experience unlike any other, feeling the grape residue gushing between my toes and watching as the new wine turned my legs the rich, deep color of Cabernet Sauvignon.

6 [*Comparison*] While this "man's work" was being accomplished, the "woman's work" was progressing in the kitchen. The heady fragrance of the crushed grapes, mingled with the savory

aromas of dinner wafting from the house, caused our feet to move in step with our growing appetites. The traditional main course for our wine-making dinner was gnocchi, a small, dumplinglike pasta that would be cooked to perfection and topped with a wonderful sauce that had been simmering for hours. *Description*

7 Like Christmas Eve, this particular night was unique in many ways. Throughout the rest of the year, we routinely sat down to dinner by 5:30 each evening. But for this occasion dinner was never served until the wine making was finished, sometimes as late at 10 P.M. By then, we were all purple from grape juice, exhausted, and famished. *Process analysis*

8 No matter how tired and hungry we were, however, Papa always prefaced the dinner with a dissertation on "the wine experience." This ceremony called for his finest wines, which had been aging in his modest but efficient wine cellar. Drinking wine, he would remind us, was a highly respected activity, not to be taken lightly. The nectar of the grape had brought joy to human beings long before recorded history. *Definition*

9 "Wine is a delight and a challenge and is never meant to be drunk quickly. It's to be savored and sipped slowly," he'd tell us. "All the senses are awakened when you drink wine. You drink with your eyes, your tongue, your throat, your nose. Notice the colors the wine makes in the glass — all the way from dark purple, like a bishop's robe, to the golden amber of an aspen leaf."

10 He would hold up the glass to the light as if we were about to share a sacrament, then swirl the wine around in his glass, guiding us through the whole ritual, from the first sip to the final, all-important swallow. *Description*

"Alla salute!"

Jessica Mitford

Embalming Mr. Jones *(p. 209)*

Mitford's essay shows students that process analysis need not be a dull series of directions and demonstrates how the method can be used to explain and support a strongly held belief. But her sardonic view of funeral customs may shock some students. Discussing the underlying seriousness of the essay and Mitford's probable reasons for choosing such an approach helps answer those concerns. As an alternative, you may want to elicit defenses of funeral directors, their profession, and American funeral customs.

Content Quiz

1. In what part of the world is embalming most widely used? [North America.]

2. Is embalming required by law?
   [No.]

3. What is a dermasurgeon?
   [An embalmer.]

4. What is the first step in the embalming process?
   [Removing the blood from the body.]

5. When is the best time to begin the embalming process?
   ["Before life is completely extinct—that is, before cellular death has occurred."]

Vocabulary Quiz

1. *Mortuary* (paragraph 1) is closest in meaning to
   a. graveyard b. funeral home c. morgue
   [b. funeral home]

2. *Decedent* (3) is closest in meaning to
   a. deceased b. relative c. mortician
   [a. deceased]

3. *Intractable* (6) is closest in meaning to
   a. stubborn b. unclear c. consistent
   [a. stubborn]

4. *Rudimentary* (10) is closest in meaning to
   a. refined b. undeveloped c. secondary
   [b. undeveloped]

5. *Somatic* (10) is closest in meaning to
   a. bodily b. brain c. technical
   [a. bodily]

ANSWERS

Meaning

1. Embalming and restoration make the corpse suitable for viewing by using costly measures to erase all traces of the cause of death. They are performed, Mitford seems to believe, because people are ignorant of the procedures (paragraphs 4, 5).

2. Americans know as little as they do because no effort is made to erase their ignorance. Mitford aims most of her attack at the funeral industry, which, she says, perpetuates the practices without any clearly defined legal rights and seems deliberately to keep relatives and the general public in the dark.

Purpose and Audience

1. Mitford analyzes the processes of embalming and restoration in the hope and expectation that readers will then question the practices themselves. An undertaker would be offended by nearly every sentence in the piece, including the quotations from embalming textbooks.

2. Mitford assumes that her audience is completely ignorant about the process of embalming — what is done, how it is done, why it is done, even what it costs.

3. Students will find their own examples of humor. Mitford uses humor to show how ludicrous funeral customs are when they are examined objectively, rather than under the emotional stress of bereavement. Humor also mitigates some of the gruesomeness of the process.

Method and Structure

1. Process analysis helps Mitford expose the custom of embalming for the morbid and absurd practice she sees it to be, allowing her to present the process in all its unsettling detail. She hopes to convince readers to reexamine their tacit approval of the practice by exposing the ugly secrets that lie behind a beautified corpse. The unusual process anlaysis allows her simultaneously to shock and to amuse her audience.

2. Mitford explains the process quite clearly. The main steps are removing the blood and replacing it with embalming fluid (paragraphs 9–11); removing entrails and replacing them with cavity fluid (13); replacing missing parts and repairing defects (15–16); "lip closure" (17); applying cosmetics, washing hair, manicuring, and so on (18–19); and "casketing" (20).

3. In paragraph 8 Mitford describes the undertaker's tools. In paragraph 10 she explains the "time element" in the process (while also illustrating the rudimentary quality of information on embalming). And in paragraph 14 she explains the objective of the process of restoration.

4. The contrast suggests that we, unlike our ancestors, are fearful and shy about death and the dead and thus acquiesce in the funeral industry's wish to keep us ignorant of its practices.

Language

1. Mitford's tone is bitingly sarcastic, overlaid with a good dollop of black humor. Some examples: the brand names of the "aids" she mentions, such as "Throop Foot Positioner" (paragraph 8); sentences such as "Head off?" (15); words such as "jabbed" (13) and "routinely handled" (15).

2. Mitford's irony contributes substantially to her sarcastic tone and to the humor of the piece. Other examples of irony: "Beautiful Memory Picture" (paragraph 2), when the trussing, trimming, and slicing earlier in

the sentence would produce quite the opposite effect; "For those who feel that there is something a little rudimentary, not to say haphazard, about this advice, a comforting thought is offered . . ." (10); "The funeral industry is equal to the challenge" (14).

3. The contrast of informal style and formal textbook style underlines the discrepancy Mitford sees between the outward dignity and solemnity of funeral practices and their actual grotesqueness and humorousness. Other examples of informal style: "Just how soon should one get going on embalming?" (paragraph 10); "jabbed into the abdomen, poked around the entrails" (13). Other examples of textbook style: "any of the better funeral establishments" (8); "the embalmer has at hand a variety of restorative waxes" (15).

Chapter 10

COMPARISON AND CONTRAST

Challenging Misconceptions

Stephen Manes

The Endangered Book? *(p. 233)*

Manes compares the book *Material World* with its CD-ROM counterpart. To establish their advantages and disadvantages, Manes compares and contrasts their components. (Though full of data, the essay is not difficult to follow.) In almost every category, Manes concludes that the bound volume is the stronger. The essay will surely engage studetns who are interested in computer technology — whether enthusiastically or skeptically. And being a review, this piece may also be attractive to students who are interested in reviewing movies, restaurants, or other arts or entertainments. Question 5 under "Method and Structure" suggests a possible topic for class discussion: Is Manes objective or subjective toward the two products? On one hand, he relies almost exclusively on factual comparisons; on the other, he obviously has a strong opinion.

Content Quiz

1. What advantages over the book do the creators of the CD-ROM version of *Material World* claim for their product?
   ["Spectacular video, breathtaking photography, and stereo sound."]

2. How many colors are used in the CD-ROM? In the book?
   [256; millions.]

3. What is the book's standard information-retrieval device?
   [The table of contents.]

4. Which has more photos, the CD-ROM or the book?
   [The CD-ROM.]

5. Which can display more information at once?
   [The book.]

Vocabulary Quiz

1. *Palpable* (paragraph 6) is closest in meaning to
   a. touchable b. overpowering c. bright
   [a. touchable]

2. *Icon* (8) is closest in meaning to
   a. button b. camera c. symbol
   [c. symbol]

3. *Interludes* (11) is closest in meaning to
   a. chapters b. introductions c. intermissions
   [c. intermissions]

4. *Tantalizing* (11) is closest in meaning to
   a. useful b. teasing c. lewd
   [b. teasing]

5. *Methodology* (12) is closest in meaning to
   a. procedure b. commentary c. results
   [a. procedure]

ANSWERS

Meaning

1. Manes clearly thinks such reports are premature, if not entirely unfounded. The essay attempts to show that the book holds its own in a comparison against electronic media: it is here to stay.

2. The book requires no equipment or installation, its graphics are better, it is easier to navigate, it can display more information at once, it has detailed source notes and three introductory articles, and it is $10 cheaper. In contrast, the CD-ROM has more photos, it includes certain information missing from the book, it can show data as bar graphs, it has an introduction by Charles Kuralt (but this is described as "simplistic" [paragraph 12]), and it comes with a technical support number (but this of course is a disadvantage in disguise).

3. This is the computer screen.

Purpose and Audience

1. "A comparison between bound volume and CD-ROM should help reveal whether reports of the death of the book are greatly exaggerated" (paragraph 2).

2. Manes reveals his bias in his statement of purpose, saying even before he begins his comparison that reports of the death of the book are "greatly exaggerated" (paragraph 2), and he continues to reveal this preference for books throughout the essay. He also wants to amuse.

3. Although this essay was published as the "Personal Computers" column in the *New York Times,* Manes does not necessarily expect his readers to be computer-savvy. He deliberately piles on the techno-speak in paragraph 3 for effect: the overwhelming technical detail is meant to

indicate that a lot of expensive, high-tech equipment is required to use the CD-ROM. (In contrast, the book requires only a source of light.) The reader doesn't need to know what any of the computer jargon means to understand Manes's point. In fact, the less readers know about computers, the more likely they may be to agree with him.

Method and Structure

1. Comparison and contrast allows Manes to be more objective, or at least appear to be. A narrative essay might be persuasive in its own way, illustrating the continuing value of reading through the example of Manes's own expeience, but a comparison allows Manes to show readers more specifically, point by point, why a CD-ROM can never replace a book.

2. The fact that the CD-ROM is a version of the book in this case gives Manes built-in points of comparison, enabling him to look at the way each organizes and presents the same content. This approach is more convincing than if he had tried to compare books and CD-ROMs in he abstract.

3. The points of comparison are prerequisites for use (paragraph 3), ease of installation (4), quality of graphics (5–6), ease of navigation (7–8), quantity and quality of information and interpretation (9–12), and cost (13).

4. The tongue-in-cheek conclusion gives perhaps Manes's strongest point: we don't need help to read a book.

5. Description is an essential part of the essay because the book and CD-ROM Manes has chosen to compare are largely pictorial. The description is mostly objective, as befits a comparison meant to be detached and factual.

Language

1. Manes's tone is mostly matter-of-fact, almost bland, like a catalog or manual. The deadpan approach contributes to the humor — as when Manes lists the equipment required for the CD-ROM (paragraph 3). But occasionally Manes shows exasperation ("infuriating," [8]) or dislike ("simplistic," [12]), and he uses irony to promote the book ("The book requires only a source of light," [3]; "Digital placeholders commonly known as 'fingers' are not supplied," [7]; "The book does not come with a number you can call for technical help," [13]). Students may disagree on whether these moments work well. Some may find them heavy-handed, others welcome or amusing.

2. Manes says the book "is a fascinating volume" (paragraph 1), while the CD-ROM's claims of greatness are "according to the jacket flap" (2). The qualifier "If these claims were true" (2) suggests that they are not, and "greatly exaggerated" further suggests that Manes believes the book's doomsayers are mistaken.

Bryan Garvey

Drugs vs. Drugs *(p. 238)*

Garvey, a student, takes an unusual approach in the debate over drugs, maintaining that legal drugs (over-the-counter or prescription) have negative side effects that make them as problematic as the illegal drugs that dominate the debate. Students should find Garvey's thesis itself debatable. Some will vehemently disagree with him, perhaps especially if they rely on any of the legal drugs he mentions. Other students will appreciate his attempt to expose hypocrisy in our attitudes toward drugs.

To open class discussion, ask students the difference between marijuana, cocaine, prozac, and codeine. Which drugs are worse for the user, and why? which should be legal and illegal? (See also the first "Writing Topic.")

Content Quiz

1. How does Garvey define the word *drug*?
   ["Any foreign substance that elicits a change in the body."]

2. What was the harmful side effect of Fen-Phen?
   [It caused liver and heart valve problems.]

3. When did it become illegal to possess marijuana in the United States?
   [1937.]

4. Who appoints the head of the FDA?
   [The president of the United States.]

5. What is the most common cause of FDA-approved pills' being taken off the market?
   [Liver damage.]

Vocabulary Quiz

1. *Ubiquitous* (paragraph 2) is closest in meaning to
   a. annoying b. overhwelming c. present everywhere
   [c. present everywhere]

2. *Elicits* (3) is closest in meaning to
   a. brings about b. solicits c. prevents
   [a. brings about]

3. *Disdain* (4) is closest in meaning to
   a. disrespect b. contempt c. disgust
   [b. contempt]

4. *Quelled* (6) is closest in meaning to
   a. inflamed b. suppressed c. ignored
   [b. suppressed]

5. *Alleviation* (9) is closest in meaning to
   a. elimination b. suppression c. easing
   [c. easing]

ANSWERS

Meaning

1. In paragraph 1: "It can be misleading to make the distinction, because both drugs and Drugs can be harmful and helpful."

2. Garvey defines a *drug* in paragraph 3 as "any foreign substance that elicits a change in the body." The distinction between drugs and Drugs, he maintains, is artificial, based entirely on the different ways society sees them: drugs as beneficial and Drugs as dangerous. But both have both good and bad effects; there is no clear-cut dividing line between the two except for their legality.

3. The FDA's decisions are subject to pressure from powerful lobbyists with political and financial clout (paragraph 8).

Purpose and Audience

1. The last paragraph makes it clear that Garvey wants readers to be more alert to the potential harmful effects of *all* drugs.

2. Garvey seems to assume that his readers will not have seen the similarities between legal and illegal drugs. To demonstrate their similarities, he provides a "basic definition of *drug*" (paragraph 3), examples of the harmful effects of legal drugs (4, 6, 8, 9), and background on the reasons for criminalizing marijuana (7) and approving legal drugs (8).

Method and Structure

1. Garvey's purpose is to lead readers to see the similarities in substances usually considered different. He wants to shift the balance away from contrast and toward comparison.

2. Paragraph 2 shows that the author has a personal interest in his subject because he grew up confused by mixed messages about drugs and continues to confront such messages as an adult. The example in paragraph 4 serves as first-hand evidence that legal drugs can have bad effects when abused.

3. The passage illustrates the arbitrariness of society's determination of whether a drug is good or bad. It shows that marijuana became illegal for an essentially bad reason — prejudice against the people perceived to use it most.

Language

1. The tone is mostly serious, somewhat vexed, occasionally ironic — appropriate given Garvey's wish to make readers reexamine their assumptions about drugs. Strong word choices include "ubiquitous" (paragraph 2), "stuffed" (2), "scourge" (4), "quelled," "as American as red, white, and blue" (6), "outcast," "stigmatizing," "debilitating" (7), "push through" (8), and "distort" (10).

2. It indicates a transition in the essay, from setting up the problem by asking questions to answering those questions.

3. He means it can cut both ways, for good (drugs for AIDS and cancer patients) and for bad (frivolous, potentially dangerous drugs like Fen-Phen).

Leanita McClain

The Middle-Class Black's Burden *(p. 243)*

McClain's essay addresses the significant issues of race and class relations both thoughtfully and uncompromisingly. Positioning herself among middle-class African Americans, McClain directly confronts the mistaken assumptions she faces among both other African Americans and middle-class white Americans. Throughout her essay, she poses some rather difficult rhetorical questions, as indicated in question 3 under "Purpose and Audience." You might direct students' attention to these questions: what does McClain hope to gain with them?

Content Quiz

1. What has McClain "had it" with?
["Being patted on the head by white hands and slapped in the face by black hands for [her] success."]

2. What do other African Americans call the middle-class African Americans like McClain?
["Oreos . . . black on the outside, white within."]

3. What has happened to some of McClain's childhood friends?
[Old classmate waits on her table, girl she played with has five children on welfare, boy from church imprisoned for murder, pal died of drug overdose.]

4. What is McClain's relationship to the middle class?
[She is "uncomfortably" in it.]

5. What is it that blacks and whites will not believe about McClain?
["Whites won't believe I remain culturally different; blacks won't believe I remain culturally the same."]

Vocabulary Quiz

1. *Proverbial* (paragraph 2) is closest in meaning to
   a. desired b. commonly expressed c. everywhere evident
   [b. commonly expressed]

2. *Berate* (3) is closest in meaning to
   a. scold b. punish c. frown at
   [a. scold]

3. *Nemesis* (11) is closest in meaning to
   a. friend b. rival c. source of harm
   [c. source of harm]

4. *Vernacular* (12) is closest in meaning to
   a. idiom b. rule c. advice
   [a. idiom]

5. *Assuage* (13) is closest in meaning to
   a. inflame b. erase c. calm
   [c. calm]

ANSWERS

Meaning

1. *Incongruities* are inconsistencies (Latin *in-*, "not," and *congruere*, "to agree"). As a middle-class African American, McClain feels she fits well in neither the predominantly white middle class nor the angry and fear-ridden African American community. Her examples include being called an "Oreo" (paragraph 3), a trip to Paris back-to-back with a back-country funeral (6), and an aunt who cleans for one of her neighbors (6). See also paragraphs 10, 13, 14.

2. Paragraph 1 sums up the "middle-class black's burden" and states McClain's main idea — that she's "had it with being patted on the head by white hands and slapped in the face by black hands for my success." (See also "Language" question 2.)

3. McClain's "ancestors" are, of course, slaves and the oppressed African Americans who descended from them. "The purposeless present" of her contemporaries presumably refers to the endemic poverty and social problems of many present-day African Americans (paragraph 8).

Purpose and Audience

1. McClain is trying to communicate the burden she feels and ultimately to promote change: "We [middle-class blacks] know the black and white worlds can meld, that there can be a better world" (paragraph 4); "Rac-

ism still dogs my people" (9); "Inasmuch as we all suffer for every one left behind, we all gain for every one who conquers the hurdle" (20).

2. McClain addresses both whites and blacks, trying to educate members of both her worlds about the prejudice she experiences and convince both to change their attitudes and behavior.

3. McClain's questions are rhetorical: they do not have easy answers, if they have answers at all. She includes them because they are the questions she confronts every day; writing the essay is a way of posing them to those who may not have thought of them.

Method and Structure

1. McClain is comparing her feelings among and misjudgment by African Americans and whites. Her points of comparison include life goals (paragraph 2), respect for roots (3–4, 19–20), congruence (5–6), racism (9–12, 15–16, 18), and tokenism (13).

2. At paragraph 6 McClain shifts from her life among other African Americans to her life among whites. The paragraph merges the two worlds.

3. Other clarifying expressions: *too* (paragraph 5), *however* (8), *still* (9), *yet* (11), *two worlds* (13), *each world* (14), *but* (16), *As for* (19), *nor* (20).

4. Description, narration, and example all appear in paragraphs 5 and 6. The entire essay analyzes the causes and effects of McClain's "burden" as a middle-class African American; specific instances appear in paragraphs 5 and 20.

Language

1. McClain's tone is angry, her language strong and uncompromising: "who has had it" (paragraph 1), "pencil pushing" (2), "antiquated ideology" (3), "wretched past . . . purposeless present" (8), "hollow victory" (10), "simplistic reproach" (11), "transparent deceptions . . . bitter hopelessness" (14), "lulled themselves" (15), "freak" (16), "No" (19), "drowning" (20). Some students will find her moral outrage appropriate given the gravity of her subject and what is at stake: the state of race relations in America. Others may wish she had tempered her anger.

2. McClain does not use *patted* and *slapped* literally, of course; they are metaphors for her experiences. Whites pat her on the head by applauding her for succeeding when they might not have expected her to; blacks slap her by berating her for her success and insisting that she has forsaken her people.

3. Parallelism reinforces McClain's comparisons because similar grammatical structures encompass contrasting ideas. Other examples: "patted on the head . . . and slapped in the face" (paragraph 1); "I have overcome

. . . , but I have not overcome" (11); "Life is easier, being black is not" (11); "I know how tenuous my grip on one way of life is, and how strangling the grip of the other way of life can be" (14).

4. The use of quotation marks around *liberal* emphasizes the term and also questions its sincerity, given the context. We are meant to distrust McClain's white acquaintances and their avowed respect for her.

ANNOTATED ESSAY

1 I am a member of the black middle class who has had it with being patted on the head by white hands and slapped in the face by black hands for my success.

THESIS

2 Here's a discovery that too many people find startling: when given equal opportunities at white-collar pencil pushing, blacks want the same things from life that everyone else wants. These include the proverbial dream house, two cars, an above-average school, and a vacation for the kids at Disneyland. We may, in fact, want these things more than other Americans because most of us have been denied them so long.

Comparison

Example

3 Meanwhile, a considerable number of the folks we left behind in the "old country," commonly called the ghetto, and the militants we left behind in their antiquated ideology can't berate middle-class blacks enough for "forgetting where we came from." We have forsaken the revolution, we are told, we have sold out. We are Oreos, they say, black on the outside, white within.

Definition

4 The truth is, we have not forgotten; we would not dare. We are simply fighting on different fronts and are no less war weary, and possibly more heartbroken, for we know the black and white worlds can meld, that there can be a better world.

5 It is impossible for me to forget where I came from as long as I am prey to the jive hustler who does not hesitate to exploit childhood friendship. I am reminded, too, when I go back to the old neighborhood in fear — and have my purse snatched — and when I sit down to a business lunch and have an old classmate wait on my table. I recall the girl I played dolls with who now rears five children on welfare, the boy from church who is in prison for murder, the pal found dead of a drug overdose in the alley where we once played tag.

Example and cause and effect

6 My life abounds in incongruities. Fresh from a vacation in Paris, I may, a week later, be on the milk-run Trailways bus in Deep South back-country attending the funeral of an ancient uncle whose world stretched only fifty miles and who never learned to read. Sometimes when I wait at the bus stop with my attaché case, I meet my aunt getting off the bus with other cleaning ladies on their way to do my neighbors' floors.

Example and narration

7 But I am not ashamed. Black progress has surpassed our greatest expectations; we never even saw much hope for it, and the achievement has taken us by surprise.

Comparison

8 In my heart, however, there is no safe distance from the wretched past of my ancestors or the purposeless present of some of my contemporaries; I fear such a fate can reclaim me. I am not comfortably middle class; I am uncomfortably middle class.

9 I have made it, but where? Racism still dogs my people. There are still communities in which crosses are burned on the lawns of black families who have the money and grit to move in.

Example

10 What a hollow victory we have won when my sister, dressed in her designer everything, is driven to the rear door of the luxury high rise in which she lives because the cab driver, noting only her skin color, assumes she is the maid, or the nanny, or the cook, but certainly not the lady of any house at this address.

Example and narration

11 I have heard the immigrants' bootstrap tales, the simplistic reproach of "why can't you people be like us." I have fulfilled the entry requirements of the American middle class, yet I am left, at times, feeling unwelcome and stereotyped. I have overcome the problems of food, clothing, and shelter, but I have not overcome my old nemesis, prejudice. Life is easier, being black is not.

Cause and effect

12 I am burdened daily with showing whites that blacks are people. I am, in the old vernacular, a credit to my race. I am my brothers' keeper, and my sisters', though many of them have abandoned me because they think that I have abandoned them.

13 I run a gauntlet between two worlds, and I am cursed and blessed by both. I travel, observe, and take part in both; I can also be used by both. I am a rope in a tug of war. If I am a token in my downtown office, so am I at my cousin's church tea. I assuage white guilt. I disprove black inadequacy and prove to my parents' generation that their patience was indeed a virtue.

14 I have a foot in each world, but I cannot fool myself about either. I can see the transparent deceptions of some whites and the bitter hopelessness of some blacks. I know how tenuous my grip on one way of life is, and how strangling the grip of the other way of life can be.

15 Many whites have lulled themselves into thinking that race relations are just grand because they were the first on their block to discuss crab grass with the new black family. Yet too few blacks and whites in this country send their children to school together, entertain each other, or call each other friend. Blacks and whites dining out together draw stares. Many of my coworkers see no black faces from the time the train pulls out Friday evening until they meet me at the coffee machine Monday morning. I remain a novelty.

Example

Some of my "liberal" white acquaintances pat me on the 16
head, hinting that I am a freak, that my success is less a matter of talent than of luck and affirmative action. I may live *Cause and*
among them, but it is difficult to live with them. How can *effect*
they be sincere about respecting me, yet hold my fellows in
contempt? And if I am silent when they attempt to sever me
from my own, how can I live with myself?

Whites won't believe I remain culturally different; blacks 17
won't believe I remain culturally the same. *Comparison*

I need only look in a mirror to know my true allegiance, 18
and I am painfully aware that, even with my off-white trappings, I am prejudged by my color.

As for the envy of my own people, am I to give up my 19
career, my standard of living, to pacify them and set my conscience at ease? No. I have worked for these amenities and
deserve them, though I can never enjoy them without feeling guilty.

These comforts do not make me less black, nor oblivious 20
to the woe in which many of my people are drowning. As *Cause and*
long as we are denigrated as a group, no one of us has made *effect*
it. Inasmuch as we all suffer for every one left behind, we all
gain for every one who conquers the hurdle.

Chapter 11

DEFINITION

Clarifying Our Relationships

Judy Brady

I Want a Wife *(p. 261)*

Brady's definition uses carefully selected examples to present an angry statement about the wife's place in the home and in society. Some students may initially misunderstand the essay and think that Brady really does want a slave of her own. Other students may see the essay as excessively hostile toward wives, husbands, and marriage. And still other students may find Brady's sense of oppression somewhat passé, not as much of an issue now as it was in the less liberated early 1970s. Class discussion may be guided by questions 1–3 under "Purpose and Audience" and by "Writing Topics" 2 and 3.

Content Quiz

1. With whom does the child of Brady's recently divorced male friend live?
   [The child's mother.]

2. Why does Brady want to go back to school?
   [So she can become economically independent and support herself and her family.]

3. Why should a wife go on family vacations?
   [To continue caring for her partner and for the children.]

4. According to Brady's definition, which partner in a marriage must remain sexually faithful to the other?
   [The wife.]

5. What should the first wife do if a new wife is taken?
   ["Take the children and be solely responsible for them."]

Vocabulary Quiz

1. *Nurturant* (paragraph 3) is closest in meaning to
   a. compassionate b. gentle c. nourishing
   [c. nourishing]

2. *Hors d'oeuvres* (6) is closest in meaning to
   a. appetizers b. cocktails c. napkins
   [a. appetizers]

3. *Replenished* (6) is closest in meaning to
   a. removed b. refilled c. rewashed
   [b. refilled]

4. *Adherence* (7) is closest in meaning to
   a. indifference b. attachment c. attention
   [b. attachment]

5. *Monogamy* (7) is closest in meaning to
   a. sexual faithfulness b. equality in a marriage
   c. marriage to only one person
   [c. marriage to only one person]

ANSWERS

Meaning

1. A wife is a person whose entire function is the selfless serving of others, especially the husband.

2. The wife's chief responsibilities are to work when doing so is beneficial to the spouse, to care for the children, to care for the house and to cook, to meet the spouse's physical and emotional needs, and to arrange and run social events. The wife's behavior should be entirely selfless. The spouse's responsibilities are to attend school and study and eventually to support dependents "if need be"(paragraph 3) — but nothing is required or contributed at home. The spouse's behavior may be entirely selfish.

Purpose and Audience

1. Brady's purpose is to attack society's — and men's — attitudes toward the role of wife. She presents a deliberately one-sided definition, exaggerating to achieve this purpose.

2. Brady seems to assume that her readers are mostly women who will understand and appreciate her anger. Her perspective seems to be that of a middle-class woman in her twenties or early thirties: the wife works to put the spouse through school; the children are relatively young; the family lives in a house; and the couple has an active social life.

3. Answers will vary widely.

Method and Structure

1. Readers may take the role of a wife for granted — or may have in 1971 — but Brady sees a need to show how the wife is taken advantage of. By presenting a slanted definition, she encourages readers to see things her way.

2. The definition is highly specific and clearly distinguishes the role of a wife from, say, the role of a housekeeper or a lover. It is also thorough in that it covers a wide range of responsibilities and behaviors. But some readers may think that the omission of any positive elements in the relationship between wife and spouse — what keeps the wife at the job: love? security? — makes the definition less than complete.

3. Paragraph 1 suggests that the author is defined by society according to her role as a wife. Paragraph 2 presents a man who seems to view a wife's role just as Brady goes on to define it: he is divorced; he has left his child to his wife; and he wants "a wife" — as if anyone might do. The question at the end of the introduction leads into the definition; once the earlier question is answered, the final rhetorical question opens up the divorced man's wish and Brady's wish to everyone.

4. With classification, Brady makes the definition more manageable. She classifies the wife's responsibilities into financial support and child care (paragraph 3), housekeeping and cooking (4), emotional support (5), social organization (6), and sexual fulfillment (7). The categories are increasingly personal and intrusive, thus emphasizing the exploitation of women in marriage.

Language

1. Brady's tone is angry and contemptuous, and it is achieved largely through irony: for example, "It may mean a small cut in my wife's income . . . , but I guess I can tolerate that" (paragraph 3); "I want a wife who will not bother me with rambling complaints about a wife's duties" but "will listen to me when I feel the need to explain a rather difficult point I have come across in my course of studies" (5).

2. The repetition portrays the spouse as childish, demanding, selfish.

3. Use of the phrase *my wife* emphasizes the spouse's depersonalization and possession of the wife. At the same time, the phrase allows Brady to avoid expressing a wish for another woman, which might be more distracting than the occasionally awkward sentences now in the essay.

4. Such expressions underline the irony.

Gloria Naylor

The Meanings of a Word *(p. 266)*

Some students may approach this essay with apprehension. The word *nigger* is so highly charged that it's difficult for many people to utter, even when discussing it objectively. To ease students into the subject, you might ask them to do some journal writing as preparation for discussion of the essay. Possible questions: What does the word *nigger* mean to you? Who uses it? What effect does it have? Students can then compare their responses with one another's and with Naylor's. (Small groups might alleviate some students' discomfort with the topic.)

Content Quiz

1. If words themselves are "innocuous," what gives them "true power"?
   [The consensus of people who use the words.]

2. When did Naylor first really "hear" the word *nigger*?
   [In third grade.]

3. Where did Naylor's maternal grandparents live?
   [Harlem.]

4. When were older children sent out of the room during the gatherings at Naylor's grandparents' apartment?
   [When the topics of conversation were sexual misconduct or death.]

5. What is the "unforgivable sin," according to the adults in young Naylor's life?
   [A lack of self-respect.]

Vocabulary Quiz

1. *Consensus* (paragraph 2) is closest in meaning to
   a. positioning b. use c. agreement
   [c. agreement]

2. *Innocuous* (2) is closest in meaning to
   a. harmful b. harmless c. insignificant
   [b. harmless]

3. *Inevitable* (3) is closest in meaning to
   a. unlikely b. direct c. certain
   [c. certain]

4. *Unkempt* (10) is closest in meaning to
   a. dingy b. messy c. noisy
   [b. messy]

5. *Impotent* (14) is closest in meaning to
   a. ineffective b. powerful c. meaningless
   [a. ineffective]

ANSWERS

Meaning

1. Words don't mean anything in themselves; they only take on meaning within a specific social context. *Nigger* meant one thing among black people and another when used by whites.

2. Naylor states her main idea in the last sentence of paragraph 2: the power of a word derives from a consensus about its meaning among the people who use the word.

3. Naylor says that by reaching their own consensus about the meanings of *nigger,* African Americans have developed a powerful word for their own uses and simultaneously rendered the word powerless when spoken by whites. Responses to the last part of the question will vary.

4. Prior to the incident with the little boy, Naylor had known the term only in the context of her own community, where it was not designed to humiliate. As she says in paragraph 5, "the word *nigger* was used in my presence, but it was set within contexts and inflections that caused it to register in my mind as something else." In fact, it's a term of both endearment and approval. Even when it is used negatively, it reinforces the value of self-respect in the community. Thus when Naylor hears it from a white person clearly intending to hurt her, the word is something quite new.

Purpose and Audience

1. Naylor seems to have written her essay for at least two interlocking reasons: to express some childhood memories and through them to explain how words acquire meaning and power. A third purpose may be revealed in paragraph 14: in disputing the view that the use of *nigger* among African Americans was an "internalization of racism," Naylor seems to want to convince readers that the African American use of *nigger* was instead a "head-on" confrontation with racism.

2. Naylor's careful picture of life in Harlem (paragraphs 4–5), as well as her precise explanation of the terms *nigger* and *girl,* indicates that she's writing to a primarily white audience. Presumably, many African American readers would already be familiar with this information. In addition, Naylor takes pains to dispel any sense her readers may have that she and her family were victims. She presents her young self as somewhat bratty, given to lording it over a classmate (3), and she presents her extended family as a warm and lively group of hard workers (4–5) who had struggled against and survived "hard times, unemployment, the occasional bout of depression" (10).

Method and Structure

1. Naylor's point is that words always need to be placed in context, no matter how well we think we know what they mean.

2. When the white boy "spit[s] out" (paragraph 3) the word, Naylor knows it's something nasty, even without fully understanding the meaning. (This is confirmed by the teacher's scolding him.) Later, we hear that the word's meaning depends on who says it, whether it's singular or plural, and who is being described. In Naylor's community, the singular *nigger* is a term of approval or endearment — approval when spoken by acquaintances, endearment when spoken by spouse or girlfriend. The plural term changes from being a positive to a negative term, and reflects lack of self-respect. *Girl* is the feminine equivalent: when spoken directly to a woman and drawn out, it signifies worth; when used in the third person and shortened, it signifies disapproval.

3. In the two introductory paragraphs Naylor establishes the importance of the spoken word (paragraph 1) and states her main idea (2). In paragraphs 3–5 she sets the scene for discussions of particular words by stepping back to recall a childhood incident (3) and to re-create the experience of being among her family (4–5). In the body of the essay she clarifies the varied meanings of the terms *nigger* and *girl* and comments on why blacks adopted *nigger* (14). The final paragraph returns us to the childhood experience and its connection to a cultural problem.

4. The childhood incident is recounted in paragraphs 3 and 15. The narrative is important because Naylor is talking about the emotional content of words, the attitudes they convey, and the feelings they engender in different contexts. Without the narrative, the discussion would be one-sided (only the positive uses of *nigger*), and the hurtful power of words would not be explicit.

Language

1. Naylor's tone is matter-of-fact and imperturbable ("I consider the written word inferior to the spoken," paragraph 1; "I will simply take the position . . ." [2]; "she took me in her lap and explained," [15]). From the first, aphoristic sentence, her style tends toward the academic ("nonsensical arrangement of sounds or letters without a consensus that assigns 'meaning,'" [2]; "In the singular," [6]; "When used with a possessive adjective," [9]; "In the plural," [10]; "used in third-person reference," 13; "social stratum," "internalization of racism," [14]). Some students will appreciate the tempered, anthropological way she treats a sensitive subject; others may wish the essay were more contentious.

2. After hearing what the boy says, Naylor the child tattles to the teacher "in a loud voice" (paragraph 3). And in 4–11 she reinforces the sense of a child growing aware of her world by separating herself from the adults in her family: the people speaking are *they*, not *we* (4–6, 9–10). Also, the use of passive verbs such as *was used* (5), *was applied* (6), and *was drawn out* (11) further emphasizes that Naylor was listening in on adult conversations. That she chooses to convey this information from the child's perspective heightens the effect of her message: the words we hear as

children influence the way we look at ourselves and those around us, and the context in which we hear those words can make all the difference. By placing herself and her readers directly in those contexts, Naylor demonstrates the power of words.

3. Examples include the following: in the apartment the "clamor" was often "punctuated by the sound of a baby's crying somewhere in the back rooms or out on the street" (paragraph 5). Naylor's "countless aunts, uncles, and cousins" and their "assorted friends" came to the apartment "to let down their hair and put up their feet after a week of labor in the factories, laundries, and shipyards of New York" (4). They experienced "triumphs and disappointments in the various workings of their lives" (5), and admired men of "strength, intelligence, or drive" (6) and women of "wit, nerve, or daring" (11). They savored "their past history of struggle and present survival against the odds" (9), and despised the "lack of self-respect" of those "who neglected their children, . . . fought in public," and otherwise "overstepped the bounds of decency" (10). This language brings the community to life. Readers are not expected to take Naylor's word for it; they see the variety and complexity of these people.

4. Demonstration is one of the most effective forms of explanation, so by using it here Naylor reinforces her definitions. While the dialogue does interrupt the expository prose, it heightens the reader's sense of "being there." Furthermore, Naylor is trying to convey to the reader that these people are indeed "varied and complex human beings" (14). How better to do that than to let them speak for themselves?

ANNOTATED ESSAY

Language is the subject. It is the written form with which I've managed to keep the wolf away from the door and, in diaries, to keep my sanity. In spite of this, I consider the written word inferior to the spoken, and much of the frustration experienced by novelists is the awareness that whatever we manage to capture in even the most transcendent passages falls far short of the richness of life. Dialogue achieves its power in the dynamics of a fleeting moment of sight, sound, smell, and touch. *1* *Comparison*

I'm not going to enter the debate here about whether it is language that shapes reality or vice versa. That battle is doomed to be waged whenever we seek intermittent reprieve from the chicken and egg dispute. I will simply take the position that the spoken word, like the written word, amounts to a nonsensical arrangement of sounds or letters without a consensus that assigns "meaning." And building from the meanings of what we hear, we order reality. Words themselves are innocuous; it is the consensus that gives them true power. *2* *THESIS*

I remember the first time I heard the word *nigger.* In my 3
third-grade class, our math tests were being passed down the rows, and as I handed the papers to a little boy in back of me, I remarked that once again he had received a much lower mark than I did. He snatched his test from me and spit out that word. Had he called me a nymphomaniac or a necro- *Narration*
philiac, I couldn't have been more puzzled. I didn't know what a nigger was, but I knew that whatever it meant, it was something he shouldn't have called me. This was verified when I raised my hand, and in a loud voice repeated what he had said and watched the teacher scold him for using a "bad" word. I was later to go home and ask the inevitable question that every black parent must face — "Mommy, what does *nigger* mean?"

And what exactly did it mean? Thinking back, I realize 4
that this could not have been the first time the word was used in my presence. I was part of a large extended family that had migrated from the rural South after World War II and formed a close-knit network that gravitated around my maternal grandparents. Their ground-floor apartment in one of the buildings they owned in Harlem was a weekend mecca for my immediate family, along with countless aunts, uncles, and cousins who brought along assorted friends. It was a bustling and open house with assorted neighbors and ten- *Narration and*
ants popping in and out to exchange bits of gossip, pick up *description*
an old quarrel, or referee the ongoing checkers game in which my grandmother cheated shamelessly. They were all there to let down their hair and put up their feet after a week of labor in the factories, laundries, and shipyards of New York.

Amid the clamor, which could reach deafening propor- 5
tions — two or three conversations going on simultaneously, punctuated by the sound of a baby's crying somewhere in the back rooms or out on the street — there was still a rigid set of rules about what was said and how. Older children were sent out of the living room when it was time to get into the juicy details about "you-know-who" up on the third floor who had gone and gotten herself "p-r-e-g-n-a-n-t!" But my parents, knowing that I could spell well beyond my years, always demanded that I follow the others out to play. Beyond sexual misconduct and death, everything else was considered harmless for our young ears. And so among the anecdotes of the triumphs and disappointments in the various workings of their lives, the word *nigger* was used in my presence, but it was set within contexts and inflections that caused
it to register in my mind as something else. *Definition*

In the singular, the word was always applied to a man 6
who had distinguished himself in some situation that brought their approval for his strength, intelligence, or drive:

"Did Johnny *really* do that?" 7

"I'm telling you, that nigger pulled in $6,000 of overtime 8
last year. Said he got enough for a down payment on a house."

Definition

When used with a possessive adjective by a woman — 9
"my nigger" — it became a term of endearment for her husband or boyfriend. But it could be more than just a term applied to a man. In their mouths it became the pure essence of manhood — a disembodied force that channeled their past history of struggle and present survival against the odds into a victorious statement of being: "Yeah, that old foreman found out quick enough — you don't mess with a nigger."

Example

In the plural, it became a description of some group within 10
the community that had overstepped the bounds of decency as my family defined it. Parents who neglected their children, a drunken couple who fought in public, people who simply refused to look for work, those with excessively dirty mouths or unkempt households were all "trifling niggers." This particular circle could forgive hard times, unemployment, the occasional bout of depression — they had gone though all of that themselves — but the unforgivable sin was a lack of self-respect.

Example

A woman could never be a "nigger" in the singular, with 11
its connotation of confirming worth. The noun *girl* was its closest equivalent in that sense, but only when used in direct address and regardless of the gender doing the addressing. *Girl* was a token of respect for a woman. The one-syllable word was drawn out to sound like three in recognition of the extra ounce of wit, nerve, or daring that the woman had shown in the situation under discussion.

Description, example, and comparison

"G-i-r-l, stop. You mean you said that to his face?" 12

But if the word was used in a third-person reference or 13
shortened so that it almost snapped out of the mouth, it always involved some element of communal disapproval. And age became an important factor in these exchanges. It was only between individuals of the same generation, or from any older person to a younger (but never the other way around), that *girl* would be considered a compliment.

I don't agree with the argument that use of the word *nigger* 14
at this social stratum of the black community was an internalization of racism. The dynamics were the exact opposite: the people in my grandmother's living room took a word that whites used to signify worthlessness or degradation and rendered it impotent. Gathering there together, they transformed *nigger* to signify the varied and complex human beings they knew themselves to be. If the word was to disappear totally from the mouths of even the most liberal of white society, no one in that room was naive enough to believe it would disappear from white minds. Meeting the word head-on, they proved it had absolutely nothing to do with the way they were determined to live their lives.

Cause and effect

So there must have been dozens of times that *nigger* was spoken in front of me before I reached the third grade. But I didn't "hear" it until it was said by a small pair of lips that had already learned it could be a way to humiliate me. That was the word I went home and asked my mother about. And since she knew that I had to grow up in America, she took me in her lap and explained. 15

Narration

Allison Amend

Taking Issue with Problems *(p. 273)*

Surely more than a few students will admit to using an expression such as "I have issues with authority," but few may have given the word *issue* serious thought before now. Amend, a student herself, writes an extended definition of the word, contrasting it with *problem* to demonstrate that the former is not a harmless substitute for the latter but influences how we think about and attempt to resolve our difficulties. Some of the distinctions Amend makes are subtle, so it may be worth class time to discuss the two questions under "Meaning," including the vocabulary list.

Once students grasp the difference between an issue and a problem, ask them to give examples of current uses of *issue* like the one in the first sentence of the preceding paragraph. (The first "Writing Topic" prompts the collection of examples.) What, as Amend sees it, is the speaker really saying about the person's difficulties? What is he or she *not* saying?

Content Quiz

1. Which term, *issue* or *problem,* does Amend consider a euphemism?
   [Issue.]

2. Which term enables people to place blame on something outside themselves?
   [Issue.]

3. Which term do people associate with "weakness, mental laziness, intellectual inflation," according to Amend?
   [Problem.]

4. According to the essay, is it more socially acceptable to talk about problems or issues?
   [Issues.]

5. Which is more important to Amend, settling conflicts or understanding their causes?
   [Conflicts need to be settled before digging for causes.]

Vocabulary Quiz

1. *Perplexity* (paragraph 3) is closest in meaning to
   a. astonishment b. discomfort c. bewilderment
   [c. bewilderment]

2. *Malaise* (6) is closest in meaning to
   a. malady b. discomfort c. maladjustment
   [b. discomfort]

3. *Culpable* (7) is closest in meaning to
   a. guilty b. faulty c. wrong
   [a. guilty]

4. *Visceral* (11) is closest in meaning to
   a. vivid b. important c. instinctive
   [c. instinctive]

5. *Tirades* (13) is closest in meaning to
   a. rants b. sobs c. discussions
   [a. rants]

ANSWERS

Meaning

1. *Problems* are tangible, discrete, and the responsibility of the person who has them. *Issues* are a formless flow of negative energy that become the concern of everyone they touch: the person who has issues tends to point the blame for them on other people. Solving a problem is useful; it accomplishes something. Dealing with an issue, in contrast, is circular, a never-ending activity whose only result is to perpetuate itself.

2. A problem, unlike an issue, is specific and finite; its borders are well defined. An issue, in contrast, is fluid, an end in itself.

Purpose and Audience

1. Amend seems to have written for all three reasons stated, but she reveals an additional (perhaps the paramount) purpose in the last paragraph: she wants to urge people to take responsibility for their own problems, not blame them on other people or justify rude behavior by calling their problems *issues.*

2. Students' responses will vary, of course, with some perhaps finding the distinction between *issue* and *problem* informative and others thinking Amend splits hairs. Students may project their own responses onto Amend's original Stanford readers.

Method and Structure

1. Definition might seem an unlikely method for an essay whose purpose is to change people's behavior. But Amend's impetus is the increasing use of the word *issue.* Defining *issue* and *problem* allows her to show what's wrong with the former while exposing the wrongheadedness of celebrating people's issues while making them ashamed of their problems.

2. Buying an issue and issuing a ticket are different uses of the word from the one Amend discusses in the essay. But Amend makes no claim that her definition is exhaustive. She is only interested in the kind of issue that results from, and in, human conflict.

3. The definitions serve as springboards to the distinctions Amend draws between the two words. She is especially sensitive to the meaning of *issue* as "flowing," using this as a metaphor to describe the way people interact with each other when they have issues (paragraph 5).

4. The two methods are mutually dependent here: Amend compares meanings and uses.

Language

1. Amend's formal vocabulary (such as "euphemism," "malaise," "expiate," and "appellation" in paragraph 6) suggests her own educated background and her expectation that her readers are also educated. At the same time, the occasional informalities ("Everyone's got 'em," [1]; "Wow," [4]) reveal a presumed closeness between writer and reader. Overall, Amend's style falls between extremes of formality and informality, especially in its vigorous images ("Freudian field-day," [6]; "throw around blame like confetti on New Year's," [7]; "issues are served up," [13]).

2. An *issue* is in one sense a pouring fourth. Amend shows how this literal meaning can be applied to the figurative one: an *issue* in the sense that a problem is fluid; it never stops.

Chapter 12

CAUSE-AND-EFFECT ANALYSIS

Exploring the Influence of Gender

Deborah Tannen

Gender Gap in Cyberspace *(p. 292)*

Tannen's essay presents a topic about which students will most likely have much to say: gender as it pertains to technology. Some students may be put off by Tannen's assertion that men are more computer-literate than women; indeed, computer-savvy women and computer-shy men in the classroom may personally contradict Tannen's thesis. This contradiction can be a good opportunity to discuss the use of generalizations and specific examples in writing, and you could have students locate instances of each in Tannen's essay. Does the existence of exceptions undermine Tannen's analysis of causes and effects? It should be interesting to notice the range of computer literacy in the classroom and whether, as Tannen claims, the men are more adept.

Content Quiz

1. Who was the first in Tannen's neighborhood to get a computer?
   [Her colleague Ralph.]

2. How did Tannen spend her free time when she first got a computer?
   [Talking on the telephone with friends.]

3. What "hooked" Tannen on computers and why?
   [E-mail, because it's "souped-up conversation."]

4. Why are boys more likely to be interested in computers than girls are?
   [Boys want to dominate the balky machines.]

5. Why doesn't Tannen do bibliographies or tables of contents on the computer?
   [She doesn't want to take time to learn how.]

Vocabulary Quiz

1. *Obliqueness* (paragraph 6) is closest in meaning to
   a. indirectness b. clarity c. difficulty
   [a. indirectness]

2. *Incited* (7) is closest in meaning to
   a. angered b. frustrated c. provoked
   [c. provoked]

3. *Vituperative* (10) is closest in meaning to
   a. boring b. abusive c. spirited
   [b. abusive]

4. *Rapport* (12) is closest in meaning to
   a. argument b. relationship c. discussion
   [b. relationship]

5. *Waned* (13) is closest in meaning to
   a. ended b. peaked c. diminished
   [c. diminished]

ANSWERS

Meaning

1. Even though Tannen and Ralph started using computers at about the same time, Ralph was much more interested in the new device. The differences in their responses illustrate that men and women generally respond differently to computers, reflecting fundamental differences in their ways of functioning in the world.

2. The paradox (repeated in the last paragraph) is that Tannen was one of the first to own a personal computer, but she still knows little about the machine. The explanation lies in Tannen's being a woman and thus, typically, a computer user but not a tinkerer or master (as a man would more likely be).

3. Unlike in casual conversation, women are focused on information with a computer because they're not responding to the challenge of getting the computer to submit (paragraph 12).

4. In paragraphs 10 and 11, Tannen offers two reasons: women do not tolerate or enjoy having their messages attacked, a practice of some men, and frequently they are sexually harassed.

Purpose and Audience

1. The response to e-mail by men and women provides a point of overlap between them, yet it also underscores a difference between them: for men, e-mail provides "a combination of the technology (which they enjoy) and the obliqueness of the written word" (paragraph 6); for women, it's a point of connection with others (8).

2. Given that this essay appeared in *Newsweek*, the audience is well educated and middle class, both men and women. Tannen assumes that readers are at least somewhat computer-literate, since she does not define terms such as "e-mail" and "online."

Method and Structure

1. Tannen's own experiences led her to explore her subject. Men avoid intense face-to-face conversation (paragraphs 5–6), compete for dominance (7), and don't mind vituperation (10). Women prefer cooperation (7), like to connect personally (8), do mind vituperation (10) and harassment (11), and do not respond to a computer's challenges (12).

2. Tannen's sentence fragment is in keeping with the conversational tone she uses throughout, and separating it as a paragraph of course calls attention to it. The final paragraph restates the first paragraph, bringing the essay full circle and stressing that everything in between explains why.

3. This example makes the phenomenon she's describing more concrete, showing us how a specific man and woman differed in their responses to computers. The fact that Tannen is writing about her own experience helps establish a sympathetic bond with readers.

Language

1. Tannen's language is colloquial, which suits discussion of her personal experiences. Examples include "souped-up" (paragraph 4), "dribs and drabs" (6), "gulp" (8), and the final paragraph with its sentence fragment and "pretty much."

2. Tannen's tone is impatient, almost foot-stamping, thus underlining her attitude toward the balky machine. The figure is personification, attributing human characteristics to a machine.

Jon Katz

How Boys Become Men *(p. 298)*

In an excellent analysis of causes and effects, Katz offers an insightful piece about how the socialization of boys contributes to insensitivity and remoteness in men. He presents concrete examples of boyhood behavior, drawing on his perspectives as both witness and participant. Students will easily recognize the behavior Katz details from their own experiences or observations. You might focus discussion on the intent and effect of these examples, as addressed in questions 3 and 4 under "Method and Structure." Students might also consider how audience shapes a piece: appearing as a column for *Glamour* magazine, this essay appeals to young women. (Question 2 under "Language" explores how Katz's pronoun shift from *we* to *they* works to align him with his audience.)

Content Quiz

1. What happens in the incident Katz observes involving two boys and a book bag?
   [One boy hits the other with the bag.]

2. How do women view men?
   ["As a giant problem in need of solution."]

3. What is the one thing boys don't want to be?
   [Weird.]

4. What causes the fight Katz has as a fifth-grader?
   [Pushing a bigger boy and taking the last chocolate milk.]

5. What does the boy being picked on in the playground do when Katz comes along?
   [Says he's fine and begins to swing.]

Vocabulary Quiz

1. *Audible* (paragraph 2) is closest in meaning to
   a. visible   b. forceful   c. heard
   [c. heard]

2. *Ethics* (3) is closest in meaning to
   a. principles   b. stepping stones   c. compromises
   [a. principles]

3. *Empathy* (5) is closest in meaning to
   a. feeling   b. helping   c. understanding
   [c. understanding]

4. *Intervening* (18) is closest in meaning to
   a. coming between   b. watching   c. calling for help
   [a. coming between]

5. *Stigmatized* (18) is closest in meaning to
   a. nicknamed   b. considered   c. branded
   [c. branded]

ANSWERS

Meaning

1. The code is detailed in paragraph 5: "Don't be a goody-goody"; "Never rat"; "Never admit fear"; don't empathize with or assist anyone except "your best buddy"; don't talk about "anything of substance." Paragraph

18 details adult male behavior: men struggle with sensitivity; prove unable to request help and support; hide weaknesses and fears; avoid helping others in trouble.

2. Katz's main idea is stated most succinctly in paragraph 15: "Men remember receiving little mercy as boys; maybe that's why it's sometimes difficult for them to show any."

3. "Frontier Justice" (paragraph 12) is Wild West talk: gunslinging, saloon brawls, showdowns, ambushes. Katz obviously overstates to make his point: Boy Justice is merciless.

Purpose and Audience

1. The stories are too painful to be entertaining, and the somber, melancholy tone reveals a serious purpose. Katz wants readers to understand the sources of men's limitations.

2. *Glamour* is a young women's magazine. Katz is explaining men to women. The stories seem designed to gain sympathetic understanding, and the limitations Katz claims for men would be familiar to many women.

3. Answers will vary.

Method and Structure

1. In paragraph 4, Katz states: "But if you don't understand something about boys, you can't understand why men are the way we are, why we find it so difficult to make friends or to acknowledge our fears and problems."

2. The opening anecdote gives the essay concreteness and immediacy and also offers support up front for what we will later see as Katz's thesis. The concluding anecdote drives the point home. Both, because they are current, emphasize that this "Code of Conduct" continues among boys today and that much needs to change before men change.

3. As noted previously, the informal, personal details seem designed to gain the sympathetic understanding of *Glamour*'s women readers; a more formal, academic approach would be out of place in a magazine column (though expert opinions and statistics might support a detailed examination of the issue in a feature article in *Glamour*). Essentially, Katz is his own authority, showing himself to be sensitive and perceptive.

4. The narratives and the examples overlap in paragraphs 1–2, 7–14, 20–23. Both provide evidence for Katz's thesis, explaining the cause of the effect.

Language

1. Katz seems to regret that male culture is the way it is ("A chicken probably would have had the sense to get out of the way," paragraph 3; "ruthless, unspoken, and unyielding rules," [5]; "It may be a long while . . . before male culture evolves to the point that boys can learn more from one another than how to hit curve balls," [20]). But there are moments of irony, where he is clearly exaggerating for humorous effect ("Never discuss anything of substance with anybody," [5]; "Boys are rewarded for throwing hard. Most other activities . . . are considered weird," [6]).

1. With *we* in paragraph 4, Katz stresses his authority to write about his subject. With *they* in paragraph 18, he is aligning himself more with his readers. His approach at this point is less personal as he lays out the meat of his analysis.

2. Capitalization creates emphasis and elevates the terms to a more inclusive and more permanent status, as if they were laws engraved in stone.

ANNOTATED ESSAY

1 Two nine-year-old boys, neighbors and friends, were walking home from school. The one in the bright blue windbreaker was laughing and swinging a heavy-looking bag toward the head of his friend, who kept ducking and stepping back. "What's the matter?" asked the kid with the bag, whooshing it over his head. "You chicken?"

Narration and example

2 His friend stopped, stood still, and braced himself. The bag slammed into the side of his face, the thump audible all the way across the street where I stood watching. The impact knocked him to the ground, where he lay mildly stunned for a second. Then he struggled up, rubbing the side of his head. "See?" he said proudly. "I'm no chicken."

3 No. A chicken would probably have had the sense to get out of the way. This boy was already well on the road to becoming a *man*, having learned one of the central ethics of his gender: Experience pain rather than show fear.

4 Women tend to see men as a giant problem in need of solution. They tell us that we're remote and uncommunicative, that we need to demonstrate less machismo and more commitment, more humanity. But if you don't understand something about boys, you can't understand why men are the way they are, why we find it so difficult to make friends or to acknowledge our fears and problems.

Cause and effect

5 Boys live in a world with its own Code of Conduct, a set of ruthless, unspoken, and unyielding rules:

Definition

> Don't be a goody-goody.
> Never rat. If your parents ask about bruises, shrug.
> Never admit fear. Ride the roller coaster, join the fist-fight, do what you have to do. Asking for help is for sissies.

> Empathy is for nerds. You can help your best buddy, under certain circumstances. Everyone else is on his own.
>
> Never discuss anything of substance with anybody. Grunt, shrug, dump on teachers, laugh at wimps, talk about comic books. Anything else is risky.

Cause and effect

Definition

6 Boys are rewarded for throwing hard. Most other activities — reading, befriending girls, or just thinking —are considered weird. And if there's one thing boy's don't want to be, it's weird.

Narration and example

7 More than anything else, boys are supposed to learn how to handle themselves. I remember the bitter fifth-grade conflict I touched off by elbowing aside a bigger boy named Barry and seizing the cafeteria's last carton of chocolate milk. Teased for getting aced out by a wimp, he had to reclaim his place in the pack. Our fistfight, at recess, ended with my knees buckling and my lip bleeding while my friends, sympathetic but out of range, watched resignedly.

8 When I got home, my mother took one look at my swollen face and screamed. I wouldn't tell her anything, but when my father got home I cracked and confessed, pleading with them to do nothing. Instead, they called Barry's parents, who restricted his television for a week.

9 The following morning, Barry and six of his pals stepped out from behind a stand of trees. "It's the rat," said Barry.

10 I bled a little more. *Rat* was scrawled in crayon across my desk.

11 They were waiting for me after school for a number of afternoons to follow. I tried varying my routes and avoiding bushes and hedges. It usually didn't work.

12 I was as ashamed for telling as I was frightened. "You did ask for it," said my best friend. Frontier Justice has nothing on Boy Justice.

13 In panic, I appealed to a cousin who was several years older. He followed me home from school, and when Barry's gang surrounded me, he came barreling toward us. "Stay away from my cousin," he shouted, "or I'll kill you."

14 After they were gone, however, my cousin could barely stop laughing. "You were afraid of *them*?" he howled. "They barely came up to my waist."

THESIS

15 Men remember receiving little mercy as boys; maybe that's why it's sometimes difficult for them to show any.

Example

16 "I know lots of men who had happy childhoods, but none who have happy memories of the way other boys treated them," says a friend. "It's a macho marathon from third grade up, when you start butting each other in the stomach."

17 "The thing is," adds another friend, "you learn early on to hide what you feel. It's never safe to say, 'I'm scared.' My girlfriend asks me why I don't talk more about what I'm feeling. I've gotten better at it, but it will *never* come naturally."

You don't need to be a shrink to see how the lessons boys 18 learn affect their behavior as men. Men are being asked, more and more, to show sensitivity, but they dread the very word. They struggle to build their increasingly uncertain work lives but will deny they're in trouble. They want love, affection, and support but don't know how to ask for them. They hide their weaknesses and fears from all, even those they care for. They've learned to be wary of intervening when they see others in trouble. They often still balk at being stigmatized as weird.

Cause and effect

Comparison

Some men get shocked into sensitivity — when they lose 19 their jobs, their wives, or their lovers. Others learn it through a strong marriage, or through their own children.

It may be a long while, however, before male culture 20 evolves to the point that boys can learn more from one another than how to hit curve balls. Last month, walking my dog past the playground near my house, I saw three boys encircling a fourth, laughing, and pushing him. He was skinny and rumpled, and he looked frightened. One boy knelt behind him while another pushed him from the front, a trick familiar to any former boy. He fell backward.

Narration and example

When the others ran off, he brushed the dirt off his el- 21 bows and walked toward the swings. His eyes were moist and he was struggling for control.

"Hi," I said through the chain-link fence. "How ya do- 22 ing?"

"Fine," he said quickly, kicking his legs out and begin- 23 ning his swing.

Amy L. Beck

Struggling for Perfection *(p. 303)*

This student essay analyzes the causes of two complex problems that are experienced much more by women than by men: eating disorders and physical abuse. Beck's report of her work at a psychiatric hospital, meeting and observing women with these problems, gives immediacy to her analysis. Students will undoubtedly respond to this essay and to its thesis (that objectification of women in the media contributes to both problems), though their responses may vary from complete agreement to complete disagreement.

The essay offers several approaches to class discussion. For instance, raising question 4 under "Method and Structure," you might focus on Beck's evidence — primarily (but not exclusively) her experiences in the psychiatric hospital: Do students find the evidence adequate and convincing? Or you might take a broader approach, following the lead of the third "Writing Topic": Do students believe that American culture emphasizes the female body, and, if so, why?

Content Quiz

1. When did Beck first become convinced of the link between unrealistic images of women in the media and eating disorders?
   [When she took a job at a psychiatric hospital.]

2. What are some other factors Beck identifies as possibly contributing to eating disorders?
   [Family problems, alcoholic parents, and histories of abuse and clinical depression.]

3. Who were the majority of the sexual abuse victims Beck encountered abused by?
   ["People close to them: relatives, ex-boyfriends, or family friends," who were "rarely pathological rapists or batterers."]

4. Does Beck believe men's disrespect for and abuse of women is due more to nature or more to nurture?
   [Nurture.]

5. What proportion of American women suffer from eating disorders?
   [5 percent to 15 percent.]

Vocabulary Quiz

1. *Gurus* (paragraph 1) is closest in meaning to
   a. experts b. geniuses c. millionaires
   [a. experts]

2. *Proliferation* (2) is closest in meaning to
   a. distribution b. growth c. sale
   [b. growth]

3. *Debilitating* (6) is closest in meaning to
   a. unpleasant b. horrifying c. weakening
   [c. weakening]

4. *Heinous* (8) is closest in meaning to
   a. hateful b. criminal c. sickening
   [a. hateful]

5. *Predisposed* (8) is closest in meaning to
   a. programmed b. condemned c. susceptible
   [c. susceptible]

ANSWERS

Meaning

1. Beck's persuasive thesis is formulated at the end of the essay: "I am absolutely convinced that the objectification of women by the media is an integral part of both of these problems, presenting women with unrealistic role models while encouraging men to think of women solely in terms of their sexuality" (paragraph 10). Parts of this thesis, which undergirds the entire essay, are stated earlier, but Beck waits until the end to bring all the elements of her cause-and-effect analysis together in one statement.

2. Unrealistic standards of physical attractiveness (cause) lead to eating disorders in women (effect). And pornography (cause) leads men to abuse women (effect).

3. Beck wants to stress that even seemingly "normal" men are susceptible to the influence of pornography, which trains them to think of their girlfriends and wives as "objects that exist solely for their pleasure and convenience" (paragraph 8). She's not excusing these men; she's showing how banal and widespread this kind of abuse can be.

Purpose and Audience

1. Beck was clearly deeply affected by her experience at the psychiatric hospital, an experience that compelled her to learn more about the two major problems she encountered there: abuse and eating disorders. Her purpose is to convince readers that "sexually charged images of women in the media . . . play a central role" (paragraph 11) in both of these problems.

2. One assumption Beck seems to make, judging from her language, is that her audience is well educated. She does not seem to assume readers' agreement, being careful to present opposing views (as in paragraphs 2, 5, 9, and 10) and to provide evidence of her thesis (as in 4–7 and 10).

Method and Structure

1. These two problems raise the question "Why" — the question this method is best equipped to answer. Beck's main purpose is to convince that there is a causal link between media images of women and abuse and eating disorders — a goal that could only be achieved by some form of cause-and-effect analysis.

2. Problems in their lives lead certain women to low self-esteem, which they try to overcome by making their bodies look like those they see in the media.

3. Beck knows that both problems are complicated, with multiple causes. Anticipating skeptics' objections that she's overstating her case, she insists only that media portrayals do have some influence, however large or small. Her balance and objectivity strengthen the essay; she would lose credibility if she tried to suggest that these images are the only cause of abuse and eating disorders.

4. The women Beck met serve as concrete examples of the abstract problems she discusses, making these problems seem more real. Although the evidence could be considered anecdotal, Beck clearly read a great deal and asked questions about what she saw; she provides specific details; and she qualifies her cause-and-effect assertions. She might have offered other data to back up her experience, but the experience alone is quite persuasive.

Language

1. Beck's tone is fairly impassioned — for instance, "My first reaction was to ask how anyone could possibly believe . . ." (paragraph 3), "every time I saw them I experienced the same shock" (4), "I am absolutely convinced" (10). Students' opinions of the tone's appropriateness will vary. It does underline Beck's sincerity and the importance of her subject, and she is careful to balance her views. But some students may prefer a more dispassionate view of such loaded issues.

2. "Sex sells" (paragraph 1) grabs the reader's attention and enables Beck to position herself as straight-from-the-hip and no-nonsense.

3. She tells us that she has done research ("After listening to and reading countless case histories, I began to recognize the patterns," (paragraph 7). She emphasizes that she is writing from one person's subjective point of view ("I am writing from a starkly different perspective," [3]). And she emphasizes her subjectivity ("I disagree," [9]; "I am absolutely convinced," [10]).

Chapter 13

ARGUMENT AND PERSUASION

Debating Cloning

Charles Krauthammer

Of Headless Mice . . . and Men *(p. 329)*

This essay and the two following it take divergent views of human cloning: Krauthammer opposes cloning, Hamner favors it, and Backous finds a middle ground. Krauthammer's essay is the most impassioned, and he raises interesting and chilling questions: Is cloning the "technology of narcissism" (paragraph 12)? Should it be banned, even (in some forms) made a capital offense? Cloning is a technological issue that can be debated not on its technological merits but on its ethical implications, allowing nonspecialists to participate on the basis of their own beliefs.

You might focus class discussion on the particular form of cloning addressed by Krauthammer and Hamner: the creation of headless humans as organ banks. Or you might approach the topic more narrowly (and rhetorically), asking students how Krauthammer's tone informs his main idea and influences reception of it. (See question 1 under "Language.")

Content Quiz

1. What caused the mice without heads, created at the University of Texas, to die?
   [They had no way to breathe.]

2. Why, according to Lee Silver, would it be legal to produce human bodies without a forebrain?
   [They wouldn't have a consciousness and thus would not be considered persons.]

3. What does Krauthammer mean by "normal" cloning?
   [Cloning of humans with the intention of letting them live autonomous lives.]

4. How much federal funding has been appropriated for human cloning research?
   [None.]

5. What action does Krauthammer recommend be taken to prevent the cloning of headless humans?
   [He wants it to be made a capital crime.]

Vocabulary Quiz

1. *Ominously* (paragraph 5) is closest in meaning to
   a. criminally b. threateningly c. dangerously
   [b. threateningly]

2. *Breached* (7) is closest in meaning to
   a. broken b. severed c. surpassed
   [a. broken]

3. *Acquiesce* (8) is closest in meaning to
   a. consent b. deny c. participate
   [a. consent]

4. *Quasi-* (8) is closest in meaning to
   a. super- b. semi- c. sub-
   [b. semi-]

5. *Totalitarian* (14) is closest in meaning to
   a. advocates b. unreasonable c. harsh
   [c. harsh]

ANSWERS

Meaning

1. "The time to put a stop to this is now" (paragraph 13). "Congress should ban human cloning now. Totally" (14).

2. The only "benefit" Krauthammer sees is satisfaction of human vanity (paragraphs 9, 11). "Human beings are ends, not means," he says (8); they are not collections of parts.

Purpose and Audience

1. It is conceivable that an opinion essay in a publication such as *Time* might play a small part in legislative change. Readers of such publications include policymakers, to be sure, but, more important, major news magazines influence public opinion, which in turn influences congressional opinion and action.

2. The ideal reader would probably be a member of Congress, since Krauthammer's stated purpose is to effect legislation banning cloning. Geneticists will probably already have strong opinions on cloning, and their ideas are not likely to be changed by a journalist writing in a mainstream publication. But average Joes and Janes are important to Krauthammer, because a groundswell of anticloning sentiment could force Congress to act.

Method and Structure

1. The essay appeals largely to readers' emotions: the assumption underlying the argument (that human beings are ends, not means) is a belief, not a conclusion from facts; the argument depends as well on other beliefs (such as statements about vanity); and the tone is adamant.

2. The first half of the essay (paragraphs 1–7) is more expository, the last half (8–14) more argumentative. But Krauthammer injects his opinion into even the most explanatory of passages, sometimes explicitly — "the scariest news of all" (1); "Frankenstein wattage," "animal monsters" (2); "deformed and dying quasi-human life" (8) — and sometimes through loaded words — "plundering" (3), "mutant" (5), "disemboweling" (8).

3. With the quotations, Krauthammer does give voice to two scientists who would disagree with him but neither scientist's view is compelling. The quotations from Silver, out of context as they are, have something of the chilly ring of the mad scientist, detached from all human considerations.

4. Headless cloning would allow for the constant replacement of defective body parts, thus theoretically making it possible for a persón's consciousness to survive once the original body was gone. Krauthammer shows through this comparison that cloning appeals to people's vanity and narcissism, not to some lofty humanitarian impulse.

Language

1. Krauthammer does not attempt to disguise his horror at the prospect of human cloning: a strong sense of disgust and dread pervades the essay. The tone becomes more dogmatic and prescriptive in the last paragraph, with such word choices as "This is not enough," "Totally," "draconian," "must be," "capital crime," "barbarity," and "hell." Krauthammer leaves no uncertainty as to his position.

2. This is a somewhat sensationalistic pronouncement, with the effect of frightening readers into listening to Krauthammer's elaboration.

3. Acquiescing is passive; encouraging is active, "deliberate" (paragraph 8) and "purposeful" (2). Someone who encouragers something wrong is guiltier than someone who merely acquiesces.

ANNOTATED ESSAY

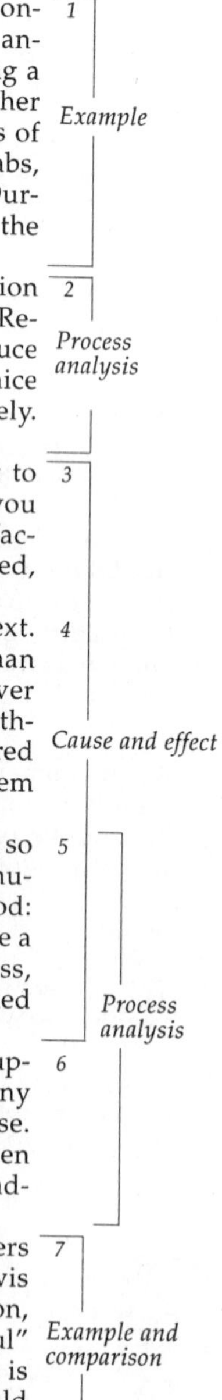

Last year Dolly the cloned sheep was received with won- 1
der, titters and some vague apprehension. Last week the announcement by a Chicago physicist that he is assembling a team to produce the first human clone occasioned yet another wave of Brave New World anxiety. But the scariest news of all — and largely overlooked — comes from two obscure labs, at the University of Texas and at the University of Bath. During the past four years, one group created headless mice; the other, headless tadpoles.

For sheer Frankenstein wattage, the purposeful creation 2
of these animal monsters has no equal. Take the mice. Researchers found the gene that tells the embryo to produce the head. They deleted it. They did this in a thousand mice embryos, four of which were born. I use the term loosely. Having no way to breathe, the mice died instantly.

Why then create them? The Texas researchers want to 3
learn how genes determine embryo development. But you don't have to be a genius to see the true utility of manufacturing headless creatures: for their organs — fully formed, perfectly useful, ripe for plundering.

Why should you be panicked? Because humans are next. 4
"It would almost certainly be possible to produce human bodies without a forebrain," Princeton biologist Lee Silver told the London *Sunday Times*. "These human bodies without any semblance of consciousness would not be considered persons, and thus it would be perfectly legal to keep them 'alive' as a future source of organs."

"Alive." Never have a pair of quotation marks loomed so 5
ominously. Take the mouse-frog technology, apply it to humans, combine it with cloning, and you are become a god: with a single cell taken from, say, your finger, you produce a headless replica of yourself, a mutant twin, arguably lifeless, that becomes your own personal, precisely tissue-matched organ farm.

There are, of course, technical hurdles along the way. Sup- 6
pressing the equivalent "head" gene in man. Incubating tiny infant organs to grow into larger ones that adults could use. And creating artificial wombs (as per Aldous Huxley) given that it might be difficult to recruit sane women to carry headless fetuses to their birth/death.

It won't be long, however, before these technical barriers 7
are breached. The ethical barriers are already cracking. Lewis Wolpert, professor of biology at University College, London, finds producing headless humans "personally distasteful" but, given the shortage of organs, does not think distaste is sufficient reason not to go ahead with something that would save lives. And Professor Silver not only sees "nothing wrong, philosophically or rationally," with producing headless hu-

mans for organ harvesting, he wants to convince a skeptical public that it is perfectly O.K.

8 When prominent scientists are prepared to acquiesce in — or indeed encourage — the deliberate creation of deformed and dying quasi-human life, you know we are facing a bioethical abyss. Human beings are ends, not means. There is no grosser corruption of biotechnology than creating a human mutant and disemboweling it at our pleasure for spare parts.

Classification and comparison

9 The prospect of headless human clones should put the whole debate about "normal" cloning in a new light. Normal cloning is less a treatment for infertility than a treatment for vanity. It is a way to produce an exact genetic replica of yourself that will walk the earth years after you're gone.

10 But there is a problem with a clone. It is not really you. It is but a twin, a perfect John Doe Jr., but still a junior. With its own independent consciousness, it is, alas, just a facsimile of you.

Division or analysis

11 The headless clone solves the facsimile problem. It is a gateway to the ultimate vanity: immortality. If you create a real clone, you cannot transfer your consciousness into it to truly live on. But if you create a headless clone of just your body, you have created a ready source of replacement parts to keep you — your consciousness — going indefinitely.

Cause and effect

12 Which is why one form of cloning will inevitably lead to the other. Cloning is the technology of narcissism, and nothing satisfies narcissism like immortality. Headlessness will be cloning's crowning achievement.

13 The time to put a stop to this is now. Dolly moved President Clinton to create a commission that recommended a temporary ban on human cloning. But with physicist Richard Seed threatening to clone humans, and with headless animals already here, we are past the time for toothless commissions and meaningless bans.

THESIS

Cause and effect

14 Clinton banned federal funding of human-cloning research, of which there is none anyway. He then proposed a five-year ban on cloning. This is not enough. Congress should ban cloning now. Totally. And regarding one particular form, it should be draconian: the deliberate creation of headless humans must be made a crime, indeed a capital crime. If we flinch in the face of this high-tech barbarity, we'll deserve to live in the hell it heralds.

Kenneth Hamner

Move Over, Ichabod Crane *(p. 334)*

Kenneth Hamner, a student majoring in microbiology and biology, directly opposes the previous author, Charles Krauthammer, in this essay on the morality of someday creating headless human clones to serve as organ banks. Hamner devotes more attention than Krauthammer does to teasing out the ethical implications of cloning. His careful reasoning leads him to conclude that producing headless clones, having no consciousness and thus no natural rights, would not be immoral.

Hamner contrasts cloning with abortion (see question 3 under "Meaning"), and the difference he sees may be a good starting point for class discussion centering on natural rights. Alternatively, you could begin with Hamner's final question, "Is that morally wrong?" (Although Hamner has answered the question, many students will disagree with his answer.) Or, if you examined Krauthammer's tone, you might also examine Hamner's, as suggested in the fourth "Writing Topic."

Content Quiz

1. Who is Dolly?
   [A sheep — the world's first cloned mammal.]

2. What are natural rights?
   [The rights of all creatures to "live their lives as nature intended."]

3. What examples does Hamner cite of violations of humans natural rights?
   [Slavery, abortion, some cases of euthanasia, creation of conscious clones.]

4. Why does Hamner see no moral dilemma in cloning headless humans?
   [There is "no brain and thus no consciousness to violate."]

5. How would headless humans be like bridges, toasters, or computers in Hamner's opinion?
   [They would serve as tools.]

Vocabulary Quiz

1. *Genomes* (paragraph 3) is closest in meaning to
   a. genes b. DNA c. chromosomes
   [c. chromosomes]

2. *Inherent* (3) is closest in meaning to
   a. intrinsic b. hereditary c. natural
   [a. intrinsic]

3. *Fascism* (7) is closest in meaning to
   a. totalitarianism b. autocracy c. dictatorship
   [a. totalitarianism]

4. *Regressive* (7) is closest in meaning to
   a. old-fashioned b. backward c. immoral
   [b. backward]

5. *Guise* (7) is closest in meaning to
   a. disguise b. ribric c. pretext
   [c. pretext]

ANSWERS

Meaning

1. "More important, would this be immoral?" (paragraph 2) is the question the essay will attempt to answer. The thesis sentences are "I see no moral dilemma. The result of this procedure would have no brain and thus no consciousness to violate" (7).

2. Paragraphs 5 and 6: Many of the same people who make this argument have no compunctions about violating the natural rights of animals, especially in the interest of humans, whose needs and comforts are seen to be more important.

3. Abortion is the disruption of a natural process — humankind interfering with nature. Cloning, in contrast, is artificial to start with: since humans create the clones, they own them and have the right to do what they want with them. And the use to which the clones would be put — as organ banks — would serve the irreproachable purpose of saving "real" human lives. But Hamner is in favor only of creating headless, and thus unconscious, human organ banks; he would be against creating conscious clones for this purpose.

Purpose and Audience

1. Hamner wants to persuade readers that at least one specific use of human cloning would be ethical.

2. Hamner writes more for readers who think all cloning is wrong, since these are the people in need of persuasion. To this end, he is careful to present the other side fairly, without caricature or ridicule, which would alienate these readers.

Method and Structure

1. Hamner's appeal is partly rational. He is encouraging readers to overcome their emotional (irrational in his view) resistance to cloning, which he calls "a major advancement both for the livestock industries and for our understanding of how genes work" (paragraph 3). And he provides careful reasoning to demonstrate that producing headless human clones would not be immoral. But at bottom his appeal is emotional, requiring readers to accept both his depiction of natural rights and his claim that headless clones would not violate these rights.

2. Hamner evidently expects that readers have accepted his point about sheep, it will be easier to persuade them about cloning humans. Hamner is pulling the reader along gently, gradually upping the stakes.

3. This information shows that Hamner has more than a passing interest in the issue of cloning and implies that he may have specialized knowledge of the subject. It helps to establish his credibility.

4. Hamner objects to "prevent[ing] or inhibit[ing]" the rights of animals to "live their lives as nature intended" (paragraph 4) and to several violations of humans' natural rights (slavery, abortion, some cases of euthanasia, creating a conscious clone — all in paragraph 5). Offering these examples makes Hamner seem a moral person, contributing to his ethical appeal, and also defines the limits he sees to tampering with other beings.

Language

1. Hamner is mostly serious, especially about science (for example, "the few dangers inherent with all genetically undiversified populations," paragraph 3), natural rights ("all creatures have the right to live their lives as nature intended," [4]), and the potential value of cloning headless humans ("No natural fetuses are being killed, nor will thinking slaves be made," [8]). But he is also occasionally casual, even flippant ("If scientists were stupid enough to make nuclear bombs and Olestra," [3]; "being the masters of hypocrisy that we are," [5]). These instances sharpen Hamner's points. Students may vary over whether they detract from the essay's overall seriousness.

2. By comparison, Hamner's list establishes the grotesqueness of headless people. However, it operates as a paper tiger. Eventually we come to understand Hamner's belief that — as Halloween costumes are only costumes — headless clone only *appear* unethical.

3. This is a rhetorical question. By this point, Hamner hopes that readers see the answer as "No."

Timothy Backous

Making Sheep: Possible, but Right? *(p. 339)*

Neither vehemently opposed to cloning (like Krauthammer) nor wholeheartedly accepting of at least some of its forms (like Hamner), Backous finds a middle ground, arguing that "toying with the very essence of creation" (paragraph 5) requires first that we "ponder the consequences of our actions (5)." Though writing from a deeply religious perspective (he is a priest), Backous makes his argument very accessible. Even students who are not religious should respond to his question of just how far we should go (or should allow others to go) in attempting to perfect human life.

This question could spark class discussion as students consider what, if any, limits our society should place on biotechnology. The entire essay can also prompt discussion of moderation in argument, following the lead of the fourth "Writing Topic": ask students if Backous gains anything that Hamner and especially Krauthammer do not. Of course, this final essay on the subject of cloning also provides a chance to consider the arguments of all three essays as well as the sample paragraphs by Elshtain and Chu in the chapter's introduction. The first of the "Writing About the Theme" topics at the end of the chapter offers a starting point for discussion or student writing.

Content Quiz

1. How could cloning help alleviate world hunger?
   ["Animals could be engineered to provide milk, meat, and labor."]

2. What is the only current limit to cloning technology?
   ["The skill and the scientific talent of those doing the laboratory work."]

3. Why does Backous think it is unrealistic to believe that cloning research can be halted?
   [Too much work has already been put into cloning research, and too much money is at stake.]

4. Who stands to benefit the most financially from a cloning breakthrough?
   [The company that corners the market on the technique.]

5. What contradiction does Backous see in the fact that humans have been able to use technology to alter God's nature?
   [God has granted humans the intelligence to change nature, and yet by doing so we are assuming a godlike role, "toying with the very essence of creation itself."]

Vocabulary Quiz

1. *Proponents* (paragraph 1) is closest in meaning to
   a. those in favor b. those against c. experts
   [a. those in favor]

2. *Circumventing* (1) is closest in meaning to
   a. slowing down b. postponing c. avoiding
   [c. avoiding]

3. *Fodder* (3) is closest in meaning to
   a. soil b. fertilizer c. food
   [c. food]

4. *Arid* (5) is closest in meaning to
   a. dry b. remote c. impoverished
   [a. dry]

5. *Ingenuity* (5) is closest in meaning to
   a. intelligence   b. inventiveness   c. wisdom
   [b. inventiveness]

ANSWERS

Meaning

1. "Perhaps the only thing we can do at this point is recognize that what was only a fantasy is now real and that education might be our first step in helping to shape the future of genetic engineering" (paragraph 4); "Perhaps the best way to stifle the march toward technological wonders is to ponder the consequences of our actions and realize that we know neither what those are nor what it means to accept responsibility for them" (5).

2. Cloning promises both enormous potential and enormous risk. To oppose it entirely would be to deny its promise of easing suffering and pain, but to advocate it unreservedly would be to play God.

Purpose and Audience

1. Backous does not have a rigid opinion on cloning. His purpose is precisely to convince readers that dogmatic views on such a morally complex problem are unreasonable and to call for more education and reflection on the issue.

2. The way Backous didactically presents both sides' arguments suggests that he is writing for readers who have not necessarily given the subject much thought or who, like himself, might be on the fence. Readers with strong opinions are not likely to be swayed to the other side by this essay — it doesn't present the arguments of either side strongly enough and leaves too many questions unanswered.

3. Backous assumes that readers believe in God. Students' responses may vary, depending on whether they share this assumption. The author does keep the notion of God general enough to include almost anybody's version of a higher being or consciousness.

Method and Structure

1. Backous's indecision, stemming from his intense awareness of the complexity of the issue, serves as an example to readers: "We must ask ourselves yet again, 'just because we can do it, should we?'" (paragraph 1); "Something feels wrong with that scenario" (2); "we have a very complex situation here" (3); "No matter where you stand on this issue, there is a nagging questions left unanswered" (5). It also helps convince readers that Backous is reasonable and objective.

2. He involves readers directly in the issue, forcing them to admit that anyone would take advantage of cloning technology if it meant saving the life of a loved one.

3. The generalization: "To say that we can stop the proliferation of experiments and research altogether seems naive (paragraph 4)." The evidence: (1) 80,000 animals were created artificially in Great Britain in the past year; (2) scientists have obtained results too spectacular to turn back the clock now, including creating a sheep whose cells all contain human genes; (3) there is too much money at stake for the company that eventually corners the market on cloning technology.

4. These examples of science being used to humane ends lend support to the side of the argument that favors cloning.

Language

1. Backous describes a "very complex situation," notes that we are "hesitant," calls cloning "frighteningly critical to the future," compares "play[ing] God" and "sav[ing] our own flesh and blood," and describes a strictly moral choice as "difficult" (all in paragraph 3).

2. The tone is calm, reasoned, and impartial: "OK. So now we can clone sheep" (paragraph 1); "Something feels wrong with that scenario" (2); "No matter where you stand on this issue," "Most of us would be forced to agree," "ponder the consequences" (5). Backous does not pretend to have the answers to the many rhetorical questions he poses. He is not championing one side or the other, and so his tone is neutral.

3. Backous seems to be saying, "We have a situation to contend with." Beginning the essay this way suggests that he understands the complexity of the issue.

Chapter 14

COMBINING METHODS OF DEVELOPMENT

Articulating a Vision

The essays in this chapter may serve several functions.

- They may be used to summarize and tie together the methods of development and to focus on the ways the methods may be combined (as the chapter introduction and the annotations point out).
- They may be used as additional examples of particular methods of development. King's "I Have a Dream," for instance, includes many examples, and Kayman's "Can Technology Make Us Colorblind?" includes substantial cause-and-effect analysis.
- They may be read for their common theme of articulating a vision.
- Since the essays are *not* followed in the text by a battery of questions, they may be used to exercise students' analytic skills, especially late in the course when the analytic framework presented by the questions should be familiar. The discussions that follow here include sample questions (and answers) and writing topics, which you can also use to initiate and focus class discussion and essays.

Martin Luther King, Jr.

I Have a Dream *(p. 349)*

King's inspirational speech offers an excellent opportunity to explore the use and effectiveness of emotional appeals. It also, of course, provides a context for discussing the improvements or lack of improvements in African American civil rights since King delivered the speech in 1963.

As effective as it is in print, the speech was even more effective in King's original delivery. A recording or film of his delivery — sonorous and movingly cadenced — can help students appreciate why the speech is so memorable. It can also encourage comparison between written and spoken persuasion: what are the strengths and weaknesses of each form?

Questions

1. What reasons does King give for refusing to resort to violence? What comfort does he offer those who have been jailed or beaten?

   [Violence would deprive the civil rights movement of "dignity and discipline," and it would lose supporters (paragraph 6). Those who have been jailed or beaten should view their suffering as "creative" and have "faith that unearned suffering is redemptive" (8).]

2. What is King's purpose in this speech, and what about this purpose and audience leads him to rely primarily on emotional appeal (see pp. 314–16)? Where does he appeal specifically to his listeners' pride and dignity? To their religious beliefs? To their patriotism?

   [King wanted to inspire his listeners to continue their struggle nonviolently — while also sending a message to the nation about the movement's determination to achieve its goals. Because King's listeners are already convinced of the need for change, they do not require a rational argument. Emotional appeals are particularly effective in inspiring an audience to act. King appeals to pride and dignity in paragraphs 6–9; to his listeners' religious beliefs in paragraphs 8, 18–19, and 23; and to their patriotism in paragraphs 1, 3, 11, and 20–22.]

3. Analyze the organization of King's speech. What is the main subject of paragraphs 3–5? 6–9? 10–23? How does this structure suit King's purpose?

   [King first establishes the common ground with his listeners (paragraphs 3–5); then urges them to continue struggling nonviolently, whatever the emotional or physical costs (6–9); and finally creates a picture of the better world they can help achieve with their action (10–23). Thus he builds to an inspirational crescendo.]

4. In paragraph 6 King says, "Let us not seek to satisfy our thirst for freedom by drinking from the cup of bitterness and hatred." To what extent in this speech does King follow his own suggestion? How would you characterize his attitudes toward oppression and segregation? Choose words and phrases in the speech to support your answer.

   [King's language does not convey bitterness or hatred. Only once does he refer to those responsible for oppression and segregation ("whose governor's lips are presently dripping with the words of interposition and nullification," paragraph 16). Otherwise, he focuses on the condition of African Americans and the work they have to do, and his words convey compassion, fervor, resoluteness: "lonely island of poverty" (2), "dark and desolate valley of segregation" (4), "There will be neither rest nor tranquility" (5), "We can never be satisfied" (7), "battered by the storms of persecution" (8), "Mississippi, a desert state sweltering with the heat of injustice and oppression" (13).]

5. King depends heavily on two stylistic devices: repetition of sentence openings, as in "I have a dream" (paragraphs 11–18); and parallelism within sentences, as in "the manacles of segregation and the chains of discrimination" (2). Locate other instances of these two related devices. How do they contribute to King's purpose? (If necessary, see the discussion of parallelism on p. 48.)

   [Other examples of repetition: "one hundred years later" (paragraph 2), "*Now*" (4), "We can never be satisfied" (7), "Let freedom ring" (20–23). Other examples of parallelism: "a lonely island of poverty in the midst of a vast ocean of material prosperity" (2), "from the dark and desolate valley of segregation to the sunlit path of racial justice" (4), "their destiny is tied up with our destiny and their freedom is inextricably bound to our freedom" (6), "will not be judged by the color of their skin but by the content of their character" (14), "to work together, to pray together, to struggle together, to go to jail together, to stand up for freedom together" (19). The repetition and parallelism, suggesting an incantation or hymn, make an almost religious appeal to listeners and thus reinforce King's inspirational purpose.]

6. King's speech abounds in metaphors, such as the "manacles of segregation" and the "chains of discrimination" in the sentence quoted above. Locate as many metaphors as you can (consulting p. 52), and analyze what five or six of them contribute to King's meaning. Which metaphors are repeated or restated, and how does this repetition help link portions of the speech?

   [Throughout the speech, King's metaphors depict oppression as low, hot, dry, and dark: "the flames of withering injustice," "the long night of captivity" (paragraph 1); "the dark and desolate valley of segregation" (4); "This sweltering summer of the Negro's legitimate discontent" (5); "a desert state sweltering with the heat of injustice and oppression" (13). Freedom and equality, in contrast, are depicted as elevated, cool, moist, and light: "a joyous daybreak" (1); "the sunlit path of racial justice" (4); "an invigorating autumn of freedom and equality," "the bright day of justice" (5); "justice rolls down like waters" (7); "an oasis of freedom and justice" (13); "From every mountainside, let freedom ring" (20–22).]

Writing Topics

1. King's speech had a tremendous impact when it was first delivered in 1963, and it remains influential to this day. Pick out the elements of the speech that seem most remarkable and powerful to you: ideas, emotional appeals, figures of speech, repetition and parallelism, or whatever you choose. Write an essay in which you cite these elements and analyze their effectiveness.

2. King says that his dream is "deeply rooted in the American dream" (paragraph 10). Write an essay in which you provide your own definition of the American dream. Draw on the elements of King's dream as you see

fit. Make your definition specific with examples and details from your experiences, observations, and reading.

3. **Cultural Considerations** Most people, whatever their background or circumstances, have experienced some sort of injustice. In paragraph 6 King outlines a strategy for achieving racial justice. In an essay, briefly explain an unjust situation that has affected you directly — in school, in your family, at work, in your community — and propose a strategy for correcting the injustice. Be specific about the steps in the strategy, and explain how each one relates to the final goal you want to achieve.

4. **Connections** King delivered this speech in 1963. Leanita McClain wrote "The Middle-Class Black's Burden" (p. 243) in 1980, just seventeen years later, yet much had changed in American race relations. Write an essay comparing the attitudes of King and McClain toward the condition of African Americans, using the authors' own words as your evidence.

Brian Kaufman

Can Technology Make Us Colorblind? *(p. 355)*

This student essay offers a worthy complement to King's "I Have a Dream": Kaufman envisions a way that computer technology could help us achieve the race-neutral society of King's dream. For the many students who participate in computer bulletin boards, chat rooms, and other electronic forums, Kaufman's essay should provide an itneresting perspective on familiar territory. Even students who are not Internet-savvy should be able to relate to Kaufman's point that the new forms of communication may overcome "the limitations of who and what we are."

This essay offers many possibilities for discussion. In conjunction with King's "I have a Dream," you could ask students whether they believe a race-neutral society is possible or even desirable: Kaufman refutes contemporary ideas about diversity in which "personal identities are based on differences" (paragraph 7) and "collective identifications" (9), but some students may share these views. Alternatively, Kaufman's essay raises hopes for computer technology that could open up debate. For instance, is the anonymity afforded by electronic communication entirely beneficial? And, even if so, what will become of people, such as the poor, who may not have access to the technology?

Questions

1. How does Kaufman's assessment of the Internet differ from that of his wife?

   [Kaufman's wife "complains" that "you don't ever really know who you're talking to" in computer chat rooms. Kaufman considers this anonymity a strength of the Internet, offering the possibility of a colorblind society.]

2. Kaufman's essay can be divided into four major parts. What is the main subject of paragraphs 2–4, 5–6, 7–11, and 12–13? What does each part contribute to Kaufman's main idea?

   [Paragraphs 2–4 establish the potential of the Internet for anonymity, as well the Internet's wide influence in everyday life. Paragraphs 5–6 point out how the Internet, then, offers a chance to achieve Martin Luther King's dream of colorblindness. Paragraphs 7–11 wonder if our current preference for separation and difference will undermine the Internet's potential. And paragraphs 12–13 conclude that technology is so widespread and powerful that it may change communication and enact King's dream, with or without our effort.]

3. How does Kaufman, in the body of the essay, answer the question he asks in the title, "Can Technology Make Us Colorblind?" What factors make the answer more complicated than a simple "yes" or "no"? Where does Kaufman indicate that the answer may be more complicated?

   [Kaufman's answer to the question in the title is generally "yes." However, he qualifies this answer throughout the essay — particularly when discussing ebonics in paragraphs 8–10 — by suggesting that in a "splintered" society, our impulse is to highlight rather than downplay difference. Kaufman seems to be saying that we can become colorblind only "to the extent that we can ignore the limitations of who and what we are" (paragraph 2) — that is by eliminating visual and other clues of difference.]

4. Kaufman says that technology may "drag us, kicking and screaming, into King's dream" of a colorblind society (paragraph 13). What does the phrase "kicking and screaming" suggest about society's willingness to be colorblind?

   [Kaufman suggests that we may no longer want a colorblind society: we tend to relish differences, and the relevance of King's speech "may lie in the symbol, not the substance" (paragraph 11).]

5. Analyze the examples Kaufman uses in paragraphs 2, 3, and 8. How do these examples serve Kaufman's point about the potential of technology?

   [All of these three examples highlight differences among people: men and women, heavy and thin, frowning and smiling, old and young, black and white. Kaufman emphasizes differences in order to establish the need (and the potential) to erase them through the anonymity of computer communication.]

6. Kaufman's vision depends on a future of widespread, even universal, use of computers, at least in the United States. Does such a spread of computer technology — however far in the future — seem feasible to you? Why, or why not?

   [Students answers will vary. Some students may observe that Kaufman's vision of colorblindness depends on equality in education, income, and other factors he does not address.]

Writing Topics

1. How do you respond to Kaufman's essay? Do you think that electronic communication could significantly improve society, or are its potential benefits outweighed by its potential damages? Consider, for instance, the frustration Kaufman's wife feels at discovering the deception of someone in a chat room (paragraph 1): does the anonymity of much electronic communication make us more vulnerable? Write an essay explaining your own vision of where electronic communication may take us, agreeing or disagreeing with Kaufman.

2. Although "technology offers a chance at an old dream," Kaufman says, "we seem to wish to separate and alienate. . . . [P]ersonal identities are based on differences and similarities are viewed with suspicion, as if every shared moment is a potential shackle" (paragraph 7). Write an essay exploring the extent to which your *own* identity depends on aligning yourself with some people and separating or even alienating yourself from others. Be specific, giving examples from your experiences.

3. **Cultural Considerations** Kaufman hopes that technology can help achieve a "colorblind society" in which people do not suffer discrimination because there are no "visual labels." Think of a group you belong to that includes people from varied backgrounds — it could be a religious group, your extended family, a club, even a writing class. How do the differences in the group's members affect their communication now? How might the members interact differently if they communicated entirely through computers? Would existing labels, visual or otherwise, disappear? Would existing barriers fall? Would new barriers arise? In an essay, explore the changes you imagine.

4. **Connections** Kaufman's idea of a "colorblind society" depends on Martin Luther King's "I Have a Dream" (p. 349), but of course King (speaking in 1963) didn't envision equality brought about by computer technology. Compare and contrast Kaufman's and King's views of how racial equality could come about in the United States. How are the views similar? What does King's view include that Kaufman's doesn't, and vice versa? What does your comparison lead you to conclude about the possibility of achieving racial equality in this country, or about the ways to achieve equality?